TREATMENT OF INDIVIDUALS WITH ANGER-CONTROL PROBLEMS AND AGGRESSIVE BEHAVIORS: A CLINICAL HANDBOOK

Donald Meichenbaum, Ph.D.
University of Waterloo
Department of Psychology
Waterloo, Ontario
Canada N2L 3G1

and

Research Director of The Melissa Institute
for Prevention of Violence and Treatment of Victims
Miami, Florida

Published by:

INSTITUTE PRESS

1560 Gulf Blvd.

Clearwater, Florida

33767

Manufactured in United States of America

This **Clinical Handbook** is dedicated to the memory of **Melissa Aptman**. Melissa, a native of Miami, was murdered on May 5, 1995. She was just two weeks away from graduating from Washington University in St. Louis. Her family, friends, neighbors and supporters established an Institute in her name to prevent violence and treat victims of violence. I am privileged to serve as the Research Director of The Melissa Institute for Violence Prevention and Treatment of Victims of Violence located in Miami, Florida. Hopefully this **Handbook** will foster the mission of the Institute.

(See **www.melissainstitute.org** for a description of the Institute's activities.)

TREATMENT OF INDIVIDUALS WITH ANGER-CONTROL PROBLEMS AND AGGRESSIVE BEHAVIORS: A CLINICAL HANDBOOK

Donald Meichenbaum, Ph.D.
446 Pages – Softcover

ORDER INFORMATION

Make check and money order payable to Don Meichenbaum
   (No credit cards accepted)
All checks must be payable in <u>US Funds</u> or payable on a US bank or send a
   US International Money Order

US Orders	$50.00 + $5.00 handling and postage, = $55.00 US FUNDS taxes included
Canadian Orders	$65.00 + $5.00 handling and postage, taxes included = $70.00 CDN FUNDS
International Orders	$50.00 + $25.00 handling and postage, taxes included (Shipped Airmail) = $75.00 US FUNDS
International Orders	$50.00 + $10.00 handling and postage, taxes included (Shipped by boat – 4 – 6 weeks) = $60.00 US FUNDS

Mail check and orders to: Dr. Donald Meichenbaum
                             1560 Gulf Blvd.
                             Apt. 1002
                             Clearwater, FL 33767

Email: dmeich@watarts.uwaterloo.ca

TABLE OF CONTENTS

DETAILED TABLE OF CONTENTS

LIST OF TABLES

Page

LIST OF FIGURES

LIST OF PATIENT HANDOUTS[1]

[1] *The reader has permission to copy and use the Patient Handouts.*

HOW TO USE THIS HANDBOOK

It is not expected that this **HANDBOOK** will be read from cover to cover, but rather that it will be used as a **Reference Guidebook** like a fine cookbook. The connoisseur will refer to it on multiple occasions for suggestive guidelines. But like the "expert" chef, the Reader will creatively alter the recipes and procedures to meet his or her needs. In order to facilitate this referral process, the following list of **CONTENT** is offered. Also, see the **SUBJECT INDEX (p. 446).**

I WANT TO <u>LEARN MORE ABOUT</u> OR <u>HOW TO:</u>

BY WAY OF INTRODUCTION

For the last 30 years I have taught at the University of Waterloo, Ontario Canada, been in private practice, and I have also had the opportunity to consult to a number of psychiatric, educational, and occupational facilities. One common theme that has cut across each of these consultative activities is the need to assess and treat individuals who have problems controlling anger and who often become aggressive. A brief enumeration of the variety of populations that I have worked with will put the present **Clinical Handbook** into perspective.

Populations Worked with on Anger-control / Aggressive Behavior

1. Psychiatric inpatients and outpatients (children, adolescents, adults)

2. Children and adolescents in residential programs – asked to train clinical and frontline staff

3. Incarcerated populations such as juvenile offenders and adult prison populations, sex offenders

4. Spouse abusive couples in the military

5. Special needs populations of individuals with traumatic brain injury and individuals with developmental disabilities who have anger-control problems; VA veterans who have comorbid problems of PTSD, substance abuse, depression and anger-control problems

6. Individuals who are extremely angry following victimization experiences, as well as various psychiatric groups (bipolar disorder, borderline personality disorder, antisocial personality disorder) where anger and aggression play important roles

7. Occupational groups such as policemen, military personnel, UN peacekeepers, psychiatric nurses

8. Educational personnel who are implementing school violence prevention programs

9. Private practice population including adult patients with "rage disorders", parents of children and adolescents who have anger-control problems, and aggressive children and adolescents

10. Finally, I have taken early retirement from the University of Waterloo in Ontario and I now **direct The Melissa Institute in Miami, Florida** that is designed to prevent violence and treat victims of violence.

In each setting, the clinicians I work with have requested a **practical, user-friendly guidebook** on how to treat individuals with anger-control and aggressive behavior. The present **Clinical Handbook** with its **emphasis on procedural guidelines** is designed to provide such a clinical tool. The focus is on **working with adults**, although a **life-span developmental perspective** is offered in order to appreciate how angry and aggressive behaviors develop and to consider the implications for assessment and treatment.

My last **Clinical Handbook for Assessing and Treating Adults with Post Traumatic Stress Disorder** was well received and proved very popular. I received many requests to do a break-out Handbook just on anger-control. Hopefully, the present **Handbook on Anger-Control** will prove equally useful. I welcome your feedback and suggestions. I can be reached in the following ways:

Address: **University of Waterloo**
                 Psychology Department
                 Waterloo, Ontario
                 Canada N2L 3G1

Fax: **(519) 746-8631**
Phone: **(519) 885-1211, extension 2551**
Email: **dmeich@watarts.uwaterloo.ca**

If you would like more information about **The Melissa Institute**, call up our **WEBSITE** which is **www.melissainstitute.org**. Also see **Appendix B** which includes **WEBSITES** and **email addresses** of programs related to **violence prevention**. I have taken the liberty of including on the next two pages order information on the **Clinical Handbook for Assessing and Treating Adults with Post Traumatic Stress Disorder**.

Although the focus of the present **Handbook** is anger and aggressive behavior, many of the assessment and treatment strategies described herein could readily be applied to patients with other psychiatric disorders (anxiety, depression, impulse-control and Axis II disorders).

Finally, I would like to express my appreciation to two people whose help, patience and encouragement made this venture doable. First, my wife Marianne who endured sacrifices as I put in the many hours to write this **HANDBOOK**. Secondly, Renata Snidr, my secretary and assistant, who typed this entire manuscript. Thank you **RENATA**. I also wish to acknowledge the financial aid of the **MELISSA INSTITUTE**.

A CLINICAL HANDBOOK / PRACTICAL THERAPIST MANUAL
For Assessing and Treating Adults with PTSD
Donald Meichenbaum, Ph. D.
600 Pages -- Softcover

Section I	--	Epidemiological And Diagnostic Information
	--	Consider the nature and impact of natural, technological, and human-made disasters as evident in specific "victim populations"
	--	Critique diagnostic alternatives and "stage" theories
Section II	--	Conceptualization of PTSD
	--	Reviews alternative conceptualizations and offers a "constructive narrative perspective"
Section III	--	Assessment of PTSD
	--	Comprehensive enumeration of PTSD and related measures of comorbidity
	--	Describes a sequential gating assessment strategy
	--	Considers potential "positive" effects
	--	Includes the "best" clinical questions you can ask
Section IV	--	Cautions About Assessment
	--	Consider the controversy over so-called "false memories"
	--	How to help the helpers
Section V	--	Treatment Alternatives: A Critical Analysis
	--	Critically evaluates pharmacological, exposure, eye-movement desensitization, group interventions and other procedures
	--	Provides treatment guidelines and considers factors that influence the length of treatment
Section VI	--	Specific Treatment Procedures: Practical "How to" Guidelines
	--	"How to": Educate clients about PTSD; deal with flashbacks; intrusive ideation; guilt; anger; addictive behaviors; depression; anxiety; conduct "memory work"; and address issues of multiple and borderline personality disorders
	--	Techniques include Stress inoculation training, cognitive restructuring, problem-solving, relapse prevention and family-based interventions
Section VII	--	Post Disaster Interventions
	--	Consider who is most at "high risk"
	--	Describes and critiques Critical Incident Stress Debriefing; When can CISD make individuals "worse"?
	--	Workplace, accident, community interventions
	--	Consider the role of religion and rituals
	--	Over 1500 references

Order Information

Make check or money order payable to Don Meichenbaum (no credit cards accepted)
All checks must be payable on a US bank, or send US International Money Order
US Orders: $60 + $5 handling and postage = $65 US Funds
Overseas Orders: $60 + $15 handling and postage = $75 US Funds
Mail check and order to: Donald Meichenbaum
University of Waterloo
Psychology Department
Waterloo, Ontario, Canada N2L 3G1
email: dmeich@watarts.uwaterloo.ca

Reviews of Meichenbaum's <u>PTSD Handbook</u>

"A **comprehensive** reference work **unsurpassed** in richness,
depth and utility for the clinician and scientist."

"This book will be *new* **for years** to come; thus, if the reader plans
to buy only one book on trauma this year, it should be Meichenbaum's <u>Handbook</u> -
it's an **extraordinary volume**, a **crowning contribution** to traumascience."

"This reviewer recommends the <u>Handbook</u> unhesitatingly."

"It is written by a giant in the clinical field."

Ervin Randolph Parson
<u>Journal of Traumatic Stress</u>
1996, <u>9</u>, 911 - 913

"Meichenbaum has provided clinicians and researchers with a **marvelous resource**. This
is the single most comprehensive compilation of information on PTSD known to me."

"The Handbook is impressive for its **usefulness**, if not for its **polish**."

"The amount of information contained and cited is **staggering**."

"The <u>Handbook</u> is as **eclectic** as any one source could be."

"Meichenbaum has a remarkable ability to make use of
exemplary work of others in the field."

Jon G. Allen
<u>Bulletin of the Menninger Clinic</u>
1996, <u>60</u>, 264 - 265

"Gathered together in one volume, this summary of the many facets of PTSD
is more than a "manual" - it is a gift of many years of research
and deduction to the understanding and impact of PTSD.
Adjectives like **"definitive"** and **"indispensable"** come to mind."

Claude Barbe
<u>Journal of Religion and Health</u>, 1996

SECTION I : THE NATURE OF ANGER

This **Clinical Handbook** begins with a **definition of anger** and a consideration of the **impact of angry and aggressive behavior**. The seriousness of the problem is underscored by a consideration of the widespread **incidence of angry episodes** and **aggressive behavior**.

SECTION I will consider briefly the **variety of factors** that have been found to contribute to angry and aggressive behavior. A **social information-processing model** is offered as an heuristic way to understand the influence of these factors.

CONTENTS SECTION I

ANGER: DEFINITION

1. **Anger** is a **feeling** an individual may have when he[2] thinks he cannot get something which he wants to obtain or to do and believes that he deserves it and is being blocked from obtaining it. **Anger may also reflect a feeling of disapproval** of the actions of another, often accompanied by **tendencies to retaliate or undo** the perceived wrongdoing. **The feeling or affective state** may vary in intensity from mild irritation to unfettered rage. Anger also includes a **cognitive** or **attitudinal component**, which underlies one's **interpretation of situations as having been provoked**. This anger may be **situational and occasional (state anger)** or it may be **persistent, long-standing, cross-situational** and reflect a **stable interpretive framework (trait anger)** (Spielberger, 1995).

2. **Anger is an accusatory response to some perceived misdeed**. The typical **instigation** is an **attribution of blame to others**, often associated with judgments of *"ought," "should have,"* or *"could have."* Because anger usually occurs as a result of a **perceived injustice** and **involves other-blame**, there is often an **element of self-justification** in the experience of anger.

3. **Anger attacks** may take various forms including irritability, overreaction to minor annoyances, frustration, fury, and rage with accompanying physical reactions including chest tightness, sweating, dizziness, shortness of breath, racing heart, feeling out of control, feel like attacking others. Anger may take the form of verbal and physical assaults (sarcasm, swearing, hitting) or passive indirect aggression (become silent, do something to hurt others).

4. Anger may also elicit **adaptive positive responses** designed to correct a wrong or an injustice (e.g., an assertive response, conflict resolution, setting limits, disengaging, avoiding conflict situations). *Note: Some anger does not produce aggression and some aggression does not involve anger.*

5. The multidimensional concept of **hostility** is used to describe a stable set of personal expectations and beliefs in which one frequently **attributes harmful intent** to the actions of others. This chronic negative attitude reflects an **antagonistic and mistrusting mindset**. Hostility involves the devaluation of work and motives of others and the expectation that others are likely sources of wrongdoing, a view of being opposed to others, and a desire to inflict harm or see others harmed. It may take the form of anger, irritation, arrogance, contempt, resentment, suspiciousness, and the like. Hostile individuals are more prone to become angry and aggressive (Donker et al. 2000).

---

[2] The masculine pronoun will be used throughout since such a large percentage of the aggressive individuals to be discussed are male. We will consider **gender differences** below.

6. Deffenbacher (1999) observes that the probability and intensity of **anger increases** if the event is judged as being:

   a) **intentional** -- someone or something **purposefully** and **willfully** made the event happen or inflicted it upon the individual;
   b) **preventable** -- the event could have been controlled or prevented and by implication it "should have" been prevented;
   c) **unwarranted** or **unjustified** -- that it is **unfair** and **undeserved**;
   d) **blameworthy** -- someone is responsible and should be punished or suffer.

Thus, anger and often the accompanying aggression not only reflects an act, but an intention as well.

7. Researchers (e.g., Crick & Dodge, 1994; Vitiello & Stoff, 1997) have highlighted a distinction between **two types of aggressive acts, impulsive (reactive)** and **premeditated (proactive)**:

   Impulsive aggression, often called **reactive aggression**, is <u>unplanned</u> aggressive acts which are **spontaneous** in action: either **unprovoked** or **out of proportion** to the provocation and occurs among persons who are characterized as *"having a short fuse."* Such **reactive aggression** involves retaliatory intent, often driven by frustration, biological impulses and relatively independent of premeditated cognitive processes.

   Premeditated or instrumental or predatory aggression is related to personal or social **gain**, or to the expression of **dominance**, or to the **achievement of some goal**. This form of aggression has been described as being nonimpulsive, predatory, or **proactive**. It is <u>not</u> usually considered to have a large emotional component, but rather is considered "cold blooded," purposeful and organized. This form of aggressive acts is seen as goal-oriented, planned and controlled. It involves hurting another person as **a means to an end,** especially when the individual or group feels there is a good chance of getting away with it. Such aggressive behavior may arise out of a power struggle, territorial disputes, as a means to achieve or maintain social status, as a form of gang ritual, self-defense, retaliation, or as a way to obtain material gain. For example, Kopel (2000) reports that of 218 homicides in New York City classified as drug-related, almost all were the result of turf wars and robberies. In Los Angeles, 59% of homicides are perpetrated by males committing other crimes.

   It is important to keep in mind that there are <u>rarely</u> pure types of reactive and proactive aggression.

Another factor, as Anderson (1994) and Cohen (2001) highlight, is that an individual may behave violently because he fears violence from others if he is perceived as a "suck" or as a "wimp". An individual fears shame of others or fears potential attacks and thus behaves in a violent fashion as a **protective act**. As Anderson observes (1974, pp. 89-90)

> *"When a person ventures outside, he must adopt the code – a kind of shield really – to prevent others from "messing with" him. In these circumstances, it is easy for people to think they are being tried or tested by others even when this is not the case."*

The observations by Anderson about the **"code of the streets"** have been aptly conveyed by a young man who was shot while involved in an altercation. As he described, he did <u>not</u> want to be perceived as a "sucker":

> *A <u>sucker</u> is a person that if someone does something to them or says something to them, they don't retaliate. You know they just sit there and take it. Nobody wants to be called – if you are living in the inner city you wouldn't want to be called a sucker, cause everybody will take advantage of you. That's why half the people get shot, stabbed these days – trying to defend themselves and not be a sucker. (Rich & Stone, 1996, p. 79)*

These young men experience their environment as a hostile place and perceive that if they are seen as weak by their peers, they will be targeted for even more victimization. Respect is earned by projecting an image of "toughness," where one "stands up for what is theirs".

> *"If you are a sucker, you're a nobody."*
> *"Not retaliating, has a clear cost."*
> *"Status in the community is tied to one's ability to stand up for oneself."*
> *"Present yourself as being capable of instilling fear in others and if necessary able to cause injury."*

The **code of the streets** can act as a catalyst for aggressive behavior.

In summary, individuals with **reactive or emotionally hostile aggression**

- have "hot tempers", are easily riled into anger-aggression at the slightest provocation

- evidence less control over emotional reactions (have a shorter "shorter fuse")

- manifest aggressive behavior (fight back) in response to being teased or provoked

- tend to be hypervigilant and misinterpret social cues

- attribute hostile intentions to the actions of others

- attack someone when feeling bad, angry, or bored, even when the perpetrator may not benefit from it and may even pay a price for his aggression

- are more likely to ruminate and have a longer maintenance of grudges, and desire for revenge

- become aggressive, especially when a favorable opinion of self is challenged – (See Baumeister et al., 1996)

Individuals who evidence **reactive aggression** have a **hostility bias**. They tend to think of their peers as behaving with aggressive intent, even when none was intended. They believe the world is hostile, that they can't trust anyone, and that people cannot be counted on.

They **take pride** in their ability to fight and they place **value** on **aggression**. They behave in an aggressive manner that pulls for counteraggressive behavior that confirms their expectations. They have poor peer relations and they tend to associate with aggressive peers.

They have a social information processing deficit as they tend to misinterpret prosocial overtures as aggressive and these expectations become self-fulfilling prophecies. They tend to use fewer social cues and focus on aggressive cues.

Individuals who evidence **reactive aggression** are more likely to fight back when teased, blame others for fights. Harsh parenting or being continually exposed to violence in the neighborhood are contributing factors to the development of reactive aggression.

In summary, individuals with **proactive or instrumental aggression**

- behavior is carried out for an extrinsic purpose or to achieve some external goals

- evidence less observable emotion

- use physical force to dominate other individuals and to achieve their goals (e.g., threatens and bullies others in school) or get others to gang up on peers

- evidence leadership qualities and an agreeable sense of humor

Combination of reactive and instrumental aggression

Often aggression may reflect a **combination** of both forms of aggression. For example, in a study of aggression in sports Kirker et al. (2000) noted that athletes may have an intention to get back at a particular player due to a previous conflict, but will refrain from acting out until they are particularly frustrated. The individual's aggressive behavior reflects the **joint influence of premeditation and reactive frustration**. The fuse was lit before the game began, but specific circumstances were necessary to trigger the response. As the athlete may observe, *"I did it accidentally on purpose."; "Circumstances took over. I had no choice."*

The mode of intervention will need to be tailored to the specific forms of aggressive behavior. But, whatever the specific forms of aggression with its accompanying anger and hostility, they can take a toll, not only psychologically and societally, but also in terms of the **individual's physical well-being** – to which we now turn our attention.

PHYSICAL IMPACT OF ANGRY AND AGGRESSIVE BEHAVIOR

Besides the social and societal costs of angry, hostile and aggressive behavior, there is increasing evidence of the impact of such behaviors on an individual's physical health.

Impact on physical well-being. Physiological correlates of anger include increased heart rate and muscle tension, pupil dilation, shallow breathing, and higher blood pressure. Over a prolonged period, these bodily changes can contribute to health problems. **Anger, chronic hostility and cynicism** have been implicated as co-factors in contributing to **physical illness** such as **heart disease** and **hypertension** (Brummett & Williams, 1998; Harburg et al., 1991; Miller et al., 1996; Suls & Wan, 1993; Williams & Williams, 1993).

As Suinn observes (2001, p. 32), *"Anxiety and hostility have been consistently demonstrated to increase vulnerability to illness, impair the immune system, increase levels of cholesterol, prevent adjustment to chronic pain, increase risk of arteriosclerosis, and even increase mortality from cardiovascular disease."*

Traditional risk factors for coronary heart disease (CHD) such as a family history of heart disease, smoking, physical inactivity, elevation of blood pressure and serum cholesterol levels, account for about **half** of the variance in cardiovascular disease. Hostility is a significant predictor of CHD and of premature mortality. Hostile individuals who have low levels of social support and who evidence high levels of social conflict may be particularly vulnerable to CHD. Kauppinen and Keltikangas-Jarvinen (2000) have reported that the relationships between hostility and physiological coronary heart disease may be mediated by depressive tendencies.

As Donker et al. (2000) have reported, the relationship between hostility and Coronary Heart Disease is complicated by the multidimensional features of hostility. Different aspects of hostility may differentially influence physical well-being. As Booth-Kewley and Friedman (1987) observed, the psychological processes that contribute to CHD such as Type A Behavior Pattern may be a "container construct" and that only certain elements may be related to ill-health. The following list illustrates some of the **physiological concomitants** of violent behavior. Future research will be needed to determine if these physiological changes are correlates, contributing factors, or mediators of aggressive behavior. Whatever the exact relationships, the following illustrative findings underscore the complexity of the anger-aggression cycle.

ILLUSTRATIVE FINDINGS OF PHYSIOLOGICAL PROCESSES EVIDENT IN VIOLENT INDIVIDUALS

(See Beckham et al., 2000; Malta et al., 2001; Scarpa & Raine, 1997; Siegman & Smith, 1994; Volavka, 1995)

Neurophysiological and Psychophysiological Processes

- Functional imagery studies of violent psychiatric patients have demonstrated decreased brain metabolism in prefrontal and medial temporal cortices, as compared to controls (i.e., decreased prefrontal activity with increased left-side limbic activity)

- Violent behavior has been associated with temporal lobe epilepsy and partial complex seizures

- Low serotonin levels combined with alcohol consumption predispose individuals to aggressive behavior

- Anger has been associated with elevated heart rate and blood pressure. There is a fairly consistent relationship between hostility and elevated reactive systolic and diastolic blood pressure. In contrast, antisocial adults display decreased electrodermal responses to aversive stimuli.

- Aggressive drivers exhibit significant increase in muscle tension and blood pressure when provoked relative to controls.

- Anger produces a pattern of facial muscle activity that is distinct form other emotions, even when expressions are not overt.

- Highly aggressive boys have been found to have lower resting heart rate than nonaggressive boys, but display a sharp surge in heart rate following interpersonal provocations relative to nonaggressive boys.

INCIDENCE: HOW WIDESPREAD ARE SUCH ANGRY EPISODES?

The history of humankind is the story of angry and aggressive behaviors. Violence, brutality, hate and victimization are all too common. But one does not have to turn to the six o'clock news report for the daily occurrence of anger and violence. One needs look no further than one's own life. Averill (1982, 1983) has studied the incidence of angry behaviors in **normal nonclinical populations**. His findings are very instructive in illustrating just how widespread angry episodes are.

1. Nonclinical populations experience about one **incident of anger per day** (7.3 per week and 23.5 episodes of annoyances per week).

2. In 88% of these anger episodes, the anger was directed at another person and in 75% of these instances the targeted individual was familiar, well known, and liked by the angry individual. Only 13% of anger episodes involved strangers.

3. Although overt physical aggression is rare (i.e., occurring in less than 10% of these episodes), individuals report frequent impulses toward verbal (80%) and physical (40%) aggression when they are angry.

4. Most interpersonal violence results from disputes between individuals who have an ongoing relationship.

5. Over 85% of the acts that led to anger were considered to be voluntary and justified or potentially avoidable (e.g., being treated with little respect, people failing to fulfill their commitments).

6. Most importantly, **low and high angry individuals** encountered a **similar number of provocative situations**, but high anger individuals responded with a greater emotional response.

7. In the nonclinical population, most anger episodes did not progress to aggressive action.

But, such anger is not always controlled and often escalates to the point of aggression. For example, the U.S. Department of Justice (1991) reports that 50% of murder victims are known to their assailants and an estimated 34% of all murders are preceded by an argument or disagreement of some kind. In only about 15% to 25% of violent instances are aggressive acts engaged in by strangers. In the remaining instances of violent episodes, aggressive acts occur between family members, relatives and acquaintances. *(See the discussion below (p. 102) on Intimate Partner Violence for further examples of the incidence of violence.)*

8. Anger is related to not only aggressive behavior and family violence, but also to substance abuse, suicide, antisocial behavior and physical health problems, as discussed below.

9. In recent years, greater attention has also focused on **aggressive drivers** and **"road rage."** Aggressive driving has been associated with anger, as well as hostility and general aggressiveness. It has been estimated that 50% of motor vehicle accidents involve some form of aggressive driving (Arnett et al., 1997; Deffenbacher et al., 2000; Larson, 1996). Malta et al. (2001) have conducted an exploratory study that found that aggressive drivers exhibit significant increases in muscle tension and blood pressure relative to controls. This particular psychophysiological profile may accompany their reactivity to road provocations. More recently, the concept of "road rage has been extended to "airplane rage."

10. Given the widespread incidence of anger and aggression, it should <u>not</u> come as a surprise that a survey of psychologists and psychiatrists indicated that they worked with angry clients as frequently as they did with anxious clients (DiGiuseppe & Tafrate, 2001). **At the clinical level, anger is one of the most common symptoms that cut across 19 psychiatric disorders (Barratt 1993).**

We will consider the incidence of angry/aggressive behaviors in psychiatric patients below, when we consider Diagnostic Issues.

What factors determine whether angry episodes escalate to the point of physical violence and aggressive behavior?

FACTORS THAT INFLUENCE AGGRESSIVE BEHAVIOR

Research on the development and the prediction of violence has implicated a number of factors that contribute to, maintain and foster angry and aggressive behaviors. These factors include:

1. **Characteristics of the Individual** (e.g., age, gender, race, IQ, dispositional features such as impulsiveness, psychopathy, severity and type of mental disorders, history and presence of substance abuse, history of violent behavior, level of hostility, cynicism, preoccupation with violence)

2. **Developmental Influences** (e.g., victimization experiences, neglect, parental influences, such as paternal antisocial behavior and substance abuse, maternal depression, history of ADHD, Conduct Disorder, academic failure, peer rejection, bullying behaviors, relationship instability)

3. **Past and Current Stressors** (e.g., unemployment, daily hassles, marital distress, absence of social supports, exposure to traumatic events)

4. **Ecological and Contextual Variables** (e.g., neighborhood factors such as concentrated poverty, exposure to community violence, social disorganization, availability of weapons, cultural norms and expectations)

While an integrative **Case Conceptualization Model** of these factors will be considered in **Section II**, the following discussion provides some examples of the influence of these factors on aggressive behavior.

1. <u>**Role of alcohol consumption and other substances**</u>. What does it take for angry behavior to escalate to the point of aggression towards others or toward oneself? We begin with the role of alcohol consumption and other illicit substances. Sege and Licenziato (2001) report that **alcohol increases** the **risk of violence** by a **factor of 12**. Alcohol dependence is among the most common psychiatric disorders, effecting 20% of men and 8% of women over the course of their lifetime (Kessler et al., 1994). In short, **alcohol consumption and violence go hand-in-hand**.

    Permnanen (1991) in Canada found that 42% of violent crimes involved drinking by the assailant, victim, or both. The relationship between violence and alcohol consumption is most evident in the area of **intimate partner violence (IPV)** (Bushman & Cooper, 1990; Felson & Tedeschi, 1993). In the U.S., approximately, one-third of the reported violence between couples involves alcohol with the male partner drinking at the time of the violent incident. Over 50% of alcoholics have been violent to a female partner in the year before alcoholism treatment (Murphy & O'Farrell, 1996). Male alcoholics who abuse their wives or girlfriends are more likely to be **binge drinkers**, have severe and early onset alcohol dependence (including a family alcohol history primarily to male relatives), have frequent arrests and engage in negative communication styles with spouses (Trezza & Pope, 2000). Nearly 80% of **binge drinkers** reported assaults in the previous year compared to only 11% of abstainers. Thus, there is a need to assess the severity and pattern of alcohol use in patients.

Pan et al. (1994), in a sample of 11,000 men, found that being younger, having a lower income and an alcohol problem were predictors for husband-to-wife physical aggression. Leadley et al. (2000) report that couples share similar drinking habits and when there is a discrepancy in the couple's drinking patterns, alcohol-related arguments and physical violence are most likely to co-occur.

The increased risk of domestic violence in substance abusing partners is _not_ delimited to heterosexual couples, but has also been found in **homosexual relationships** (Irons & Schneider 1997; Schilits et al., 1990; West, 1998).

Substance use has also been found to potentiate the risk of **self-injurious behaviors** (attempted and completed suicides). (See Greenwald et al., 1994; Kleespies et al., 1999) Hufford (2001) has noted that alcohol intoxication can lead to aggressive behavior toward oneself, as well as toward others, but aggression can also lead to drinking. Moreover, acute alcohol intoxication is a greater risk for suicidal behavior than an habitual pattern of alcohol consumption. Alcohol intoxication can lead to increased negative affect, depression, feelings of helplessness, constricted thinking, or what Steele and Josephs (1990) described as "alcohol myopia" or an inhibition of considering options, and to a heightened desire to escape from self (Baumeister, 1990; Dean & Kange, 1999). The end result is that alcohol puts one at high risk for suicidal and aggressive behaviors.

The relationship between alcohol abuse and violence is further underscored by the finding that 60% of murderers were under the influence of alcohol and one-half of individuals incarcerated in State prisons for violent behavior consumed alcohol just prior to their offense. These violent outcomes fit with the observations that intoxicated persons act more aggressively when provoked than do sober persons, as alcohol tends to boost aggression (Baumeister, 1997; Chermack & Taylor, 1995; Sayette et al., 1993).

But alcohol alone is _not_ an adequate explanation for violence. While alcohol can increase the degree of aggression, it does _not_, by itself, cause aggression. Alcohol should be viewed as a moderating variable that acts as a contributing factor, but is neither a necessary nor sufficient factor.

Research has indicated that **substance abuse treatment is effective in reducing violent behavior** (Orwin et al., 2000). For example, O'Farrell et al. (1999) found a two year decrease in domestic violence posttreatment in a study of male alcoholics who attended a behavioral marital therapy alcoholism treatment program.

But alcohol is only one of several substances that have been found to increase the likelihood of aggression (See Hoaken et al., 1998). Among **illicit drugs**, **amphetamines**, phencyclidine **(PCP)** and **cocaine** have also been **linked to violence** (Friedman et al., 2001; Moss & Tarter, 1993).

2. **Role of co-occurrent mood disorders.** Many individuals who have problems controlling anger and substance abuse problems, also have other comorbid psychiatric disorders, as discussed in **Section III**. One comorbid disorder that plays a critical role in risk for violence is **depression**. Approximately 1/3 of depressed outpatients present with anger attacks (Fava, 1998; Fava et al., 1993). A good example of the relationship between depression and anger comes from the research of Pan et al. (1994) who examined 11,000 US Army men and found that for every 20% increase in **depressive symptomatology**, the odds of their using moderate physical aggression (e.g., pushing) against their wife increased 30%, and the odds of their using severe physical aggression (e.g., beating) increased by 74%.

    Depressed patients with anger attacks also show higher scores on anxiety. Indeed, anger has also been found to co-occur with anxiety disorders such as panic attacks (George et al., 1989) and agoraphobia (Fava et al., 1993). Such anger attacks often remit in response to antidepressants and anti-anxiety medications. Patients with eating disorders and Borderline Personality Disorders have also been found to have emotional regulation problems in the area of anger control (Linehan, 1993).

3. **Role of stress factors.** Background, situational, or ecological factors can influence the likelihood of anger / aggressive responses. For example, **job loss** increases the risk of violent behavior toward the spouse by six-fold. In turn, violent behavior increases the likelihood of job loss by 15-fold. **Commuting** can increase the likelihood of violence, as does **continual exposure to chronic daily hassles** (See Novaco, 1993). Another from of stress that has been found to be related to aggressive and violent behavior is the experience of **traumatic stress** that may take the form of **PTSD**. For instance, several observers (Grossman, 1995; Hallock, 1998 and Hendin & Haas, 1984) have observed that **combat veterans**, especially those who have engaged in killing are more likely to have violent outbursts, become alienated, be hostile, hypervigilant (perceive combat as *"never ending"* and engage in a *"counter-attack mode"*), and may experience survivor guilt. As Shay (1994, p. 191) observes:

    > *"Some survivors, have learned the worthlessness of words and conclude that the only way to be heard is through action – guerilla theater. Intimidation, acting out, and creating impossible situations sometimes aimed at coercing the therapist to feel the fear and helplessness that the survivor felt. It recreates terror and helplessness at work, in the family, on the street and in the clinic."*

These observations were supported by the findings of Beckham et al. (1997, 2000) who reported that male Vietnam Veterans with PTSD committed between 13 and 22 acts of interpersonal violence in the previous year in contrast to 0.2 acts of violence in the non-PTSD veterans. The repeated aggression was <u>not</u> associated with alcohol problems, nor with childhood physical abuse. Unemployed veterans with PTSD have the highest incidence of violence. The level of severity of PTSD symptomatology has been linked to the level of aggression and to the degree of interpersonal violence (Frueh et al., 1997). Mayne and Ambrose (1999) report that anger and rage are ***"the most salient and prevalent emotional responses in men with PTSD"*** (p. 306) and they rate anger-management difficulties in social situations as one of their most distressing problems. The relationship between anger and PTSD is likely cyclical with anger expression predicting later PTSD severity, but PTSD severity is also predictive of the level of anger (Dalenberg, 2000). Their angry behaviors can produce interpersonal problems leading to shunning and avoidance behaviors that reinforce the cycle.

Illustrative of these relationships are the findings of Chemtob et al. (1997a) who reported that Vietnam veterans with PTSD scored two standard deviations higher on an Anger Scale than did psychiatric patients in state hospitals. They reported that 46% of combat veterans with PTSD have committed at least 1 violent act during the previous 12 months and 37% have had 6 or more such violent episodes during this period of time. Those veterans with PTSD averaged 12 acts of violence compared to 3.5 such acts by veterans without PTSD, consistent with the findings of Beckham et al. (2000). A similar profile of the relationships between anger, hostility, aggression and PTSD in veterans has been reported by Byrne & Riggs (1996); Carroll et al. (1985); Frueh et al. (1997); Kubany (1994); Kulka et al. (1990); Lasko et al. (1994); and Matsakis (1998). Abe et al. (1994) have reported on the role of anger and PTSD with refugees and Green et al. (1994) have highlighted the role of anger and PTSD in disaster victims.

Traumatized individuals, out of fear of losing their temper and hurting others, may withdraw and isolate themselves as a form of protection. In fact, **symptoms of avoidance-numbing were significantly associated with violence**, more so than reexperiencing and arousal symptom clusters (McFall et al., 1999). Coping styles of escape, avoidance and distancing were more likely to be related to measures of aggression and hostility (McCormick & Smith, 1995).

In a study of over 2500 violent individuals, Orwin et al. (2000) observed that 74% reported a history of victimization. Most perpetrators were victims and vice versa. Only about 1 out of 10 clients were "pure" perpetrators (not victims as well). See Creamer (2000) for a discussion of the relationships between PTSD, anger and violence. Anger has been found to interfere with the natural healing processes following PTSD (e.g., combat, rape, motor vehicle accidents).

4. __Neighborhood poverty__ with high rates of unemployment, racial segregation, rapid population turnover, low income levels, density of single parent families with children, overall lack of economic opportunities, social disorganization, and the accompanying "code of the streets" or the set of informal rules that value aggression as a means of resolving conflicts have each been seen as breeding grounds for aggressive behavior (Anderson, 1997; Sampson & Lauritsen, 1994; Silver et al., 1999).

5. __Role of proximal factors such as the availability of weapons__ (See Berkowitz, 1993). In the U.S., half of all homes contain guns, or approximately 240 million guns are in circulation. The sobering statistic is that half of parents who acknowledge having a gun in the home do not lock the gun away from their children, putting children at a high risk for handgun-violence. A handgun in the home is 43 times more likely to be used for murder or suicide than for self-defense (Sege & Licenziato, 2001).

   Nevertheless, the major reason offered for owning and carrying a gun is "for protection." As Kopel (2000) observes, most individuals possess guns as a means of protecting themselves, especially if they live in a perceived high-risk area. For example, it has been estimated that 6,000 students carry a gun to school in the U.S. on a given day. When asked, 65% of students indicated that they knew "how to get a gun with little or no trouble." 87% of incarcerated youths responded positively to this item. Moreover, most students expressed the opinion that "nothing could be done to prevent access to guns." Kopel (2000) makes a convincing case that just focusing on gun control legislation would prove insufficient to reduce violence. As one violent youth observes:

   > *"We need better schools and jobs. That's the way you stop the killing. You have to offer hope. If there is no hope, the killing will go on whether there is a gun ban or not." (p. 100).*
   > *(See the discussion of school shooters below, p. 62)*

6. __Role of cultural factors.__ Approximately 25,000 Americans die in homicides each year. These numbers are not equally distributed throughout the U.S. __There are sharp regional differences in the homicide rate__ (Daly & Wilson, 1988). For example, the South (consisting of the States of the old Confederacy) has a homicide rate almost double that of the Northeast. This is particularly true of small towns in the southern part of the U.S. Nisbett (1993) reports that in medium-sized cities with populations between 50,000 to 200,000 __Southern white males__ commit murder at a rate __twice__ that of their counterparts in the rest of the nation. In small Southern cities, with populations from 10,000 to 50,000, the murder ratio is 3 to 1, and in rural Southern areas it is 4 to 1, relative to the rest of the country. To put this in context, consider that the Southern States' murder rate is the key factor behind America's high homicide rate (e.g., 7.4 per 100,000 in U.S., as compared to France's 1 per 100,000, or Japan's .6 or Britain's .5).

What accounts for these regional differences? Some suggestion comes from the pattern of homicides. **In the South, many murders are of a personal nature** (e.g., a result of a barroom brawl, a quarrel between acquaintances, or a fight between lovers). In contrast, elsewhere is the U.S. homicides usually begin with another crime, like a robbery and usually involve strangers. Nisbett (1993) proposes that a **perceived violation of an acculturated "code of honor" which derives from a cultural norm** contributes to the high homicide rate in Southern States. Nisbett and Cohen (1996) observe that Southerners, especially young white men, develop a greater tendency to focus on the need to gain and defend their prestige (honor) by fighting. They are more prone to think that physical retaliation is called for whenever someone insults or offends them.

Cohen (2001) notes that the frontier of the South and the historical roots of where people come from in Europe led to a **culture of honor** and an emphasis on *"masculine toughness"* that was different from the less violent milieu of the agricultural North. Men in the South came to value their reputation for toughness – as an "individual not to be messed with." They adopted a "tit for tat" interpersonal strategy where one reciprocates for the very last action the other does or that the other might do, as violence often begets more violence. *"Do onto others as they do unto you or do unto others before they do unto you."* In the Southern culture, toughness and preemptive belligerence became normative and the backdrop to honor-related homicides. Southerners (both men and women) tend to hold pro-violence attitudes about honor concerns.

Cohen (2001) goes on to observe that the **norms of violence** may be accompanied by **enhanced norms of courtesy and politeness**, as Southerners embrace politeness as a means to avoid the enmity of others. But such politeness can have the negative results of making insults and affronts all the more offensive when they occur and politeness can sometimes prevent people from directly working out their interpersonal difficulties before a conflict escalates.

The tendency of young men in the South responding in such an aggressive fashion goes back to the origin of the county, as noted by Alexis de Tocqueville in 1835. Fox Butterfield (1995) in his Pulitzer Prize award winning book, All God's Children, provides a moving sociological and historical account of how culture impacts on the development of violent behavior.

7. **Role of Biological Process.** Scarpa and Raine (1997) review the biological findings on violence (genetics, biochemistry, neuropsychology, psychopathology) and conclude that violent and criminal behavior "may indeed be partly mediated through biological mechanisms", but while biological factors may lead to a criminal behavior, it is an "insufficient explanation" of violent behavior. [For a discussion of the role of genetics and aggression see Eley et al., (1999), Lesch and Merschdorf (2000) and Tescott and Barondes (1990).] Asceltine et al. (2000) have proposed that violence should be seen as the consequence of stressors occurring in the context of some underlying social or constitutional vulnerability.

Moreover, social and psychological factors have also been found to predispose individuals to violence. The works of Mednick and Kandel (1988), Scarpa (1998) and Volavka (1995) illustrate that a combination of **biological vulnerability factors** (e.g., perinatal influences, attentional and emotional dysregulation) and **psychosocial risk factors** (unstable, non-intact, victimizing environments) **interacts** in contributing to aggressive and violent behaviors. It is important to keep in mind that a number of physical conditions can contribute to the expression of aggressive behaviors. These **physical conditions** may include low blood sugar, diabetes, hypoglycemia, hyperthyroidism, chronic pain, fatigue, too much caffeine, organic brain problems, such as brain tumors, Alzheimer's, cerebrovascular disorders, sleep deprivation, withdrawal from a mood altering substance and Vitamin B-12 deficiency (Tardiff, 1994). (See Matsakis, 1998, pp. 49-51 for a discussion of the impact of prescription drugs and how they interact with alcohol and drug abuse in contributing to aggression.) When changes in anger accompany physical disorders, DSM-IV characterizes these as a **Personality change owing to general medical conditions, aggressive type**. Also see Morrison (1997) for a discussion of how psychological problems can mask medical disorders.

How do these various factors exert their influences on the individual's likelihood to become angry and aggressive? A **social information-processing model** has been offered as a framework to understand the nature of anger / aggression. For an historical perspective of the various theoretical models to explain anger and aggressive behavior see Fesbach, 1986; Hall, 1998; Kemp and Strongman, 1995; Mandler, 1980; and Richardson, 1998.

A SOCIAL INFORMATION-PROCESSING ANALYSIS

(See Baron & Richardson, 1997; Baumeister et al., 1996; Crick & Dodge, 1994; Epps & Kendall, 1995; Feshbach & Zagrodzka, 1997; Greenberg & Paivio, 1997;Holtzworth-Munroe, 1992; Rusting & Nolen-Hoeksema, 1998; and Tsytsarev & Grodnitzky, 1995 for further discussion of the social information.)

A **social-cognitive model of angry behavior and aggression** offers a useful framework to understand the relationships between perceived provocations, accompanying feelings and thoughts, and aggressive behavior. Crick and Dodge (1994) and Holtzworth-Munroe (1992) have provided a **social information processing model** of **aggressive behavior** that highlights the following interdependent component processes of chronically aggressive individuals:

ENCODING PROCESS

- **selectively attend to cues**
- **hypervigilant for hostile cues**
- **failure to attend to relevant neutral and prosocial cues**

REPRESENTATION PROCESS

- **hostile attributional intentional bias**
- **failure to consider alternative explanations**
- **underperceive own aggression and overperceive others' responsibility**

RESPONSE SEARCH PROCESS

- **aggressive responses are most salient in memory**
- **poor ability in generating prosocial verbal assertive solutions**
- **implicit "if-then" rules, choose primarily aggressive goals**

RESPONSE DECISION PROCESS

- **failure to employ consequential thinking**
- **biased outcome estimates**
- **place value and derive satisfaction from aggressive behavior**

RESPONSE SELECTION PROCESS

- limited experience with non-aggressive responses
- preference for direct action aggressive solutions ("get even")
- scheme activation of intentionality elicits "cognitive scripts" that act as learned guides for aggressive responses

---

EMOTIONAL VULNERABILITY

- high sensitivity – low threshold for emotional reactions and immediate reactions
- high reactivity – extreme reactions and high arousal
- slow return to baseline – long-lasting reactions

According to the **social information-processing model**, how individuals **encode and interpret social cues**, and how they engage in **memory search, evaluation** and **enactment,** each influence the development and expression of anger/aggression. Aggressive individuals have **distorted and deficient social information-processing mechanisms.** They are prone to have **hostile interpretations, evidence hostile attributional biases, hold unrealistic expectations,** and have **cue-detection deficits** (misread social and situational cues and misread the intentions of others) that lead them to experience anger in situations where nonaggressive individuals are more likely to view the situation in a more benign manner. More specifically, **angry individuals** tend to:

a) maintain a **hostile attributional bias** (blame the cause of an event on the malicious and **hostile intentions** of another person(s); contains both the misperception of intent, but also the assumption of hostile motivation – (*"She meant for this to happen just to get back at me!"*);

b) **presume hostile intent** on the part of others, **be distracted from relevant social cues, choose aggressive responses to situations, evaluate aggressive responses as leading to successful outcomes, generate less constructive problem-resolving responses;**

c) **misattribute causes** (quickly and automatically perceive events as negative, even when information suggests alternative possibilities); have an **exaggerated sense of violation** and **feelings of having been wronged;**

d) be **poor estimators of probabilities** (overestimate the probability of negative outcomes, events, and/or personal resources and underestimate the possibility of positive outcomes);

e) **mind read** and believe in the **certainty of future events** (believe they know what others are thinking, how others will behave, and the consequences of their behavior);

f) **overgeneralize** - use broad constructs when evaluating **time** (e.g., *"always"*, *"never"*) and view **others** as being *"stupid, crazy, worthless"*;

g) use **dichotomous** black and white **thinking** (e.g., victim – aggressor; winners – losers; right – wrong; likes me - hates me);

h) use **inflammatory** or **provocative labeling** (use emotionally-charged language, *"Idiots"*, *"Jerks"*);

i) use **catastrophic evaluations** (e.g., *"horrible"*, *"awful"*, *"unbelievable"*, *"hate"*);

j) be **high demanders** and use **dictatorial thinking** (e.g., values cease to be preferences and become "sanctified dogma." Desires become commandments, expectations become absolute [Deffenbacher, 1999]);

k) engage in **self-focused rumination** (i.e., focus of attention is on the causes of a negative state, brooding on those causes, the perceived injustice and blame -- *"Why do other people treat me the way they do?"* **Focus on "why" questions**, the answers to which are not readily available and are highly inferential, as compared to "what" and "how" questions). This often leads to angry associations in memory *("Let it grow.", "Let it brood.")*;

l) view events as a **trespass** to a personal domain, as **insults to self** or to valued others, as **violations of values and expectations** (violate "code of honor", "code of the streets") (*"He dissed me*, -- show disrespect in front of my peers where I lose face.");

m) view anger and aggression as **justified**, appropriate, natural, and an **automatic response** to an unjust world; tend to **blame others** and not take responsibility for actions and consequences;

n) have **low frustration tolerance** - severe intolerance for discomfort as evident in the use of such phrases as: *"I can't stand it.", "I can't take it.", "I can't tolerate it."*; *"They should have done it my way."*

These **patterns of thinking** and accompanying **learned scripts** predispose angry individuals to become aggressive. They respond **more frequently** and **intensely** with angry emotions and in an uncontrolled manner with more negative consequences. The individuals' anger is also influenced by the **nature of the social knowledge and beliefs they hold,** as described next.

ROLE OF BELIEFS

DiGiuseppe et al. (1994) has highlighted that individuals with chronically high levels of anger **hold beliefs** that:

a) their anger is **justified, fitting** and **appropriate** (feel that he has been *"wronged, hurt, put down, treated unjustly"*) and now has a **"right"** to **get back** at the person (e.g., desire for retribution, *"evening the score"*);

b) reflect a **lack of emotional responsibility** for becoming angry (tendency to blame others) and **assign responsibility to external events** (e.g., *"Anger just happens to me."; "I just blew it."; "She hurt me (with words, and deeds), now it is my time to get back."; "An eye for an eye, a tooth for a tooth*);

c) other people are **being unreasonable** (e.g., *"They wanted me to follow some dumb, unfair rule."*);

d) they tend to **condemn** and **disparage** others (e.g., *use prejudicial racial epithets*);

e) reflect feelings of a **narcissistic self-righteousness**, demandingness, entitlement, deservingness, and unfairness (e.g., *"Feel wronged and have every right to retaliate"*);

f) reflect **long-standing** personal **grudges** and **cynicism**(e.g., *"It is a way of showing that I will not be pushed around."*);

g) the use of anger expression and aggression are the **only ways** to get attention, **gain respect** (e.g., *"This is the only way to get them to listen."*) and **avoid being further victimized** (e.g., *"Show that I am not a suck, or they will get me next."*);

h) they **must release** or **discharge** their emotions of anger (i.e., they hold an **"hydraulic"**, **cathartic-discharge** model of anger expression) as conveyed in such metaphoric expressions as *"Fuse lit", "Pressure pot", "Powder keg ready to blow", "Pump primed"; "Only way to get rid of my anger."*;

i) views the world as **"negative"** and depicts others as being antagonistic, threatening harmful and untrustworthy. Particularly of clinical concern is when the patient evidences **dichotomous thinking** (good-bad, friend-enemy) and refers to **diffuse others** -- *"They are out to get me."; "They betrayed me."* This may lead to a **justification position.** *"If they don't*

care about me, why should I care about them?"; "They don't deserve
the air they breath. I'm expendable and so are they."

The following quotes offered by <u>teenage murderers</u> further illustrate the **nature of beliefs** and the accompanying **lack of remorse** and **regret**. (Kopel, 2000, pp. 69-70)

"He brung it on himself."
"It must have been his time to go."
"I feel as though it wasn't my fault. This thing just happened. I ain't seen no
*   blood or nothing."*
"Everybody is vulnerable to mistakes. Mistakes will happen."
"I'm not a violent person. I didn't kill nobody. He killed himself."
"I killed him, but not in cold blood. I didn't shoot him two, three or four times.
*   I shot him once. I'm not really a violent person."*
"I looked at my right hand 'cause it pulled the trigger. I blame my right hand."
"If somebody see you with a gun, they gonna turn the other way – if not, they
*   must want to get shot."*
"It's not like I'm no serial killer. I didn't kill a lot of people."

Baumeister et al. (1996) have noted that a main source of anger and violence is **threatened egotism**, thinking well of oneself. Such **heightened self-esteem may be inflated or ill-founded** and when this heightened sense of self-esteem is challenged with an external evaluation that threatens or damages this self-view, angry aggressive behaviors may ensue. As Baumeister (1996) observes,

*The **most potent recipe for violence** is a **favorable view***
*of oneself that is disputed by someone else** – in short,*
'threatened egotism' (p. 141) ... Egotism is behind most
violent acts of revenge. (p. 132)

When individuals who are conceited, arrogant, consumed with thoughts of superiority and who view themselves as the "center of the universe" are threatened, this is a formula for aggression. **"Narcissists mainly want to punish or defeat someone who has threatened their highly favorable view of themselves."**

As noted, Cohen et al. (1996) report that when an event challenges an individual's or a groups' **"cultural code of honor"** (e.g., their status, masculine reputation) individuals are more likely to become upset and angry, especially if such insults occur in front of friends. Similarly, Anderson (1997) has noted that when adolescents are "dissed" (dishonored, disrespected, challenged) in front of their peers, this is an occasion to emotionally overrespond and become aggressive. Kopel (2000) reported that 18% of arrested juveniles agreed that *"It is okay to shoot someone who disrespected you."* 34% of gang members agreed.

Individuals who become angry and aggressive readily carry with them **prepotent schemas** that reflect concerns with **fairness, equity, justice, and a sense of entitlement**.

But, many individuals have similar concerns about fairness, equity, justice, then **what distinguishes those individuals who are chronically aggressive from nonclinical populations**?

It is proposed that it is _not_ the presence of their concerns or schemas _per se_, but rather:

    (1)   how <u>central</u>, compelling, or predominant the schemas are and how strongly the incident/beliefs are held;

    (2)   how <u>easily</u> and <u>readily</u> is the individual's core concerns or "<u>fuse</u>" lit or their "button is pressed";

    (3)   how <u>frequently</u> their concerns are <u>tapped</u> (situational generality);

    (4)   how readily disposed they are to <u>express anger overtly</u>;

    (5)   how <u>emotionally intense</u> their reactions are and <u>how long</u> their reactions <u>last</u> ("Can't let it go!");

    (6)   how <u>disruptive</u> their reactions are (interpersonally and intrapersonally);

    (7)   how easily the individual can be <u>interrupted</u> or <u>redirected</u> (distracted) once their schema has been triggered;

    (8)   how <u>impermeable</u> and how readily <u>open to disconfirming information/data</u> they are;

    (9)   how <u>long-standing</u> are the core concerns (developmental history of victimization and exposure to violence);

    (10)   how <u>culturally shared</u> and <u>normative</u> are their beliefs;

    (11)   how <u>responsive to treatment</u> or to other modes of intervention are they.

It is interesting to compare this current model of anger with that offered by the 18th Century French philosopher Rousseau in his discourse on the education of Emile. As Dent (2000) observes, Rousseau highlighted the role of **perceived demandingness** (feel deprived, denied, thwarted), **sense of entitlement** (feel something owed to them), **perceived unwarranted injury** (see events as an affront, having been ill-used), **sense of ownership** (deserving something in a form of placing a claim upon it as being one's own; being deprived of what is <u>rightfully</u> their due just by virtue of having laid claim upon it). Rousseau highlighted that it was this **habit of constructive interpretations** that sets the stage for anger and aggressive behaviors. A modern-day version of this is called a **constructive narrative perspective**.

CONSTRUCTIVE NARRATIVE PERSPECTIVE (CNP)

"We are lived by the stories we tell."

"We live in and through stories."

"Stories inform life."

"Individuals see everything that happens in terms of stories."

These observations reflect the emergence of a **narrative perspective** to explain goal-directed behaviors such as aggression. McAdams (2001) has proposed that individuals **construct stories** that make sense to them given their circumstances. These constructions are culturally influenced and reflect the values and norms of the individual's communities, as the discussion of the differential homicide rates in the former Confederacy States highlight. An individual's or group's current goals influence the ways in which socio-cultural and biographical information is retrieved, organized and the ways in which new information is processed. At the personal level, Elkind (1981) proposes that individuals generate "personal fables" that become self-fulfilling prophecies as they **come to live the stories they create about themselves and about others.**

Meichenbaum (1994, pp. 102-108) has reviewed the history of the **CNP** and has employed the narrative perspective to explain the impact of trauma exposure on the development of PTSD and the implications for assessment and treatment. He notes that traumatic events can create self-defining memories with vivid, affectively-charged, repetitive unresolved stories that are linked to other similar memories. It is proposed that in the same way that **CNP** can be used to understand therapeutic interventions with PTSD, the **CNP** can also be used to frame therapy procedures with angry and aggressive patients. In both the case of PTSD and anger, one of the tasks of therapy is to help patients co-create or refashion a different, more adaptive set of stories. For aggressive patients, the therapeutic goal is to collaborate in helping them generate a story about their "possible selves" as being "nonviolent individuals" who can exert self-control and achieve their goals in a nonaggressive fashion.

Many of the cognitive behavioral procedures that will be discussed below can be viewed from a **CNP** as a means of not only educating patients and teaching skills but also as a means of helping patients tell different stories about themselves and others. As a preview, consider that the cognitive-behavioral therapist will:

(1) **educate** patients about the nature of the anger-aggression cycle so they do not see themselves as mere "victims" of anger and of the reactions of others;

(2) **engage** patients in **goal-setting activities** that nurture their hope;

(3) **employ time-lines** that trace the patients' survival skills and "strengths", thus helping reframe their histories;

(4) have patients **self-generate reasons** for engaging in therapeutic activities;

(5) have patients **share** their **new accounts** with others;

(6) have patients **take credit** and **ownership** for changes;

(7) have patients **plan-ahead** and **view lapses as learning opportunities**.

In short, one can view the remainder of this **HANDBOOK** as a set of procedural guidelines designed to use assessment procedures, patients' feedback, and various therapeutic procedures as a means to have patients construct different stories, as well as learn how to employ more adaptive coping skills. A central component of the patients' stories are the **metaphors** that they use and how these come to be changed over the course of therapy.

METAPHORICAL LANGUAGE TO DESCRIBE ANGER

While psychologists may discuss anger in terms of information-processing terminology, such as encoding and decoding, belief systems and a constructive narrative perspective, aggressive individuals who are angry have their own ways of talking about anger. The manner in which they speak is relevant to the pattern of their thinking and to their implicit theories about the nature of anger. These implicit theories are often conveyed in the **language, narratives**, and **metaphors** they use to describe how they feel. As Lakoff (1987) aptly noted, the metaphors concerning anger often reflect the notion that anger needs to be **"emotionally discharged"** in some way, as the following list of patient metaphors denotes.

> *"There is no better metaphor for anger than a <u>hot fluid in a container</u>, when pressure reaches a critical point an explosion of anger emerges as a new property." (Robins & Novaco, 1999, p. 336)*

"Pressure cooker ready to blow." / "Reached my boiling point."

"Just letting off steam." / "All steamed up." / "Anger bottled up inside."

"Anger simmers." / "Doing a slow burn." / "Burned up." / "Breathing fire."

"Blew a fuse." / "Blew my top." / "Push my buttons." / "Last straw."

"You make my blood boil." / "Constantly on edge."/ "Powder keg."

"Like a blown up balloon ready to pop." / "Tied up in knots."

"Nerves shot." / "Volcanic outburst." / "Full of rage."

"Lash out in rage." / "Blinded by rage." / "Seething with rage, fuming."

"Feed my anger." / "Fueled my rage."

"Explosion of rage." / "Vent my spleen." / "Gripped, seized, torn by anger"

"Anger is a force that just takes charge."

"Anger is like witches' brew – bubbling and fermenting."

"Feel like a deer caught in headlights." / "Anger is in my nature."

These are not idle metaphors, but reflect the belief that **anger is something that wells up from within and just happens**. There is an accompanying belief that releasing anger and related emotions is a natural process that needs to, and invariably must run its course, be discharged and that there may be little one can do to control it.

Moreover, as Baumeister (1996) observes, an individual's or group's language can act as a "smoke screen" that can conceal, confuse, mislead, "sanitize" and deny responsibility for aggressive behavior. Consider the following examples of **elaborate justification of aggression**:

> *"Ethnic cleansing" / "Final solution" / "Special handling" / "Waste*
> *someone" / "Order a hit" / "Have someone whacked" / "Rub him out" /*
> *"Snuff her out" / "Getting a body" /*
> *"Pop someone" / "Exterminate" / "Knock him off" / "Even the score"*
> *Dehumanize victims – "Vermin, Slime, Filth, Use Racial Epithets"*

By employing such language to describe aggressive behavior, the perpetrator **avoids feelings of guilt and shame**. Guilt and shame can be prosocial emotions that strengthen bonds and that foster personal responsibility. These emotions of guilt and shame arise out of a fear of losing relationships. Without such concerns, the restraints for engaging in aggressive behavior are reduced.

As to be discussed below, a major function of the assessment and educational processes is to help patients appreciate the role and responsibility they play in **inadvertently, unwittingly**, and perhaps even **unknowingly**, contributing to their anger and aggressive behavior and learning alternative ways to control anger and prosocial ways to achieve their goals.

Before considering these assessment and treatment procedures, we will first consider the **developmental** features of anger/aggressive behavior. We will consider three questions:

(i)   **How does angry, aggressive, and violent behavior develop?**

(ii)   **How do you make a violent person?**

(iii) **What can be done to alter this developmental trajectory or "career path" toward violent behavior?**

A **Case Conceptualization Model** will be offered as a framework to understand the influence of multiple factors in contributing to aggressive behavior.

SUMMARY:
WHAT YOU SHOULD TAKE AWAY FROM SECTION I

1. An appreciation of just how widespread are angry and aggressive behaviors.

2. The societal, psychosocial and physiological consequences of chronic anger and aggressive behaviors.

3. That anger and aggression not only reflect an act, but also a complex set of cognitive and emotional reactions.

4. That social information processing deficits and the "stories" or narratives that angry individuals offer to themselves and to others, help to explain the nature of anger and how it escalates to aggression.

5. That aggressive behavior may take different forms (reactive, proactive, and the combination).

6. That what distinguishes high and low angry individuals is not the type or number of provocations they are exposed to, but the beliefs and meanings those events hold for them.

7. That a number of factors (**individual** – in terms of stress, alcohol consumption, mood disorders and biological processes; **societal and ecological** – cultural beliefs, poverty and availability of guns) influence the likelihood of anger escalating to the point of becoming aggressive behavior.

In order to test your knowledge and understanding, each **SECTION** of the **HANDBOOK** will conclude with a set of questions where you can **TEST YOUR EXPERTISE**.

TEST YOUR EXPERTISE[3]: SECTION I

1. Consider when you become angry. How often do you become angry? How intense is your anger? On a 0 to 10 point scale, where 0 equals mild annoyance, irritation and 10 equals intense rage, where would you fall? What does it take to get your anger to increase on this scale?

2. Close your eyes and replay in your mind's eye a situation when you, or someone you treat, becomes angry. What factors do you think contributed to the anger onset, and most importantly, what does the person have to do (say to himself) in order to foment and sustain the anger?

3. What would it take for your anger to escalate to the point of aggression? What about your patients? You may need help from others *(accomplices)* to escalate your anger. What do they have to do to escalate your anger to the point of aggression?

4. Can you or someone be aggressive without being angry? In answering this question, comment on the differences between reactive and proactive aggression? What are the differences between these forms of aggression? Give an example of when these two forms of aggression can be combined.

5. How aggressive are you as a driver? What about the drivers around you? How can aggressive driving be an example of the combination of reactive and proactive aggression?

6. When and how can anger be an adaptive and a useful emotion? Give two examples.

7. A friend or relative comes to you and asks you to explain why there is so much violence in the U.S. How would you answer this question? In your answer include comments about:

    (1) Who commits which kind of violent acts and where they come from or live geographically in the U.S.

    (2) The role of developmental histories, highlighting the role of victimization. *(Discussed in more detail in Section II.)*

---

[3] *This Handbook can be used in various training programs. The Questions and Exercises included at the end of each SECTION provide a basis for the reader to assess his/her knowledge and understanding. The QUESTIONS are designed to stimulate critical thinking and group discussion. Find two colleagues and work your way through this HANDBOOK as a team. In subsequent SECTIONS, I have included a number of 3 person role-plays and exercises. Performing these role plays, will increase all of the participants' expertise.*

(3) The influence of biological and psychological factors.

(4) The role of availability of weapons and role that substance abuse plays.

8. Clinicians need to be on the lookout for the possibility that a patient's aggression may be a consequence of a variety of physical disorders. List the physical disorders that can contribute to aggressive behaviors.

9. Did you grow up in a state in the U.S. that was part of the Confederacy? If not, interview someone who grew up in the South. Ask them about the "cultural code of honor" and the norms for politeness. How do these contribute to the high incidence of violence in this part of the U.S.?

10. Revisit your recollection of when you became angry. Now analyze this angry incident using the **social information-processing model**. Or use an account of aggression offered by a patient. Use each of the components of the model to explain the aggressive behavior (namely, encoding, representation, search, decision and selection processes, and emotional vulnerability).

11. What role do the following concepts play in the explanation of aggressive behavior?

> a) hostile attribution bias
> b) belief systems
> c) egotism
> d) cultural code of honor
> e) code of the streets

12. Finally, what are your favorite **metaphors** for anger? Listen to your patients talk about their anger. What metaphors do they use? What are their meta-theories about controlling anger and other emotions?

13. What role do the feelings of guilt and shame play in inhibiting aggressive behaviors? What are the implications for assessment and treatment?

SECTION II: A DEVELOPMENTAL LIFE-SPAN PERSPECTIVE OF AGGRESSIVE BEHAVIOR

(The information summarized in this SECTION came from research and reviews offered by Baron & Richardson, 1997; Blechman et al., 1995; Dodge & Crick, 1990; Dodge et al., 1995; Fraser, 1996; Frick, 1998; Goldstein, 1999; Karr-Morse & Wiley, 1997; Loeber, 1990; Loeber, Burke et al., 2000; Loeber & Stouthamer-Loeber, 1998; Maugh & Rutter, 1998; Moffitt, 1993; Osofsky, 1997; Schlesinger, 2000)

If we wish to understand, prevent, and treat adults who have problems controlling their anger and aggressive behavior, our intervention efforts would prove to be more effective if we took into consideration the multiple developmental pathways of such aggressive behavior. The career adult criminal tends to have roots in juvenile delinquency. Moreover, our intervention efforts should be informed by an appreciation of what interventions "work" and "don't work" and by knowledge of those programs that can inadvertently make the situation "worse."

A **life-span perspective** provides a framework for addressing such questions as:

> *"How does one make an aggressive and violent individual?"*
> *"How does an individual get from the point of conception to the point of where he murders someone, like Melissa?"*

A number of authors (Adams, 1974; Cornell, 1989; Ewing, 1990; Heide, 1999, 2001) have indicated that the answers to these questions are complex, and yet incomplete. But, a consideration of the current "state of the art" will highlight what we now know and what we still need to find out.

CONTENTS SECTION II

With this information in mind, we can then turn our attention to the issues of assessment and treatment of adults with anger-control problems and aggressive behavior. As we will see, an intervention program needs to be sensitive to developmental, ecological, cultural and gender factors. There is a need to view adults problems in the context of a **life-span perspective**.

EPIDEMIOLOGY OF AGGRESSIVE BEHAVIOR
IN CHILDREN AND YOUTH

(See Dahlberg, 1998; Kopel, 2001; Sege & Licenziato, 2001; Websites – Appendix B)

In the same way that we considered the epidemiology and the widespread incidence and seriousness of aggressive behavior in adults, we begin the discussion of a **life-span perspective** by considering the incidence of angry and aggressive behavior in children and adolescents. For example:

- In the U.S., one million minors come into contact with the Juvenile Justice system each year. 90% of incarcerated youths are held for nonviolent offences. Overall, youths are responsible for 19% of all violent crime.

- The seriousness of the problem is underscored by the findings that between 1980 and 1997 there were 20,000 murders in the U.S. committed by juveniles (2% were by children under the age of 12).

- Murder is the fourth leading cause of death among children younger than 14 years of age. On average, there are 17 Americans between the ages of 15 and 24 murdered each day. Teens are $2^{1/2}$ times more likely than adults to be victims of violence.

- In a National Survey of high school students, 36% had been in a physical fight more than once during the past year, with 4% requiring medical attention. Victims frequently become perpetrators in future assaults.

- A small percentage of youth account for a disproportionately large number of offences against people and property. **6% of boys account for 50% of crimes**, often beginning their careers of crime before age 12

- Approximately 4% to 10% of children are diagnosed with **Conduct Disorder – CD** (average 6% of boys and 1.6% girls)

- Among a psychiatric CD population, 75% are boys and 33% are girls *(See discussion below about gender differences in CD)*

- CD usually begins before age 10 and **Oppositional Defiant Disorder - ODD** usually precedes CD. It is rare for CD to appear after age 18. As described below, there may be late-starter CD individuals, who also have a 15+ age onset. There is also evidence for some CD individuals desisting from aggressive antisocial behaviors.

- Antisocial behavior among high school students correlates with other high-risk behaviors such as sexual acting out, smoking, alcohol and other substance abuse, academic difficulties and sexual acting-out.

EVIDENCE FOR THE STABILITY OF AGGRESSIVE BEHAVIOR

(See Derzon, 2001; Furlong et al., 2001; Lahey et al., 2000; Loeber & Farrington, 2000; Miller, 2001; Morrison & Skiba, 2001; Pajer, 1998; Reddy et al., 2001; Sprague et al., 2001; Walker & Sprague, 1999)

The **consistency of aggressive behavior** over the lifespan was highlighted by Olweus (1979) who had reported results of 16 longitudinal studies. He reported a stability coefficient of .68 between childhood aggression at age 8 and young adults (age 21). More recent meta-analysis of 58 prospective studies (including 38, 000 subjects) revealed far less consistency of aggressive behavior over time. Derzon (2001) reported a **correlation between childhood and adult aggression of .34**. Morrison and Skiba (2001, p. 176) in their qualitative review concluded:

> **_Less than 50%_ of children with extreme antisocial behavior become antisocial adults or continue to exhibit antisocial behaviors in their later childhood or teen years.**

> **_Not_ all aggressive children become violent youthful offenders and _not_ all violent youthful offenders become violent adults (Jonson-Reid, 1998, p. 160).**

Most children and youth who engage in antisocial or substance-using behaviors <u>are</u> <u>unlikely</u> to engage in later violence. Selection criteria will **fail to identify 60%** of those who will display later aggressive and violent behavior (60% false negative rate) and 60% of those who engage in antisocial and/or substance-abusing behaviors were not later violent offenders (60% false positive rate) (Derzon, 2001).

While there is evidence for relative consistency in aggressive behaviors (as enumerated below), **there is also <u>much hope</u> that among those who are initially aggressive a large percentage will desist**. We will consider below some of the "protective" and "resilience" factors that may contribute to desistance. The following findings highlight that among the core group of aggressive children there is evidence for **relative stability**.

- Noncompliance in preschool predicts school-age aggression (e.g., 18 months predicts 2 years of age). *(Note that temper tantrums and physical aggression peak around the end of two years of age and the beginning of year 3.)* 50% of boys and 40% of girls at preschool evidence aggressive behavior - hits, bites, kicks, grabs.

- 50% of children as young as 4 and 5 years of age who evidence externalizing symptoms will develop persistent psychosocial problems. Age 3 children with undercontrolled temperaments have been linked to interpersonal conflicts at age 21. *(Note however that externalizing behaviors are relatively common in young children.)*

- 38% of kindergartens who evidence aggressive behavior will fail grade 3, and in turn, of those who fail grade 3, there is a 1 in 3 chance of their evidencing adolescent delinquent behavior.

- Antisocial behavior in grade 4 leads to peer rejection at grade 6 and accompanying academic failure. Academic failure has been most clearly identified as a significant risk factor for later use of alcohol and drugs.

- Two-thirds of aggressive boys are rejected by peers, while only 20% of nonaggressive boys are rejected.

- The onset of minor aggression (e.g., annoying others) tends to precede the onset of violence, with most violent behavior appearing after age 10. Aggressive behavioral patterns become increasingly stable during the early school years.

- Bullies have a fourfold increase in criminality as adolescents (60% of bullies between grades 6 and 9 have one conviction by age 24; 40% of bullies vs. 10% of nonbullies engage in criminal activities – 3 or more arrests). *(Note, that bullying is negatively related to peer status at grade 3, but not at grade one. Bullying has different meaning and functions at different grade levels.)*

- Bullies evidence aggressive behavior toward teachers, parents and sibs. Bullies are more likely to be physically active, impulsive and physically strong. The rate of overt bullying decreases over grade levels (in grade 2, 16% of children are bullied; in grade 9, 5% of children are bullied). Parents of bullies tend to lack warmth, model aggressive behavior, use harsh physical punishment, and evidence poor parental supervision. The bully at school is often a bullying victim at home.

- Boys are more likely to be bullies than girls and boys are more likely to be victims of bullies. Bullies evidence aggressive behavior toward teachers, parents and sibs.

- Aggressive behavior is stable by grade 3. Grade 3 and 4 troublesome behaviors correlate .42 with being an adolescent offender.

- The prevalence of overt conduct problems increases from childhood to adolescence, while the incidence of physically fighting tends to decrease. But serious forms of aggression such as robbery, rape and attempted or completed homicide tend to increase during adolescence.

- Conduct problem behavior is more likely to begin before drug abuse than vice versa. The escalation of delinquent behavior is often accompanied by substance abuse.

- Peer-directed aggression at age 8 correlates with spousal abuse at age 30. Childhood aggression (as determined by peer nominators) significantly predicted the number of convictions for driving while intoxicated 22 years later.

- Half the children with serious violent offenses *(SVO)* prior to age 11 continue violent adult careers, but half do not. 30% of youths continue violent behavior into adulthood if their first violent acts occurred during preadolescence (ages 11-13). 10% of youths continue violent behavior into adulthood if their first violent act occurred during adolescence. The highest age risk of SVO is 15 to 16 years of age.

- 75% of convicted juvenile offenders are reconvicted between ages 17 to 24.

- Over half the persons who become involved in SVO prior to age 27 committed their first violent offense between ages 14 to 17.

- Antisocial behavior and **Disruptive Behavior Disorders (DBD)** ("externalizing" behaviors) are transmitted across generations. Early offenders often come from families in which assaultive, predatory behaviors are evident in parents and relatives. For example, there is a correlation between antisocial criminal behavior of fathers and sons. Maternal delinquent activity during adolescence predicts single-parent family status and accounts for the relationship between family status and externalizing behavior among their children. Mothers who evidenced delinquent behaviors during adolescence are 50% more likely to have a child with externalizing behavior problems.

- There is a correlation between mothers' and fathers' criminal convictions; a direct effect of parent convictions on child convictions, and a criminality socialization effect among siblings.

DIVERSE DEVELOPMENTAL PATHWAYS TO AGGRESSIVE BEHAVIORS: EARLY AND LATE STARTER MODELS

Moffitt (1993) has proposed **three developmental pathways** to antisocial and violent behaviors, each defined by the **age of onset.**

1) **Life-course persistent type (early starters – prior to age 14)** – begin evidencing conduct problems early to middle childhood. By adolescence account for almost half of all adolescent crimes and the majority of violent crimes. Associated with both chronic juvenile offending and adult recidivism. Late onset is significantly <u>less</u> related to both of these outcomes.

2) **Late-onset adolescent limited type (late starters)** – initiate offending in adolescence and usually desist by late adolescence or early adulthood as they marry and enter the workforce. (14+ age onset, rare to appear after 18)

3) **Limited-duration type --** child / adolescent usually desists (start and stops)

LIFE - COURSE TYPE: EARLY STARTER MODEL

(The following list indicates the predicative value of factors that are related to the making of a violent individual. In considering these <u>risk factors</u>, it is the <u>total number of risk factors</u> present which is more important than the specificity of the risk factors.)

Early -onset externalizing or antisocial behavior problems are **relatively stable** across the lifespan. The factors that may contribute to such a persistent life-course include:

During **pregnancy**, mother may use hard drugs, consume alcohol, smoke, engage in poor nutrition, exposure to environmental toxins, experience high stress levels resulting in premature births, low birth weight, developmental delays

Child born with a **difficult temperament** (irritable, impulsive, uninhibited, novelty-seeking). The level of distress proneness in infants can evoke in parents avoidance, hostility, criticism, with the result of a transactional, bi-directional coercive exchange. Researchers have found that the infant characteristics of a difficult temperament and impulsivity elicit harsh parenting by age 4, which in turn predicted externalizing problems by age 10. (Bates et al., 1995; O'Connor et al., 2001)

Difficult to socialize (evidence preschool noncompliance, stubbornness, resistance to
control, difficult to manage, tantruming, can begin a coercive- parent-child
escalating conflict cycle).

Attentional deficits, hyperactivity, language-delay, socially unskilled, negative
emotionality and risk-taking behaviors precede childhood and adolescent antisocial
behavior. The onset of CD is particularly early in boys with ADHD and ODD. In
half of the cases ADHD boys will become antisocial depending upon the level of
parenting skills. Parental absence of cognitive assistance and little help learning
new skills, parental nattering, explosive discipline and escalating coercive cycles
are contributing factors.

Overt conduct problems (oppositional behavior, disobedience, rebelliousness,
aggressiveness, bullying,). Aggression is usually accompanied by ODD symptoms
(negativistic, defiant, hostile, which usually starts before age 7). This **overt
pathway** of minor aggression at age 7 contributes to physical fighting at 14 and
aggressive antisocial late teenage years. Teenagers who are most likely to get hurt
in fights are those who are most likely to abuse drugs, be sexually precocious,
engage in reckless driving, and drop out of school (Arnett et al., 1997). *The
discovery of risky behaviors in any one of these domains should lead to inquiry
into the other areas.*

Early onset of CD problems is often preceded by **persistent ODD symptoms**. Physical
fighting and ODD is predictive of CD.

Poor peer relations and peer rejection (difficulty playing cooperatively), social
withdrawal and isolation limits social opportunities with other children. ADHD
children tend to be socially immature, interruptive, intrusive, disruptive and
aggressive. Peer relations and academic failure are often correlated, approximately
.40.

Poor academic progress and low academic achievement (low IQ and reading problems).
Defiance and avoidance of authority -- truancy, running away. Low bonding to
school. (Ask student: *"If you were absent from school, who, besides your friends
would notice you were not present and miss you?"* Taps positive contact with
adults in school.)

There is a link between **developmental reading problems** and delinquency.
Incarcerated adolescents are on average 5 years below expected grade level. Poor
readers are more likely to be incarcerated for crimes of greater violence than better
readers, and they are 3 times more likely to be injured in a fight requiring medical
intervention and more likely to miss school (Davis et al., 1999; Maugh et al., 1996).
Up to 80% of incarcerated youth are functionally illiterate (Karr-Morse & Wiley,
1997).

<u>Disciplinary contacts with Principal</u> – 6% to 9% of children account for 50% of office discipline referrals. The number of discipline contacts with the Principal during the school year predict arrest status in 5th and 10th grades. If student has 10+ disciplinary referrals to Principal's office in a year, he is a serious risk for school failure, delinquency, drug and alcohol use. Up to 40% of school suspensions are likely to be repeat reoffending. School aggressive behavior and substance abuse predicts weapon possession, gang membership and marijuana use. (Morrison & Skiba, 2001)

A **<u>covert pathway</u>** of concealing conduct problems such as shoplifting, stealing, vandalism, property damage, animal cruelty, fire-setting, manipulating peers into antisocial acts can lead to moderately serious delinquency. These children often lack empathy for victims, guilt or remorse. The overt pathway can escalate this covert pathway. The converse is <u>not</u> usually true. CD children who evidence callous and unemotional symptoms have more serious behavioral problems and have more contact with the police.

<u>Associates with deviant peers</u>. Individuals select like-minded friends. Friends of antisocial youth are more likely to experiment with drugs, engage in substance abuse, experiment with sex and other risk-taking behaviors. Youth murderers are more likely than older murderers to act as part of a group. Moreover, a number of researchers have highlighted the dangers and **negative effects of pull out programs that bring together antisocial peers** into some form of interventions program. Dishion (1994) and Dishion et al. (1999) have characterized such programs as a way to inadvertently conduct **deviancy training**. As a result of participating in these treatment programs, antisocial children receive increased attention and interest from participants that reinforce antisocial behaviors. (See Eddy et al., 2001; Gottfredson, 1987). Also, having an **older sibling** who is aggressive and engages in substance abuse increases the likelihood of antisocial behavior.

<u>Substance use</u> – early drunkenness predicts later aggression, but <u>not</u> the converse. Multiple or <u>polydrug use</u> (alcohol, smoking, marijuana) put youth at most risk for developing aggression. Substance use, police arrests and health risk taking behaviors are highly intercorrelated.

Availability and **<u>ready access to weapons</u>**, cruelty to people and animals, and weapon use predicts subsequent CD. Recall Kopel's (2000) observation that it is <u>not</u> just the mere availability of weapons that accounts for the high incidence of juvenile violence.

Living in violent communities – violence exposure, (re)victimization, lack of feelings of safety, and communal attitudes condoning violence, each contribute to the development of violence (Johnson-Reid, 1998). See Flannery et al. (2001), Moffitt (1996), Singer et al. (1995) for a discussion of how to assess children's exposure to violence. Sege and Licienziato (2001) highlight that injured teenagers in a fight, robbery, or assault have been found to be **six times more likely to be injured again** in a fight. Following such an episode, the principal, teacher, doctor, parent should ask the youth such questions as:

> *Do you feel safe leaving here (hospital, office)?*
> *Is there a safe place to go to while things cool off?*
> *What plans do you have regarding the other person(s) involved in the fight?*
> *Are you thinking about revenge?*
> *Is there someone (an adult) who can help mediate the fight (help as a go-between)?*
> *Is there a peer mediation program in your school (community) that you can use to settle this conflict?*

Ineffective parenting practices such as **inadequate parental supervision** (poor monitoring of child's activities, whereabouts, peers), parental uninvolvement and indulgence, parental rejection, inconsistent harsh punishment, humiliation (receive comments about "essential badness" and punish for who he is and not for what he did). As a result, children learn to avoid parents' attempts to discipline. This coercive bi-directional process is exacerbated by the parents not setting and not imposing limits with their children; inconsistent rule enforcement; lack of nurturance and warmth. The importance of ineffective parenting was highlighted by Patterson et al. (2000) who reported that **parent training** effectively increased parental discipline effectiveness, and this, **in turn**, was associated with reduced child noncompliance and antisocial behavior. These reductions, **in turn**, were accompanied by significant improvements in peer relations. The results of the Patterson et al. (2000) study underscore the interdependence of the multiple factors included in the developmental pathway toward antisocial and aggressive behavior.

Unstable familial environment – level of marital distress, occurrence of domestic violence, conflictual divorce, parents never wed or out of wedlock child. Note that in the U.S., 40% of children are born to married parents who will eventually divorce. The children of conflictual divorced parents are at high risk for a variety of behavioral, emotional and academic problems.

Parent-child and parent-adolescent conflict – Poor quality of parenting and high incidence of parent-adolescent conflict predicts association with deviant peers one year later (Ary et al., 1998). The process of acculturation (discrepancy between parents and adolescent can also contribute to familial conflict). The adolescent's natural striving for independence combined with acculturation to values of individualism can occur in contrast to the parent's values to preserve strong family cohesion and parental controls. Szapocznik and Williams (2000) highlight the need for **bicultural effectiveness training** to address conflicting cultural values between parents and their adolescent children..

Child maltreatment increases the probability of violent delinquency 11%, while abuse and neglect increases the risk of violent crime by 29%. Early physical abuse predicts the development of children being hypervigilant to hostile cues, having hostile attributional biases and using aggressive problem-solving strategies. While most maltreated children do not engage in delinquent behavior, having been abused or neglected as a child increase the likelihood of arrest as a juvenile by 53%, as an adult by 38%, and being involved in a violent crime by 38%. Children identified prior to kindergarten as having been abused by an adult during the first 5 years of life are 4 times more likely to engage in acting out behaviors by the 4th and 5th grades. *(See discussion below for further examples of the role that trauma exposure plays in the development of aggressive antisocial behaviors.)*

Develops **insecure attachment relationships** with parents and with other prosocial adults and lacks attachment to conventional societal organizations or activities. Absence of positive role models and preoccupation with **violent media**.[4]

Presence of other problems (**comorbid disorders**) such as depression, anxiety, learning disability substance abuse, somatization. *(See discussion below on examples of comorbidity with CD.)* There is a **high incidence of psychiatric disorders** among youths in the **juvenile justice system**, including conduct disorder, depression, ADHD, learning disability and developmental disabilities, as well as medical problems. 50% - 75% of juvenile offenders also have substance abuse problems. 32% of juvenile offenders have PTSD (higher among female offenders – 70%) (Cauffman et al., 1998; Steiner et al., 1997). Also true of a community sample of dangerously violent adolescents (Flannery et al., 2001).

Delinquency (arrest and authority conflicts), school suspension, expulsion, **drop out of school** and **gang membership** each accelerates illegal activity. (Low parental monitoring, poor academic skills and peer rejection predict association with deviant peers by early adolescence.) Dropouts have high rates of violence exposure and psychological problems.

Boys who engage in **dating violence** are more likely to demonstrate risky sexual behavior, engage in forced sex and threaten others with physical violence. Girls who report dating violence are more likely to attempt suicide, engage in risky sexual behaviors, become pregnant, ride in a car with a drunk driver, and use injectable drugs.

---

[4] The importance of obtaining a **media history** is underscored by the fact that the average American child spends more than **21 hours per week** viewing television which translates into viewing 10,000 acts of violence per year. In addition, preadolescent boys spend approximately 4 hours per week playing video games, 50% of which have violent content (Villani, 2001). See Bushman and Anderson (2001) for a fascinating account of media violence. *Also see Websites on Media Literacy.*

Recidivism – early (< 11 years of age) and repeated involvement with juvenile justice system, rearrest, multiple agency involvement. (Cornell et al., 1999 discuss the role that anger plays in contributing to recidivism in adolescence.)

Incarcerating adolescents in adult prisons. As Talbot (2000) observes, within the last 10 years the number of teenagers doing time in adult prisons has more than doubled. One in 10 juvenile offenders are incarcerated in adult prisons in the U.S. **60%** of youth who had been released from adult prisons for murder or attempted murder were **returned**. Of those returned, 80% were released again. (Heide et al., 2001). The follow-up data also indicated that most failed within the **first three years of release**. Bishop et al. (1996) and Winner et al. (1997) have reported a significantly higher recidivism rate among youth transferred to adult prisons with more serious offences than those youth who were sent to the juvenile justice system. Parenthetically, it is interesting to note that the follow-up data on juvenile murderers who had <u>killed their parents</u> was <u>more favorable</u>, with a successful reintegration into society being crime-free, as compared to juvenile murderers who had killed strangers, acquaintances and relatives (Heide, et al., 2001).

Without intervention delinquent youth are likely to go on to lead lives characterized by heavy drinking, polydrug use, sexual promiscuity, reckless driving, marital violence, occupational marginality and criminality.

System failures may also contribute to the escalation of violent behavior. For example, agencies and schools may ignore parents' pleas for help; ignore the youth's escalating threats of violence; lack of communication and collaboration across social system agencies, failure to work with each other or with parents, provision of inadequate assessment and treatment, limited after-school programs, no interested adults. A good example of how the lack of communication contributed to school violence is the **Columbine High School shooting** – see the Governor's report at *http://www.state.co.us*

Minority differences. 18 to 25 years of age the overall rate of aggressive behavior begins to decline, but this decline is <u>not</u> similarly evident among African-Americans. The criminal career lasts longer for African-American males. Minority youth are also more likely to be victimized by peer violence. Thus, some aggressive behaviors may be self-protective. African-Americans who comprise about 14% of U.S. population, account for half of all juvenile homicide arrests.

Almost all offenders commit their first offence before age 21.

Antisocial behavior wanes after age 40.

Dutton (1998, 1999) and Jones (1996) have highlighted **three classes of factors that contribute to the development of aggressive behavior**. These include:

1) **Exposure to trauma history** in the form of violence directed toward self or others (e.g., 3.3 million children in U.S. witness parental violence; 70% of perpetrators of physical violence had experienced victimization [physical/sexual abuse], however most abused men do <u>not</u> become perpetrators). Exposure to urban violence, neighborhoods characterized by high crime rates and social disorganization. For example, studies in California estimate that 10% to 20% of all homicides are witnessed by children (Pynoos & Eth, 1986). "Virtually all" of the inner city ethnic minority children in South Central Los Angeles witness a homicide by age 5 (Parsons, 1994). In New Orleans, 90% of fifth grade children witness violence, and 40% have seen a dead body (Osofsky, 1997). 39% of children living in medium to high crime neighborhoods in Chicago have witnessed a shooting, 35% have seen a stabbing, 24% have seen someone murdered (Osofsky, 1997).

2) **Insecure attachment relationships** which contribute to high rejection-sensitivity and to externalizing defenses. As a result, such individuals have the tendency to attribute relationship conflict to traits in the other person or to external sources.

3) **Shaming experiences** and **rejection by fathers** in the form of public humiliation; comments about the individual's essential "badness"; global attacks, ***"You are never going to amount to anything."***; and random punishment which conveys the message that he is punished for who he is, <u>not</u> for what he did.

SUMMARY OF EARLY PATHWAY TO AGGRESSION

High-risk intrauterine environment

↓

Difficult temperament / Difficult to socialize

↓

Parental rejection, neglect, escalating coercive disciplinary cycles, victimization, exposure to violence

↓

In about half the cases, around age 10, ADHD and oppositionality progress to conduct disorders with accompanying callousness that takes covert and overt delinquency pathways

↓

Aggressive behavior, social incompetence, peer rejection, academic difficulties, especially reading comprehension and math deficiencies

↓

Discipline problems (especially bullying behavior), affiliate with deviant peers, substance abuse, and other risk –taking behaviors, preoccupation with violent media), dating violence

↓

Accompanying inadequate parenting (especially absence of supervision and low parental involvement in academics), coercive parent-adolescent conflict

↓

Exposure to high-risk family and neighborhood violent environment

↓

Involvement with the justice system and related agencies (especially being sent to adult prison)

LATE-ONSET TYPE: A CASE STUDY OF SCHOOL SHOOTERS[5]

(See Discussion Below on Predicting Violence pp. 187)

The developmental pathway just described covers the **Early Starter Model** and illustrates how the variety of biological, psychological and social factors can "conspire" in contributing to violent behavior.[6] A second developmental pathway to violent behavior is that of the **late-starter model** (14 years +). An example of this late-starter model is that of the recent study of **school shooters**. While school shooters vary, the recent research indicates yet another developmental pathway to make a violent individual.

While schools are still the safest place for children and adolescents with less than 1% of all child/youth homicides occurring in schools, the recent rash of school shootings in the U.S. have caused great concern and the search for possible risk factors. The following list of **risk factors** which is a summary of a compilation offered by Dwyer et al. (1998), McGee and DeBarnardo (1999), Verlinden et al. 2000, and The FBI Report on school shooters *(see Website in Appendix B)* underscore the observation that the factors that have been implicated in predicting general aggressive behavior of **early starters** such as child abuse and neglect, poverty, academic failure, lack of educational opportunities and substance abuse do not seem to apply in the case of school shooters. While each school shooting has its own particular signature, assailants of school shootings have been primarily from middle class or affluent families, many of whom had no previous criminal records. One factor that is often common across both generally aggressive youth and school shooters is being involved in **bullying** (being a bully or victim of bullying, or both).

In most instances, the school shooter has been someone who more readily fits the **late-onset type** and fits what McGee and DeBarnardo (1999) call the **classroom avenger** with the following features:

---

[5] In 1998, 6000 students were expelled from schools in the U.S. for possessions of firearms. Nevertheless, **violent deaths at schools** are not only extremely rare, but **on the decline**.

[6] For example, instruments designed to identify such early starters and predict juvenile recidivism include the youth's age at first referral or adjudication; number of prior arrests; number of out-of-home placements or institutional commitments; level of academic achievement; school behavior and attendance; substance abuse; family stability; parental control; and peer relationships (Heilbrun et al., 2000). **Note, many of these indicators do not apply to the school shooter.**

Features of the Perpetrator

Primarily an adolescent male

Raised in middle class family in suburban or rural area

Not have a history of severe conduct problems, nor an extensive history of legal activity

Tends to be rejected by peers (labeled as "geek" or "nerd"). Social outcast or loner.

Experienced repetitive severe bullying.

> *"I killed because people like me are mistreated everyday. I did this to*
> *show society; push us and we will push back."*
> *(School shooter, Pearl, Mississippi)*
>
> *"This is what you get for the way you treated us."*
> *"I hate you people for leaving me out of so many fun things."*
> *"You made me what I am. You added to my rage."*
> *(School shooters, Columbine High School, Colorado)*

May belong to a group of other similarly ostracized teenagers

Has a negative image of self (view self as physically unattractive)

From early age has difficulty bonding and establishing attachment relationships

May engage in covert vandalism and dishonesty developmentally

Interested in real and fictional violence, preoccupied by violent fiction, movies, music and engages in violent fantasy, racist's beliefs

Academic achievement within normal limits or above average, but academic performance tends to decline within weeks or months preceding the violent outburst

Has access to guns and other forms of destruction. May be proficient with weapons.

Depressed, but often manifested as being sullen, angry, irritable and reclusive

Lack of parental supervision

Lack of communication across social services (lack of collaboration and shared information / responsibility about the perpetrators across agencies)

Nature of the Violent Act

Considered a "crime of vengeance", often precipitated by disciplinary action from an authority figure and/or rejection by peers or from a girlfriend

Target victims may be popular or high achieving school peers and/or aggrieved adult and/or victim of hatred and racism

At the time of the shooting, the perpetrator may express a wish to kill, a wish to be killed, and a wish to die

Prior to the violent act, the perpetrator is prone to express his intent to kill someone, commit suicide, and do something highly dramatic prior to the violent attack. This threat may be in the form of boasts or warnings. These communications are most likely to be conveyed to peers, rather than to adults (authority figures).

Prior to the violent act, the perpetrator may be preoccupied with thoughts of revenge (feel justified) about performing violent acts; ("getting even") and has developed elaborate plans.

Quite often, the violent act is done with another peer.

SUMMARY OF RISK FACTORS IN SCHOOL SHOOTINGS

(See Dwyer et al., 1998; Verlinden et al., 2000; and Time Magazine March 19, 2001, as well as WEBSITES on School Safety – APPENDIX B)

INDIVIDUAL FACTORS

Threatens violence
Has a detailed plan
Blames others for problems
Uncontrolled anger
Depression
Suicidal threats
History of discipline problems
Violent writings or drawings
Cruelty to animals
Substance abuse
Previous mental health treatment
Has brought weapon to school

FAMILY FACTORS

Lack of warm family relationship
Lack of parental supervision
Perceived lack of family support
Victim of abuse or neglect

SCHOOL / PEER

Poor coping and social skills
Feels rejected by peers
Feels picked on, persecuted (bullied)
Socially isolated
Member of antisocial peer group
Lacks school commitment / achievement
Intolerance / prejudicial attitudes m/ Preoccupation with hate literature

SOCIAL / ENVIRONMENTAL

Access to firearms
Fascination with weapons and explosives
Preoccupation with violent media / music

SITUATIONAL FACTORS

Stressful event / Loss of status / Rejection
Sudden decline in functioning

ATTACK-RELATED BEHAVIORS

Interest in targeted violence / Weapons
Interest in similar aggressive acts
Is organized for attack
Has communicated violent intentions to peers
Lack of prosocial support system
Experience of recent loss that lead to feelings of desperation (e.g., loss of relationship)
Harrassing or menacing behavior (Motivated by desire for revenge, obtaining justice, acquisition of status or fame, suicide)

THE RELATIONSHIP BETWEEN CHILDHOOD VICTIMIZATION AND THE DEVELOPMENT OF AGGRESSIVE BEHAVIORS

Childhood trauma exposure may include physical and sexual abuse, neglect, exposure to domestic violence and urban violence, natural and man-made disasters or the combination of these stressors. What is the impact of exposure of such traumatic events on the child's development of aggressive behavior? While the following summary of research findings illustrate the long-term consequences, perhaps the best example comes from one child who reported:

"I live like I was treated." (Widom, 1997b)

Early childhood maltreatment significantly increases a child's risk by 11% for arrest during adolescence (from 17% to 26%); abuse and neglect increase the risk of violent crime by 29% and arrest by 53% as a juvenile.

Abused and neglected children begin their criminal activity almost a year earlier and have twice the number of arrests and they are more likely to be repeat violence offenders than nonabused children.

Being **neglected** as a child also increases the risk of defiant acting out behavior and the risk of arrest for violence. Note that the incidence of neglect is more than twice that of physical abuse.

In addition to developing antisocial behavior and Antisocial Personality Disorder, abused and neglected children are also more likely to manifest PTSD and higher rates of suicide attempts. Academic failure, substance abuse, unemployment and poor social relationships as adults are also evident.

The rate of childhood physical abuse is significantly higher among violent juveniles, among homicidal and violent adults, among adults who abuse children, their dating partners and spouses.

Children who witness their fathers engage in domestic violence have poor relationships with their partners, have more impulse-control problems, more hostile cognition about women and a larger number of antisocial peers (Geffner et al., 2000; McClosky & Walker, 2000).

In the U.S., the number of incarcerated youths is approximately 500,000. Ulzen and
    Hamilton (1998) report that 63% of their sample of incarcerated youth has 2 or
    more psychiatric disorders and 24% met the DSM-IV criteria for PTSD (15% males
    and 54% females). Steiner et al. (1997) found that among incarcerated adolescents,
    32% fulfilled the diagnostic criteria for PTSD and 70% of incarcerated youths have
    learning and emotional disturbances. Those youth with PTSD showed elevated
    distress, anxiety, depression, and lowered restraint and poorer impulse and anger
    control.

70% of girls in the juvenile justice system have histories of physical abuse vs. 20% of
    females in the general population. 32% of boys in the juvenile justice system have
    been victimized. There is a high potential of self-harm in violent adolescent
    females (Flannery et al., 2001).

Dodge et al. (1995) found that early physical abuse results in the children developing a
    hostile attributional bias, as they become hypervigilant to hostile cues, become
    distracted from relevant prosocial relevant cues and tend to attribute hostile intent to
    peers. They are also more likely to choose aggressive response options, aggressive
    problem-solving strategies and they evaluate aggressive responses favorably. Thus,
    being victimized can directly affect the ways in which children process social
    information.

Early victimization has also been found to lead to **neurological impairments** (prefrontal
    involvement, delayed language development, altered habituation to startle response,
    and to a compromised immune system) (Perry & Pollard, 1998; Pynoos, 1994).

DEVELOPMENTAL COMORBIDITY

(Co-occurrence of CD with other psychiatric disorders)

While epidemiological research indicates that children and adolescents with **Conduct Disorders (CD)** often receive diagnoses for other psychiatric disorders (as enumerated below), Patterson et al. (2000) provide a much needed **caveat**. They note that the various forms of Disruptive Behavior Disorders change developmentally and may reflect **different aspects of the <u>same</u> disorder**. Child problem behaviors such as hyperactivity, oppositional behavior, antisocial behavior, peer rejection, depressed mood, academic failure, substance abuse and police arrest may be all manifestations of a **single process**, rather than different disorders with distinct etiologies, prognoses, and the like. With this caution in mind we can consider the evidence for concurrent and sequential comorbidity.

- 1/2 of children with CD have additional diagnoses

- Between the ages 4 to 11 there is a 60% overlap between CD and ADHD, by age 11+ one-third overlap

- ADHD in childhood, especially if accompanied by ODD – oppositional defiant disorder - is often a precursor of aggression, CD and delinquency which subsequently creates risk for involvement with illicit drugs and antisocial behavior

- CD with ADHD boys have a worse outcome than CD boys without ADHD, earlier onset of CD boys exhibit more physical aggression and more persistent CD

- ODD is often a precursor to CD which is thought to be a precursor to Antisocial Personality Disorder (APD). The presence of ADHD exacerbates these processes

- College students with ADHD <u>versus</u> non-ADHD students report more trait and state anger, more problems with temper and with their temper leading to hurting others and damaging property, and less social skills in expressing anger (Ramirez et al., 1997). Also see Barkley (1995) and Wender (1995) for descriptions of the difficulties adults with ADHD have in controlling their anger.

- Overlap CD and emotional disorders (anxiety and depressive disorders) 1:6 among adolescent boys, 1:2 among adolescent girls (There is a need to treat affective component). In particular, the combination of CD and ADHD is associated with increased risk for anxiety and depression. Anxiety often precedes depression.

- Overlap CD and somatization disorder 1:5 adolescent boys and 1:3 adolescent girls

- Close link between suicidal behavior and aggression; 2/3 of suicidal adolescents have a history of aggressive behavior; 39% of aggressive adolescents have a history of suicide attempts

- Positive relationship between CD and "consumptive" behaviors including cigarette and marijuana use, alcohol and caloric intake. The level of substance abuse disorder (SUD) has been found to be related to the severity of CD. 80% of adolescents with SUD meet criteria for some form of comorbid psychiatric disorder (1/3 to 1/2 have CD).

- The combination of Substance abuse disorder and PTSD results in more externalizing behaviors with delinquent and aggressive features, poorer school performance, absences, more course failures, suspensions, expulsions and an increased likelihood of criminality, risk-taking behaviors and suicidal behavior.

- Frontal lobe dysfunction, impulsivity and learning disabilities and often accompany CD (see Moffitt, 1993)

- Several disorders have been associated with CD including APD, substance abuse, mania, schizophrenia and obsessive-compulsive disorder

- Nationally, approximately 30% of adolescent chronic offenders aged 12 to 18 years, in the juvenile prison system have a mental disorder (U.S. Department of Justice, 1997).

GENDER DIFFERENCES IN AGGRESSIVE BEHAVIORS

(See Artz, 1998; Burtle, 1985; Chesney-Lind & Brown, 1999; Crick et al., 1999; Hoyt & Scherer, 1998; Leschied et al., 2001; Pajer, 1998; and for a discussion of gender differences.)

For eight years I was a consultant at a correctional facility for **female adolescent offenders**. This experience highlighted for me the **multiple** and **unique programming needs of girls** versus boys. While boys commit more violent crimes than girls, the rate of girls being charged with violent crimes has increased twice as fast as for boys (Lescheid et al., 2001). In the U.S., almost three-quarters of a million girls under 18 are arrested, accounting for 26% of the total juvenile arrests (Sege & Licenziato, 2001). *(See below for a FACT SHEET on incarcerated women.)* If we are to be of most help to these female offenders, it is critical that we be informed about **gender differences** in terms of **expression, developmental course** and **correlates** and **unique treatment needs** of aggressive, antisocial and violent females.

Expression

- Girls tend to use **more indirect**, **relational** and **verbal forms of aggression**, for example social exclusion, gossiping, rumor spreading, character defamation, name-calling, ostracism, threatening to end valuable friendships, threatening to disclose personal information and mean-spirited teasing. This **relationship aggression** consists of efforts to harm others through manipulation or control of relationships with others. Such relational forms of aggression are more common in **same sex peer groups**. The differences in expression of anger between boys and girls tend to emerge at about age 8. Girls in early adolescence tend to be more verbally aggressive than girls in later adolescence. But the exact form of gender differences may vary across cultures.

- At all ages, girls are less verbally aggressive and tend to engage in less competitive, grabbing aggressive behaviors than boys. Friendships among highly relationally aggressive girls involve high levels of intimacy, jealousy and exclusivity. Girls shift to a more indirect form of aggression at the beginning of adolescence. Boys are more likely to express their aggression as an impulsive act.

- Adolescent boys commit the majority of violent crimes with a prevalence ratio compared to girls of from 3:1 to 12:1 depending upon the exact type of violent offense reported. Boys have a higher drug use than girls.

- Females are <u>less likely</u> than males to engage in serious forms of violence. Boys carry weapons and engage in physical fighting at rates double that of girls. When girls carry a weapon they are more likely to get into a physical fight. Youth homicide rates and serious crime are overwhelmingly male. 92% of people in prison are males.

- Nonnormative aggressive behaviors among girls (e.g., physical aggression) result in more severe maladjusted outcomes than normative aggression or nonaggression (Crick, 1997). Girls who fight and who engage in cruel behaviors (gender atypicality) are most likely to develop Conduct Disorder (CD). CD in girls is associated with developing Antisocial Personality Disorder (APD). Other adjustment problems may include depression, anxiety and loneliness. Peer rejection is related to relational aggression and the relationship between rejection and aggression increases over time.

- Since most of the aggressive behavior of females is nonassertive and covert, females tend to be arrested more frequently for covert forms of delinquency, such as shoplifting and fraud and for non-violent offenses, usually drug-related crimes. Girls who use drugs are also more likely to be involved in stealing, fighting and gang membership. Girls are arrested most for status offenses (e.g., runaway, juvenile prostitution).

- Boys are four times more likely to appear in Juvenile Court than girls. Girls who are taken into custody besides status offences are likely to be more deviant than their male counterparts. Females have to reach a higher threshold before becoming involved in the juvenile justice system.

- More recently, there is an increase in the prevalence of female delinquency and the emergence of girl gangs. In recent years, female offenders are entering the juvenile justice system at younger ages and at a higher rate. Male to female ratio is higher for early as compared to late onset offenders. Boys and girls are more similar in the rate of aggression in urban schools than in rural schools

- Females are more likely to direct anger toward themselves rather than toward others. Such self-directed anger may be manifested in the form of self-injurious behaviors (e.g., Horesh et al., 2000). As the level of suicidality increases, so does the frequency of violent externalizing behaviors.

Developmental Course

- The age of onset for violence is later for girls than boys. Girls develop antisocial behavior mainly during adolescence rather than earlier.

- The stability of disruptive aggressive and antisocial behavior tends to be as high for females as it is for males.

- Abused and neglected girls are more likely to become violent at a later age than are maltreated boys. Maltreatment (abused / neglect) is more of a risk factor for girls than for boys.

- Girls diagnosed with ADHD are more likely than boys with ADHD to develop CD.

- Bullying is much more of a concern among boys than girls, especially physical bullying. Cross-gender aggression is higher for girls than boys.

- Girls tend to outgrow the tendency toward oppositional behavior at an earlier age than do boys. Girls tend to withdraw from competitive situations, whereas boys play in larger groups and engage in more public and rougher play.

- Aggressive girls tend to have more sibling conflict than do boys.

- Aggressive girls are more attracted to aggressive boys than are nonaggressive girls. Girls with CD are more likely to select antisocial partners than men select antisocial women.

- Early maturing girls with a history of behavior problems are more likely to have more adjustment problems in adolescence than late maturing girls.

- The developmental course of substance abuse appears to be different for boys and girls. A stronger link exists between early problem behaviors such as aggressiveness, shyness and antisocial behavior and substance abuse among boys than girls. Girls tend to link drug use to coping with stress, whereas boys associate drug use with pleasurable effects.

- CD girls are more likely to become adolescent mothers, single parents, be less competent mothers, have a higher incidence of psychiatric symptoms such as depression and accompanying suicide attempts, phobias and obsessive compulsive disorders and they are more likely to have children who evidence externalizing behavior problems than girls without CD.

- Adolescent girls are more likely to have conflict with their mothers than their fathers and girls have more conflicts than boys have with their mothers and fathers.

Risk Factors
(See Battle et al., in press; Lederman & Brown, 2000)

- Girls who get into trouble with the law often have a different developmental life course than do incarcerated boys.

- 70% of girls in juvenile justice system have histories **of <u>physical abuse</u>** vs. 20% females in general population. 32% of boys in the juvenile justice sample have been victimized. Often girls runaway from home to escape such victimization. *(Note: Most maltreated children do <u>not</u> engage in delinquent behavior.)*

- 95% of incarcerated girls lack a stable home life.

- 54% of incarcerated girls report mothers who had been arrested.

- 40% of incarcerated girls had fathers who had been arrested.

- Parental rejection, parental verbal and physical aggression, negative family communication style by parents, and low parental involvement are related to daughter's aggression at home and with peers.

- Females are more likely to be raped, physically assaulted by partners and as a result they have a higher incidence of depression, PTSD and comorbid Substance Abuse Disorders.

- Women have heavier and more frequent drug use before offense than do men.

- Importantly, this same pattern is evident for a **community sample** of dangerously violent (DV) female adolescents. For example, Flannery et al. (2001) reported clinical levels of severe anger, depression, suicidal potential, PTSD and disassociation were evident in DV females relative to matched control nonviolent females.

The following **FACT SHEET** summarizes the scope and seriousness of the problem.

FACT SHEET ON INCARCERATED WOMEN

- 3.2 million women in the U.S. were arrested in 1998, making up 22% of all arrests.

- The largest percentage of incarcerated women in the U.S. are unmarried women of color between the ages of 25 – 34.

- Half of incarcerated women were unemployed at the time of the arrest.

- 6% of the incarcerated women were pregnant at the time of the arrest.

- 1.3 million children in the U.S. have mothers in correctional prisons.

- 58% of incarcerated women grow up in homes with one parent.

- 46% have one family member who was incarcerated.

- 33% have a parent with a history of drug/alcohol abuse.

- 64% to 80% of incarcerated women are likely to have a psychiatric disorder in their lifetime.

In summary, girls who have been maltreated and victimized, who enter puberty early, who have learning problems and a depressed mood and who associate with antisocial peers and antisocial boys are at most high risk to become serious violent offenders and to experience the accompanying behaviors of early sexual activity, substance abuse, covert antisocial activity initially, followed by overt antisocial activity. They are also most likely to have children who will evidence externalizing problems.

Implications of Gender Differences for Assessment and Treatment

A consideration of the differential development of aggressive behavior in girls highlights the need for therapists to:

(1) **Systematically assess** for **relational aggression** and for the variety of **co-occurrent clinical problems** in incarcerated females. These include depression, anxiety (General Anxiety Disorder an PTSD), Polysubstance abuse and Conduct Disorder. In particular, the therapist should asses for a history of victimization, suicidal ideation and self-injurious behaviors.

(2) Collaboratively develop a **Time-line** of the history of life-stressors, intergenerational exposure to antisocial models, as well as assessment for "strengths" (abilities, positive prosocial role models and attachment history)

(3) Treatment planning needs to be multifaceted addressing:

    a) prior victimization (e.g., physical abuse and sexual abuse by family members and strangers);

    b) ways to avoid subsequent revictimization;

    c) health-related needs of sexuality (vulnerability to sexually transmitted diseases, pregnancy prevention, family planning, child-rearing);

    d) interpersonal skills (conflict resolution, communication, problem-solving skills, empathy and perspective-taking skills);

    e) job-skills and career planning (e.g., computer-literacy skills);

    f) issues of gender-identity – "rites of passage" and exposure to positive same-sex role models (use mentors);

    g) issues of generalization and transfer (e.g., follow-through case management, ongoing supervision and ongoing contact). For example, teach the juvenile offenders computer-literacy skills so they can maintain Internet contact with their therapists and access other resources.)

As example of such a program that gives the girls a voice in the program is offered by Judge Cindy Lederman in Miami, Florida. *(See Websites: www.gapgirls.org)*

THE ROLE OF RESILIENCE AND "STRENGTHS"

A third developmental pathway was a **limited-duration type** of children who evidence early aggressive behavior and then desist. How children and youth come to give up aggressive and antisocial behavior is a critical research question. If we could determine the processes and factors that interrupt the aggressive "career path," then we could use that information to formulate more effective intervention and prevention programs. At this point, we do not know the exact factors involved, but we can obtain some hints by looking at the literature on "resilient" children who "overcome the odds" and who do not engage in aggressive behaviors even though they have been exposed to numerous risk factors. The literature on resilience and protective factors is quite extensive, but perhaps can be most succinctly summarized in quotes from Norman Garmezy and C. R. Snyder.

"The resilient child is one who works well, plays well, loves well and expects well." Norman Garmezy, 1987

"The hero in a child's eyes is the adult who takes the time to give the gift of hope." Snyder et al., 2000

There is a radio commentator in the U.S. named Paul Harvey whose anecdotal reports always include the phrase, *"And now, for the rest of the story!"*, to highlight the "strengths" that individuals employ in the face of adversity. When it comes to a consideration of aggressive children who come from "high-risk" environments it is critical to consider "the rest of the story." Keep in mind that approximately 50% of children who evidence aggressive and antisocial behavior will desist. If we wish to explain this dramatic decline there is a need to focus on **protective factors** that may "moderate, counterbalance, avert," the influence of negative events and consider how interventionists can prevent damage, restore, compensate for the impact of adversities and build assets by facilitating, mobilizing, boosting strengths. Masten (2001) defines **resilience** as a class of *"phenomenon characterized by good outcomes in spite of serious threats to adaptation or development"* (p. 228). The transactional concept of resilience is characterized by patterns of positive adjustment in the context of significant adversity. While a comprehensive review of the literature on resilience is beyond the scope of the present **HANDBOOK**, the major findings have been summarized by Matsen and Reed (in press, p. 22).

"The most striking conclusion arising from all of the research on resilience in development is that the extraordinary resilience and recovery power of children arises from ordinary processes. The evidence indicates that children who "make it" have basic human protective systems operating in their favor. Resilience does not come from rare and special qualities."

Rather, the data indicates that resilient children and youth take advantage of "second chance opportunities" and that they make choices and create opportunities at critical junctures that play an important role in their life course. They are able to rebound from, transcend, overcome the odds and successfully adapt." As Masten (2001) observes, they may "find a mentor, enter the military, find a new and deeper faith, marry healthy partners, have a supportive peer group or take actions that have positive consequences." Resilient youth tend to place themselves in healthier contexts – "niche seeking" behaviors. **It is important to keep in mind that a child's resilience may be area specific.** What constitutes protective factors in one domain may not be as relevant in other domains. Moreover, resilience should be viewed as being fluid over time and the nature of resilience factors will vary developmentally and across gender, race and cultures.

The major categories of resilient factors include:

   a)   **Individual Characteristics**

        Cognitive and behavioral capabilities
        Temperament personality factors
        Social abilities

   b)   **Family Factors**

        Social Supports / Attachment Relationships

   c)   **Community Resources**

The specific features of strengths and protective factors are reviewed in the following **Case Conceptualization Model**. The work of Masten and her colleagues was most helpful in generating the list of protective factors.

CASE CONCEPTUALIZATION MODEL
FOR ANTISOCIAL YOUTH

How does one make sense and integrate all of the information about **mediating, moderating** and **mitigating** factors that contribute to antisocial and aggressive behaviors? How does one not get overwhelmed with the diversity of violent behaviors and juvenile delinquency and the role of gender, developmental, cultural and contextual factors in order to formulate an assessment and treatment plan? These questions became salient for me when I was asked to consult at the **Juvenile Assessment Center (JAC)** in Miami. Each year, the JAC in Miami-Dade apprehends and processes some 18,000 youths between the ages of 8 and 18. Yes, 18,000! Moreover, this is only one of several such Centers in Florida. Imagine you were asked to help them formulate a framework that taps relevant information and that guides assessment, placement and treatment planning.

I have consulted at a number of child, adolescent and adult psychiatric and correctional settings. In each setting, I developed a **Case Conceptualization Model (CCM)** that summarizes and integrates various sources of current, developmental , social and biological information. **FIGURE 1** provides a **Generic CCM** or a **procedural flow chart** of various sources of information that clinicians can use in formulating assessment and treatment decisions. Each of the **Boxes** in the **CCM** could be conceived as a window on your computer with its own break out sub-boxes. Obviously, the nature of the presenting problem (Box 2A) and the specific content of the Boxes will vary across clinical populations and the relevance of the accompanying risk, protective and barrier factors will change accordingly. In this **HANDBOOK,** we will consider how the **CCM** works for two angry and violent populations:

a) Juvenile offenders in the JAC

b) Men who engage in Intimate Partner Violence (Domestic Violence)

What do the various Boxes of information look like for these two populations and how can they inform decision making? Before I attempt to answer this question, it is worth highlighting some of the advantages of the CCM in clinical practice. First, the clinical staff I have worked with have found that the CCM is a useful way to:

a) summarize relevant clinical information
b) communicate both to patients and to colleagues
c) formulate a treatment plan
d) monitor progress and conduct outcome studies using Goal Attainment Scaling.

For example, using the Box numbers in the **CCM**, the therapist can indicate how he/she plans to spend time with the patient and his family members. Following the collection of relevant information in each Box (as discussed below) , the therapist can note that he/she spent the therapy session working on **current presenting problems (Box 2A)** and then plans to work on **issues of treatment nonadherence (Box 5B)** and will conclude by building on **individual strengths (6A)**. Therapists can not only use the CCM to communicate to colleagues, but also to patients and their family members, as the following example illustrates. The therapist can convey:

> *Let me see, what brought you in was (Presenting Problems) and this has been going on for some time. (Give description.) In addition, (Box on Comorbidity), you are also struggling with X which is a problem as evident by ….. These problems are made worse (exacerbated, maintained) by (Box on Stressors), not only now but also what lingers from the past is …. For these you have received the following treatments some of which have worked well, but some other treatments were difficult to follow or stick to because … You were specifically satisfied with and would recommend that we try or continue with … (Box on Treatment)*

But, *in spite of* (whenever the phrase "in spite of" is used this means that the clinician has gone to the Box on Strengths) you have X going for you or you can count on or use.

> *If I am understanding your situation some of the things you have had to deal with (struggle with) are … But, on the other hand, you were able to … in spite of.. Is that the way you see it? If indeed, we have captured what you have been through, then where should we begin (or what additional information do we need to obtain)? (The therapist negotiates with the patient where and how to begin the therapy process – collaborative goal-setting).*

> *As we consider our treatment options, let's consider what barriers or obstacles might get in the way (Box on Barriers) and how we can anticipate and address them should they arise.* (Note that the discussion of Barriers should not be introduced too early, otherwise it might deflate the patient's motivation.)

The therapist concludes by exploring:

> *Finally, how will we know if you are making progress (Introduce Goal Attainment Scaling).*

Let's consider how the **CCM**, as depicted in **Figure 2**, integrates various sources of information that includes demographic, risk and protective factors for **juvenile offenders**. The importance of considering various sources of information is highlighted by Stouthamer-Loeber et al. (in press) who reported that:

> *"Children with 3 risk domains more than protective factors have an 8 fold increase in the likelihood of becoming persistent serious delinquents in adolescence" (p. 756).*

Figure 3 provides examples of the **Break-out Boxes** and the information that would facilitate decision-making. Obviously, not all such information will be available. Nevertheless, an enumeration of the desired sources of information will help guide the assessment process. One of the advantages of representing clinical data in such a flow-chart fashion is that it lends itself to be incorporated in a **computer-generated report**, as included below (p. 99). (We will also see how this **CCM** can be employed with **men who engage in Intimate Partner Violence** - p. 104.)

FIGURE 1
GENERIC CASE CONCEPTUALIZATION MODEL

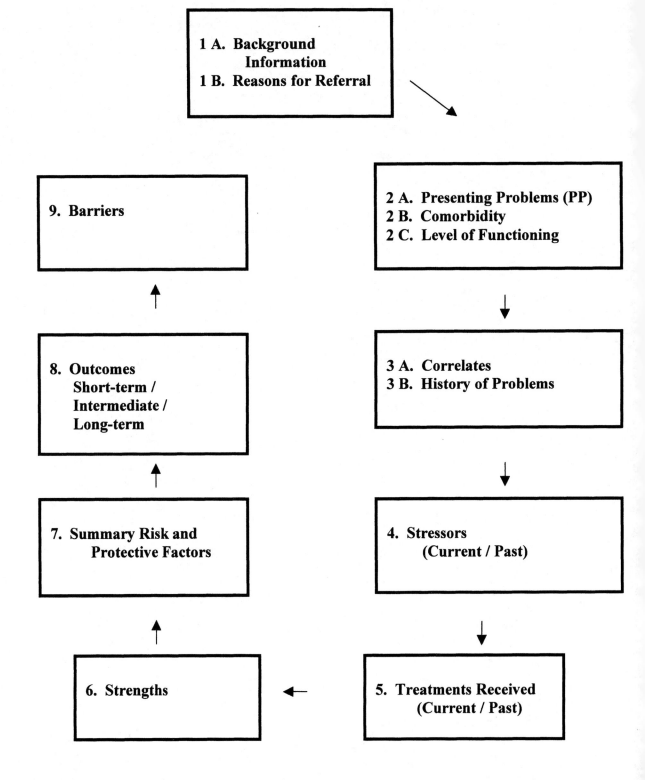

FIGURE 2
CASE CONCEPTUALIZATION MODEL
FOR JUVENILE OFFENDERS

```
┌──────────────────────────────────┐
│ 1 A.  Background Info             │
│ 1 B.  Current Living             │
│            Conditions             │
│ 1 C.  Reasons for Referral        │
└──────────────────────────────────┘
```

```
┌──────────────────────────────────┐
│ 2 A.  Presenting Problems (PP)    │
│ 2 B.  Comorbidity                 │
│ 2 C.  Level of Current            │
│            Functioning            │
└──────────────────────────────────┘
```

```
┌──────────────────────────────────┐
│ 9.  Barriers                      │
│     9 A.  Individual              │
│     9 B.  Social                  │
│     9 C.  Systemic                │
└──────────────────────────────────┘
```

```
┌──────────────────────────────────┐
│ 3 A.  History PP                  │
│          Criminal / Substance /   │
│          Media / Temperament      │
│ 3 B.  Medical History             │
│          Youth / Family members   │
│ 3 C.  Academic History            │
│          Performance /            │
│          Motivation / Discipline  │
│ 3 D.  Peer and Sibling Influences │
└──────────────────────────────────┘
```

```
┌──────────────────────────────────┐
│ 8.  Outcomes                      │
│     8 A.  Short-term              │
│     8 B.  Intermediate            │
│     8 C.  Long-term               │
│                                    │
│ Wavs to Address Barriers          │
└──────────────────────────────────┘
```

```
┌──────────────────────────────────┐
│ 7.  Summary Factors               │
│     7 A.  Risk                    │
│     7 B.  Protective              │
└──────────────────────────────────┘
```

```
┌──────────────────────────────────┐
│ 4.  Stressors                     │
│     4 A.  Current                 │
│     4 B.  Ecological              │
│     4 C.  Developmental           │
│     4 D.  Familial                │
└──────────────────────────────────┘
```

```
┌──────────────────────────────────┐
│ 6.  Strengths                     │
│     6 A.  Individual              │
│     6 B.  Social                  │
│     6 C.  Community               │
└──────────────────────────────────┘
```

```
┌──────────────────────────────────┐
│ 5.  Treatments Received           │
│        (Current / Past)           │
│     5 A.  Efficacy                │
│     5 B.  Adherence               │
│     5 C.  Patient Satisfaction    │
└──────────────────────────────────┘
```

FIGURE 3
CASE CONCEPTUALIZATION MODEL
FOR JUVENILE OFFENDERS: BREAKOUT BOXES

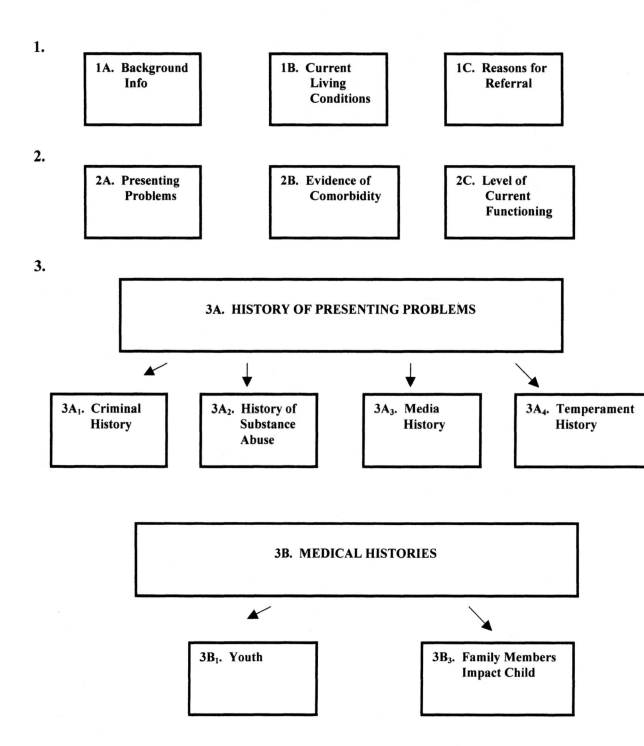

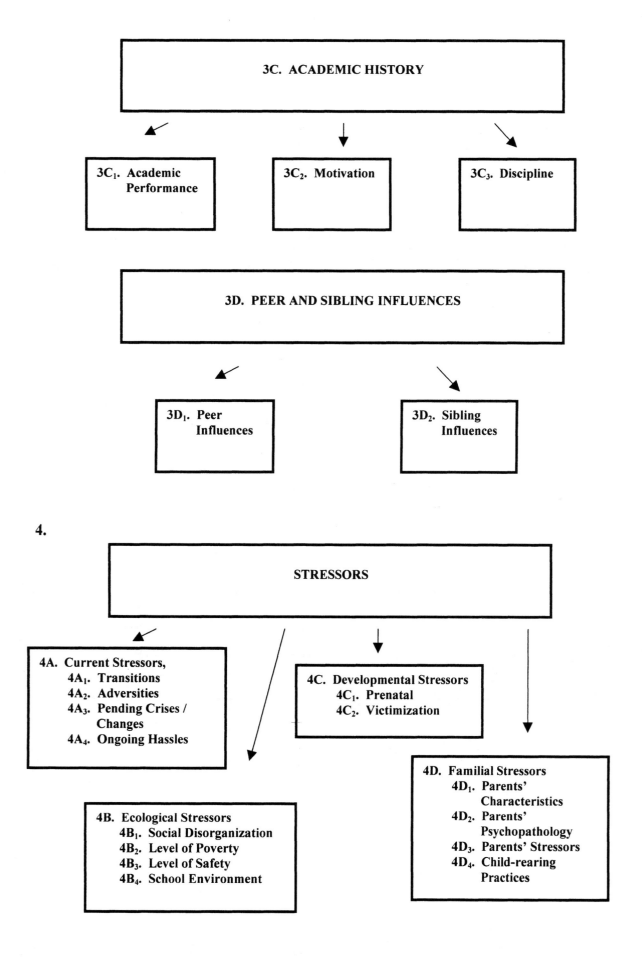

3C. ACADEMIC HISTORY

3C₁. Academic Performance

3C₂. Motivation

3C₃. Discipline

3D. PEER AND SIBLING INFLUENCES

3D₁. Peer Influences

3D₂. Sibling Influences

4.

STRESSORS

4A. Current Stressors,
 4A₁. Transitions
 4A₂. Adversities
 4A₃. Pending Crises / Changes
 4A₄. Ongoing Hassles

4C. Developmental Stressors
 4C₁. Prenatal
 4C₂. Victimization

4B. Ecological Stressors
 4B₁. Social Disorganization
 4B₂. Level of Poverty
 4B₃. Level of Safety
 4B₄. School Environment

4D. Familial Stressors
 4D₁. Parents' Characteristics
 4D₂. Parents' Psychopathology
 4D₃. Parents' Stressors
 4D₄. Child-rearing Practices

5.

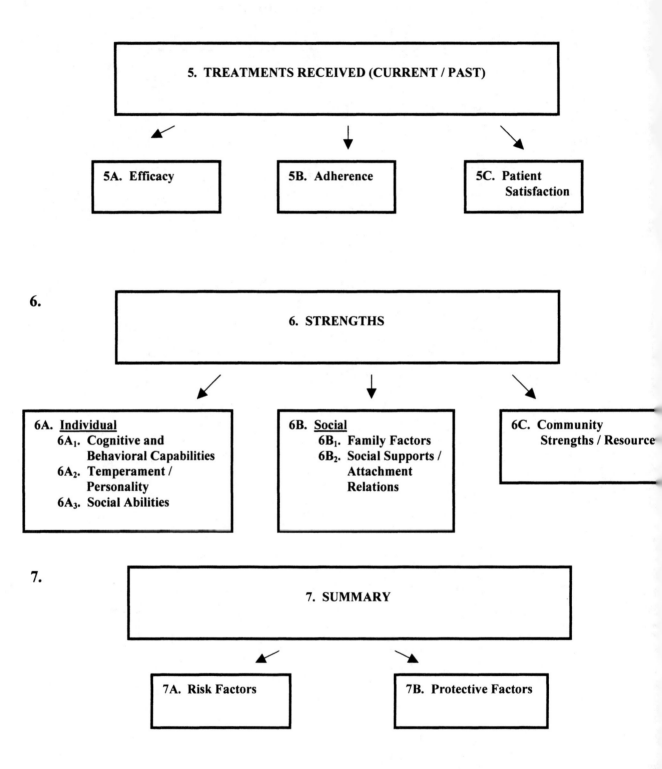

5. TREATMENTS RECEIVED (CURRENT / PAST)

5A. Efficacy

5B. Adherence

5C. Patient Satisfaction

6.

6. STRENGTHS

6A. Individual
- **6A₁. Cognitive and Behavioral Capabilities**
- **6A₂. Temperament / Personality**
- **6A₃. Social Abilities**

6B. Social
- **6B₁. Family Factors**
- **6B₂. Social Supports / Attachment Relations**

6C. Community Strengths / Resource

7.

7. SUMMARY

7A. Risk Factors

7B. Protective Factors

8.

```
┌─────────────────────────────────────────────────────┐
│                                                       │
│              8.  GOAL ATTAINMENT SCALING              │
│                                                       │
└─────────────────────────────────────────────────────┘
```

```
┌──────────────────┐   ┌──────────────────┐   ┌──────────────────┐
│  8A.  Short-term │   │ 8B.  Intermediate│   │  8C.  Long-term  │
│       Tx Goals   │   │      Tx Goals    │   │       Tx Goals   │
└──────────────────┘   └──────────────────┘   └──────────────────┘
```

9.

```
┌─────────────────────────────────────────────────────┐
│                                                       │
│                     9.  BARRIERS                      │
│                                                       │
└─────────────────────────────────────────────────────┘
```

```
┌──────────────────┐   ┌──────────────────┐   ┌──────────────────┐
│  9A.  Individual │   │  9B.  Social     │   │  9C.  Systemic   │
└──────────────────┘   └──────────────────┘   └──────────────────┘
```

DETAILED BREAK-OUT INFORMATION

1A. BACKGROUND INFORMATION

Child's name / Age / Gender / Minority status – ethnicity / English second language – child, parents / Family constellation (parents, single parents, stepparents, others) / School currently attending

1B. CURRENT LIVING CONDITIONS

Location – obtain Zip code for ecological assessment / History of residence – number of moves and reasons / Who else is present in the home – relationships to patient / Marital and employment status / Public Assistance / SES level and standard of living -- income, education, and occupation / Substandard housing / Overcrowding and density of family – three or more siblings at home before age 10 / Homeless teens and runaways are particularly at high risk

1C. REASONS FOR REFERRAL

Referral source / By whom / When / Reasons for referral

2A. PRESENTING PROBLEMS

Nature of aggressive behaviors (reactive, proactive, relational, combo) / Seriousness of crimes against persons, property, or drugs, or combination / Weapons involved / Alone or with others – play lead role, coerced / Evidence behavior, dress, language of gang member / Who were the victims of violence – family members, stranger, acquaintance / Current legal status / Use of illicit drugs at time of criminal activity / Availability, familiarity, competence with weapons / Other presenting problems such as being prejudiced toward others

2B. EVIDENCE OF COMORBIDITY (AXES I, II, III)

"Externalizing" problems – ADHD, ODD, CD
"Internalizing" problems – Anxiety, PTSD, depression, level of hopelessness, pessimism about future and view self as at risk for early untimely death, loneliness
Substance abuse disorders / Personality disorder, especially Antisocial Personality and Borderline Personality Disorders
Learning Disabilities
Health-related Problems (sleep disorders)
Combination of disorder / Record present and past diagnoses

2C. LEVEL OF CURRENT FUNCTIONING

Performance in various roles — school, peers, family, sibling relations, outside activities
Evidence of sudden disruption or downward progression of functioning

3A. HISTORY OF PRESENTING PROBLEMS

3A$_1$ Criminal History

Number of previous criminal episodes / History of violent behavior / Number and
        type of prior arrests / Most serious offence – persons, property, both / Age
        at first arrest – first contact with criminal justice system / History of
        sentencing, amount of time served, probation / Weapon use history /
        Exposure to delinquent peers / Gang involvement – note role
Evidence of covert and overt delinquency / Bully, victim of bullies, both

3A$_2$ History of Substance Abuse

History of substances used / Age fist used / How pay for drugs / Motivational
        analysis and impact (e.g., DUI charges) / Family members and peers use
        illicit drugs

3A$_3$ Media History

Excessive viewing and preoccupation with violent media (e.g., television, music.
        literature, videogames)

3A$_4$ Temperament History

Level of irritability, inattentiveness, impulsivity, oppositional / Difficult to manage
        (not "easy going") / Angers easily – frequent arguments, temper outbursts,
        throw objects, fights / Disposition to violence
History of risk-taking behaviors, harm avoidance, daring and sensation-seeking
        behaviors / Level of emotionality and expressivity – strong negative
        feelings / Level of callousness / Degree of self-regulation / Chronically
        bored
Level of aggressiveness – reactive aggression and hostile attribution bias /
        Accompanying attitudes that support aggressive-violent behaviors /
        Inflated sense of self-worth – sensitive to threats to self-image and to
        rejection / Extent of attachment relationships / Rebelliousness and
        alienation / Use of emotional-focused coping strategies tied to higher
        levels of problems among adolescents

3B. MEDICAL HISTORY

3B$_1$ Youth

Medical records of low birth weight / Premature birth / Developmental illnesses / Medical services accessed – regular checkups, hospitalization / Chronic illness – e.g., asthma, allergies, diabetes, etc. (Obtain medical time line including current conditions.)

3B$_2$ Family Members

Acute and chronic physical and psychiatric disorders that impact child / youth (Describe nature of the impact at the time and ongoing) / Obtain Time Lines including current medical conditions

3C. ACADEMIC HISTORY

3C$_1$ Academic Performance

Poor academic performance, especially reading comprehension and math performance / Low overall academic achievement / Evidence of grade retention – old for grade / Poor organizational skills – study and test-taking habits / Diagnosed as learning disabled / Special education placement / Requires tutor and mentor

3C$_2$ Motivation

Number of schools attended / Weak bonding to school / Low school interest and commitment / Low academic aspirations / Low involvement in extracurricular actives / Little homework time / Low parent involvement who hold low academic expectations *(To assess the degree of school bonding ask the youth, "If you were absent from school, who besides your friends would notice you were absent and miss you?")*

As Heide (2001, p. 149) observes:

> *Youths who felt that <u>teachers treated them fairly</u> and who felt <u>close to people at school</u> were significantly less likely than youths who felt disconnected from school, to be violent, to smoke cigarettes or marijuana, to drink alcohol, and to have had sexual intercourse. Adolescents who identified with their schools were also less likely to be emotionally distressed and to have engaged in suicidal thoughts or behaviors, than youths who felt estranged from the school experience.*

3C₃ <u>Discipline</u>

Poor attendance / Truancy / School dropout / Serious disciplinary problems –
number of referrals to principal's office / Bully, victim of bullies, both /
Suspended and expelled – number of times and reasons / Carry weapon to
school – number of times and reasons

Summary of school adjustments – rated as **"good"** / minimally disruptive, no
fighting, seems to enjoy school, involved in activities; **"fair"** (somewhat
disruptive, no fights, school seems OK, few or no activities; **"poor"** /
disruptive, involved in fighting, dislike school, not involved in school
activities) (Heilbrun et al., 2000)

3D. PEER AND SIBLING INFLUENCES

3D₁ <u>Peer Influences</u>

Rejection (liked by few peers, actively disliked / Victim of bullies / No close
friends
Associates with deviant antisocial peers who do not abide by the law, who
engage in antisocial behavior, substance abuse, risk-taking daring
behaviors, have low academic performance, high school dropouts and who
have authoritarian parents *(Ask for names of friends spend most time
with at school and with after school. Assess social supports.)*
Gang member who does not want to get out (does <u>not</u> know how to desist from
gang activities, nor has the confidence to disengage from gang)

3D₂ <u>Sibling Influence</u>

Negative role model and influence, especially older same-sex sibling who is
aggressive, antisocial and abuses substances / Sibling rivalry and conflict /
Sibling who provides little guidance and support

4. STRESSORS

4A. CURRENT STRESSORS

4A₁ <u>Family transitions</u> – separation, divorce / <u>Recent losses</u> – death, material
losses, employment, status, friendships

4A₂ <u>Family adversities</u> – financial, legal, illness, injury

4A₃ <u>Pending crises and changes</u> - Potential loss of resources (e.g., disasters)

4A$_4$ **Ongoing stressors** – youth works more than 20 hours a week while attending school, see Life Event Scales[7]

4B. Ecological Stressors[8]

4B$_1$ Level of Social Disorganization

High percentage of residential turnover – population instability / Few social ties nor neighborhood cohesion nor neighborliness – absence of Neighborhood Watch or report public crime / Community sense of isolation – "we – they" attitude / Distrust police / Ethnic heterogeneity with accompanying stereotyping, discrimination and racism / Exposure to community trauma with accompanying loss of resources and loss of "social capital" / Low collective efficacy – absence of involvement and trust

4B$_2$ Level of Poverty[9]

High population density / High unemployment – lack of local employment and absence of public transportation to employment sites / Percentages of single adults head of households, fathers absent in neighborhood, neighbors who graduated from high school / Signs of economic deprivation and poverty (physical deterioration, graffiti, garbage, etc.)

4B$_3$ Level of Safety

Level of community violence / High availability and easy access to handguns and other weapons / Drugs and drug sales / Presence of gangs / Neighborhood norms and expectations for use of violence to resolve conflicts and to advance social status through the use of violence / Lack of supervision – absence of informal and formal social controls / Exposure to violence, bullying / Lack of safe places for children to play and for youth to engage in after-school activities

---

[7] For example, see Compas et al. (1985) measure of ongoing stressors in adolescence.

[8] See Sampson et al. 1997 and *Website http://phdcn.harvard.edu* for examples of ecological assessment and impact on violence. Community risk factors have been found to include how often the following occurred in the neighborhood a) a fight in which a weapon was used; b) a violent argument between neighbors; c) a gang fight; d) sexual assault; e) a robbery or mugging; f) availability of guns.

[9] 27% of children in U.S. live in poverty

4B₄ School Environment and School Climate

Characteristics of the school environment – overcrowded, high student-teacher ratio, no breakdown into smaller schools within larger schools / Lack of supervision in halls, lunchrooms, afterschool activities / <u>Absence</u> of active violence prevention programs such as anti-truancy programs, peer mediation program, hotlines, etc. / Lack of clarity of rules, consequences, expectations / Teachers threatened / School climate one of "get tough" <u>versus</u> "student-centered," nonpunitive / *(Use of corporal punishment in school is related to a higher ratio of student interpersonal aggression)*

Characteristics of student body - Percentage of transfer student / Percentages in special education programs / Daily absentee rates / Referrals to principal and vice principals / Out-of-school suspensions / Expulsions / Presence of gangs / Bullying / Degree to which students feel "safe" / High perceived level of drug use among peers, as well as the actual prevalence of drug use

4C. DEVELOPMENTAL STRESSORS

4C₁ Prenatal Stressors

Expectant mother used drugs and alcohol during pregnancy / Poor nutritional habits / Expectant mother exposure to high stress levels / Premature birth / Exposure to pollutants – lead toxicity

4C₂ Victimization

Abuse (Physical, sexual, emotional) / Latch-key child, absence of supervision / Neglect / Exposure to violence – domestic/urban / Homelessness / Transient lifestyle / Multiple out-of-home placements *(Note: Children may be exposed to multiple types of violence, both within and without the home)*

4D. FAMILIAL STRESSORS

4D₁ <u>Parent's Characteristics – Demographics</u>

Current ages / Ages at the time child was born – teenage motherhood / Current
    SES levels / Current occupations – unemployment, on Public Assistance /
    Marital status – single parent, inexperienced mother

4D₂ <u>Parent's Psychopathology</u>

Parent's criminality and antisocial behaviors – history of arrests and trouble
    with the law / History of substance abuse disorders – current usage of
    drugs / Favorable attitude toward violence and drugs / Depression,
    especially in mothers / Anxiety disorder, especially PTSD as a result of
    parent being a victim of violence (past/present) / Irritability / Chronic
    medical conditions / Poor history of education – drop out of high school

4D₃ <u>Parental Stressors</u>

Marital conflict – ongoing, history of separations, divorces / Coercive parent-
    child interactions – presence of negative bi-directional feedback loop /
    Parent-adolescent conflict—adolescent runaway, kicked out of house,
    gone without permission / Stressors on parents – employment, financial,
    legal, health, community violence / Acculturation stress – cultural
    differences – parent and adolescents / Stress fulfilling parenting role –
    child care burden / Maternal insularity and isolation from others / Presence
    of intrusive, high critical kin – high Expressed Emotion (EE) environment

4D₄ <u>Child-rearing Practices</u>

Nonexistent or limited parenting – poor supervision, low monitoring / Lack of
    knowledge or limited involvement in child's/youth's activities, friends,
    school

Authoritarian parenting – use of power assertive coercive discipline, use of
    excessive, severe physical punishment, especially with teenage sons / Use
    of inconsistent discipline – overly strict and/or too permissive – fail to set
    clear limits and clear expectations

Low family cohesion – little and poor communication, little familial bonding,
    warmth and support / Harsh criticisms – high Expressed Emotion
    environment / Absence of family or parent involvement in religious and
    community organizations and activities

Parent family connectedness has been found to be a consistent correlate of protecting youth from engaging in high-risk behaviors that threaten their health. Heide (2001, p. 146) observes:

"Youth who felt love, warmth and caring from one or both parents, in contrast to those who do not, were significantly less likely to engage in violent behavior and associated high-risk behaviors (e.g., substance abuse, be depressed, and engage in precocious sexual activity)."

Heide (2001) goes on to observe:

When asked in follow-up interviews how parents could help children, young men who had killed someone during their adolescent years repeatedly emphasized the need for greater parent involvement and the importance of parents setting limits on behavior.

5. TREATMENTS RECEIVED – CHILD/FAMILY, CURRENT/PAST

5A Efficacy

Current Treatments – by whom, where, how often – how effective / Involvement of others – school, family members, peers / Pharmacotherapy

Past history of treatments – Age at first referral for treatment / History of service utilization / Out of home placements – both psychiatric and behavioral such as history of contacts with juvenile justice system / History of pharmacotherapy / Evidence of efficacy

5B Adherence / Compliance[10]

Evidence of treatment nonadherence with pharmacotherapy and other training / Discontinuance, no shows, fail to follow-through, Parole violations, Reoffense
Reasons of nonadherence – Barriers to compliance – e.g., beliefs, social, systemic

5C Patient Satisfaction

Patient's and families' impressions of past and current interventions / Program satisfaction measures

---

[10] 45% to 77% of child and adolescent patients do not enter treatment or they terminate prematurely. See Kazdin et al. (1997) and Kazdin and Wassell (1999) for ways to **assess barriers to treatment**.

6 STRENGTHS

6 A. INDIVIDUAL STRENGTHS

6A₁ <u>Cognitive and behavioral capabilities</u>

Intellectual functioning (IQ) / Attentional and problem-solving skills / Self-regulation skills of arousal, impulsivity, emotions and behaviors / Talents valued by self and society / Academic achievement

6A₂ <u>Temperament / Personality Factors</u>

Easy temperament in infancy / Adaptable personality in response to stress (not readily upset, evidences perseverance) / Positive outlook on life – hopeful, goal-directed thinking, maintain a personal dream, faith and a sense of meaning or purpose in life / Positive self-perception, confident – perceived control of environment and circumstance / Good sense of humor, happy

6A₃ <u>Social Abilities</u>

General appealingness or attraction to others (healthy) / Social competence with others, especially peers / Empathy, sympathy skills, perspective taking / Ability to avoid violent conflict or deescalate a violent situation (e.g., not plan retaliation or revenge after experiencing violence / If minority, bicultural competence – establish a cultural and racial identity / Win recognition for involvement in positive prosocial activities

6 B. SOCIAL STRENGTHS

6B₁ <u>Family Factors</u>

Authoritative parents (high on warmth, structure/monitoring and expectations) – establish agreed-upon family rules / Family feels they can trust child / Positive family climate with low discord between parents / Child feels loved and enjoys being with family members / Organized home environment – meal times, family time / Parents' involvement in child's education / Motivational support from family members / Post secondary education of parents / Socioeconomic advantages *(Note: Effective parental monitoring includes knowing where child is at all times; Knowing child's friends; Getting to know the parents of child's friends; finding out if there is adult supervision.)* See Steinberg (2001) for a discussion of the critical role that authoritative parenting plays as a protective factor.

> *"Authoritative parents are warm and involved, but firm and consistent in establishing and enforcing guidelines, limits,*

> *and developmentally appropriate expectations." (Steinberg, 2001, p.)*
>
> *"Adolescents from authoritative homes achieve more in school, report less depression and anxiety, score higher on measures of self-reliance and self-esteem and are less likely to engage in antisocial behavior, including delinquency and drug use." (p. 8)*

Importantly, adolescents benefited from having friends whose parents were authoritative.

6B₂ Social Supports / Attachment Relations

Close relationships to competent, prosocial and supportive adults / Association with prosocial rule-abiding peers / Positive attachment relationships and involvement in affectional ties outside of the family / Sense of belonging to family and involvement in the community activities, groups who hold prosocial values *(Who was an adult figure in your life you could trust? / Who was kind to you?)*

6C Community Resources

Collective efficacy and cohesion as measured by community involvement and trust among residents / Effective schools / Ties to prosocial organizations and activities (e.g., church attendance, clubs, scouting) / Availability of positive adult models, especially same sex models / Support of cultural and religious organizations and traditions / Availability of neighborhood center or recreation hall / Involvement in community sports / Youth engages in community services where he helps others and feels needed and respected *(See Lyons et al., 2000 for a discussion of strengths.)*

7 SUMMARY

7A Risk Factors

7B Protective Factors

8 GOAL ATTAINMENT SCALING

8A Short-term Goals

8B Intermediate Goals

8C Long-term Goals

9 BARRIERS

9A Individual

Older the child's age / Externalizing symptoms / Substance abuse / Social disability and level of psychopathology / Denial and minimization / Feeling hopeless

9B Social

Low SES / Parents' level of psychopathology – maternal depression / Substance abuse / Antisocial behavior / Beliefs and feelings that it is useless to struggle against the odds, incapable of change / Unsupportive family attitude toward treatment

9C Systemic

Long waiting list / Transportation difficulties / Inaccessibility to treatment facilities / Absence of child care / Absence of follow-through by social service agencies *(N.B. Treatment should focus on beliefs that underline motivational deficits.)*

COMPUTER-GENERATED REPORT BASED ON
CASE CONCEPTUALIZATION MODEL (CCM)
FOR ANTISOCIAL YOUTH

(The numbers and letters in the report refer to information in the Boxes in the CCM –
Figure 2)

Introduction

This (age, gender, race) (**1A** – information) who currently lives indicate geographic area)
with (**1B** – information). The housing situation (note any specific concerns about threats
to safety – *"red flags"*). The date and reasons for referral by .... were **1C**.

Presenting Problems

The **presenting problems** include **2A** (Note the source of information and if violence is
indicated, the role of weapons, injuries, substance abuse and peers – (violence was an
isolated act or part of a peer group).

In addition, the youth s also experiencing difficulties with (**2B** – comorbidity). These
presenting and comorbid problems are having an impact on the level of functioning as
evident by ...

An examination of the youth's **developmental history** reveals (review prior record and
history of presenting problems and history of comorbid problems – **3A**). These
behavioral problems were accompanied by (exacerbated by) – medical history (**3B**) and
academic history (**3C**) and by peer and sibling influences such as (**3D**).

An examination of **current** and **past stressors** for both the youth and his family members
reveals (**4A to 4D**). *[Note: In particular, the source of information for developmental
stressors such as victimization (4C) and familial stressors (4D).]*

For these various presenting and comorbid problems and stressors, the youth and his
family are currently receiving (or have received) the following treatments (cite specific
interventions, by whom, when) with what effects (**5A**) *(cite source of information).*
Some of the difficulties encountered with this treatment included .. (cite source of
information for **treatment nonadherence** – **5B**). Based on their treatment experiences
the youth and his parents were particularly satisfied with (dissatisfied with) ... because
... (**5C**).

In spite of the difficulties and the presence of ... (list "risk" factors, stressors) the youth
and his parents were able to achieve ... (cite source for **individual and familial
strengths** – **6A** and **6B**). The "strengths" that the youth and his family have going for
them are ... They can also access (note, **community** and **agency** resources – **6C**).

In **summary**, an examination of the "risk" factors and adversities indicate (**7A**), but a consideration of protective factors (**7B**) also reveals (Note: "challenges" and "opportunities").

In terms of the **goal attainment scaling (GAS),** the major three target behaviors to be addressed initially include … The agreed-upon signs of improvement negotiated with the youth and his family are … *(For each target behavior note what the specific change would look like.)*

Specific Ways Behavior Should Change

	Minimal Improvement		Moderate Improvement		Significant Improvement
	0% change	25% change	50% change	75% change	100% change
Target Behavior 1					
Target Behavior 2					
Target Behavior 3					

In collaboration with the youth and his family, the following assessment and treatment goals and plans have been established, as noted on the **Goal Attainment Scaling (GAS)** procedure. The short-term (**8A**), intermediate (**8B**), and long-term (**8C**) goals that will be worked on are … More specifically, the individualized treatment plan for the youth and his family indicates that a **follow-up assessment** should include … *(What additional information is needed and how and when is it to be obtained)*; placement *(Amount of supervision required – least to most restrictive in light of likelihood of further offences);* treatment options *(What should be done , by whom, when and how will generalization / transfer and evaluation be built into the treatment plan).*

In order for these changes to occur, the following **barriers** at the individual (**9A**), familial-social (**9B**) and systemic levels (**9C**) have to be addressed. *(Note, how these barriers were identified.)* The intervention plans to address these barriers include … The evidence that they have been addressed successfully include data that *(Note data like that included on GAS – 0% to 100% change.).*

INTIMATE PARTNER VIOLENCE (IPV)

Another clinical population that I have been involved with, both as a therapist and as a consultant, is the area of **domestic violence** or **intimate partner violence (IPV).** For example, as a trainer for the military, I used the **Case Conceptualization Model (CCM)** as a way to help them formulate assessment and treatment decisions. But, before we turn our attention to the **CCM**, it is important to put the **IPV** into a larger social context in order to underscore the seriousness of the problem and the "state of the art" concerning possible interventions. The following **FACT SHEET on Marital Distress and IPV** sets the stage for a consideration of the CCM.

FACT SHEET ON MARITAL DISTRESS AND IPV

(Data in these FACT SHEETS derived from Arias, 2000; Eckhardt, et al., 1997; Edelson, 1999; Holtzworth-Munroe & Bates, 1997; Gottman, 1994; Jacobson & Gottman, 1998; O'Leary et al., 2000; O'Leary & Maiuro, 1999; Straus et al., 1980; Tjaden & Thoennes, 1998)

- In the U.S., approximately 90% of adults will marry

- In the 1920's, 1 in 7 marriages ended in divorce. By the 1950's, the divorce rate was 1 in 5, and by the turn of the century **1 in 2 marriages will end in divorce** in the U.S.

- Approximately 25% of couples are divorced within 3 years of marriage. The average divorcing couple will stay married for approximately 7 years.

- Following divorce, 80% of individuals will eventually remarry; with an average 3 year period before remarriage.

- 60% of remarriages will end in divorce. The average length of the second marriage is 5 years.

- The higher the level of marital distress, the higher the level of **IPV.**

- Intimate partner violence (**IPV**) is frequently cited as grounds for divorce, but it is important to recognize that **psychological abuse** is often a **better predictor** of marital discord, partner depression and divorce than is physical abuse.

- **IPV** refers to kicking, punching, hitting with a closed fist, hitting with an object, threatening with a weapon, destroying property, threatening others like children, pets. *(See measures of Conflict Tactics Scale by Straus 1979; Straus et al., 1996 for examples of items designed to assess IPV – Also see Section below on Assessment.)*

FACT SHEET : HOW WIDESPREAD IS IPV?

- In the U.S., the incidence of spouse abuse has been found to be **1 in 8 couples**. Every year, in approximately **16%** of couples at least one spouse **commits a violent act**.

- 1.8 million wives are assaulted by their spouse or partner each year, in the U.S.

- Over the course of their marriage in the U.S. approximately 15 million couples, out of 50 million couples, have experienced violence in the marriage, at some point.

- **13%** or **5 million wives** have been **chronically and severely abused** by their husbands. Women are 3.7 times more likely to be killed by their male partners than by strangers. 30% of all female homicide victims in the U.S. are killed by their husbands, boyfriends or former partners. Half of these homicides occur during the course of an argument. The most conflictual topics include finances, household management, personal disagreements, and sexual relations. While arguments over childrearing practices are <u>not</u> the most frequent source of marital distress, they are most strongly related to physical partner aggression.

- 50% of the couples seeking marital treatment involve physical aggression. Aggression is in the form of self-defence in less than 20% of the cases. Aggression is often mutual between partners contributing to an escalating cycle.

- Violence is more likely to be used by males as a means to assert or maintain power and control and by females as a form of self-defence. But, **IPV** is multifaceted and can serve several diverse functions.

- **40% of newly married couples** report physical aggression against their partners. While serious violence is relatively uncommon prior to marriage, a developmental pattern is seen where verbal aggression is often followed by throwing objects. The majority of these violent incidents are directed at young child-bearing women who are between the ages of 16 and 24.

- When violence occurs, it tends to be **repeated**. Once battering has begun, it is likely to continue to occur and will often escalate in frequency, intensity and severity.

- Marital conflict increases the likelihood of parent-child and parent-adolescent conflict. **Spouse abuse and child abuse/neglect often co-occur.**

- It has been estimated that the **co-occurrence** of physical aggression toward the child and partner within the same family is approximately **6% in a community sample** and up to **50% in a clinical sample. The implication is that aggression toward a child or a partner warrants assessment of the other kind of aggression.** It is important to obtain information about the use of physical aggression within the **entire family.** For example, physical aggression of a man to his wife has been found to result in more aggression of the wife to the child. **The more serious the child abuse by the father, the greater the likelihood that the mother may need protection.**

- Children under 12 years of age are present in more than half of the homes where violence occurs. Witnessing abuse within the family during childhood has been linked to negative mental health outcomes (e.g., conduct problems, anxiety, PTSD).

- Consider that women in women's shelters report over 60 acts of husband's violence per year. 87% of their children are exposed to "wife beatings." In contrast, in community samples of **IPV**, the average incidence of husband violence is about 6 acts of violence per year.

- Such partner aggression is <u>not</u> delimited to heterosexual couples. Partner abuse is common in **same gender male and female relationships**; with some estimates being close to 50% (Renzetti, 1992; West, 1998).

- Burke and Follingstad (1999) report that,

    > *"Research suggests that <u>lesbian</u> and <u>gay men</u> are just as likely to abuse their partners as heterosexual men, although it is unknown whether the severity of abuse is comparable between these two groups. <u>Risk markers and correlates</u> of intimate violence in same-sex relationships are <u>notably similar</u> to those associated with heterosexual partner abuse." (p. 508)*

- Over 1 million women in the U.S. seek medical care for injuries relating to battering each year.

- 20% of all women emergency room visits are the result of battering.

- Health care costs for women who are victims of **IPV** are 2.5 times the costs for nonvictimized women.

- **Physicians detect only 5% of all cases of partner violence.** However, when emergency department nurses were trained to administer partner violence screening protocols, the identification rate jumped to 30%.

INTERVENTIONS WITH BATTERERS:
INTIMATE PARTNER VIOLENCE

Given the widespread incidence and seriousness of **IPV**, we can consider what interventions have been developed to treat batterers and how effective are such programs. To anticipate, the **outcome data for the relative effectiveness of interventions with batterers is <u>indeed humbling</u>**.

Most **IPV** treatment programs for male batterers employ a weekly group format ranging from 8 to 36 weeks. These multifaceted interventions focus on:

1) Anger-management procedures -- helping batterers become aware of their anger-aggression cues, and developing a number of self-regulation procedures including learning to take time-outs, using relaxation, self-talk, emotional disengagement, and violence cessation skills, psychoeducational and cognitive restructuring procedures, including treating anger as a secondary emotion;

2) Efforts to change attitudes and behaviors that derive from a feminist perspective – sex role attitudes, discussion of patriarchal male power roles, attitudes toward women and use of aggression;

3) Training in communication, conflict resolution, negotiation, empathy training, and social problem solving skills;

4) Treatment of comorbid problems such as substance abuse (e.g., see O'Farrell et al., 1999)

Illustrative of these group programs is the work of Hamberger (1996) and Hamberger and Hastings (1993) who provided a 16-week cognitive behavioral treatment program to batterers. The initial 3 sessions focused on assessment, feedback, and motivational engagement activities that were followed by 12, 2 hour weekly sessions., with 10 participants in each group. Geffner (2000), O'Farrell et al. (1999), O'Leary (1996) and O'Leary et al. (1999) have indicated the potential of using **couples therapy** with batterers under certain circumstances.

Whatever the format of the treatment, the major challenge is the **high incidence of treatment nonadherence** as the following numbers underscore.

- Of the batterers offered treatment, only 7% to 16% will complete 12 sessions of treatment. The dropout rates between initial contact and program completion are often greater than 90% (Gondolf & Foster, 1991).

- Among court-mandated men, 1/3 do <u>not</u> keep initial appointments and 30% of those who initially participate terminate treatment prematurely

- Large number of men never keep their initial appointments, whether or not they are ordered by the court to do so

- Men who drop out of abuse treatment programs are more likely to repeat violence then those who complete treatment

(See Gondolf & Foster, 1991; Hamberger et al., 2000; Holtzworth-Munroe. 2000; Saunders, 1999a for a fuller discussion of treatment nonadherence.)

Of those who participate in batterers treatment programs, just how effective are these diverse treatment programs? Rosenfeld (1992) reviewed 25 outcome studies of batterers and found that the **average recidivism rate** (i.e., at least 1 act of violence by the time of the follow-up) **was 27%.** This is consistent with other estimates that 25% to 50% of men who batter who attend treatment programs repeat their violence during the periods of 6 months to 2 years following treatment (Gondolf, 1997; Saunders, 1996a). Rosenfeld (1992) highlights, however, that the batterers who completed treatment had only **slightly lower rates of recidivism** than batterers who had refused treatment, who had dropped out of treatment, who were arrested and <u>not</u> referred to treatment.

A similar conclusion was offered by Koss (2000) who observed:

> *<u>None</u> of the alternative treatments for battering, which include counseling diversion, adjudicated counseling, or traditional sentencing have been shown to have a <u>unique</u> <u>preventative effect</u> on the prevalence, severity or frequency of battering (Koss, 2000, p. 5).*

Overall, these intervention programs are relatively effective, but as Rosenfeld and Koss highlight, they do <u>not have unique nor differential preventative effects</u>. This point was most impressively highlighted in a major intervention study conducted by Dunford (2000). Dunford reports on the comparative results of three different 12 month interventions for servicemen who engaged in battering behaviors. 861 couples were randomly assigned to 4 groups: a men's group; a cojoint group; a rigorously monitored group; and a control group. Cognitive-behavioral interventions were implemented in both the men's groups (Wexler, 2000) and the cojoint group (see Geffner, 2000). Outcome data was collected at 6 months and 18 months. The cognitive-behavioral groups met weekly for 6 months and then monthly for an additional 6 months for a total of 1 year of treatment. The weekly meetings included both didactic and process activities. The didactic weekly sessions addressed the perpetrator's attitude concerning women and violence and taught a variety of skills. *(Copies of the treatment manuals are available from Franklyn Dunford, Institute of Behavioral Science, University of Colorado, Boulder, Colorado, 80309)*

The results indicated a **nonsignificant difference** between the various groups. The interventions were successful in the majority of cases in having men discontinue their physical abuse of their wives or cohabitant partners. The humbling aspect of this study is that the **rigorous monitoring group** that used systematized and official monitoring in order to hold perpetrators accountable for their abusive behaviors **was equally effective.** 83% of the men in the treatments (men's groups, conjoint interventions and rigorous monitoring) did <u>not</u> reinjure their wives during a 1 year outcome period.

> *"This finding ranks among the best of the evaluations found in the literature. However, when the results are examined in the context of the behavior assigned to the control group, it is apparent that the treatment interventions <u>were not responsible</u> for the relatively low recidivism rates." (Dunford, 2000, p. 475.)*

This important study obviously bears replication, especially with a civilian population, where the consequences of rigorous monitoring (e.g., discharge from the Navy) would not be as powerful. Dunford (2000) offers yet another explanation of the absence of treatment effects, namely, the imposition of **one-size-fits-all approach** to the treatment of batterers and their spouses. Such a treatment approach fails to consider the **heterogeneity of the population of batterers.** Recent attempts to create **typologies** of batterers (e.g., Hamberger & Lohr, 1996; Holtzworth-Munroe & Stuart, 1994; Holtzworth-Munroe et al., 2000; Langhirichsen-Rohling et al., 2000; Tweed & Dutton, 1998) highlight the potential of matching the treatment content and format to the differential motivations and needs of men who abuse their wives/partners. As Holtzworth-Munroe et al. (2000, p. 628) observe:

> *"Violent men have varying levels of problems with criminal behavior, substance abuse, psychological distress, attachment, demanding behavior, jealousy, impulsivity, social skills defects, attitudes toward violence and hostility toward women."*

A similar conclusion was drawn by Levesque et al. (2000) who reported that a meta-analysis of batterer treatment programs only yielded an Effect Size of .06 and that treatment attrition averaged 40% across programs. (Also see the report of the National Research Council and the Institute of Medicine (1998) that question the efficacy of such treatment programs.) These highly structured, psychoeducational, and "one-size-fits-all" programs **fail to attend to individual differences** (e.g., see some promise of tailoring interventions by Saunders, 1996).

Thus, what is needed is a **Case Conceptualization Model (CCM)** that would attend to individuals' differences and guide assessment needs and inform treatment planning accordingly. In my capacity as a consultant to the military and to various treatment battering programs, I have put together a **CCM for IPV.** In the same way as I employed the **CCM with juvenile offenders**, I have been able to use the **CCM** in formulating

treatment planning with batterers. Depending upon the nature of the data, the treatment can, in collaboration with patients, be used to differentially decide on whether individual, and couples, or group interventions are warranted, moreover, whether the treatment focus should be on anger management skills, victimization experiences, adherence problems, bolstering strengths and the like. The **CCM** also provides a framework for monitoring progress.

The information in the following **CCM** and the accompanying **Breakout Boxes** was derived from the literature reviews offered by Archer, 2000; Babcock & Steiner, 1999; Dutton & Golant, 1995; Gelles et al., 1994; Gondolf, 1997; Gondolf & Russell, 1987; Hamberger, 1996; Healey et al., 1998; Holtzworth-Munroe, 2000; Holtzworth-Munroe, 1990, 1997 – Parts I, II, III; Jacobson & Gottman, 1998; Leadley et al., 2000; Neidig & Friedman, 1984; O'Leary & Arias, 1988; Saunders, 1996b, 1999; Stordeur & Stille, 1989; Wexler, 2000; White et al., 2000).

Since **IPV** is multifaceted and influenced by a variety of risk and protective factors, there is a need for a comprehensive conceptual case formulation that guides clinical decision-making.

FIGURE 4
CASE CONCEPTUALIZATION MODEL:
INTIMATE PARTNER VIOLENCE

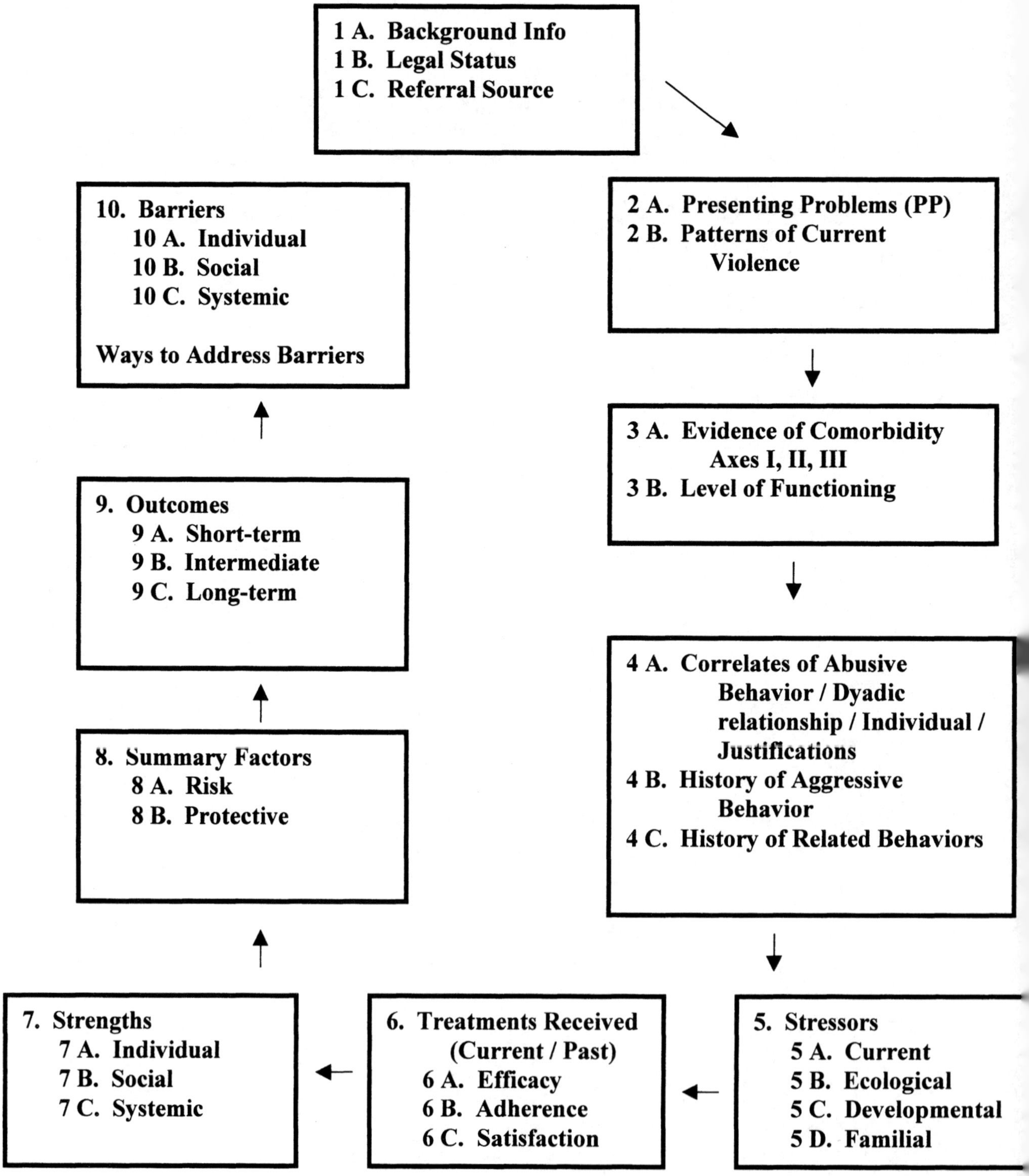

1 A. Background Info
1 B. Legal Status
1 C. Referral Source

2 A. Presenting Problems (PP)
2 B. Patterns of Current
       Violence

3 A. Evidence of Comorbidity
       Axes I, II, III
3 B. Level of Functioning

4 A. Correlates of Abusive
       Behavior / Dyadic
       relationship / Individual /
       Justifications
4 B. History of Aggressive
       Behavior
4 C. History of Related Behaviors

10. Barriers
     10 A. Individual
     10 B. Social
     10 C. Systemic

Ways to Address Barriers

9. Outcomes
    9 A. Short-term
    9 B. Intermediate
    9 C. Long-term

8. Summary Factors
    8 A. Risk
    8 B. Protective

7. Strengths
    7 A. Individual
    7 B. Social
    7 C. Systemic

6. Treatments Received
     (Current / Past)
    6 A. Efficacy
    6 B. Adherence
    6 C. Satisfaction

5. Stressors
    5 A. Current
    5 B. Ecological
    5 C. Developmental
    5 D. Familial

DETAILED BREAK-OUT INFORMATION

1A. BACKGROUND INFORMATION

Current age / Race, ethnicity, religion / Language spoken / Marital status – length of
        marriage, divorced, separated, cohabitation / Highest level of education /
        Employment status / Occupation / Level of SES – welfare, public assistance /
        Living arrangements – people present in home / Children – number, age, gender /
        If combat veteran, then post combat adjustment, employment status,
        compensation-seeking, substance abuse and PTSD

Notes: *While IPV can occur across all SES and education levels, there is a higher*
        incidence in lower SES. Age has <u>not</u> been found to correlate with level of IPV;
        Cohabitating individuals are more likely to engage in abusive behaviors <u>versus</u>
        those not living together. Unemployed men are more likely to dropout of
        treatment.

1B. LEGAL STATUS

Court involvement – Restraining order / Deferral or mandated treatment / Prosecution –
        probation, parole / History of involvement with legal and judicial systems

1C. REFERRAL SOURCE

Court mandated / Probation ordered / Partner, relative, friend, colleague, employer
        referral / Women's shelter / Voluntary self-referral

(Court mandated patients have a greater likelihood of dropping out of treatment.)

2A. PRESENTING PROBLEMS

(Note both men and women tend to underreport both the incidence and severity of
        violence.)
Current levels of aggression and hostility
Frequency, severity, duration and chronicity of physical and psychological aggression –
        include verbal, emotional and sexual abuse toward partner / *(Obtain description*
        of most recent, worst and first violent incident)
(Verbal aggression often predicts physical violence in a pattern of hostile conflicts that
        escalate overtime.)
Co-occurrent violence toward children – frequency, severity, duration, chronicity,. Ask
        about child management problems. *(Parent-child, parent-adolescent conflict.*
        Children are at an increased risk of physical abuse and/or severe physical
        punishment when wife abuse occurs. – See discussion by Appell & Holden,
        1998)

2B. PATTERNS OF CURRENT VIOLENCE

Situational specificity <u>versus</u> **generality of aggressive behavior**; family <u>versus</u> family violence <u>plus</u> violence outside of home.

Typology of batterers *(See below for descriptions)*
- **Family only**
- **Dysphoria Borderline type**
- **Generally violent (Antisocial type)**

Types of aggressive behavior
- **Reactive aggression** – reactions to perceived provocations, reflects emotional dysregulation
- **Proactive aggression** – goal-directed and premeditated – reflects level of belligerence, contempt, brooding, stalking, harrassment
- **Self-defence aggression** – tries to prevent onset of violent attack or in defence of self and others

Current level of interpersonal control – demean, intimidation, threaten, economic restrictiveness, hypersensitive, dominate, isolate, suspicious, jealous, moody, feel powerless

TYPOLOGY
A **tripartite typology** of men who batter female partners has been proposed that recognizers the heterogeneity of batterers. Holtzworth-Munroe et al. (1994, 2000) propose that
   (1) **severity** and **frequency** of **IPV**,
   (2) **generality** of violence – within family and also outside of family
   (3) batterer's **degree of psychopathology** and/or personality disorders
provide an organizing framework for clustering various forms of **IPV**.

Family-only – proposed that they engage in low levels (severity and frequency) of violence; least amount of emotional and sexual abuse against partner, and typically no violence outside of family; little or no psychopathology; mild social skills deficit; low levels of impulsivity

Dysphoria-borderline – proposed that they engage in moderate to severe forms of **IPV**; violence is primarily confined to wife, but some extrafamilial violence also may occur; show symptoms of borderline personality disorder, emotional liability and volatility; depressed, anxious symptoms and also likely to have substance abuse problems; fearful and preoccupied about abandonment and rejection; high dependency; intense unstable relationships and difficulty establishing attachment relationships; high likelihood of victimization as child and adolescent; experienced parental rejection; high dependency on spouse and poor interpersonal skills

Generally violent – proposed that they engage in moderate to the most severe forms of IPV, including psychological and sexual abuse. Engage in extrafamilial violence and criminal activity, antisocial behavior, arrest record; alcohol and drug problems.

3A. EVIDENCE OF COMORBIDITY
Level of Psychopathology: Axes I, II, III
(It is estimated that only 3% of individuals who engage in IPV suffer severe forms of psychopathology.)

Symptoms associated with anger attacks
- Depression, anxiety – PTSD, Intermittent Explosive Disorder
- Antisocial Personality Disorder, Borderline Personality Disorder
- Substance abuse disorder – SUD, especially alcohol

(50% of alcoholics have been violent toward their partners; SUDs involved in half of all wife beatings; Binge drinking is more closely related to IPV than other forms of alcohol abuse; Wife assault increases with the severity of alcohol abuse. Need to assess for polysubstance abuse and for history of substance abuse such as arrests due to drunk driving – DUI arrests.)

3B. LEVEL OF FUNCTIONING

Ability to fulfill multiple roles – job, spouse, parent, other roles
Job loss, trouble with law, self management and interpersonal skills

4A. CORRELATES OF ABUSIVE BEHAVIOR

4A₁ Dyadic Relationship Factors

Level of marital distress *(The higher the level of marital distress, the higher the level of IPV)*
Cycles of mutual escalating violence
Interpersonal relatedness – demandingness – withdrawal patterns / Ratio of positive to negative interactions / Poor communication skills – arguments escalate rapidly
Power struggle issues of control and sex-role and egalitarian attitudes *(More violence in couples where power over decisions is confined in husband's hands, as compared to when decision making is shared. Wife beatings are 20 times more likely in couples where power over major decisions is concentrated in the husband's hands, as compared to couples where decisions are shared. Fewer everyday squabbles and conflicts build up into a reactive and routinized fashion – "not let small stuff go.")*

There is a higher incidence of marital violence where there are high level of
stress, unemployment, differences between partners in religion, race,
educational levels. **Status inconsistency** is more frequent in violent
homes than in nonviolent homes (that is, where the husband is less
educated, less verbal, makes less money, or has failed to achieve his
desired occupational status.)

Both partners use mutual aggressive behaviors that escalate.

Both partners abuse substances.

Women raised by violent parents had a husband beating rate 6 times higher than
women with nonviolent parents.

4A₂ INDIVIDUAL FACTORS

Difficulties with intimacy / Ineffective communication, assertiveness and
empathy skills / Inadequate verbal expressive skills relative to skillfulness
of partner / Poor social problem-solving skills / Emotional volatility and
high levels of emotional dysregulation

Hold attitudes that condone use of violence and part of a peer group that
condones aggression.

Negative attitude toward women and negative attitude toward sex-role
egalitarianism.

Seek power and control but not experience self as being powerful or as having
what they want.

4A₃ JUSTIFICATION

Punish –	*"She hurt me, so I need to hurt her back."* *"Consequences disregarded or viewed as tolerable."* *"It wasn't so bad."*
Justified –	*"It is revenge."* *"She's been unfaithful."* *"It is for a higher good – being a martyr."*
Forced compliance –	*"Break her will."* *"Make sure she gets some sense."* *"Make her listen."*
Dominate / Isolate –	*"Right to tell her what to do."* *"I had to put her in her place."*
Sense of entitlement –	*"Partner is considered property."* *"I am King in my home."*

Fear of abandonment– (Morbid jealousy)	*"Keep her from leaving."* *"Constantly prove her loyalty."* *"Fear of rejection."* *"I was being ignored."*
Exert control –	*"Make her obey."* *"Assert my will over her."* *"Way to maintain sense of power when other resources are perceived as insufficient."*
Feel out of control –	*"My rage took over."* *"I couldn't stop."* *"Uncharacteristic of me."*
Partner blame –	*"My partner was to blame."* *"If she treated me better."* *"If she left me alone, I wouldn't have a problem with violence."*
Worry about future attacks –	*"I need to stay away."* *"I worry about future attacks. I need to withdraw, then I'm alone."*

4B. HISTORY OF AGGRESSIVE BEHAVIORS

Conduct history of violent behavior

History of police contacts, arrests, prison, parole / Include arrests due to offenses other than **IPV** – shoplifting, traffic violations, DUI

(Individuals with a history of criminal offenses show a greater likelihood of treatment dropout.)

Developmental history of aggressive behavior (ADHD, ODD, CD, bullying behavior or being a victim of bullies, Associates with antisocial peer group) Had parents who used physical punishment when youth was in adolescence / Involved with parents in coercive interpersonal cycles / Family involved in antisocial behaviors

4C. HISTORY OF RELATED BEHAVIORS

History of Substance Abuse

History of drug-related arrests, injuries, hospitalizations / Early onset of substance abuse
History of substance abuse in family members, especially male members of family
Other relevant related behaviors – academic performance, work history

5 STRESSORS

5 A. CURRENT STRESSORS

Current life stressors (financial, legal, health, occupational)
Daily hassles – community, irritants and interruptions
Negative life events to self and family members – transitions, hassles due to illness,
      death, disaster, status
Marital and familial stressors
(Higher incidence of IPV with higher levels of stress)

5 B. ECOLOGICAL STRESSORS

Live in high crime area, poverty, exposure to community violence
Social norms and expectations that condone the use of violence as a means to
      solve interpersonal conflict
Community supports masculine entitlement role ("machismo")

5 C DEVELOPMENTAL STRESSORS

History of victimization – experience physical and sexual abuse, emotional
      victimization, neglect *(Record history, frequency and duration of abuse.
      Note that 1/3 of individuals who were abused or neglected will grow-up
      and abuse their family members; 2/3 will not. Family violence can also
      lead to depression, withdrawal and self-punishing behaviors.)*
Witness parental violence during childhood and adolescence. *(Men and women
      who had seen their parents engage in physical violence are almost 3
      times as likely to hit their spouse, as compared to those who had __not__
      witnessed such domestic violence; 17.1 incidents per 100 men __versus__ 5.4
      incidents per 100 men, per year. The more serious the violence
      witnessed, the stronger the tendency to be violent. __Note__ that family of
      origin aggression is more predictive of violence (3 to 4 times) in the early
      stages of marriage, as compared to the later stages of marriage. The
      estimated rate of intergenerational transmission of intimate partner
      violence is 30%, five times the rate of intimate partner violence in the
      general population.)*
Parental divorce with accompanying conflict and distress and use of violence
Parental use of aggression and alcoholism witnessed by the child
Received harsh inconsistent physical punishment, especially boys from fathers
      during teenage years and accompanying coercive interactions that
      contribute to feelings of powerlessness. They are 4 times more likely to
      beat spouse than those not physically punished.
Men who were reared in homes where they were being **shamed** and
      humiliated, especially by father. They were punished for "essential
      badness", rather than for specific behaviors
History of poor attachment relationships with prosocial adults

Men who developed insecure attachment to their mother
Exposure to violence in community

5 D FAMILIAL STRESSORS

Ongoing familial and marital stressors – coercive cycles
Level of psychopathology in family members – antisocial father, depression in
    mothers
Intergenerational victimization

6. TREATMENTS RECEIVED –CURRENT/PAST

6A <u>History of treatment and interventions</u>: <u>Efficacy</u>

Dates. Sites, Treatment agents, Format – such as mandated, individual, group,
    couples, Psychological – skills training, Ecologically-based treatments

6B <u>Treatment Nonadherence / Patient noncompliance</u>

*(33% of referred and court-mandated batterers do <u>not</u> keep initial
    appointments; 30% terminate treatment prematurely)*
(Men who drop out of treatment are more likely to repeat violence)
*(Treatment group's composition – when participants in the treatment group
    are consistently in racial minority, they have a higher likelihood of
    dropping out of treatment)*
*(Other risk markers of nonadherence include: younger age, lower SES, lower
    educational level, unemployed, alcohol and drug-related criminal
    record, history of violence, more severe forms of violence, drinking
    partnership with spouse)*
Obtain treatment adherence information such as dropping out, failure to take
    prescribed medication, failure to attend treatment on a regular bases,
    failure to perform agreed-upon "homework"

6C <u>Treatment Satisfaction</u>

Obtain reactions to previous and current treatment and recommendations for
    future treatment

7 STRENGTHS

7 A. INDIVIDUAL STRENGTHS

More resources available (education prestige, occupational and fulfilling and other roles, social affiliations), the less the likelihood of engaging in violent behaviors
Attachment history – past / current
Social and communication skills
Role of spiritual values

7 B. SOCIAL STRENGTHS

Commitment to relationship
Level of social supports
Participation in organizational activities (Attends meetings, activities)

7 C. SYSTEMIC STRENGTHS

Service availability
Social and cultural supportive groups and activities
(Having a secure attachment relationship to at least one adult may act as a buffer)
(Participation in prosocial group activities may act as a buffer. Men who do __not__ participate in social activities have an assault record of 10.5 per 100 men; whereas those men who attend 11 or more such group activities have an assault record of 1.7 per 100 men)

8 SUMMARY FACTORS

8A SUMMARY RISK FACTORS

8B SUMMARY PROTECTIVE FACTORS

9 OUTCOMES (GOAL ATTAINMENT SCALING)

9A SHORT-TERM GOALS

9B INTERMEDIATE GOALS

9C LONG-TERM GOALS

10 BARRIERS

10A INDIVIDUAL

Typology of violence / Beliefs and correlates / Presence of psychopathology / Comorbidity / Lack of motivation

10B SOCIAL

Condoning and nonsupportive environment / Peers condone use of violence / "Secondary gains" for use of violence / Peers and family reinforce use of aggression / Partner contributes to mutual escalation – partner abuses substances and engages in aggressive behavior

10C SYSTEMIC

Absence or delay of services / Lack of continuity of care / Practical barriers – transportation, child care / Composition of treatment group – racial makeup / Lack of preparation for treatment – engagement process

WARNING SIGNS OF POTENTIAL FOR
INTIMATE PARTNER VIOLENCE (IPV)

I was asked by a friend for help concerning her interpersonal relations. She had been divorced and had experienced domestic violence. Several years had gone by and she was beginning to date again. She wanted to know what "signs" to watch for beyond her "intuitive feel" for determining how safe she was with a potential partner. I was reluctant to give her specific advice, but soon I came to realize that as a father of four grown children, I actually had an **Implicit Checklist** that I use when they bring home a possible partner.

As this **Handbook** goes to press, a funny movie called <u>Meet the Parents,</u> starring Robert DeNiro, came out. I realized that parents and their children should be informed by what the literature says about the likelihood of predicting future domestic violence.

Moreover, since abused patients are often likely to find themselves in subsequent abusive relationships (as a result of assortive mating), therapists should ensure that they spend time with their patients discussing whom patients can "trust" and whom they "cannot trust." They need to consider the lessons to be learned from their previous victimizing relationships. Patients need to be informed of the warning signs for possible **IPV**.

The following **Checklist** which includes both **current** and **developmental factors** is my compilation from the literature on **IPV**. **CAVEAT:** This is <u>not</u> a validated Checklist that has been tested on large samples of populations and it applies more toward male partners than female partners. It is, however, a scholarly list of possible factors that can be used to evaluate the potential for **IPV**. But, as I told my friend, the Checklist should <u>not</u> replace her own sensitivity and judgment.

WARNING SIGNS OF POTENTIAL FOR
INTIMATE PARTNER VIOLENCE - CHECKLIST

CURRENT FEATURES

- High level of marital (dating) dissatisfaction

- Use of verbal aggression and physical aggression to resolve arguments and conflict (N.B. Low levels of verbal and physical aggression in dating are warning signs of future high levels of partner violence)

- Current substance abuse, especially binge drinking

- Limited social skills and verbal competence (e.g., poor communication and negotiation skills relative to that of the partner)

- Limited social resources (e.g., few social contacts outside of the relationship; not participate in same-sex, pro-social organizations and activities)

- Disparities between partners (e.g., education, income, status inconsistency, partner failed to achieve desired occupational level)

- Possible sources of conflict (e.g., interracial, interreligious)

- High level of stress (e.g., chronic unemployment, dislocation)

- Moody, irritable, impulsive, suspicious, jealous, resentful, hostile, oppositional, insecure, sense of inadequacy and feelings of powerlessness

- Argumentative, especially disagreements over child-rearing

- If male who has children, uses physical punishment as a disciplinary procedure

- Hold attitudes and beliefs that condone aggression

- Part of a peer group that condones the use of violence to resolve conflict – achieve status in peer group for use of aggression

- Male exerts control (power) over major couple decisions (e.g., nonegalitarian attitude)

- High dependence on partner (e.g., fear of abandonment, high demand of attention / love)

- Heightened egotism (inflated sense of self and narcissistic entitlement)

- Both partners drinking with mutual (bi-directional) escalating conflict

- Presence of current psychiatric disorder (e.g., Antisocial personality disorder, depression with suicidal ideation, PTSD, migraine headaches, co-occurrent mental disorders and substance abuse disorders, sudden behavioral changes following onset of disorders)

- Availability of weapons

DEVELOPMENTAL FEATURES

- History of aggressive behavior and violence (e.g., fights with resultant injury requiring medical attention)

- History of antisocial behavior (e.g., trouble with the law, more than 5 offences, delinquency, cruelty to animals)

- Age of first contact with the juvenile justice system (< age 12)

- History of substance abuse (e.g., polysubstance use, binge drinking and substance abuse in male family members)

- History of developmental problems (e.g., hyperactivity, accompanied by oppositional behavior and conduct disorder)

- Victim of abuse and / or neglect

- Parents divorced, separated (contentious and conflictual separation)

- Violence in parents' relationship, especially witnessed as a child

- Parents' history of antisocial behavior and substance abuse

- Received inconsistent, harsh punishment, especially physical punishment as a teenager (e.g., boys from father)

- Men have an insecure attachment relationship with their mother and a weak attachment relationship with other prosocial role models

- Men raised in home where they have been shamed and humiliated, especially by father who engendered feelings of powerlessness

- Developmentally exposed to community violence and to peer groups who model and condone use of violence

- Grew up in the South in the U.S. (former confederate State), especially small towns where a *"code of honor"* prevails, or grew up in an area where the *"code of the streets"* condoned and honored aggression when one was disrespected

POSSIBLE INTERVENTIONS

(Andrews et al., 1990; Heide, 2001; Lipsey, 1992; MacKenzie, 2000; Sherman et al., 1997; Sherman, 1999; Texas Youth Commission, 1997; Wilson et al., 1999)

Given the complex interplay of multiple influences contributing to the development of aggressive and violent behavior, it is not surprising that there would be a myriad of possible preventative and treatment interventions. In fact, Kazdin (2000) has noted that there are **over 550 different treatments** currently in use for children, adolescents and their families, but few of these treatments have demonstrated efficacy, nor have they been systematically evaluated. Moreover, as we consider in some instances the interventions are not only ineffective, but they have been found to inadvertently increase the likelihood of aggressive behaviors. Clinicians need to be informed about "What works", "What doesn't work", "Which are promising", "Which have the potential of making the situations worse".

A number of reviewers (see Andrews et al., 1990; Heide, 2001; Lipsey, 1992; MacKenzie, 2000; Sherman, 1999; Sherman et al., 1997; Texas Youth Commission 1997; Wilson et al., 1999; and *Websites on Crime Prevention http://www.preventing crime.org and http://www.bsos.umd.edu/ccjs/corrections*) have each reviewed these alternative treatments. Rather than reproduce this list of home-based, school-based, and community-based interventions, I have chosen to generate a list of some lessons that the field has learned in developing and evaluating interventions for children / youth and their families.

SOME LESSONS LEARNED FROM PREVENTION AND TREATMENT INTERVENTION RESEARCH FOR CHILDREN / YOUTH WITH DISRUPTIVE BEHAVIOR DISORDERS (DBD)

- Overall corrective interventions are <u>not</u> very effective

- The earlier the interventions, the more likely they are to be effective

- Identifying "high risk" children based on a single marker such as externalizing behaviors often misidentifies many children and underestimates females. There is a need for a multi-gating assessment approach that uses a variety of sources.

- The factors that place children at risk are multifaceted and are unlikely to be modified by relatively brief, time-limited interventions.

- Single factor-focused interventions are <u>not</u> likely to be successful. Need to target multiple risk and protective resources. There are <u>no</u> simple "magic bullet" solutions.

- Interventions that are conducted across multiple settings and systems (school, home, community) are more effective than single setting interventions.

- There is a need to involve prosocial peers as part of the intervention. Interventions that only involve "high risk" children and adolescents may do more harm, and inadvertently, increase the rate of violence.

- While parent management training is one the most effective interventions with oppositional and conduct disorder children/youth, parents of children with DBD have high "no show" rates. A promising alterative is to conduct an active home-based intervention program. Need to focus on engagement procedures and possible barriers from the outset and throughout training.

- Interventions need to be sensitive to cultural/racial and gender differences and sensitive to developmental differences.

- Interventions should build on participants' strengths and be collaborative and employ a guided participation model.

- Skills-oriented intervention programs should build in generalization training from the outset and explicitly train for transfer.

- Since inadequate parental supervision and lack of parent involvement are strong predictors of future antisocial behavior and delinquency, parent training is critical. But, *"parents alone <u>cannot</u> provide supervision to adolescents, let alone impulsive adolescents"* (Blechman et al., 1999). Thus, supervision and involvement by caring adults outside the family is required.

These lessons provide guidelines for planning and evaluating prevention and treatment interventions with children and youth with **DBD (Disruptive Behavior Disorders)**.

EXAMPLES OF INTERVENTION PROGRAMS

(The Melissa Institute is working on procedural guidelines on how each of these interventions can be conducted.)

SCHOOL-BASED INTERVENTIONS

- Assessment program to identify high-risk students and families

- Conduct assessment of how safe students and teachers feel

- Ensure health and safety of all students

- Create a secure environment

- Create an Inviting Learning Environment (e.g., create a school within a school., nurture a welcoming atmosphere, implement cultural/racial diversity programs)

- Actively work to involve parents in school activities and provide a variety of parents' training programs

- Designate teachers/staff who act as "beacons for nonviolence" and who act as facilitators

- Formulate and practice implementing a crisis management program

- Employ a range of in-school and out-of-school disciplinary practices

- Implement anti-truancy and dropout prevention programs

- Implement a multifaceted anti-bullying program

- Implement a peer mediation program

- Implement an anonymous peer system for reporting threats of violence

- Provide training and support programs for improving teachers' classroom management skills

- **Implement skills training programs for students**

  - **Anger management and conflict resolution skills (e.g., see Larson and Lochman, in press; Second Step, Grossman et al., 1997; Anger Replacement Training, Goldstein et al., 1987;, 1998)**

  - **Involve parents in the training programs**

  - **Follow generalization guidelines** *(see p. 334)*

- **Implement a transition program to help students move from one level of school to another**

- **Work to improve teachers pedagogical skills (e.g., ongoing training, mentoring programs for beginning teachers)**

- **Work to improve students' academic performance (e.g., focus on reading and math skills; teach study and test-taking skills; have Individualized Education Plans; mentoring programs)**

- **Help students with goal-setting (e.g., vocational counseling)**

- **Have after-school programs (supervised prosocial activities)**

- **Provide aide with summer programs (e.g., employment, job interview skills, life skills)**

- **Conduct ongoing consultation with other agencies (e.g., mental health, medical, police, courts)**

- **Have an active outreach program to the community (e.g., Big Brothers – Big Sisters; Find "mentors for hope" – usually same sex – same race)**

- **Have active preschool programs (e.g., see Perry School Project, Syracuse Family Development Program – See Heide, 2001)**

HOME-BASED AND FAMILY-BASED INTERVENTIONS

- Home-based nurse visiting programs that provide prenatal care and provide ongoing education and support following delivery (e.g., see Heide, 2001; Olds et al., 1999)

- Parent Management Training Programs (e.g., see Henggeler, 1999; Kazdin et al., 1999; Patterson, 1982; Sanders & Lawton 1999)

- Conduct home-based Multisystemic Interventions (e.g., see Borduin, 1999; Henggeler, 1999)

- Conduct Functional Family Therapy (e.g., see Alexander et al., 1976; Szapocznik & Kurtines, 1980)

COMMUNITY-BASED INTERVENTIONS

- Implement community-wide intervention programs that include members from diverse agencies such as Communities that Care, the Youth Prevention Council and Community Blueprints for Action programs (see Hawkins & Catalano, 1992; Heide, 2001; Tremlow & Sacco, 1996)

- Relocating families to a more affluent and less distressed neighborhoods (see Leventhal & Brooks-Gunn, 2000)

CAUTION -- *See Andrews et al., 1990; Arnold & Hughes, 1999; Dishion et al., 1999; Kopel, 2000; MacKenzie, 2000 and Powell et al., 1996 for a list and description of intervention programs that do not work such as Shock programs -- Scared Straight, Bootcamps, Gun buy back programs, and programs that segregate antisocial youth*

SUMMARY:
WHAT YOU SHOULD TAKE AWAY FROM SECTION II

1. An appreciation of the complexity and heterogeneity of aggressive behavior.

2. The ability to discuss the widespread incidence, impact and developmental pathways of aggressive behavior.

3. The importance of **gender differences** in understanding the nature and development of aggressive behavior and the implications for assessment and treatment.

4. How to employ a **Case Conceptualization Model (CCM)** in organizing diverse information and how to use the **CCM** in formulating an intervention program (e.g., with juvenile offenders and with batterers).

5. The importance of assessing aggressive and violent youth for <u>both</u> violence exposure and symptoms of psychological trauma and accompanying comorbidity. For example, it is critical to assess for the potential of self-harm in violent adolescent females.

6. The importance of assessing and nurturing **protective factors** and **"strengths"** (resilience factors) in any intervention program.

7. The guidelines to follow when developing an intervention program so we do <u>not</u> make the situation "worse".

TEST YOUR EXPERTISE: SECTION II

1. Just how stable is aggressive behavior over the life-span? Why does the stability data reflect as much **hope** as **concern**?

2. What are the differences between early-starter and late-starter models of aggression? What are the implications for assessment, prevention and treatment?

3. Generate a formula or describe a developmental pathway designed to make a violent individual. How can health care providers and the juvenile justice system inadvertently, unwittingly and perhaps even unknowingly, further contribute to the development of violence?

4. You have been called to Columbine High School to help them better understand the school shooting and to develop an intervention program. What suggestions would you offer? (See Website *http://www.state.co.us* for the Governor's report so your answer can be informed)

5. *"I live like I was treated"*, one violent youth commented. What is the relationship between violence and victimization that he was referring to?

6. How often do you and your colleagues systematically assess for victimization and comorbidity in your population of conduct disorder children and juvenile and adult offenders? What percentage of your clinical population has a history of victimization? If you found victimization, how does that influence your treatment approach?

7. Revisit **Question 3** about making a violent individual. Now redo the developmental pathway model separately for females. How does the pathway differ for girls <u>versus</u> boys? What are the implications of these gender differences for treatment?

8. Approximately 50% of youths who grow up in high-risk environments do <u>not</u> become delinquents, nor violent. 50% of aggressive individuals desist. Use the **Case Conceptualization Model** and the literature on resilience and "strengths" to explain what factors influence who does and who <u>does not</u> develop antisocial behavior and psychopathology.

9. The Mayor of Miami has established a committee called "Not one more," referring to not one more child death due to violence. You have been asked to be a consultant to this committee. What advice would you have to offer the Mayor? How would you identify high-risk children, families, neighborhoods? What are the dangers in your selection process? How is your advice informed by the lessons that have been learned and by an analysis of "what works"?

10. What are your reactions to the **Case Conceptualization Model (CCM)**? How useful is the **CCM**? Try it out! The next time you attend a case conference or have to write-up a case, consider the procedural flow chart. What background info do you usually collect **(Box 1A)**? What are the presenting problems, behaviorally defined **(Box 2B)** and **in addition**, what are the related problems and comorbid disorders that the patient evidences **(Box 2B)**. For these problems, what treatments have been and are being received **(Box 5A)** and moreover, how effective have the treatments been in terms of objective outcome measures and patient satisfaction? What difficulties, if any, did the patient have in following the treatment regimen (adherence data – **5B**)? What stressors, currently and developmentally, have exacerbated and helped maintain the presenting problems? **(Box 5)**. But, **in spite of** these difficulties, adversities, and risk factors, the patient has been able to achieve what, as recorded on the time lines. How did the patient do this? What individual, social and systemic strengths was the patient able to call upon? **(Box 6)** Thus, where should therapy begin? How can the therapist collaborate with the patient in taking stock of risk and protective factors **(Box 7)** and in formulating a practical means to systematically establish short-term, intermediate and long-term treatment goals so progress can be monitored? The **Goal Attainment Scaling** procedure **(Box 8)** will help the patient and the therapist to formulate not only workable goals, but also to develop a shared understanding and agreement on how to achieve the treatment goals. Finally, the therapist can help the patients and significant others to anticipate any potential barriers and develop anticipatory plans to address these potential obstacles **(Box 9)**.

Role play with your colleagues how to use the **CCM** with patients.

11. Can you code your therapeutic interventions using the **CCM**? For each intervention, what Box are you working on (Presenting Problems – Box 2; Treatment adherence problems – Box 5B; Building self-efficacy – Box 6A; Victimization – 4C; Long-waiting list – 9C – Systemic barriers). *It is proposed that there is nothing that you do in therapy that cannot be put into one of the Boxes.* As you become familiar with the **CCM**, you will be able to record and communicate effectively to patients, colleagues and managed care companies how you spend your time and why. **ENJOY THE BOXES** and consider how you would change and adapt the **CCM** for your specific clinical population. For example, apply the **CCM** to the challenging problem of domestic violence (**IPV**). Why aren't interventions with batterers more effective? How can the **CCM** be used to develop more effective treatments?

12. Consider the issue of **Intimate Partner Violence** (Spouse Abuse / Domestic Violence). Describe the various types of batterers and the implications for assessment and treatment. How would you alter your intervention program depending upon the information offered in the **Case Conceptualization Model**? How would such issues as comorbidity, victimization, correlates of abuse, treatment nonadherence, barriers, and the like, influence how you proceed in therapy?

13. You have been asked to consult to the **Melissa Institute** on how to reduce violence. What specific suggestions do you have on what programs should be implemented and what types of programs should be avoided? How can health care providers and public officials make the situation "worse" and inadvertently create programs that may increase violence?

14. This **HANDBOOK** went to press two weeks after the September 11, 2001 bombings in New York and Washington. I have wondered if the analysis of the factors that contribute to our understanding of "how to make a violent youth" or "how to make a batterer" could be applied to *"how would one make a terrorist"* who would be willing to kill thousands of innocent victims and commit suicide in the process. Calling terrorists "evil" or "crazy" are nonexplanatory concepts. What is the "mindset" and cognitive, affective and psychological processes that lead to such violent behavior? While I recognize that the answer to this question is complex, I invite you to join me in thinking through the steps that might be involved. Only after such an analysis will we begin to understand what intervention steps to undertake to prevent the development of the next generation of terrorists. Consider how the following processes may come into play in the *making of a terrorist*. The terrorist needs to:

(1)   perceive a series of provocations, threats, eliciting fears, even to the point of feeling a sense of possible annihilation and a fight for survival of person, beliefs or way of life;

(2)   attribute intentionality to the perceived provocations;

(3)   engage in justification (see themselves as being "bullied" and "victimized," both in the past and present that justifies retaliation and revenge – "Eye for an eye, tooth for a tooth.") See selves as acting in ways that any human would respond.;

(4)   perceive provocations as violating their code of honor and eliciting shame and rage;

(5)   engage in thinking patterns and hold fundamentalist beliefs that are perceived as being shared with peers and that fit religious and cultural norms – sense of entitlement, dichotomous (black – white) thinking and other cognitive errors that bolster a sense of efficacy and a purpose or mission;

(6)   use language and metaphors that dehumanize victims and that preclude feelings of guilt, blame, (victims are considered, "enemies of God", "collateral damage" and necessary to achieve their goals);

(7)   embrace a set of beliefs (e.g., religious, cultural) that transforms death into a "higher good" and as a preparation for afterlife;

(8)   receive (or their family members will receive) financial, or other practical payoffs, or martyrdom. Terrorists also believe that they should not let peer group down. Engage in violent behaviors not only for a cause, but because of public commitment to others.

Obviously, this explanation is simplistic, but how would you improve upon this preliminary analysis?

SECTION III: ASSESSMENT

From a cognitive-behavioral perspective, assessment and treatment are **highly interdependent processes.** **A great deal of treatment and education occurs during the assessment process.** The **ongoing** or recurrent assessment process over the course of treatment allows both patients and the therapist to monitor progress and to determine the degree to which mutually agreed upon treatment goals have been achieved and/or have to be revised.

SECTION III will consider how a **multiple-gating assessment procedure** can be used and concludes with a consideration of the challenging problems of how to **predict** violence and how to **manage violent individuals**. The relationship between mental disorders and violent behavior will also be examined.

CONTENTS SECTION III

GOALS AND STRATEGIES OF ASSESSMENT

The **goals of assessment** include determining:

(1) the nature and impact of the patient's present and past history of angry and aggressive behaviors and the current level of "dangerousness";

(2) the correlates of aggression and evidence of comorbidity;

(3) a psychiatric diagnoses;

(4) possible stressors, strengths, and barriers to change;

(5) and formulating a Case Conceptualization Model that will guide treatment planning.

Another major goal of assessment is to **enhance** the **patient's emotional awareness skills**. Many patients who have problems with anger have a limited emotional vocabulary and have difficulty answering questions about how they feel. They fail to appreciate how their anger escalates into rage and the ways in which anger may be a **secondary emotion** that **masks other feelings** such as shame, fear/anxiety, vulnerability.

In order to achieve these objectives the therapist can use an array of assessment procedures, employing multiple sources of information, and a **multiple-gating sequential decision-making process** (see Dishion & Patterson, 1993; Feil et al., 1998). The assessment process may include:

(1) **Interviewing** -- structured and clinical interviews designed to assess for various components of anger responses -- emotions, physiological responses, cognitions, behaviors, anger-related memories, angry and aggressive fantasies, images of revenge and retaliation

(2) **Self-report measures**

(3) **Self-monitoring procedures**

(4) **Clinical ratings**

(5) **Performance-based measures and behavioral samples**

(6) **Input from others and from records**

(7) **Physiological and biochemical indicators**

(8) **Assessment of comorbid features**

(9)   **Assessment of contextual features (ecological assessment)**

(10) **Assessment of strengths, resources and possible barriers**

The therapist can use a variety of assessment procedures **besides interviewing** and **self-report measures** in order to help patients "unpack" and understand the relationships between their thoughts, beliefs, feelings and behaviors. We will consider three such assessment procedures:

    (1) **Imagery-based assessment**

    (2) **Self-monitoring**

    (3) **Gestalt-based empty-chair**

Before we consider the list of specific measures and interview questions, we will provide an overview of an **assessment strategy** that can be used. How many elements of this strategy are included depends on the purpose of the assessment and the time available. In considering the alternatives, it is important to keep in mind that:

    (1) there is little agreement on a standardized assessment battery for anger-prone and aggressive individuals;

    (2) there is <u>no</u> agreed upon diagnostic system for anger;

    (3) different classes of assessment (self-report measures, reports from others, reduction of aggressive behaviors and increase of prosocial behaviors, physiological indices) do <u>not</u> correlate very highly with each other and that these various indices are differentially responsive to alternative treatments (Di Giuseppe & Tafrate, 2001).

The assessment process begins with an exploration with the patient of where and when he or she becomes angry and why. The therapist needs to carefully **listen to the patient's "story"** and **acknowledge the legitimacy of the patient's account.** The therapist should <u>not</u> interrupt the patient's "story." Rather, the therapist should paraphrase what you heard and ask if you understood correctly (Thomas, 1998). *(Tables 1 to 9 provide illustrative questions.)*

The interviewer guides the patient through a **functional analysis** of the vulnerability factors, emotions, thoughts, actions and events that fall along the **chain of behaviors** for a specific aggressive episode. The therapist uses a **nonjudgmental** and **noncritical manner** to elicit a descriptive account of aggressive episodes to which the therapist conveys acknowledgment and understanding.

The semi-structured functional analysis interview can be **supplemented by** conducting a
Structured Interview for Anger (DiGiuseppe et al., 1994; McElroy et al., 1998)
Determine the frequency, duration, magnitude of the anger response, range of anger-
eliciting situations, hostile outlook, mode of anger expression – anger turned
inward/outward. (Ascertain when the patient's anger is too frequent, too intense, too
prolonged, unprovoked, or managed ineffectively. Determine whether the patient's
angry feelings and aggressive behaviors are commonly impulsive or premeditated
and whether it involves anger-related memories, rumination about retaliation and
revenge. Determine whether the individual suppresses anger and harbors grudges.)
*(See Deffenbacher et al., 1996; Gottman et al., 1995; and Thomas 1997 for a
discussion of the negative consequences of suppressing anger or turning "anger-
in".)* Keep in mind that individuals may engage in anger to fend off other feelings
such as helplessness, fear, shame, humiliation, betrayal, anxiety, depression *(See
Ornstein, 1999; Paivio, 1999; Tangey et al., 1996)*.

Conduct an **Historical Interview** of when the individual was exposed to anger /
aggressive behavior and whether the patient's peers view anger and aggression as
desirable and valued. Obtain an account from the patient, collateral (others), records
of trouble with law, arrests, drunk driving, property damage, threats with and without
a weapon, physical fighting, loss of job or interpersonal difficulties resulting from
anger.

Obtain a **specific account of violent behavior**. Ask the patient to list the most extreme
aggressive/violent acts engaged in **over the past 6 months** (e.g., hitting, physically
or verbally assaultive to another person, breaking objects because of being angry or
being frustrated). Ask the patient to indicate the approximate date, duration (how
long the incident lasted) and the time of the day. Barratt et al. (1999) asked
individuals to evaluate **each aggressive act** on a 22 item 5-point scale (definitely
yes, yes, can't decide, no, definitely no). Illustrative items include:

> *Act was planned.*
> *Act was spontaneous.*
> *Act was the result of immediate peer or group pressure.*
> *I was concerned about the consequences of the act for others.*
> *I cannot accurately recall the details of the act.*
> *I was <u>not</u> under the influence of alcohol or other drugs.*
> *My behavior was too extreme for the level of provocation.*
> *I now consider the act to have been impulsive.*
> *I felt guilty following the act.*

(There is also a need to assess for "dangerousness", as described below.)

Use **Anger self-report measures for specific areas** (e.g., Deffenbacher et al. 1994, 2000, have developed a questionnaire to assess "road rage.") **(Driving Anger Scale)**

Use **Imagery-Reconstruction Procedures** -- Analyze anger scenario in terms of frustration level and perceived consequences in the future *(See below p. 167)*

Use **role-playing** and **videotape replay** of the patient engaging in anger-provoking situations (Assess problem-solving competence, empathy, perspective-taking, relationship skills)

Use **Gestalt two-chair technique** (Client expresses anger and then changes chairs and expresses how the other person feels and thinks) *(See below p. 178)*

Use **Self-report Scales: State-Trait Anger Expression Inventory** (Forgays et al., 1997; Spielberger, 1988,; 1999); **Anger Inventories** (Novaco, 1990) and Buss and Perry's (1992) **Aggression Questionnaire; Anger Consequences Questionnaire** (Deffenbacher, 1995; Deffenbacher et al., 1996; viz., *"What happens when you become angry?"* enumerates possible consequences. Covers last 2 months); **Worst Anger Incident in the last year** (Deffenbacher et al., 1996; Deffenbacher & McKay, 2000, pp. 175-177). Determine the degree to which anger and aggression are evoked by distal events and consequences. **Propensity for Abusiveness Scale** (Dutton, 1998).

Use **self-monitoring procedures** (Anger Log and Anger Attack Questionnaire, Hassle Log, Risk Diary, Keep track of "Least Miserable Moments") *(See Deffenbacher et al., 1996; Feindler and Ecton, 1986; Fava et al., 1997; Gerlock, 1996; Meichenbaum, 1994) (See examples of self-monitoring forms below, pp. 175-177)*

The **assessment should be balanced** probing the patients about those occasions when they have attempted to control and self-regulate their anger (see **Coping Strategies Measure**, Novaco, 1995) (e.g., avoid "high risk" situations and conflicts, socially isolate themselves, walk away from "risky" situations, keep busy, hide their reactions, view provocations as a "problems-to-be-solved.") Use **interviewing, self-report scales, and self-monitoring** procedures to have patients describe what they have done to **handle or cope with anger situations.**

Have the patient **observe** and **interview others** on how they handle anger-engendering situations

Assess for the **role of alcohol abuse** (e.g., Use CAGE Interview [Liskow et al., 1995, *p. 156 below*]; the **Addiction Severity Index**, McLellan et al., 1992) *(See Awalt et al., 1997; Chermack & Giancola, 1997; Meichenbaum, 1994 for a discussion of the relationship between aggression and alcohol abuse and for a list of additional assessment measures).* As noted, the levels of anger and violence are higher in substance abusers.

Assess for **comorbidity** (psychiatric disorders such as ADHD, antisocial personality disorder, substance abuse, depression, anxiety disorders, psychosis) and medical conditions. *(e.g., See Fava et al., 1991 for a discussion of anger attacks in depressed patients; See Meichenbaum, 1994 for a list of possible measures of comorbidity, as well as see the Assessment Section below)*

ASSESSMENT MEASURES OF ANGER AND HOSTILITY
FOR ADULTS
(See Biaggio et al., 1981; DiGiuseppe et al., 1994;
Eckhardt et al., 1997, and Spielberger, 1995 for reviews)

Self-Report Measures

State and Trait Anger Expression Scales	Spielberger, 1985, 1988; Spielberger et al., 1983
Anger Provocation Inventory	Novaco, 1990
Novaco Anger Scale	Novaco, 1994; Mills et al., 1998
Buss-Perry Aggression Questionnaire (BPAQ)	Buss & Perry, 1992; Harris, 1997
Anger Attack Questionnaire	Fava et al., 1991; Mammen et al., 1999
Propensity for Abusiveness Scale	Dutton, 1998; Dutton et al., 2001
Anger Proneness in Women: Anger Situations Questionnaire	VanGoozen at al., 1994
Anger Inventory for people with Intellectual Disabilities	Benson et al., 1986
Reaction Inventory	Evans & Strongeland, 1971
Anger Log (Hassle Log)	Deffenbacher et al., 1996; Feindler & Ecton, 1986; Gerlock, 1996; Meichenbaum, 1994
Aggressive Acts Questionnaire	Barratt et al., 1999; Mammen et al., 1999
Anger Expression Scale	Deffenbacher, 1995; Ramirez et al., 1997
Worst Anger Incident in the Last Year	Deffenbacher et al., 1996; Deffenbacher & McKay, 2000
Anger Attacks Questionnaire	Fava et al., 1991
Anger Consequences Questionnaire	Deffenbacher, 1995; Deffenbacher et al., 1996

Self-Report Measures (continued)

Multidimensional Anger Inventory	Siegel, 1986; 1992
Anger Self-Report	Goldstein et al., 1988; Zelin et al., 1972
Symptom Questionnaire	Kellner, 1987
Irritability, Depression, Anxiety Scale	Snaith et al., 1978
Self-report for Anger	DiGiuseppe et al., 1994
Situations-Reaction Inventory	Blackburn & Lee Evans, 1985
Overt Aggression Scale	Yudofsky et al., 1986
Aggression Inventory	Gladue, 1991
Driver's Stress Profile	Blanchard et al., 2000,; Larson, 1990; Malta et al., 2001
Driving Anger Scale	Deffenbacher et al., 1994
Risk of Eruptive Violence Scale	Shopshire & Reilly, 1996
Assaultive Behavior Survey	Mehrabian, 1996, 1997
Feelings and Acts of Violence Scale	Plutchik & Van Praag, 1990
Self-expression and Control Scale	Van Elderen et al., 1997
Impulsiveness Scale (BIS-II)	Patton et al., 1985; Barratt, 1994; Webster & Jackson, 1997
Buss-Durkee Hostility Inventory	Buss & Durkee, 1975; Buss & Perry, 1992 (See Buss & Warren 2000 for updated Aggression Questionnaire)
Cook-Medley Cynical Hostility Scale (MMPI Subscale)	Cook-Medley, 1994; Kubany et al., 1994
Hostility and Direction of Hostility Questionnaire	Maiuro et al., 1988
Hostile Automatic Thoughts Questionnaire	Snyder et al., 1997

Self-Report Measures (continued)

Hostile Interpretations Questionnaire	Simourd & Mamuza, 2000
Responses to Provocation Scenarios	O'Connor et al., 2001
Vengeance Scale	Stuckless & Goranson, 1992
Criminal Sentiments Scale – Pride in Delinquency Scale	Simourd & Mamuze, 2000
Coping Strategies Measure	Novaco, 1975; Ramirez et al., 1997
Trait Hope Scale	Snyder et al., 1991

Measures of Comorbidity and Adjustment

SCID (Nonpatient Edition)	Spitzer et al., 1992
Social Adjustment Scale	Weissman & Bothwell, 1976
Symptom Checklist-90 (SCL-90-R) Also see Hostility Subscale)	Derogatis et al., 1994
Beck Depression Inventory (BDI)	Beck, 1967; Beck et al., 1988
PTSD Assessment	Carlson, 1997; Meichenbaum, 1994 for overview (For specific PTSD measures see Blake et al., 1990; Coffey et al., 1998; Falsetti, 1993; Foa, 1995, 1997; Green, 1996; Kubany et al., 2000; Norris, 1990; Norris & Riad, 1997; Wolfe et al., 1996)
Early Trauma Inventory	Bremner et al., 2000
Addictions Severity Index (ASI - Semistructured Interview)	McLellan et al., 1980
Short Michigan Alcohol Screening Test (MAST)	Skinner & Allen, 1982; Pokorny et al., 1992
Timeline Followback Procedure	Sobell & Sobell, 1992

Measures of Comorbidity (continued)

Substance Use Measure (SUDDS) *(Note: There is a need to conduct an assessment of polysubstance use.)*	Harrison & Hoffman, 1985
Psychopathy Checklist – Revised	Hare, 1991; Forth & Burke, 1998; Hart et al., 1995
McArthur-Maudsley Delusional Assessment Schedule	Appelbaum et al., 1999
Screening Questions for Threat/Control Override Delusions	Appelbaum et al., 2000
Schedule for Imaginal Violence	Grisso et al., 2000
Personality Assessment Inventory (PAI)	Morey, 1991
MMPI (High scores on Pd-Psychopathic Deviate, Hypomania, Hy-Hysteria and Pa-Paranoia)	Dutton, 1999
Millon Clinical Multiaxial Inventory (MCMI-II)	Hamberger et al., 1996; Millon, 1987
Self-report of Borderline Personality Organization (BPO)	Oldham et al., 1985
Psychopathy Checklist Revised	Hare, 1991; Forth & Burke, 1998; Hart et al., 1995; Salekin et al., 1996

Structured Interviews

Structured Interview for Anger Disorders	Eckhardt, 1994
Structured Interview for Anger	DiGiuseppe et al., 1994
Questions About Behavior Functions Scale *(Assess factors that maintain aggression – attention, escape, tangible, nonsocial and physical.)*	Matson & Vollmer, 1995; Matson et al., 1999, 2001
Camberwell Family Interview (CFI) (Hostility rating – conveys dislike patient as person)	Vaugh & Leff, 1976
Domestic Violence Interview	Fruzzetti et al., 1999
Interview Significant Others (Co-joint/Individual) *(Note: With spouse abuse it may be safer to conduct parallel individual interviews)*	DiGiuseppe et al., 1994
Homicide Behavior Survey	Annis et al., 1997; Malmquist, 1996
Structured Interviews for Intermittent Explosive Disorder	McElroy et al., 1998
Family History of Impulse-Control and Other Disorders	Andreasen et al., 1977
Caregiver Anger Interview	Steffen & Berger, in press
Child Maltreatment Interview Schedule	Briere, 1992

Clinician-Rated Instruments

Brief Psychiatric Rating Scale   Overall, 1988

Dangerous Behavior Rating Scale   Menzies et al., 1985

(See Fava for reviews of the   Fava, 1997
multiple rating scale that can be
used on an inpatient basis)

Cognitive Assessment

Automatic Thoughts Questionnaire -   Ingram & Wisnicki, 1988
    Positive

Executive cognitive functioning   Hoaken et al., 1998

Articulated Thoughts in Simulated   Davison et al., 1983; Eckhardt et al.,
    Situations (ATSS)   1998

Imagery-based assessment   Rusting & Nolen-Hoeksema (1998)

Psychophysiological Measures

                                                Gottman et al., 1995; Malta et al.,
                                                    2001; Scarpa & Raine, 1997

Biochemical Indicators

                                                Berman et al., 1997;
                                                Trestman, 1997

Measures of Couples' Conflict

Conflict Tactics Scale (CTS)	Straus, 1979; see Straus et al., 1996, revision; Schafer, 1996; Neidig & Friedman, 1984
Modified Conflict Tactics Scale *(Added items to Straus, 1979 that cover psychological abuse)*	Pan et al., 1994; O'Leary, 1999; Margolin et al., 1990
Spouse-specific Anger and Hostility Scale	Holtzworth-Munroe et al., 2000
Sexual Experiences Survey *(Note CTS does not tap sexual aggression)*	Koss et al., 1987
Emotional Abuse Questionnaire	Jacobson & Gottman, 1998
Domestic Conflict Index	Margolin et al., 1998
Dyadic Adjustment Scale (DAS)	Spanier, 1976
Revision Dyadic Adjustment Scale	Busby et al., 1995
Marital Adjustment Scale	Locke-Wallace, 1954
Spouse Verbal Problems Checklist (SVPC)	Haynes et al., 1984
Psychological Maltreatment of Women Inventory	Tolman, 1999
Dominance-Isolation Scale	Tolman, 1989
Sphere of Control Scale	Paulhaus & Christie, 1980
Spousal Assault Risk Assessment Guide	Kropp et al., 1995
Fear of Spouse Scale	O'Leary & Curley, 1986
Attribution of Responsibility Scale	O'Leary et al., 1999
Response to Violence Inventory	Dutton, 1998

Measures of Couples' Conflict (continued)

Areas of Disagreement Questionnaire   Fincham & Bradbury,. 1992

Relationship Attribution Measure   Knox, 1997

Conflict Resolution Style Inventory   Kurdek, 1994

Communication Patterns Questionnaire   Christensen & Sulloway, 1984

Desired Change Questionnaire   Christensen & Heavey, 1990

Marital Satisfaction Scale   Snyder, 1979; 1981

Marital Problems Questionnaire   Douglass & Douglass, 1995

Intimacy of Assessment PAIR   Schaefer & Olson, 1981
   Inventory

Observational Scales of Conflict

Marital Interactions Coding System   Heyman & Vivian, 1993;
                                                Heyman et al., 1995

Observational Rating Scales of   Berns et al., 1999; Hotzworth-
   Marital Conflict   Munroe et al., 1998; Gottman et
                                                al., 1995; 1999

Behavioral Coding Scheme --   Gottman et al., 1995 (also see
   Specific Affect Coding System   Eckhardt et al., 1997)
   (SPAFF)

Violence Risk Assessment

*Risk is **not** static, but changes over time and across conditions (See Otto, 2000).*

Risk assessment varies across different jurisdictions within states
(Helbrun et al., 2000)

Violence Risk Appraisal Guide (VRAG)	Harris et al., 1993; Quinsey et al., 1998
Violence Prediction Scheme	Webster et al., 1994
HCR-20 (Historical, Clinical and Risk Management)	Webster et al., 1997; Witt, 2000
Early Assessment Risk List EARL-20-B	Augimeri et al., 1998
Structured Assessment for Violence Risk in Youth (SAVRY)	Borum et al., 2000
Sexual Violence Risk Scale (SVR-20)	Boer et al., 1997; Witt, 2000
Level of Services Inventory – Revised	Andrews et al., 1995; Hoge & Andrews, 1996
Rapid Risk Assessment of Sex Offender Recidivism (RRSAP)	Hanson, 1998
Weapon Availability / Preoccupation with Violence	Otto, 2000
Child Abuse Potential Inventory	Milner, 1989a, b

ART OF QUESTIONING

Of all the assessment tools available, the **most valuable is the clinical interview** and the most important therapeutic skill is the **art of questioning**. The questions that the therapists pose to patients are often more important than the answers that patients offer or the advice that therapists give. The questions that therapists pose help patients to co-construct new "life stories", as well as provide patients with a cognitive model for a style of thinking. As Overholser (1993) observes, questions provide patients with an opportunity for discovery and a means of enhancing their awareness of the triggers and consequences of their behavior. Effective questioning can **stimulate** the **patient's curiosity**. By asking questions for which there are no immediate answers, the therapist helps to "plant seeds" for future sessions.

In this **SECTION** we will consider the strategies therapists can use to engage, challenge, motivate and educate their patients. Specific examples of questions are offered in a series of **Tables**. Obviously, it is not suggested that the therapist cover all of these areas, nor ask all of these specific questions. The "expert" therapist samples in a flexible fashion from this array of queries. Interviews should always end with the therapist asking patients if they have any questions.

The **art of questioning** provides patients with an opportunity to discover, rather than for the therapist to didactically teach. Such questioning fosters patients' understanding as patients are more likely to remember and apply those ideas that they discover by their own reasoning processes than the information and observations that are offered by the therapist. (As described below, I contrast this **Socratic form of questioning** versus those therapists who act like **"surrogate frontal lobes"** for their patients.) The interview questioning process begins with a general overview and then focuses on specific probes about the patients' anger and aggression.

1. **Conduct a behavior-analytic interview** to obtain detailed information about the reasons for seeking help and then move toward a consideration of the patient's anger/aggressive behavioral pattern. *(See Table 1 for examples of specific questions.)*

    a)   Ascertain the degree to which the patient believes he has a problem with anger; determine what is the greatest concern he has about his/her anger; how will working on this problem make his life different. Note that many individuals believe that their feelings of anger are justified and that the focus of treatment should not be controlling their anger. They do recognize, however, that they often experience interpersonal conflicts. Thus, **the phrase "conflict resolution interventions" can be used instead of anger control interventions.**

b)   It is important that the therapist **maintain composure** when the patient relates tales of anger and aggression and when the patient acts in a provocative confrontational fashion. The therapist should <u>not</u> put himself or herself at risk and should be familiar with self-defense and self-protective behavioral skills. *(See the Section below for a discussion on how the therapist can respond when the patient becomes angry, pp. 239.)*

c)   Probe for the **various features of anger** -- frequency, intensity, duration, mode of expression, effects on performance, relationships, and impact on health and perceived consequences. Also address the degree to which the patient is fearful of expressing anger and/or whether anger acts as a defensive protective behavior for other "hurt" feelings.

d)   Determine the **settings** and **persons** with which anger is associated -- note, the pattern of events that routinely provoke anger (external and internal triggers such as frustrations, annoyances, insults, perceived inequities, memories, images, etc.). Ask if there are any times when the patient was provoked, but did <u>not</u> respond in an angry/aggressive fashion.

e)   Conduct a **situational analysis** of how anger and aggression vary across settings and over time and the role that the patient's thoughts and feelings play. (**Use an ABC analysis:** A = situation; C = how reacted; What is the B -- thoughts and feelings?; Use **imagery reconstruction procedures**, as described below, **pp. 167**.) Help the patient to understand how interpersonal exchanges unfold, noting his pre-anger state (e.g., feel overwhelmed, out of control), triggers, reactions and consequences.

f)   Assess for the **propensity for violence** and probe for any *"aggressive impulses"* or *"violent, irresistible urges"* that patient's experience prior to aggressive acts. (For example, McElroy et al., 1998 describe how patients with **Intermittent Explosive Disorders (IED)** describe the tension related to their impulses as the "need to attack", the "need to defend oneself", the "need to strike out", as an "Adrenaline rush", "seeing red", the "urge to kill someone". (See Grisso et al., 2000 for how to assess for violent thoughts and preoccupations.)

g)   Help the patient notice **"warning signs"** of anger episodes (e.g., changes in mood, energy level, presence of manic-like behaviors, racing thoughts, automatic symptoms such as tremors, palpitations, tingling, chest tightness, head pressures, loss or changes in awareness). Also, ask the patient about any relief of tension that he/she experiences when engaging in aggressive behavior (e.g., **feelings of relief and even pleasure**).

h) Explore with the patient **how distressing** such aggressive impulses and episodes have been to himself and to others. What has been the ***"impact"***, the ***"toll"***, the ***"price"*** that the patient and others have paid for their anger, their conflicts? What social, familial, vocational, legal, and financial problems have the patient experienced because of his anger problems?

i) Explore **what the patient does with his anger (brooding).** Explore what keeps the patient from acting out on his impulses. What is the patient doing to **control his level of anger** and **what gets in the way** of the patient using anger-management skills. Treat feelings, such as anger as a **"product"** or as a **"commodity"** that one does something with. The therapist can ask, ***"What do you do with the mad that you feel?"*** This **inquiry** is a productive way to have patients share their coping strategies (e.g., ***"I stuff my angry feelings."; "I blow-off steam."; "I try to work it out with the person who got me pissed off."***). The therapist can then ask patients ***"What is the impact? What is the price? What is the toll of handling anger in this fashion?"*** If the patient answers, ***"I don't know."***, then the therapist can reply, ***"I don't know either. How can we go about finding out, and moreover, how will our finding out be useful in helping you achieve your goals?"*** This exchange will lay the groundwork for the patient to engage in self-monitoring, as described below (**p. 174**).

j) Determine the degree to which anger attacks are **uncharacteristic of the individual.** (Look for other possible disorders.) For example, are the attacks in response to minor or trivial matters and is the anger response out of proportion to these provocations?

k) Explore the **developmental history** of aggressive behavior and correlates. Note the presence of high risk factors (ADHD, bullying or being a victim of bullying, truancy, poor academic performance, age of first contact with law, etc.). Assess for exposure to domestic violence, shaming episodes, history of attachment relationships. (See McClellan & Kellen, 2000)

l) Determine the presence of any feelings of **regret, remorse, guilt, blame, shame.** Such emotions can be used in therapy to bolster the patient's motivation to change.

m) Explore **familial and cultural norms** concerning anger and aggression.

n) Check for involvement of **other stakeholders** (e.g., courts, police, school, etc.).

SUMMARY OF INTERVIEW TABLES

(Note: The clinician can <u>sample</u> from these questions. Most are "<u>what</u>" and "<u>how</u>" questions, with very few "why" questions included. "What" and "how" questions are most effective in fostering change. The remainder are "when" questions.)

Table 1
INITIAL BEHAVIOR ANALYTIC INTERVIEW QUESTIONS
*(Questions for the patient or for the family members to be
employed at the outset of assessment.)*

*In order to understand your situation, I would like to ask you some questions, if that is
okay?*

*Can you take a few moments and describe what you see as the problem(s)? What
seems to be troubling you today? What would you like help with?*

Give me a recent example of the problem, as you see it …What happens before …?

What happens after …? Then what happens? After that what happens?

Who is present when the problem happens?

What does he/she (each person who is present) say or do? And then what happens?

Where does this problem of … most frequently occur?

Where is it least likely to occur?

Is there a particular time when the problem is most likely (most unlikely) to occur?

*Can you tell ahead of time when this might occur? What signs are there that this
might occur (or that this might be a "high risk" situation)? (Explore the concept of
internal and external "triggers".)*

How often does this problem (be specific) occur?

*How long does this problem last? When does your feeling X (or doing Y) usually end?
What contributes to your behaving differently (be specific)?*

*How is this a problem for you? How serious a problem is this as far as you are
concerned?*

Have you felt this way before or is this the first time?

*Who is most bothered by the problem of X? Who in your home (workplace) most wants
this behavior to change?*

*How have you handled this situation in the past? Give me an example. What else have
you tried? How have these strategies worked?*

*What do you wish you had said or done differently? Looking back on that incident,
what do you wish had happened?*

*Is there something in what he/she does that draws you into X? (Explore the bi-
directional context, notion of significant others acting as an "accomplices".)*

How long has this been going on? When did this behavior become a problem?

What do you think is causing the problems of …?

*If your wife were here now, how would she say that you were trying to solve this
problem?*

*It sounds like you have thought about this problem. What have you tried in the past?
What has worked? What do you think might be done to improve your situation?*

Table 1 (continued)
INITIAL BEHAVIOR ANALYTIC INTERVIEW QUESTIONS
(Questions for the patient or for the family members.)

What advice would you have for someone else with this problem (or who is in this situation)? (When questioning use specific patient examples.)
What else do you think I should find out about your problems (situation) to be of help?
Is there anything you would like to add?
Are there any other problems that you are experiencing that I missed?
Is there anything else you want to discuss?
What would be the risk of your telling me about X?
What goals do you think we should be working on?
What do you think I can do to help?
What do you think you can do to help yourself?
Are you interested in trying something new to see if you can improve things, work on your goals of X?

[It is important to ask if assistance for these problems has been provided previously or currently. If yes, by whom, when, with what outcomes? Is the patient (or family members) satisfied with the treatments received? Was it difficult to follow the treatment regimen? Ask about treatment adherence.]

Table 2
QUESTIONS ABOUT VIOLENCE
(Adapted from Borum et al., 1996; Otto, 2000.)

Initial Screening Questions

How can you tell when you are feeling angry? or likely to become aggressive?

How does your body feel when you are getting angry?

Can you identify any "warning signs" (cues, triggers) that you might become violent?

Do you ever worry that you might physically hurt someone?

What suggestions, if any, do you have to control your temper (aggression, violence)?

What kind of things make you mad? / feel angry?

You mentioned that you get angry when you are driving. Please describe a situation that made you the angriest ... What about a situation that made you most frightened? When this occurred, what did you do? How did you feel? What thoughts did you have? What thoughts went through your mind? What did the other driver do that provoked you further? What would you do next? What if the driver wouldn't let you pass? (Patient is stuck in a frustrating situation for a period of time ... Malta et al., 2001).

What do you do when you get really mad like you describe?

What is the most violent thing you have ever done? Has there ever been a time when you hit, slapped, punched, threatened someone with a weapon?

Have you ever threatened or used a weapon in a fight or with someone?

How did that happen?

What is the closest you have ever come to being violent?

Have you ever hurt someone in a fight?

Have you ever used a weapon in a fight?

What would have to happen in order for you to get so mad or angry that you would hurt someone?

Do you own any weapons like guns or knives? Where are they now?

Table 2 Continued
QUESTIONS ABOUT VIOLENCE

Follow-up Questions About Specific Violent Incidents

What would it take for you to use a weapon (your gun)?

Please describe in as much detail as possible the most recent experience of anger. For the moment do __not__ worry about your thoughts or feelings, but concentrate specifically on what happened during the incident. We will come back to your feelings and thoughts. In other words, if I was there, what would I see and hear?

I want us both to understand what happened when you (be specific in reflecting what the patient said about the violent incident).

Where did this incident occur?

Who was involved (injured)? What is his/her/their relationship to you?

What happened after you got mad?

Did this angry incident result in injury to others (to yourself)?

What kind of injury (harm) happened? (Ever attacked with a weapon? Ever injured in a fight so seriously that you required medical attention?)

What do you think caused the violence?

How did you feel before the fight? During the fight? After?

What were you thinking before the fight? During the fight? After?

Were you using alcohol or other drugs at the time of the argument (fight)? (around the time of ...)?

Have you had these kinds of feelings and thoughts at other times? When? What happened then?

Have you ever been this angry at X before? What did you do?

Suppose you did become that angry what would you do?

Can you tell me anything more about your anger?

How did you __not__ let those feelings and thoughts get you into trouble? What did you do to control (thoughts, feelings – be specific)?

Table 3
NATURE OF ANGER: TRIGGERS AND FREQUENCY

What makes you angry?

At work (school, home) how often do you get angry?

What kind of things "trigger" your anger, ... get you going, ... light your fuse? Please give me some examples.

Do you ever find yourself "lighting your own fuse", "Rekindling your anger, again and again"? " Making a mountain out of a molehill"? "Overreacting"? "Upsetting yourself"? (Use the patient's words.)

What sets you off?

Does anyone ever try to make you angry by teasing you? What usually happens?

Do you think this is an example of the "escalation trap", "taking the bait" that we talked about?

Let's look together at what happens when you ...

So, you start to feel X, but then it sounds like ... Is that the way you see it?

What do you notice when others are getting angry that tells you how upset they are?

How do you respond to someone who has expressed anger at you? Someone who frustrates you? upsets you? interrupts you? embarrasses you?

I can understand why you became so angry and why it was so important to you at that time. I wonder if there are other parts of your life that could add to your anger?

What happens inside of you when you feel humiliated, ashamed, abandoned, helpless? What do you do with these feelings?

Sometimes what happens at home (work) can affect how you react at work (home). Can we take a few moments to examine this possibility?

Do you find that you tend to act differently when you are on alcohol or take drugs, as compared to when you are sober or clean?

Imagine that you did have a few drinks. How do you think it would affect you?

(If there is concern about the patient's alcohol consumption, the CAGE Interview 1995, can be administered. Also ask about getting into trouble with the law because of drinking such as Driving Under the Influence of Alcohol (DUI). See Liskow et al.(1995) for a brief interview to assess Substance Abuse.

CAGE INTERVIEW
Liskow et al., 1995

"Have you ever wanted to cut down on <u>consumption</u>?" **(C)**

"Have other persons <u>annoyed you</u> with their comments about your consumption?" **(A)**

"Have you felt <u>guilty</u> about the effects on your life?" **(G)**

"Have you needed a drink / hit / etc./ as an <u>eye-opener</u> after drinking / after using the day before?" **(E)**

Table 4
NATURE OF THE ANGER RESPONSE
(Component Analysis)

How strong are these feelings of anger at work (school, home)? Can you give me an example? Please describe for me the kind of anger you experience.

What thoughts go along with your angry feelings?

When you are feeling so angry with X, what are you thinking …. What do you say to yourself when you are angry?

When you do become angry, how intense is the feeling? Would you describe yourself as being annoyed, irritated, frustrated, angry, furious, or enraged? What factors determine whether you only become irritated and annoyed <u>versus</u> furious and enraged?

Does your anger last for minutes, hours, days, months or longer?

The following is a list of some things that may happen when <u>you become angry</u>. Did you do any of these in the <u>past two months</u>?

a) *Destroy property?*
b) *Threaten someone with physical violence (without a weapon)?*
c) *Threaten someone with physical violence (with a weapon)?*
d) *Have a physical fight with someone?*

Table 4 Continued
NATURE OF THE ANGER RESPONSE
(Component Analysis)

Do you spend time and energy thinking about (ruminating) about what got you angry?

Do these thoughts make you get angrier or stay angry?

Is it difficult to just let your anger go, let bygones be bygones?

Do you think about the slight (grievance, affront, bullying) afterwards? (Choose one.) Brood about it? Do you seek "revenge," want to get even, settle scores?

When you are angry, do you usually "keep it inside", discuss it, take it out on others, get headaches, or any other physical reactions?

You mention that you keep your anger "inside", try and push it away, avoid others. What do you fear might happen if you showed all of your angry feelings?

Where do you feel your anger in your body? Please describe the sensations you feel when you get angry.

What do you think your body is telling you? What would your gut say if it could speak?

Do you think you are putting your health at risk with your anger?

To what degree is anger creating problems at work (with people in your life, in your relationships)?

Can you predict when and where you will become angry?

Do you ever find that sometimes you are "sucked into" an argument, caught up in an angry situation that escalates? Can you give me an example of a time this happened?

Can you think of a time when someone got angry with you? When were you the object of someone else's anger/aggression? How did you feel when you were treated that way? Did you want to be his friend? Did you want to cooperate with that person or help him with his work? Do you think that some times you come across in the same fashion? What can we learn from this episode?

Table 5
HOW THE PATIENT <u>COPES</u> WITH ANGER

What does it feel like to be angry?

How do you usually handle anger? (e.g., The interviewer should listen as to whether the patient suppresses anger "I stuff my feelings"; directs anger toward others in the form of verbal assaults and physical actions.) What is the <u>impact</u> or <u>toll</u> of stuffing feelings, as you describe?

What does "coping" mean to you?

If you keep the anger to yourself, what do you think prevents you from expressing it (sharing it with others)?

What do you do to control your temper? How have you attempted to cope with your anger?

How do you know when to take a time-out?

How can you tell when you are crossing the line from angry thoughts to becoming assaultive (aggressive)?

What do you do to cool down? Any other strategies that you have tried?

Do your thoughts or what you say to yourself ever help you calm down and control your temper and solve your problems?

How does what you say to yourself help you make better choices?

Were there things that you could have said to yourself that would have proved helpful with your anger control?

Can your body's warning signs (give examples) help you remember to ... ?

What do you do to prevent yourself from becoming angry in the first place?

What can you do to prevent the anger from escalating to the point of aggression?

How do you let others know that you need them to back off? ... that you need to take a time-out?

Table 5 Continued
HOW THE PATIENT <u>COPES</u> WITH ANGER

Can you remember a time when you were really angry and did <u>not</u> take it out on someone? What did you do then? How did you feel about that? How did you feel about yourself? Have you ever kept yourself from becoming really angry/aggressive? If so, how did you do that?

What is <u>different</u> about the times when you are provoked and don't get angry, <u>versus</u> the times when you lose your cool, act out, and become aggressive?

How do you get this self-control process to happen?

How (or when) did you get so good at ... ?

Who else is likely to notice how you are handling your anger? What would they notice?

How is this <u>different from</u> how you might have handled it?

<u>Apart from the anger,</u> what other feelings did you have in that situation?

Sometimes people become angry because they are feeling afraid, or sad, or ashamed, or insecure, or betrayed, or humiliated (choose one or two emotions). Has something like that ever happened to you? Please give me a recent example. Let's discuss that in more detail. If you get angry for these other reasons, what does that mean for what <u>we</u> should work on here in order to help you better control your anger and aggression? (The therapist can use <u>concentric circles</u> as a way to convey different types of emotions – "core hurts" and related feelings.)

If your life depended on it or if someone made a large bet, could you keep yourself from becoming angry/aggressive? If yes, what would you do?

When you encounter someone who is angry what have you found is the best way to deal with the situation?

When you are angry, what have you found is the best way to handle the situation?

If you were to recognize the warning signs of anger (and aggression) in you, what do you think would help you to handle the anger constructively?

If you were to ask someone to help you resolve a conflict, who would you choose? What is it about this person (or what is it that he/she does that leads you to choose him/her? Is it possible that you could do some of those things in resolving your own conflicts?

Table 6
EXPLORE THE <u>CONSEQUENCES</u> OF ANGER
(See Deffenbacher & McKay, 2000 pp. 174-175 for further examples)

What happens as a result of your expressing anger in that way? ... So you were able to get the anger off your chest and get back at him, but what happened <u>in the long run</u>?

What was your goal in that situation? Did your anger help you achieve your goal? So, is your anger getting you all you want? (Help the patient appreciate that becoming angry often leaves the problems unresolved, if not worse.)

So, in some sense your anger (aggression) is working for you? It gets you ...

What is the impact, the toll and the price (emotional, physical and interpersonal) of behaving in an angry fashion?

If the patient says, "I don't know.", the therapist can say, "I don't know either. How can <u>we</u> go about finding out? What is the impact, toll, price of your doing X? Moreover, why would it be important for us to find out? How is finding this out going to help you achieve your goal of Y?"

Table 7
CONSIDER <u>ALTERNATIVES</u> TO ANGER AND AGGRESSION

Of all the things you could have done, how did you <u>choose</u> that way of reacting? Take me through the steps of how you chose to respond.

Are there less angry ways to achieve your goals and still feel okay?

Let us revisit this angry episode and consider how you could handle it in a non-angry and non-aggressive fashion.

If you tried this, what do you think would happen? And then what? What gets in the way of your trying that?

How do you think things would turn out if you did Y instead of X? How would you feel about yourself?

If I am in tune with what you are saying, you felt you were treated unfairly and you felt unappreciated (abandoned, rejected, etc.). How are you going to live with this? What can you do about this without becoming angry? What options are there?

What advice would you have for a friend so he/she could handle this situation without becoming angry and aggressive?

Can you recall a non-angry reaction of someone whom you respected? How did he/she handle it? What advice would your friend have for you in handling this situation?

What has worked best for you in the past? Is there anything that you could use to help control your anger? Your aggression?

Are there some situations in which other people become angry, but in which you did <u>not</u> become angry? What did you do?

It sounds like you had a lot of experience coping with stress over the years. What have you done that has helped to calm you down so you do not get derailed?

From what you said so far, I get the impression, and correct me if I am wrong, that <u>in spite of</u> some major setbacks (stressors) you have been able to keep going and achieve X? <u>How did</u> you accomplish that? <u>What</u> did you do? (Questions are designed to support and promote the patient's strengths and resources and nurture hope.)

From what you said so far, I get the impression, and correct me if I am wrong, that <u>in spite of</u> the many successes that you have encountered, some very challenging obstacles still exist? Have I gotten that right? How do you plan to address these hurdles?

Table 8
DEVELOPMENTAL INFLUENCES

Tell me the story of your life, whatever you think is most important to tell, starting from as early as you can remember and going right up to the present time.

When you were growing up, was it usual for your family members to show their anger if they were feeling it? How did they show it?

Did you witness violence at home?

How were you disciplined at home when you were growing up? ... when you were an adolescent? How did that make you feel?

How old were you when physical hitting stopped?

Who treated you with anger in your life?

Were you ever made to feel ashamed (embarrassed, humiliated)? What happened? What lingers from that experience now?

What was it like to grow up (shut down, in fear, lonely, not able to reach out to others)?

What do you think the impact of that experience is on you now? What conclusions, if any, do you draw about yourself and about other people as a result of that childhood experience?

As you were growing up, were there any adults who were particularly kind to you? Who? What did they do?

As you were growing up, who were you able to count on or share your concerns and feelings with (family member, other adults such as a teacher, coach, peer)? (Obtain an attachment history and a time-line of what the individual was able to achieve or was proud of in spite of adversities. Ask him how he was able to achieve these feats.)

Is there anything else happening in your family (or has happened) that you think it would be helpful for me to know about (or for us to discuss)?

Table 8 Continued
DEVELOPMENTAL INFLUENCES

Consider the Impact of Developmental "Hurt"

Have you ever felt a lot of "hurt" in your life? What happened? How much of your present anger is influenced by (results from, due to) that "hurt"? How often do you think about those times when you have been hurt? When you think about that, what impact does it have on you ... on others?

How much of your life is driven by the "hurt" and anger inside of you? Would you say it is ..(obtain a percentage). We can work on helping you reduce the percentage of your life that is driven by your underlying "hurt".

If all of your hurt feelings inside of you went away, what would happen to your anger? How would your behavior change?

Some people wear their anger as if it was a medal, or as a sign of their personal injuries and their unhealed emotional "hurt". Does this apply in your case?

You said that you always hated everything. Sometimes hating is a way of trying to (protect oneself form feeling, keep others away, feel better). Does this make sense in your case?

Table 9
SELF-CONCEPT (RELATED TO ANGER)

Do you see yourself as "hot-headed" or as someone who is "slow" to become angry?

How would someone who knows you well describe you?

Is this the way you see yourself?

Is this the way you really want others to see you or the way you want to see yourself?

How would you like others (e.g., your children) to describe you or view you in the future? On your tombstone or in your obituary how would you like people (your children) to describe you? What do you want to be most remembered for? How does your present behavior (your anger) get in the way of that goal?

Table 9 Continued
SELF-CONCEPT (RELATED TO ANGER)

As I listen to you, it sounds like there is a "part of you" that feels (wants to) X, but there is also another "part" that wants Y? Is that the way you see it? If that is the case, what is the impact ... what can we do to resolve this?

(Note: I don't believe there are different "parts" of people. but this may be a useful description to engage individuals, as Hanna and Hunt, 1996 and Hunt et al., 1999 illustrate. Consider the following examples.)

I understand that you really don't care to talk about how anger gets you into trouble, but I wonder if there is some small part of you that does care?

I hear you when you say that you don't care, but I wonder if you ever hear a voice in the back of your mind that tells you that you maybe making a mistake?

I wonder if there is a part of you that worries about what is going to happen to you? That is the part that I would like to talk to. Is that okay with you?

Is there a small part of you that is worried about what is happening to you?

Is there a small part of you, maybe a tiny voice, that wants to talk about the tough times that you have been through and what lingers from all of that?

On a percentage basis, how much of you cares and how much does not care what happens to you?

What do you want other people to believe about you?

What is really true about yourself that you do not tell anyone else?

You are too smart to trick yourself into self-deception ... into believing that it is okay to hurt others.

When did you first learn to work others up (to use force to get your way, to intimidate others)? How did you go about learning that? It is possible to unlearn these skills. What would you replace them with?

In addition to the range of questions included in these nine tables, one can add the types of <u>questions</u> that **Solution-focused therapists** might ask patients (see deShazer, 1988). For example:

The Miracle Question

> *Suppose that one night, while you were asleep, there was a miracle and this problem was solved. How would you know? What would be different?*

> *If I pulled out a magic wand on your situation and were able to perform magic on your situation, what would be happening that is different from before?*

> *Can you envision a future without the problem and describe what that looks like?*

Before asking the Miracle questions, it is important to hear the nature of the patient's distress in order that he/she feels 'heard", before seeking a solution to the problem.

Maintaining Progress Question

> *Between now and the next time we meet, I would like you to observe so you can describe to me next time, what happens in your life that you <u>want to continue to have happen.</u>*

Surprise Task

> *Do at least one or two things that will surprise your parents (spouse, kids, friends, coworkers, boss). Don't tell them what it is. Parents, your job is to see if you can tell what it is that he is doing. Don't compare notes; we will do that next session.*

LIFE-SPACE CRISIS INTERVIEW

Additional questions suggested by Larson and Lochman (in press) and Nicholas and Long (1993) can be used to analyze the patient's awareness, knowledge, and ability to cope with anger in a specific situation.

What happened to you?	**(Stressor)**
How did you feel when that happened to you?	**(Feeling)**
How did you show that feeling in your behavior?	**(Behavior)**
How did the others react?	**(Reaction)**
Did their reactions help manage this problem <u>or</u> did it make things worse? What did you do?	**(Reciprocal Reaction)**
What were you doing before the problem started? Do you know when you are getting out of control or does it just happen?	**(Warning Signs)**
Are you telling me, are you saying to yourself, that you go from being angry to suddenly being out of control? Can you remember anything you said or did between the time you got mad and the time you lost control (had to be restrained)? What were you thinking as the problem was unfolding? What were you feeling? What did you do?	**(Assess Time Line)**
If X did not stop you when you were really angry, what might you have done? So by stopping you, X protected you from doing something that would have caused you more problems?	**(Possible Outcomes)**
What are you planning to do next? Is there anyway you can learn to "notice," "catch," "interrupt," "stop" yourself? What are your choices? How can you become your own coach, your own therapist?	**(Take Ownership)**

SEE <u>APPENDIX B</u> ON HOW TO USE THE "ART OF QUESTIONING" TO HELP INDIVIDUALS WHO ARE IN "CRISIS" BECOME BETTER PROBLEM-SOLVERS.

IMAGERY-BASED ASSESSMENT

In addition to interviewing patients and having them fill out self-report measures, clinicians can use **imagery-based assessment procedures** in order to help the patients better understand the nature of their anger/aggression experiences. This information can be used to "educate" patients (i.e., increase their awareness and provide a basis for discussion and training). Patients can be asked to imagine instances of **when they become angry** and **"loose it,"** as well as those instances when they become angry and have evidenced some form of **"control."**

In order for the **imagery assessment** to be most effective the patient should choose a specific situation in which he became extremely angry and recall the event in detail so it comes **alive in the present**. The object is to help the patient access cognitions and emotions that contribute to the escalation of his anger. Such assessment procedures will help the patient learn to **recognize emotions**, even at low intensity, **label** different emotions, **acknowledge** his anger, and **better appreciate** what he can do to **regulate, accept** and **tolerate** emotions.

For example, Rusting and Nolen-Hoeksema (1998) asked individuals who have problems with anger to:

> *"Think of a time in your life when you felt so angry you*
> *wanted to explode. During the next 10 minutes, try to re-*
> *experience the memory you've retrieved as vividly as you*
> *can. Picture the event happening to you all over again.*
> *Picture in your mind's eye the surroundings as clearly as*
> *possible. See the people or objects; hear the sounds;*
> *experience the events happening to you. Think the*
> *thoughts you actually thought in that situation. Feel the*
> *same feelings you felt in that situation. Let yourself react*
> *as if you were actually there right now. As you're*
> *reimagining the event, <u>write</u> about what is happening, what*
> *you are thinking, and how you are feeling." (p. 796.)*

Individuals may be asked to write down their thoughts or to share and **describe aloud** the feelings and thoughts they had before, during, and after, the selected episodes. In this way, individuals cannot only become aware of the **external and internal triggers (A),** and how they **responded (C),** but as Albert Ellis highlights, also the **(B) – thoughts and accompanying feelings** that mediate, fuel and exacerbate the anger and contribute to aggression.

Patients may **also** be asked to **select an angry situation or episode**, or choose an episode where they experienced aggressive impulses, but they were able to:

a) **manage**, **resist** or **suppress** enacting their aggressive impulses;

b) engage in **less destructive aggressive behaviors** (e.g., being verbally assaultive and refraining from being physically assaultive);

c) **resolve** the situation;

d) find a way to **"live with"** the situation, **accept** and **tolerate** angry feelings without brooding about or thinking about retaliation.

The therapist can ask the patients what distinguishes those situations and episodes where they attempt to exert control from those in which they "lost control"? As noted previously, the patient may answer, *"I don't know"*, to which the therapist can answer, *"I don't know either. How can __we__ go about finding out? Moreover, why will this information prove instructive and helpful?"*

Another example of how imagery assessment has been used is to have patients **visualize a specific situation** that is described on a State Anger Provocation Scale and then complete a self-report measure (e.g., Novaco's Coping Strategies Measure) as to how they would handle this situation (See Ramirez et al., 1997).

Imagery-based assessment procedures help patients to attend to data (their feelings and thoughts) that they otherwise may not have noticed. In this way, patients can come to see that they are <u>not</u> mere "victims" of perceived provocations, but rather they can come to better appreciate that how they appraise both situations and their ability to handle them play a critical role in their anger experiences.

Finally, there is a need to assess for the patient's **anger-related memories**, **angry** and **aggressive fantasies**, **images of revenge** and **retaliation**.

GUIDELINES FOR CONDUCTING SELF-MONITORING AND OTHER EXTRA-THERAPY ACTIVITIES
(Keeping Anger Log, Diary)

(See Meichenbaum, 1994, p. 245-255 for a more detailed description on how to have patients self-monitor.)

A key feature of cognitive-behavioral intervention is having patients **self-monitor** or keep track of various aspects of their behavior. Research indicates that if patients do <u>not</u> comply with the request to self-monitor, they are less likely to follow-through on more demanding therapeutic tasks. The following set of therapist's guidelines is designed to foster treatment adherence. While these guidelines have been enumerated for the clinical task of patient self-monitoring, the same principles can be used for implementing any extra-therapeutic patient activity. A **Procedural Checklist** follows so clinicians can develop an automatic subroutine whenever they ask patients to self-monitor or engage in other extra-therapeutic activities.

In order to increase the likelihood that patients will engage in self-monitoring, the therapist should:

1. Provide the patient with an **opportunity to come up with the notion of self-monitoring**. Use **situational analysis** and **Socratic questioning** in order to highlight how the patient's anger varies across situations and over time. The therapist can ask *"What's different when the anger escalates to the point of aggression <u>versus</u> those times when you are able to keep your cool and not explode?"* If the patient says, *"I don't know."* the therapist can say, *"I don't know either."* *"How can <u>we</u> go about finding out?"* Establish the need for self-monitoring collaboratively.

2. Provide a **clear rationale** for self-monitoring and for each homework task. (Discuss with the patient how self-monitoring is a means for knowing what triggers his anger/aggression or recognizes the things that set him off in order to apply the coping skills that <u>we</u> will work on.) Relate doing the self-monitoring to the therapy goals. Highlight why doing this task is a necessary component of the overall treatment program – a "stepping stone" and a way to know how he is progressing.

3. **Keep the request simple**.

   a. Use <u>foot-in-door technique</u>, **gradually increase the task demands**.

   b. Make the "homework" request <u>small</u>, rather than large.

   c. Make the homework a <u>physical</u>, <u>behavioral task</u>. (Agree on a time and location the homework will be done.)

      d. <u>Build in reminders</u>. Figure out how the individual will remember to do the "homework." *("How can you remember to do this?"; "What would help you remember?")* Provide written reminders and other supports (e.g., emails).

      e. Be careful about using the word **"homework."** Use an **analogy** of the patient becoming a *"detective, scientist, own therapist."* Often the word "homework" carries surplus meaning and triggers emotional failures.

4.   Ensure that the patient has the **skills** necessary to conduct self-monitoring. Give the patient a **choice** as to how to conduct self-monitoring. Ask the patient, *"How might you keep track of the things that trigger your anger and how you respond to them?"* Would it be better to use a written journal or a small tape recorder. **Practice in the session** how to self-monitor.

5.   Use **implementation intention statements (when and where statements – *"So you agree that whenever situation X arises, you will do Y." "So <u>if</u> you encounter X, <u>then</u> you will do Y."*)**

6.   Clarify and **check** the patient's **comprehension** (use **role-reversal procedures** of the therapist playing the role of being a "new patient" and the patient explaining what to do, and most importantly, why it is critical to do it. Help the patient **<u>generate reasons</u>** for doing the self-monitoring.) Provide a **written list** of the homework assignment and accompanying reasons.

7.   Establish **desirable rewards** and **involve peer/family supports** for conducting self-monitoring and "homework".

8.   **Anticipate possible barriers** that might get in the way of self-monitoring and consider possible reasons for nonadherence and how these potential obstacles can be addressed.

      "It is important for me to understand how you feel about the homework tasks we develop together."
      "What thoughts do you have about doing this task?"
      "Can you think of anything that could prevent you from completing this task?"

Use **covert rehearsal** (have the patient imagine doing the self-monitoring and imagine coping with any difficulties). Use role play and use reverse role-play -- patient-therapist reversal. Include in the **behavioral rehearsal** a consideration of coping tactics to deal with possible barriers. Ask the patient how likely he is to perform the self-monitoring activity. If the patient does not come up with any barriers, the therapist can raise some possible obstacles such as "forgetfulness," "busy schedule," "lack of confidence," that other patients have had and how they can be anticipated and addressed.

9. Elicit a **statement of intent** or a **commitment statement** and **review** with the patient, once again, the **reasons** for conducting the self-monitoring.

> *"Is this something you think you could complete?"* *("should take on"?)*
> *"Let's review what <u>we</u> have agreed on, and most importantly, why we have agreed on these tasks."*
> *"In order for you to get the most out of this program, it is important for you to make a commitment to completing these tasks. Each time we meet I will check on how you do with these tools. Does that sound okay?"* *(Sanders & Ralph, 2001, p. 77)*
> *"Before we finish today's session, let's just review the tasks you will complete before our next session. Remember it is important to try out the ideas we discuss to see if they make a difference. I'd like you to make a <u>commitment</u> to complete the tasks we discussed today. The next time I will check how you did with the tasks. Ok?"* *(Sanders & Ralph, 2001, p. 95)*

Lower the patient's expectations about the impact of self-monitoring. Indicate that therapy is just at the point of understanding and *"<u>not to expect major changes as a result of self-monitoring.</u>"*

10. In subsequent therapy sessions, following an initial discussion of intercurrent life events and any patient concerns, the session can begin by **collaboratively setting an agenda** for this session and highlighting where reviewing self-monitoring fits in.

> *"In today's session we will have a chance to ... "* (Provide an Advance Organizer)
> *"During today's session we will be able to check on how your self-monitoring (doing homework, keeping track) went and what you learned from this."* (Use Informed Instruction)

For example, the session can begin with the patient "checking in" using a seven point anger scale with seven representing the highest level of anger experienced during the past week, as well as assessing his current level of anger. *(What is going on that is contributing to your current level of anger?)*

Review homework from the last session. *("What did you do?"; "How did it work?")* Solicit the patient's input and feedback. Address any difficulties that arise as **"learning opportunities."** **Praise effort**, not product.

11. Set up the assignment of **self-monitoring** as *a "no-lose" situation*. Whatever the patient does or does <u>not</u> do can be reframed as a **"learning opportunity."** The therapist and patient can address noncompliance as an occasion to explore possible reasons why the patient did not complete the task, <u>as agreed upon</u>. The following questions that the therapist can ask the patient illustrate this **problem-solving approach to noncompliance.**

> *What is that you were supposed to do? How was it supposed to be done? (If the patient has difficulty explaining the task the therapist may need to teach, model and rehearse the task once again.)*
> *Do you remember why <u>we</u> said it was important to ... ? Yes, it allows us to check out ...*
> *Let's consider what got in the way of your carrying this out so we can come up with a better plan to use next week. Let's focus on ...*
> *Was the task too difficult or was it too unpleasant to complete?*
> *Was there any part of what <u>we</u> agreed for you to work on that was not clear or too confusing?*
> *Was there something that you didn't like about the plan?*
> *Was there something (or somebody) that stopped you (interfered with) you putting your plan into practice?*
> *Were you hoping for quicker results?*
> *We discussed that change won't be an easy process and will require work and commitment on your part. Is this something you are willing to undertake?*

The **therapist** can take some **responsibility** and ownership for the patient's noncompliance.

> *Did I (the therapist) fail to explain what it is you are to do and why?*
> *Did I ask you to undertake too much, before you were ready?*
> *Did I fail to check whether you had all of the necessary skills in order to perform this task?*

The therapist should **provide encouragement** for each patient's **attempt** and **reinforcement** for the patient's **effort**, not just for the completed task.

The therapist should **invite** the patient's **feedback** and **questions**.

> *Do you think this plan is useful?*
> *Do you think it will work?*
> *What are your reactions to how we are progressing?*

12. Ensure that the **patient** makes **self-attributions** ("take credit") for any changes that occurred.

   > *"Do you think doing the task was useful?"*
   > *"How were you able to do the task of ... ?"*

13. The therapist can request that the patient **drop-off his journal** or **log** before the next session so the therapist can review it ahead of time. Highlight the importance of doing homework. Refer to homework (self-monitoring) throughout therapy.

14. As the therapy progresses have the **patient generate** his or her own **homework assignments**.

15. The therapist should **keep track** of the proportion of the assignment that was completed.

When you ask patients to conduct self-monitoring or to engage in an extra-therapeutic activity, how many of the following steps in the procedural guidelines do you use?

PROCEDURAL CHECKLIST FOR CONDUCTING SELF-MONITORING <u>AND</u> OTHER EXTRA-THERAPY ACTIVITIES

1. Provide an opportunity for the patient to come up with suggestions for self-monitoring. Use situational analysis.

2. Provide a rationale. Highlight the connection between doing "homework" and the patient achieving his/her therapy goals.

3. Keep requests simple. (Use behavioral tasks and "foot in door" approach and build-in reminders).

4. Ensure that the patient has the skills to perform the task. Give the patient a "choice" as to how best to conduct the assignment.

5. Use implementation intention statements ("When and where", "If ... then," "Whenever" statements).

6. Clarify and check the patient's comprehension (use role-reversal, behavioral rehearsal).

7. Use desirable rewards and peer/family supports.

8. Anticipate possible barriers and collaboratively develop coping strategies.

9. Elicit commitment statements and patient-generated "reasons."

10. Inquire about self-monitoring (other "homework" activities).

11. Nurture patient self-attributions ("take credit" for change).

12. Reinforce effort and not just product.

13. View failures as "learning opportunities."

14. Keep record of patient's compliance.

ANGER LOGS

"Listening to Yourself with a Third Ear."
(See Deffenbacher et al., 1996; Feindler & Ecton, 1986;
Gerlock, 1996; Meichenbaum, 1994)

A number of different procedures have been used to help patients become aware of the nature of their anger and ways to cope. The **self-monitoring procedure** selected should be tailored to the patient. The demands of the **Anger Log** can be increased over the course of treatment. For example, Deffenbacher and McKay (2000) have three **Anger Log Forms** that gradually increase the amount of information requested.

ANGER LOG I: Patient is asked to record

Date / Time	Situation	Reactions Rate 0 - 100	

ANGER II

Date / Time	Situation	Thoughts	Reactions Rate 0 - 100

ANGER III

Date / Time	Situation	Reactions	Coping Efforts (*What did you do, how did it turn out?*) Rate 0 - 100 before and after

---

A rating of 0 to 100 is used, where 0 represents little or no anger and 100 represents the maximum level of anger that the patient has ever experienced (i.e., furious, as angry as ever have been).

The therapist should ensure that the patient fully understands what he is to do and why. The therapist can ask the patient to explain what he is to do, as if the therapist were a new patient who needs to record anger episodes. The therapist can ask, *"So are you clear about what you are going to do and most importantly why?"*

The patient should be told to fill-out his **Anger Log** as close to the time as the episode happens.

The patient is also told to **make an entry at least once a day**, regardless of his anger level. Record the highest level of anger that day.

When the therapist reviews the **Anger Logs** with the patient he can explore such features as:

a)   Details of the specific situation
b)   Nature of triggers
c)   Expression and intensity of anger
d)   How long angry episodes lasted
e)   Accompanying thoughts
f)   Consequences (short-term and long-term)
g)   Possible coping efforts

Another, somewhat more detailed version of the **Anger Log** *(see next page)* has been suggested by Gerlock (1996). In that format the patient keeps an **Anger Log** or **Diary** for several weeks, recording brief accounts of anger episodes. Subsequently, the patient and the therapist can analyze this data for recurrent patterns and themes. Such Anger Logs can focus on the **prompt-appraisal-anger expression sequence** and the role of anger, hostility, and the accompanying aggression cycle. The Anger Log or Diary are designed to help the patient collect data on the **frequency** of anger experiences, the **degree** of anger experienced, and the **ability to demonstrate control** and **coping responses**. Patients are encouraged to record the full range of provocations, from minor annoyance to infuriating events, in order to improve their ability to monitor and control their angry outbursts. The overall goal is to help the patients understand the daily experience of anger in their lives.

The manner in which self-monitoring is conducted should be individually-tailored to the patient. For example, Rose et al. (2000) described how a self-monitoring diary was employed with a **developmentally delayed (DD) population**. The DD patients were asked to report on their distress (anger) for the day by circling different pictures of facial expression. Patients reviewed with staff on a daily basis what had led them to evaluate their day in this manner. The need for developing cognitive-behavioral interventions with persons with mental retardation was underscored by Matson and Mayville (2001) who reported that aggressive behavior occurs in approximately 8% to 24% of the DD population. See Benson 1994, Benson et al. 1986, Rose, 1996, and Rose et al. 2000 for a description of programs for the assessment and treatment of individuals with DD. Front-line staff are active members in the treatment programs. The self-monitoring procedures are occasions to help DD patients collaboratively identify their triggers and develop and practice coping strategies.

ANGER LOG II

(Gerlock, 1996)

Trigger

Describe "what happened"

Anger Level

Use a 0 to 10 "anger meter"

Note various gradient feelings of anger

Help the patient to draw a distinction between feelings such as being "bothered, upset, irritable, hassled, annoyed, frustrated" <u>versus</u> "very angry, burned up, pissed off, irate, furious, enraged, boiling over, fit to be tied"

Anger-up thoughts and feelings

Thoughts that dehumanize, externalize, convey jealousy, sense of entitlement

Anger-down thinking

De-escalating thoughts and feelings

Behavior

What did the patient do? (Take time out, use relaxation, problem-solving)

Note other feelings and accompanying thoughts

Experience of jealousy, hostility, loathing, disgust, anxiety, depression

Another form of self-monitoring that can be used is to ask the patient to **plot the intensity of anger** on a 10-point scale on the vertical axis (1 being annoyance, 5 being angry, and 10 being rage) and plot time of anger on the horizontal axis (Beck & Fernandez, 1998). Feindler and Ecton (1994) have used a **Hassle Log** with adolescents that includes many of the same elements as Gerlock (1996). Also see Feindler (1995) and Feindler and Guttnan (1994) for a description of how these procedures can be adapted to children and adolescents.

GESTALT-BASED EMPTY CHAIR PROCEDURE

Another way to help patients become more aware of the factors that contribute to their anger and the impact of anger is to use the **Gestalt-based empty chair procedure**. For example, Paivio and Greenberg (1995) have described how patients can be taught to engage in a dialogue with an **imaginal other** and encouraged to express their feelings and needs directly to an imaginal other. The empty-chair procedure can be shifted into a dialogue of **two parts of self** (e.g., that part that suppresses anger and who is fearful of expressing feelings and that part that loses control and explodes). In one chair the patient can be encouraged to experience and express his **anger in typical ways**. When he switches chairs, he can be encouraged to experience and express how he felt as the recipient **of this anger**. The patient may be encouraged to engage in similar perspective-taking in his daily experience.

By having the patient access and express feelings, the therapist can use the procedure to tap the patient's **underlying beliefs** concerning feeling "worthless, unlovable, insecure." Often patients with anger-control problems have a fear of their disruptive impulses, fear of loosing control, fear about being different, lack of trust. The therapist needs to develop a therapeutic alliance that nurtures safety, support and fosters such self-disclosure. *(See Section below on developing a therapeutic alliance, pp. 218.)*

Therapists have also used the **Empty Chair Procedure** to have patients interact with absent others (e.g., father) in order to convey previously unexpressed feelings. See the Discussion below on **Letter-writing and Journaling** that is designed to achieve a similar therapeutic objective *(pp. 309).*

Finally, it is important to keep in mind that no matter what form of assessment is used (interviews, self-report, imagery, self-monitoring, and the like), the critical feature is how patients are **given feedback** and how this information is **shared** and **incorporated** into a **Case Conceptualization Model** that informs treatment planning and fosters goal-setting.

MENTAL DISORDERS AND VIOLENT BEHAVIOR

"Multiple factors contribute to violence and one characteristic is rarely enough to predict violence." (Meyer et al., 2000, p. 117)

(For detailed reviews see references by Arboleda-Florenz et al., 1998; Baron & Richadson, 1997; Dolan & Doyle, 2000; Hillebrand, 1995; Hiday, 1997; Hodgins & Muller-Isberner, 2000; Menzies et al., 1994; Monahan 1996; Monahan & Steadman, 1994; McConnell & Catalano, 2001; Mossman, 2000; Otto, 2000; Quinsey et al., 1998; Rice, 1997; Sampson & Lauristen, 1994; Steadman et al., 1998; Taylor & Gunn, 1999; and Volavka, 1995.)

One objective of the assessment process is to educate the patient about the nature of his anger, and secondly, to help formulate a diagnosis. Another goal of assessment is to **assess the level of the patient's dangerousness to both self and others**. In my capacity as a consultant to various psychiatric facilities, I have been asked to offer my clinical opinion on the potential violence of adolescent and adult patients. Moreover, during the course of therapy, patients often make threats concerning others or toward themselves. My ability to address the issues of mental disorders and aggression is hampered by the lack of standardized diagnostic criteria for anger and aggression. While DSM-IV enumerates 9 different categories for anxiety disorders and 10 different categories for depression, there are limited diagnostic categories for anger, namely **Intermittent Explosive disorder (IED)** (312.34) and **Adjustment Disorder with Disturbance Conduct** (309.3) and **Adjustment Disorder with Mixed Disturbance of Emotions and Conduct** (309.9). Before we consider the critical issue of predicting violence and its relationship to mental disorders, we will first briefly consider the concept of **IED** and the recent proposals to develop a classification system of Anger Disorders.

When the pathological aggression is **not** secondary to any medical or psychiatric disorder, then the DSM-IV diagnosis of **Intermittent Explosive Disorder (IED)** is applied to individuals who attack others and/or destroy property. DSM-IV defines **IED** as an **impulse control disorder** characterized by **discrete episodes of failure to resist aggressive impulses that result in serious assaultive behavioral acts or destruction of property**. The degree of aggression expressed during an episode is grossly **out of proportion** to any precipitating psychosocial stressor. Finally, the explosive episodes are not accounted for by another mental or general medical condition.

In a study of 27 cases of individuals with IED, McElroy et al. (1998) found that they all demonstrated substantial Axis I psychopathology in addition to IED, most notably major mood disorders, substance abuse, anxiety, and other impulse control disorders. Subjects also displayed high rates of comorbid migraine headaches. Childhood histories showed high frequencies of temper tantrums, ADHD, conduct disorder such as stealing and fire setting.

At this point, however, the behavioral criteria for **IED** have been **poorly operationalized**. As Coccaro (1998) has noted, there is no clear specification of what constitutes "serious assaultive behavior" or "destruction of property", nor how frequent behavioral outbursts should be in order to meet the **IED** criteria. They proposed that such impulsive aggression should average **twice weekly for at least one month**.

Several authors have called for a more developed classification system of **Anger Disorders** (Kassinove, 1995). For example, Eckhardt and Deffenbacher (1998) have proposed several diagnostic categories for patients with pathological anger and aggression. They include:

1) **Adjustment Disorder with Angry Mood** -- experienced identifiable stressor within the past 3 months

2) **Situational Anger Disorder without Aggression** -- persistent intense anger reaction to a situation for 6 months or more

3) **Situational Anger Disorder with Aggression** -- intense anger reaction with verbal and/or physical aggression

4) **General Anger Disorder without Aggression** -- anger <u>not</u> tied to specific situation, more pervasive and generalized

5) **General Anger Disorder with Aggression** -- chronic excess emotion with verbal and/or physical aggression

Exclusion Rules: Organic disorders, psychosis, PTSD, and personality disorders such as antisocial, borderline, paranoid.

With these diagnostic criteria in mind, we can **consider the relationships between mental disorders and violent / aggressive behavior**.

The recent set of publications by John Monahan, Henry Steadman, Paul Appelbaum, Ed Mulvey, and their colleagues, under the **MacArthur Violence Risk Assessment Study**, has proven most helpful in providing guidelines for making such clinical decisions (See Appelbaum et al., 2000; Grisso et al., 2000; Monahan et al., 2000; Silver et al., 1999; Steadman et al., 1994, 1998). These authors underscore the need for a **multilevel** and **multi-gating assessment process** that considers individual, clinical, developmental, familial and ecological factors. The MacArthur group have developed specific actuarial measures that can be used, as well as an **Iterative Classification Tree Approach to Risk Assessment** (Steadman et al., 2000). In this latter approach a series of <u>sequential decisions</u> are made rather than using a main effects multiple regression approach.

Their assessment approach reflects the observation that *"the accuracy of psychiatric assessment of future violent behavior is limited, but it may increase for specific subgroups within specified time frames and locations"* (Steadman, 2000, p. 265). For different assessment models see Hufford (2001) and Swets et al. (2000) who propose chaos therapy, a CUSP catastrophe model, and multi-decisional analyses to predict violence. These explanatory models are in contrast to traditional linear models.

Diagnosis and assessment take on particular importance when clinicians are called upon to make judgments about the likelihood or prediction of violent behavior. **There is a need to assess dangerousness thoroughly** given the **complex relationship** between mental disorders and violence, as noted in the FACT SHEET below. Binder (1999) provides guidelines on how such assessments should be conducted. She begins by proposing that the question *"Are the mentally ill dangerous?"* should be rephrased as a more complex question. After reviewing the research literature, she concludes that clinicians should formulate a different and a more complex question, namely,

> ***Which** mentally ill patients are dangerous, under **what** **circumstances**, in which **phase of illness** with which **comorbid diagnosis**, while considering whether they have a **history of violence** and whether they are **compliant with treatment**.*

Which -- **male, young** (late teens and early 20's) and **lower SES**, chronically unemployed, have an increased risk of violence, **apart from their psychiatric illness, chronic unemployment.** (N.B. clinicians tend to overpredict violence in nonwhite patients and **underpredict violence in women.**) This underprediction is of concern, when we learn that among more severe psychiatric populations there is little gender difference in violent and aggressive behaviors.

What circumstances -- the potential for violence is increased when an individual is placed in an environment that "pulls for" and that values violence. Do the current circumstances allow for **adequate monitoring** for drug and alcohol use; has there been a **strong therapeutic relationship** established; what is the **likelihood of potential victims** (Family members with whom patients are living and who are setting limits on patients are the most likely victims, as well as individuals who are in the caretaking role.).

Phase of illness -- when the patient's illness is in an active **acute phase**, there is a greater likelihood of violence. **Symptoms** such as high levels of thinking disturbance, hostility, suspiciousness and agitation - excitement are more valuable in predicting violence than is the patient's diagnosis. These symptoms should be systematically assessed using a Standardized Rating Scale such as the Overt Aggression Scale (See Steadman et al., 1998). (Note that agitation in depressed patients can be a side-effect of anti-depressant medication.)

Comorbid diagnosis -- there is a high correlation between substance abuse (especially alcohol abuse) and violence; also delusional jealousy (See Silve et al., 1998).

Compliant with treatment -- treatment nonadherence such as not taking medication, not attending therapy session. When patients are actively involved in collaboration with the treatment process and when a strong therapeutic relationship has been established, the likelihood of violence is reduced (See Beauford et al., 1997).

History of violence --the single greatest risk factor for predicting future violence is a history of violent behavior and criminal behavior more generally (e.g., past acts of violence, verbal threats of violence). The risk for violence increases with each prior episode of violence. The likelihood of future violent acts exceeds 50% among persons with 5 or more offences. The age at which the patient first had contact with the Juvenile Justice system (first serious offense) is also predictive (e.g., violent acts before age 12).

When clinicians take these factors into consideration and when they feel **confident**, they are more often accurate in their judgment about violence. Moreover, the prediction of violence (like the prediction of the weather) is more likely correct in the **short term**, than over the long haul where situational circumstances that are distal can change.

Using the input from significant others, past records and current patient behavior, the clinician needs to consider **a number of risk factors for aggressive behavior** that include:

a) **Current substance/alcohol abuse.** Alcohol, cocaine, PCP, and Amphetamines have been found to exacerbate anger/aggression. (See Hoaken et al., 1998 and Lau et al., 1995 for a review of how alcohol affects executive (frontal lobe) cognitive functioning and how alcohol acts as a mediator of aggression. See Chermack & Taylor, 1995, for a consideration of how expectancy effects and beliefs about the impact of alcohol also come into play.) ;

b) **Antisocial personality.** History of illegal, violent, antisocial behavior, prior violence toward others. History of agitation, irritability, impulsivity. Family history of violence. **Membership in a social group that condones and encourages violence.** (Note that the rate of mental illness is 2 to 3 times higher among those incarcerated in jails than in persons in the general population, and that the mentally ill are disproportionately arrested compared to the general population. 40% to 50% of patients in the mental health system have an arrest history [Roskes et al., 1999]).

c) **Presence of comorbid psychiatric and medical disorders.** (Incidence of violent/homicidal behaviors is highest in patients with comorbid disorders (Asnis et al., 1997). As noted, the **risk of violence is most** evident when symptoms are **acute** (Steadman et al., 1998) and among **mentally ill individuals with coexisting substance abuse** (Eronen et al., 1998) Anger may be part of other psychiatric disorders such as depression, bipolar disorder, PTSD, schizophrenia, manic patients who have a hostile suspicious mood state, Axis II Paranoid, Narcissistic, Borderline, and Antisocial Personality disorder. **Evidence of medical disorders** such as head-injury, tumor, tension and migraine headaches, elevated blood pressure, coronary heart disease. Manifest sudden changes in behavior and overactivity following illness onset, agitation and restlessness have been found to be predictive of violent behavior;

d) **Presence of psychotic symptoms**, especially those that threaten a person or that involve delusional thinking and intrusion of thoughts. These are known as **threat-control-override symptoms** where individuals see violence as a justified defense or retaliation against harmful or manipulative actions that the person believes to be directed against himself. 8% to 22% of psychiatric inpatients have had assaultive episodes within the past 2 weeks prior to their hospitalization (Mulvey, 1994). However, see Applebaum, et al. (2000) for a discussion of the relationship between delusions and violence. In their study neither delusions in general, nor threat/control override delusions were associated with a higher risk of violent behavior. Borum et al. (1999) observe that command hallucinations, delusional ideas, feelings of persecution are more likely to be followed when the command hallucination is a familiar voice, when the delusional belief is consistent with the command, and when there is evidence of a past history of compliance with such commands (Also see Hersh & Borum, 1998).

e) **Presence of self-destructive and suicidal behavior.** (depression, hopelessness, suicidal rumination);

f) **Presence of threatening behaviors - past or current.** For example, stalking another person; being found with a weapon; having a clear and specific feasible and viable plan; identified targets. *(Ask about past violent behavior and ask directly if the patient intends to commit a similar offense in the future, if released.)*;

g) **Mood and thoughts consistent with violence.** For example, resentment, hostility, preoccupying thoughts, images, fantasies of harm/assault, revenge, retaliation, aggressive impulses and urges;

h) **Lack of resources.** Isolated, few prosocial social supports, low self-esteem, doubts in their ability to cope with anger (low self-efficacy);

i) **Availability of weapons**. Assess for access to weapons and past use and interest in weapons;

j) **Victim availability**. Individual(s) with whom the patient was violent prior to hospitalization are most often attacked upon release (e.g., half of targeted victims are family members). *(Ask about intervention efforts of significant others)*;

k) **Lack of response to previous treatments.** Nonadherence to medication and failure to participate in treatment, weak therapeutic alliance, low commitment to treatment;

l) **Intensity of community supervision** and **unresponsiveness of the mental health care system**. In any predictions of violent behavior in psychiatric patients there is also a need to consider the **role of the mental health system**. Michael Winerip (1999) in a moving account tells the poignant story of Andrew Goldstein who pushed Kendra Webdale to her death on the New York subway tracks. Mr. Goldstein had frequently and voluntarily sought hospitalization as well as supervised housing, but he was repeatedly rejected because of no vacancies even though he had a history of violence (13 violence assaults over 2 years).

IN THE ASSESSMENT SECTION, VARIOUS MEASURES DESIGNED TO ASSESS RISK WERE ENUMERATED. IN CONSIDERING THESE MEASURES IT IS IMPORTANT TO KEEP IN MIND THAT RISK ASSESSMENT IS A CONDITIONAL "IF – THEN" PROCESS SINCE RISK CAN CHANGE OVER TIME, ACROSS CONDITIONS, OR IN RESPONSE TO VARIOUS INTERVENTIONS. THE PRODUCTION OF DANGEROUSNESS OR RISK SHOULD BE VIEWED AS BEING CONTEXTUALLY DEPENDENT BOTH ON THE SITUATION AND CIRCUMSTANCES, DYNAMIC (SUBJECT TO CHANGE), AND CONTINUOUS (VARY ALONG A CONTINUUM OF PROBABILITY).

FACT SHEET
ASSOCIATION BETWEEN VIOLENCE AND MENTAL ILLNESS

(See Bensley et al., 1995, 1997; Bernstein, 1981; Convit et al., 1990; Eichelman & Hartwig, 1995; Eronen et al., 1998; Haller & DeLuty, 1988, Hanson, 1996; Lanzi, 1991, 1992; Madden et al., 1976; McConnell & Catalano, 2001; Steadman et al., 1998; Thackery & Bobbitt, 1990; Tyron, 1986; Whittington & Wykes, 1994; Whittington et al., 1996; Wyatt & Wyatt, 1995; Yassi, 1994)

- Although a small percentage of violent acts are committed by the mentally ill, there is evidence of an association between violence and mental illness, as the following data indicates.

- Up to 40% of people admitted to psychiatric wards of general hospitals are violent before admission.

- Presence of an Axis I diagnosis increased violence prevalence rates by 5 times that of community residents with no psychiatric disorders.

- People with a history of psychiatric treatment are two to three times more violent than nonpsychiatric population.

- People who direct violence at others are also likely to direct it at themselves.

- Arrest rates for former psychiatric patients are higher than those of the general population.

- The risk of committing a homicidal act is about 8 times higher for men than women. Higher rates of violence were not found for the presence of delusions or hallucinations. In fact, schizophrenia has been found to be associated with lower violence rates than other forms of psychiatric disorders.

- The presence of alcohol or drug abuse increased violence prevalence rates by 10 to 15 times compared to individuals with no psychiatric disorders.

- Antisocial personality disorder increased the odds ratio of violence over 11-fold.

- Prevalence of psychiatric disorders among incarcerated males is three times higher than among the general population.

- The **combination** of mental disorders and substance disorders increases the likelihood of violence the most.

- High risk for violence was associated with males, prior violence, abuse as a child, living in disadvantaged neighborhoods, personality or adjustment disorder diagnoses, violent thoughts and psychopathy (highest risk factor).

- The majority of violence acts (86%) committed by former mental patients occurred within the context of the family and friendship networks.

- Patients receiving adequate treatment (about one session per week) were no more violent than others in the community.

- Finally, it is worth noting that:

  > **"Because serious mental illness is relatively rare and the excess
  > risk is modest, the contribution of mental illness to overall levels of
  > violence in society is miniscule." (Eronen et al., 1998, p. 22)**

Given the risk involved in working with aggressive and potentially violent psychiatric patients the following **GUIDELINES FOR MANAGING POTENTIALLY VIOLENT PATIENTS** are offered. These guidelines grew out of a request that I train frontline staff on how to respond to aggressive patients. **APPENDIX B** also provides examples of how staff can respond to patients who are in **"CRISIS."**

GUIDELINES FOR MANAGING VIOLENT PATIENTS

(See Carmel & Hunter, 1990; Davis & Boster, 1998; Dubin, 1981; Eichelman, 1995; Hackett, 1997; Harris & Morrison, 1995; Kidd & Stark, 1995; Mataskis, 1998; McNeil, 1998; Royal College of Psychiatrists, 1998; Stevenson, 1991; Tardiff, 1996; Temple, 1994; Tishler, 1996; Tishler et al., 2000; Visalli et al., 1996; Wondrak, 1989 and Zimmerman, 1996 for more detailed suggestions on how to manage potentially violent patients)

INCIDENCE OF VIOLENCE AGAINST MENTAL HEALTH STAFF

Nearly **<u>one-half of all psychotherapists</u>** will be **threatened, harassed or physically attacked** at some point in their careers by their patients. This may take the form of unwanted calls, verbal and physical attacks on self or loved ones, or even murder.

50% of all staff compensation cases at psychiatric facilities result from patient assaults. Moreover, 50% is likely an underreport. It is estimated that only 1 in 5 assaults are actively reported.

Those mental health personnel who are at the lower ladder of the organization are the most likely to be assaulted and the least likely to report such incidents.

Between **4% to 8%** of individuals brought to psychiatric emergency rooms **bring weapons**.

Emergency rooms and inpatient psychiatric units are settings in which mental health professionals are most likely to be assaulted by patients.

In psychiatric hospitals most assaults take place **in corridors**, rather than in other settings.

Homicide is the cause of **12%** of deaths in **workplaces**.

SUMMARY OF WARNING SIGNS OF POTENTIALLY VIOLENT PATIENTS

(See Borum et al., 1999; Lam et al., 2000; Mossman, 2000; Rossi et al., 1986)

Psychosis, manic state, major depression, violence-filled obsessions, substance intoxication, head trauma

Agitation, restlessness, aggressive impulses

Presence or availability of a weapon, detailed plan, identified "targets"

History of violence and history of drug and alcohol abuse (review prior records and look for prior signs of violence)

Noncompliance with psychiatric medication

Weak therapeutic alliance (e.g., mental health professionals who have been included in the patient's social support network are less likely to be victims of violence)

Access to intended victims (as noted, family members and friends are persons most likely to be targets of violence).

When a female inpatient exhibits signs of an elevated risk of violence, the significance of that risk should not be discounted on the basis of her gender.

Borum at al. (1999) have summarized these various warning signs in the form of a question that **assesses potential threat**.

> *"Has the patient engaged in recent behaviors that suggest that he/she is moving on a path toward a particular target(s)?"*

Does the patient have the:

ABILITY --   access, means, capacity, opportunity and interest (show interest in similar acts)

INTENT--   specificity of plans and actions taken toward implementing those plans

THRESHOLD CROSSED--   engage in attack-related behaviors, target selection

CONCERN EXPRESSED FROM OTHERS--   patient discussed plan, threaten others, others afraid or others support, accept or ignore threats

MOTIVES --   loss of status (public's humiliation, failure, rejection, loss of job) that contribute to feelings of desperation and despair and loss of supports; desire to achieve notoriety, fame, bring attention to personal or public problem, avenge a perceived wrong or desire to retaliate, end "personal pain", suicidal act

> *In short, the "task is to determine the nature and degree of risk a given individual may pose for certain kinds of behaviors in light of anticipated conditions and contexts" (Borum et al., 1999)*

When the level of risk for violence or dangerousness is identified, what can health care providers do? We now turn out attention to this critical question.

POSSIBLE INTERVENTION AND
VIOLENCE PREVENTION STRATEGIES

What Can Hospital Administrators and Staff Do

Obtain information based on a combination of self-report, collateral reports from significant others and agency records.

Educate staff on a regular basis on violence prevention strategies.

Collect and share data on violent incidents; be sure to pass along information about possible risk assessment; keep good records.

Conduct ongoing critical incident analyses. Watch for contagion effects of violence among patients..

Have explicit policy on using restraints and train staff on how such restraint practices should be implemented by a team.

Post and have accessible crisis intervention guidelines. Review them on a regular basis.

Provide adequate staff-patient ratios (e.g., violent incidents tend to occur where there is low staff-patient ratios).

Ensure that a policy on chemical and physical restraints is followed. (e.g., Patients should be assessed prior to the administration of neuroleptic medication for possible chemical intoxication, such as alcohol or street drugs like PCP).

Where warranted, use metal detector searches, have "emergency" buttons, cell phones, additional security staff available.

Make violence prevention and reduction priorities.

Monitor patients' symptoms regularly.

Warn or notify authorities of potential threat.

Warn identifiable potential victims.

Arrange for intensive aftercare case management. Ensure continuity of care. *(See Mueser et al., 1998 for a discussion of the importance of community follow-up and the need for educating families.)*

Finally, Flannery and his colleagues (Flannery, 1998; Flannery et al., 1991, 1994, 1995, 1996, 1998, 1999, 2000) have developed a comprehensive **Critical Incident Stress Management approach** for psychiatric health care providers. This **Assaulted Staff Action Program (ASAP)** is a voluntary, system-wide, peer-help crisis intervention program designed to assist employee victims in the aftermath of violent outbursts. **ASAP** is a Critical Incident Stress management approach that includes pre-incident training, acute care services, and post-incident assistance for victims and their family members. The **ASAP** services include individual crisis counseling, group crisis counseling, a staff victims' support group, employee victim's family counseling and private referrals. The **ASAP** teams are comprised of volunteer first line responders, **ASAP** supervisors, and the **ASAP** team leader. The **ASAP** responders provide clinical support for employee victims within 20 minutes to 10 days after each assault episode.

The **ASAP** intervention resulted in a 63% reduction assault frequency within a 2-year period, less injury, less staff turnover, less use of sick leave, less worker compensation claims, less medical and legal expenses and higher staff morale. The **ASAP** program resulted in a reduction in the frequency of assault rate greater than 40% over baseline. The **ASAP** is an effective way to reduce violence in psychiatric facilities and in the workplace.

WHAT CAN THE THERAPIST DO IF "DANGEROUSNESS" IS DETERMINED

"Therapists have a 'duty to protect' potential victims when they hear clear meaningful threats."

- Check information with collateral sources

- Conduct a careful assessment of potential threat – assess patient in terms of current plans, intentions, and history of violence and assess environment in terms of availability of weapons, access to potential victims, and level of supervision. *(Review SECTION on factors to consider in predicting violence.)*

- Notify intended victim or someone who will notify the intended victim or the police.

- Ensure that all weapons have been removed from the patient's possession

- Secure hospitalization for the patient

- Refer the patient to a more structured treatment program (e.g., partial hospitalization)

- Increase frequency of therapy sessions

- Patients receiving adequate treatment (at least one session per week) have a reduced level of violence.

- Mobilize social supports who can provide supervision

- *(See SECTION below (p. 218) on how therapists can respond when patients become angry)*

WHAT CAN FRONTLINE STAFF DO TO REDUCE VIOLENCE:
BEHAVIORS – SOME "DO'S" AND "DON'TS"
(The following list of "Do's: and "Don'ts" were derived from Tishler et al., 2000;
VandeCreek and colleagues, 1994, 2000)
(ALSO SEE APPENDIX A)

NONVERBAL BEHAVIORS

DO'S	DON'TS
Ensure safety for the patient and for those in immediate area	Disregard safety issues
Screen for **medical conditions** that result in aggression or irritability (*WHIMPS*[11])	Intervene immediately
Be **sensitive to nonverbal signs** of aggression (e.g., agitation, abrupt body movements, body tremors, heavy breathing, darting eyes)	Be self-preoccupied
Assume a non-threatening physical posture	
Approach patients from the **front or side**	Make quick erratic gestures
Maintain an **adequate distance** (at least one arm length)	Approach the patient from behind so as to startle the patient
	Violate the patient's personal boundaries; Crowd the patient

---

[11] The acronym *WHIMPS* refers to medical conditions that may result in aggression or irritability and require medical attention (Wernicke's or Withdrawal, hypoxia, hypoperfusion, hypertensive crisis, hypoglycemia, intoxication, meningitis, poisoning, status epileptucus). In children, consider lead and iron poisoning, iron deficiency, evidence of abuse and drug intoxication (Sege & Licenziato, 2001). *(__The Reader has permission to copy this List of Do's and Don't's and give it to front-line staff.__)*

NONVERBAL BEHAVIORS (Continued)

DO'S	DON'TS
Stay at **eye level** (e.g., If the patient is sitting, then sit; if standing, then stand with him. The likelihood of aggression is reduced if patient is seated.) Encourage the patient to stay seated.	Stand over a patient - this may be perceived as threatening
When walking with the patient be in a **lateral position**	Walk behind or in front of the patient; Stand behind the patient
Maintain **moderate eye contact**	Use penetrating or persistent eye contact
Be mindful of the interview space. See patients in **"safe" areas** (remove all potentially dangerous items such as ashtrays, etc.) and **notify colleagues** and ask to **be monitored**	See patient in an isolated area without notifying anyone
Area should allow for **escape** and **visibility** and quick **back-up help** should be available	Use a confined interview area
Position self by **door** and have a **"safety plan"** (e.g., **large enough area** if help is needed for team restraints)	Go in unprepared
If patient has a **gun**:	
i) **Acknowledge** - "I see you have a gun"	Reach for the gun, forcefully search, threaten the patient
ii) Ask the patient to put the gun on the **floor**	Express fear of the gun - may exacerbate patient's agitation
iii) Ask about **other weapons**	
iv) Go to **another room** with the patient and **ask a colleague** to confiscate the gun. Make this request **in front of** the patient.	
v) Maintain **calm** demeanor	Panic

VERBAL BEHAVIORS

DO'S	DON'TS
Introduce self as a **clinic staff** member, **"helping" professional** who's goal is to **help** the **patient**	Act removed or disinterested
Speak calmly and softly. Use short sentences. Keep it simple. Use a controlled voice.	Raise voice, talk fast. Interrupt the patient.
Engage patient in a **conversation**. *("I'm wondering if you are feeling …?"; "Many (some) people in your situation might feel frustrated / angry. Is this true for you?")*	
Create a respectful supportive **therapeutic alliance** that conveys compassion. Obtain a **time-line** of what events led to getting so upset that he needs a weapon	
Ask the patient for **permission to discuss** a given subject / issue *("Is it okay with you if we discuss …?"; "Would you feel comfortable discussing how you are feeling about …?")*	Use threats
Paraphrase what the patient has said and ask for **feedback** to make sure you understand the patient *(Translate the patient's anger and his use of a weapon as a means of solving a problem. Note, that "sometimes people get angry because they are feeling scared, alone, humiliated".)*	
Acknowledge the patient's being "upset", "distressed".	

NONVERBAL BEHAVIORS

<u>DO'S</u>   DON'TS

Discuss **possible causes** and likely
consequences for violence.

Offer **help** *("What, if anything, can I
do to help?")*

Refer to **prior contacts** with the patient
*("I remember the last time you were
angry, you were able to …")*

Redirect anger *("How would you like
the situation to change?")* Suggest
that the patient and you both take a
time out, use a relaxation procedure.
Give the patient as much choice and
control as possible.

Indicate consequences. *("You are
using angry words and engaging in
scary acts. Your words (acts) are
pushing me away as well as other
people who want to help. If this
continues I am required to call the
police for help.")*

Be **firm and set limits.** Remind the
patient that his present threatening
behavior violates the rules he has
agreed to follow.

Use **emergency alarm button** to call for
assistance.

Notify transition staff about possible
dangers and the potential for violence.
Implement "safety" monitoring plans.

IN SHORT, TAKE VIOLENCE PREVENTION SERIOUSLY

"The best type of management of any potentially violent patient lies in prevention."

SUMMARY:
WHAT YOU SHOULD TAKE AWAY FROM SECTION III

1. The need for a multifaceted assessment strategy that combines different sources of information and different assessment procedures.

2. How to formulate a clinical interview that taps the various aspects of anger and aggression.

3. How to increase the likelihood that your patients will engage in self-monitoring and other extra-therapeutic activities.

4. How to predict violence and the level of dangerousness – what to watch out for.

5. How to prevent violence and how to defuse patients who are in crisis (Also see Appendix A).

In order to test your knowledge and understanding try your hand at the following **TEST YOUR EXPERTISE** questions.

TEST YOUR EXPERTISE: SECTION III

1. An aggressive, angry patient has been referred to you. Generate a **clinical interview** (select questions from Tables 1 to 9) that you would employ. How do you use self-report measures in treatment? Which measures would you use (select from the list of self-report measures)? Which of these measures would you use again in order to assess progress?

2. Role play with two colleagues a clinical interview. One can be the angry patient, one the therapist, and the third can act as a coach, using Tables 1 to 9 as prompt sheets. Take turns playing these different roles.

3. What are your "key" questions that you use in treatment that are <u>not</u> included in these 9 Tables. Please email Don Meichenbaum with these "clinical nuggets." *(dmeich@watarts.uwaterloo.ca)*

4. With a patient, try the imagery-based assessment, the Gestalt-based empty chair and self-monitoring procedures.

5. How compliant patients are with a self-monitoring requests is predictive of how well they will be adherent to other more demanding aspects of the treatment subsequently. Write out the **14 steps** that the therapist should include when asking patients to **self-monitor** or to engage in any **extra-therapeutic activity**. *(See Procedural Checklist, page 174, for a reminder of the steps.)* How many of these steps do you routinely employ?

6. Have you been called upon to make predictions about the level of "dangerousness" of your patients? What factors did you include in your assessment? Compare your list of factors against those enumerated in this **SECTION**.

7. One-half of psychotherapists have been threatened or physically attacked by their patients. Are you in this half? What are the **warning signs** of patients being potentially violent? This is <u>not</u> a mere academic exercise; knowing the warning signs and knowing how to diffuse a crisis are critical. **Role play** with your colleagues ways to **defuse a crisis.** Have one person play an agitated threatening patient. The second person can play the role of the therapist. The third person can use the **Guidelines** and the interview protocol in **Appendix A (pages 401-435)** as examples of how to defuse **a patient in crisis**. Mastering these defusing skills will be helpful when such potentially violent episodes occur.

8. The administrator of your hospital or mental health center is concerned about the "dangerousness" of the patients and about the safety of the staff given some recent incidents. He/she comes to you for advice on how to set up a prevention and intervention program. What <u>specific</u> advice would you offer? What steps would you take to insure that your advice was heeded?

SECTION IV: INTRODUCTION TO TREATMENT

"Violence is a complex problem and prevention and treatment require efforts at multiple levels." (Meyer et al., 2000, p. 117).

This **SECTION** introduces the topic of **treatment options**. Following an enumeration of treatment alternatives, we examine the nature of the **core tasks** that need to be addressed in working with patients who have anger-control problems. An **overview** of the cognitive behavioral treatment (CBT) approach is offered, as well as a **listing of illustrative studies** that have used the **CBT** with **diverse populations**.

CONTENTS SECTION IV

TREATMENT ALTERNATIVES

(See Fava, 1997 and Lavine, 1997 for reviews of pharmacological treatment studies; See Beck & Fernandez, 1998; Bowman-Edmonson & Cohen-Conger, 1996; Deffenbacher, Oetting & Di Giuseppe, in press; Di Giuseppe & Tafrate, 2001; and Tafrate, 1995, for reviews of psychological treatment studies; and Whitaker, 1993, for a review with people with learning difficulties)

Di Giuseppe and Tafrate (2001) have noted the increased popularity of anger management programs, but they caution that this enthusiasm and popularity have <u>not</u> been accompanied by empirical demonstrations of their effectiveness. In an effort to address the questions of differential effectiveness of psychosocial interventions, they conducted a meta-analysis of some 50 between group studies (treatment <u>versus</u> no treatment control studies) and 7 within group treatment studies (pre-post-treatment assessments). Their comprehensive review is instructive and provides a **cautionary, but promising** cast on the field of interventions with patients who have anger-control problems. Their analyses reveled the following conclusions.

(1) Some 92 different psychosocial treatment interventions have been employed with 1841 angry subjects. The interventions with the most complete experimental designs and statistical analyses were cognitive-behavioral and included such diverse interventions as self-instructional training, problem-solving, cognitive restructuring, stress inoculation training, relaxation and exposure-based therapy, skills training, psychoeducation and the combination of these treatments.

(2) The meta-analysis that compared effect sizes revealed that **cognitive-behavioral interventions for anger reduction** were **moderately successful**. Subjects in the between group designs who received **cognitive-behavioral treatment (CBT) were better off then 76% of control untreated subject**. The results of the within subjects designed studies indicated that **83% of the CBT treated subjects improved in comparison to their pretest scores**. Di Giuseppe and Tafrate found that the CBT had an **effect size of .70**, as compared to no-treatment controls. This effect size was significant and relatively homogenous across studies. These findings are similar to the conclusions drawn by Beck and Fernandez (1998) who conducted a meta-analysis of 50 treatment studies that involved 1640 subjects, but included studies across the full age range.

(3) Di Giuseppe and Tafrate report that the level of improvement was generally maintained at a follow-up period that ranged from 2 to 64 weeks. The maintenance of treatment gains was lower for behavioral indicators of anger than for self-report measures of anger. (Only 18 of the 50 between group studies were included in the meta-analysis of follow-up data.)

(4) There were <u>no significant treatment differences</u> between the <u>various forms of CBT</u>, but the limited N and power may have restricted the possibility of finding treatment differences. The average number of treatment sessions was 12 among the various forms of interventions.

(5) The meta-analysis of effect sizes revealed that the treatment format of **individual treatment was more effective than group treatment**. This conclusion should be treated as preliminary given the limited number of such comparative studies.

(6) There was some initial suggestion that the relative effectiveness of the various CBT treatments have differential impact on the various classes of measures (e.g., self-report of anger, behavioral indicators of anger reduction, production of prosocial interpersonal behaviors, signs of comorbidity). Overall, anger treatments produced low effect sizes for the improvement of interpersonal relationships. Thus, anger reduction may be the first step in a comprehensive treatment program that needs to focus on social skills training, as discussed below. There is a need to consider the effectiveness of treatment separately for each class of outcome measures.

(7) In comparison to the meta-analysis for other emotional disorders (anxiety and depression), the treatment of anger in adults yields lower overall **effect sizes (d = .70 anger)** than for the meta-analysis of **anxiety disorders (d = 1.00),** and an **effect size of 2.00 for depression**. The respective meta-analyses indicate that the treatment of anger is <u>not as effective</u> as the treatment of other emotional disorders. This difference may be in part due to the characteristics of angry and aggressive patients who often have a lifetime history of aggression (Early Starter model) and who also have high levels of victimization and comorbidity. The present **Handbook** is designed to improve the quality of care for such angry and aggressive patients. The need for such a standardized, comprehensive, life-span perspective is underscored by the last major conclusion drawn by Di Giuseppe and Tafrate (2001).

(8) A major finding of the meta-analysis revealed that those programs that used **standardized treatment manuals and which conducted treatment fidelity checks were found to be most effective**. To quote Di Giuseppe and Tafrate (2001):

> *"Practitioners working with aggressive clients should choose structured interventions, delivered in an individualized format and employ safeguards to ensure that the treatment is delivered in a manner consistent with the manual."*

(9) A **meta-analysis** of anger-management programs for **children** and **youth** (DeBaryshe et al., 2001) covering the period between 1980 and 2000 yielded **27 studies**. Most studies had a modest sample of 30 and covered 10 sessions in duration. The **overall effect size** was a quite **modest .18** which is characterized as small-to-medium in size. This result indicates that on the average 64% of treatment children have posttest scores above the median posttest score for the control group. Thus, in both the interventions with adults and children, we have a long way to go to improve our interventions. Hopefully, this **HANDBOOK** will improve our preventative and treatment efforts.

The following list of interventions offers an overview of the types of interventions that have been provided to patients with anger-control problems and aggression.

- **Pharmacological interventions** (such as SSRIs, lithium carbonate, beta-adrenergic blockers, mood stabilizers, antidepressants, anxiolytics, neuroleptics) (See Coccaro & Kavoussi, 1997; Citrome & Volavka, 1997; Horne & Lindley, 1995; Shay, 1992). Note, some medications may have paradoxical effects of occasionally increasing aggression (e.g., Librium, Valium, and Xanax). Also, some drugs such as PCP, hallucinogenics and anabolic steroids are capable of inducing aggressive behavior (Lavine, 1997). Fava (1998) reports on the favorable response of depressed patients with anger attacks to fluoxetine. Any consideration of pharmacotherapy must address the issue of treatment nonadherence and patient noncompliance. *(See next SECTION.)*

- **Psychoeducational intervention** (educate patients about specific aspects of anger such as situational or personal triggers, the link between cognition, affect and behavioral expression, and about the functional adaptive aspects of anger.)

- **Cognitive-behavioral interventions** that include multicomponent interventions and exposure-based treatment of anger where patients experience sufficiently realistic and anger-provoking situations repeatedly during sessions (e.g., Brondolo et al., 1997). The interventions may include stress-inoculation training, self-instructional training, cognitive-restructuring procedures.

- **Emotion-focused treatment** techniques for arousal regulation and reduction (applied relaxation, systematic desensitization, affect self-awareness and developing empathy for others).

- **Skills training** (cognitive relaxation coping skills training -- see Deffenbacher & McKay, 2000; Fehrenbach & Thelen, 1981; Rimm et al., 1974) social skills training including assertiveness, communication and problem-solving training, parenting and supervisory skills, substance abuse, relapse prevention training)

- **Exposure-based treatments** involves cognitive behavioral interventions in conjunction with in-clinic and in-vivo practice.

- **Behavior management interventions** (functional communication training, self-control training, contingency management, alter individual routines, ecologically-based interventions)

- **Family-oriented interventions** involving significant others in treatment, multisystemic interventions

- **Community-based interventions** involving ecological changes

- **Multicomponent interventions** -- combinations of the above.

ADDRESSING ISSUES OF TREATMENT NONADHERENCE

Any discussion of **pharmacotherapy** should also consider the critical issue of **patient noncompliance**, as Meichenbaum and Turk (1987) have highlighted. Following a discussion of the high incidence of nonadherence with treatment regimens, they provide a set of guidelines for both the prescribing physicians and for all health care providers who should counsel the patient on the importance of adherence to the treatment regimen.

The following **Guidelines** should be reviewed by the patient's therapist, even if he or she is not prescribing the medication. If medication is deemed as an appropriate treatment of choice, then health care providers <u>cannot</u> assume that the patient will readily comply and take the medication. The following points should be reviewed with the patient.

- Make sure the patient **knows the name of his disorder** that is being treated *("So you are taking the medicine that the doctor prescribed for you in order to treat X.")*

- **Name the medication**

- **Provide reassurance** that his disorder is treatable and that taking the medication will help the patient achieve his treatment goals.

- Review the **schedule of medication** (When the patient is to take the medication – time, dosage, course – for how long)

- **Highlight the importance of treatment adherence.** Ensure that the patient knows what to do if he misses a dose

- **Probe about previous adherence problems**, and note short and long-term dangers of non-compliance

- Help the patient **anticipate potential problems** or barriers that might contribute to nonadherence and jointly explore how these potential obstacles can be anticipated and handled

- **Check the patient's comprehension.** Make sure that the patient clearly understands the treatment rationale and can offer **self-generated reasons** why taking the medication will be of help. Repeat critical points as necessary.

- **Reemphasize** the **importance** of **adherence** to the full therapeutic regimen.

- Provide **written** back-up information

- In follow-up meetings, ask about compliance and address difficulties encountered in patient compliance. Collaboratively consider possible solutions.

CORE TASKS OF PSYCHOTHERAPY WITH PATIENTS WITH ANGER-CONTROL PROBLEMS

Before we consider the specific features of the **cognitive-behavioral treatment**, it is useful to provide an **overview** of the **core tasks of treatment**. Although, these core tasks are enumerated in a sequential fashion, the "expert" therapist is able to integrate these tasks in a **flexible and interlocking fashion**. They should <u>not</u> be viewed as a lock-step format.

DEVELOP AND MAINTAIN A THERAPEUTIC ALLIANCE

PROVIDE ONGOING EDUCATION TO THE PATIENT
Conduct assessments, have the patient engage in self-monitoring, enhance patient awareness, use modeling films, employ bibliotherapy.

NURTURE HOPE
Foster a shared understanding using a Case Conceptualization Model, collaboratively engage in goal-setting, highlight patient's strengths, include examples of individuals who have benefited from treatment.

TEACH SKILLS
Emotional regulation, self-control, relaxation, self-instructional, "rethinking", problem-solving, interpersonal skills, tolerance and acceptance

ENSURE APPLICATION IN CLINICAL TRAINING SETTING AND IN VIVO

BUILD IN GENERALIZATION AND MAINTENANCE PROCEDURES
Involve significant others as "allies"; follow generalization guidelines

TREAT COMORBID PROBLEMS
Substance abuse, Axis I, II, and III disorders such as depression, PTSD, personality disorders, medical disorders

CONDUCT RELAPSE PREVENTION

ENSURE PATIENTS "TAKE CREDIT" AND "OWNERSHIP" FOR CHANGES

BUILD IN FOLLOW-THROUGH AND BOOSTER SESSIONS

WHERE INDICATED, ADDRESS ISSUES OF VICTIMIZATION
Address sequelae of trauma exposure – PTSD and Complex PTSD, Conduct memory work, help patients find meaning and avoid revictimization *(See Meichenbaum, 1994 for a detailed discussion on how to achieve these core tasks with victimized patients)*

EXAMPLES OF COGNITIVE BEHAVIORAL AND RELATED INTERVENTION PROGRAMS

(See Beck & Fernandez, 1998b; Chambless & Ollendick, 2001; Bowman-Edmondson & Cohen-Conger, 1996; Lipsey & Wilson, 1993; Mayne & Ambrone, 1999; Tafrate, 1995 for major reviews.)

Treatment of Individuals with Anger-Control Problems

Anderson-Malico, 1994; Brondolo et al., 1997; Cottrell, 1999; Dahlen & Deffenbacher, in press; Deffenbacher, 1988, 1994, 1995a, 1996a, 1999, 2000; Deffenbacher & McKay, 2000; Deffenbacher & McNamara, 1990; Deffenbacher & Oetting, 1990; Deffenbacher & Stark, 1992; DiGiuseppe et al., 1994; Dryden, 1990; Dua & Swinden, 1992; Hazaleus & Deffenbacher, 1986; Kassinove, 1995; Kirman, 1995; Levy & Howells, 1990; Meichenbaum, 1985; Meichenbaum & Novaco, 1998; Messer, 1999; Norcross & Kobayashi, 1999; Norcross et al., 1999; Novaco, 1975, 1976, 1996; O'Donnell & Worell, 1973; Ornstein, 1999; Paivio, 1999; Paivio & Greenberg, 1995; Robins & Novaco, 1999; Sharkin, 1988; Suinn & Deffenbacher, 1988; Warren & McLellarn, 1982 (Elderly – Johnson & Wilborn, 1991)

Treatment of Aggressive Drivers

Deffenbacher, Huff et al., 2000; Deffenbacher, Lynch et al., (in press); Larson, 1996

Treatment of Aggressive Psychiatric Patients

Awalt et al., 1997; Bullard, 1994; Corrigan et al., 1993; Dvoskin & Steadman, 1994; Koerner & Dimeff, 1998; Linehan, 1993; Maier, 1993; McElroy, 1999; Nemeroff et al., 1999; Preston, 1997; Renwick et al., 1997; Solomon, 1992; Stermac, 1998

Treatment of Aggressive Psychiatric Patients With PTSD and Comorbidity Problems (Includes Veterans)

Carroll, 1985; Chemtob et al., 1997a, 1997b; Gerlock, 1990, 1994; Grossman, 1995; Kubany et al., 1994; Lehmann, 1997; Matsakis, 1996, 1997; Meichenbaum, 1994; Najavits et al., 1998; Najavits & Weiss, 2000; Reilly et al., 1994; Wolpow et al., 2000; Yehuda, 1999

Treatment of Incarcerated and Community-Based Offenders

Andrews and Bonta, 1995; Bush, 1995; Fabiano & Ross, 1985; Feshbach et al., 1983; Forbes et al., 1992; Henning & Frueh, 1996; Holbrook, 1997; Knott, 1995; Maruna, 2001; Novaco, 1997; Novaco et al., in press; Raynor & Wanstone, 1996; Roskes et al., 1999; Serin & Kuriychuk, 1994; Waldman, 1999; Wang et al., 1999; Wang & Diamond, 1999

Treatment of Individuals with Hypertension and Type A Behavior

Bennett et al., 1991; Chesney & Rosenman, 1985; Davison et al., 1991; Haaga et al., 1994; Hart, 1984; Larkin & Zayfert, 1996; Nakano, 1990; Roskies, 1983; Shapiro et al., 1997; Siegal, 1992; Suls & Wan, 1993; Thurman, 1985

Treatment of Spouse Abusers

Berns et al., 1999; Brannen & Rubin, 1996; Browne et al., 1997; Carden, 1994; Carrillo & Tello, 1998; Dunford, 2000; Dutton et al., 1995; Dutton, 1998; Edelson & Tolman, 1992; Feldman & Ridley, 1995; Geffner, 2000; Gottman et al., 1976; Hamberger, 1996; Hamberger & Lohr, 1996; Harway & Evans, 1996; Heyman & Neidig, 1997; Holtzworth-Munroe et al., 1990; Jacobson & Gottman, 1998; Jacobson & Margolin, 1979; Jenkins & Davidson, 2000; Koss, 2000; Mantooth et al., 1987; Neidig & Friedman, 1984; O'Leary, 1996; O'Leary et al. 1999; Sana-Loue, 2001; Saunders, 1996a,b; Schlee et al., 1998; Sonkin & Durphy, 1984; Stordeur & Stille, 1989; Stosny, 1995; Sugarman & Frankel, 1996; Tolman, 1996; Tolman & Edelson, 1995; Wallace, 1999; Wexler, 2000; Wile, 1981; Williams, 1995

Treatment of Substance Abusers

O'Farrell et al., 1999; Orwin et al., 2000

Treatment of Lesbian and Gay Batterers

Burke & Follingstad, 1999; Goldfried, 2000; Kurdek, 1994; Margolies & Leeder, 1995; Renzetti, 1992; West, 1998; Wise & Bowman, 1997

Treatment of Abusive Parents

Acton & During, 1992; Nomenelli & Katz, 1993; Whiteman et al., 1987

Treatment of Special Populations

Traumatic Brain Injured: O'Leary, 2000; Uomoto & Brockway, 1992; Whiteman, 1994

Pain patients: Fernandez & Turk, 1995

Developmentally Delayed: Benson, 1994; Benson et al., 1986; Carr & Newsom, 1985; Gardner & Cole, 1993; Mace et al., 1986; Rose, 1996; Rose et al., 2000; Schloss et al., 1989

Learning Disabled: Moore et al., 1997

Caregivers of Dementia Family Members: Gallagher-Thompson et al., 1992; Steffen, 2000

Blind Individuals: David et al., 1998

Treatment of Sexual Offenders

Fernandez & Marshall, 2000; Haaven et al., 1990; Laws et al., 2000; Mann, 2000; Mann et al., 1999; Marques et al., 2000; Marshall et al., 1999; Murphy & Page 2000

Treatment of Occupational Groups Who Experience Anger-Control Problems

Police officers: Sarason et al., 1979; Meichenbaum & Novaco, 1977; Novaco, 1977

City traffic agents: Brondolo et al., 1998

Probation officers: Novaco, 1980

Treatment of Juvenile Offenders and Aggressive Adolescents

Anderson, 1994; Ashford et al., 2001; Blechman et al., 1995, 1999; Brestan & Eyeberg, 1998; Brondolo et al., 1994; Cornell et al., 1999; Davis & Boster, 1992; Dishion et al., 1999; Ecton & Feindler, 1990; Feindler, 1995; Feindler & Ecton, 1986; Feindler & Guttman, 1994; Goldstein, 1988, 1990; Goldstein et al., 1987; Hammond & Yung, 1991; Hanna et al., 1999; Hanna & Hunt, 1999; Henggeler et al., 1998; Hollin, 1999; Howells & Hall, 1989; Lipsky & Wilson, 1998; Lochman & Lenhart, 1993; Nugent, 1991; Ross & Fabiano, 1985; Tate et al., 1995; Wexler, 1991; Wilcox & Dorwick, 1992

Treatment of Violence in Schools and Residential Settings

Budlong et al., 1993; Feshbach et al., 1983; Howard et al., 1999; Long & Dorf, 1994; Long & Morse, 1996; Redl & Wineman, 1952; Stage & Quiroz, 1997; Swaffer & Hollin, 1997- Wood & Long, 1991

COGNITIVE BEHAVIORAL TREATMENT PROGRAM:
AN OVERVIEW OF A FOUR-PHASED TREATMENT APPROACH

*(Note, these treatments can be conducted on an
individual, couples, family and group basis.)*

PHASE I:
INITIAL EDUCATION AND CONCEPTUALIZATION

Establish a therapeutic alliance, build rapport and nurture trust (see DiGiuseppe, 1995; DiGiuseppe et al., 1994; Meichenbaum, 1994)

Conduct assessment procedures (Interview, self-report measures, self-monitoring) *(See the SECTION on Assessment strategy and measures p. 138.)*

Enhance the patient's personal awareness (Consider developmental and family of origin patterns; use imagery reconstruction, role playing.) Collaboratively explore and help the patient understand his anger and increase the patient's motivation for learning anger-reduction techniques.

Collaboratively develop a treatment rationale, an individualized case conceptualization and engage in mutual goal-setting. Note that the patient's goals are likely to change over the course of treatment. Underscore that the goals of treatment are to:

> *"learn how to manage anger and cope more effectively. The goal is anger reduction, not anger elimination. Frustrations, disappointments, hassles are part of life. How you handle them is what therapy is all about."*

In short, the therapist can say to the patient:

> *"We are trying to find out how things are now. How would you like them to be and what we can do to help you achieve these goals. We also need to find out what you have tried in the past so we can learn from those efforts".*

Educate patients about the components and functions of anger and its relationship to stress and aggression. Have the patient and therapist agree on acceptable goals and the means of treatment to achieve these goals. *(See the Section on Education below p. 253.)*

Consider the **nature and functions of anger** (Highlight that anger is a normal human reaction to a variety of perceived insults and that angry feelings have both positive and negative consequences.) **Negative** in the form of social, personal and physiological consequences (e.g., individuals with high levels of anger and hostility are at high risk for coronary heart disease). Anger can also have a **positive consequences** in terms of warning someone that something is wrong and that some form of self-protective action is called for or that there is a need to correct an injustice.

Develop an **individual profile** -- help the patient identify the chain of angry feelings, thoughts, and behaviors and obtain information about specific anger-evoking triggers. For example, have the patient tell or act out a "story" of the provocation-anger response. Along the way, ask the patient about:

Triggers -- physical, emotional, cognitive, behavioral (sources of anger and accompanying beliefs) *"What lights the patient's fuse?"*

Early warning signs – intra- and interpersonal cues that indicate he is becoming angry and that his behavior is escalating toward violence

Setting events -- identify high risk situations (where, when, with whom) and **pre-anger states**

Role of exacerbating factors -- alcohol, drugs, presence of peers

Role of coping responses -- ways to help the patient identify existing "strengths" or abilities in anger management and conflict resolution. Ask the patient about a time that he felt angry or mad, but handled the anger in an "effective" and "reasonable" way.

Move to a problem-solving mode. Highlight that the patient has options in order to increase his sense of personal control.

a) **Intrapersonal** (e.g., what coping techniques used)

b) **Interpersonal** (e.g., discuss the value of sharing feelings about troubling events such as quarrels, relationship conflicts, or more serious incidents with a supportive listener -- see Pennebaker, 1992; Thomas, 1997)

Engage in collaborative mutual goal setting (short-term, intermediate and long-term goal setting -- *See the SECTION on Goal-setting below p. 227*).

Use bibliotherapy (See Clancy, 1990; Gottman et al., 1976; Mataskis, 1996; McKay et al., 1989; Sonkin & Durphy, 1984; Tavris, 1989; Thomas & Jefferson, 1996; Williams & Williams, 1993)

Note that the treatment plan should flow naturally from the assessment process and the collaboratively-generated case conceptualization. The treatment rationale should be in simple clear language that the patient can easily understand.

PHASE II:
SKILLS TRAINING AND STRESS INOCULATION TRAINING

Teach patients how to:

1) develop **self-control skills** (identify provocation situations to which they are vulnerable, self-management relaxation training, taking time out, self-instructional training by means of behavioral and imaginal rehearsal, cognitive-restructuring, role playing, and how to conduct practice in clinic and in vivo);

2) take **constructive action** on precipitants of anger <u>whenever possible</u> (problem solving, communication, bargaining, assertive, parenting, supervisory skills training);

3) employ **acceptance, distraction and emotional-soothing** coping techniques when no constructive action is possible (e.g., use vigorous physical exercise, talk about angry incidents with a confidant).

Arousal-reduction techniques including applied relaxation training -- use slow deep breathing, cue-controlled relaxation which includes the use of calming imagery and slowly repeating the word "relax" and relaxing more with each repetition. Help the patient learn how to switch off anger images and anger-engendering self-dialogue and learn to visualize relaxation images. (See Suinn & Deffenbacher, 1988 and Deffenbacher and McKay, 2000) *(Note, relaxation training usually precedes cognitive-based intervention by 2 or 3 sessions)*

Build in homework (address concerns about adherence - practice initially in nonstressful situations and then with a hierarchy of imaginal coping scenes). Eventually, **practice in vivo.** *(See Guidelines p. 169 on how to have patients do homework.)*

Use taking time out procedures *(see below p. 275)*

Use self-instructional training *(see below p. 281)* - patients are encouraged to generate their own self-statement package and self-control scripts

Use guided coping imagery training - use hierarchical scenarios from mildest to most anger-arousing

Use role playing ("barb" or challenge techniques) *(see below p. 329)*

Use stress inoculation training (See Meichenbaum, 1985; Novaco, 1977; Awalt et al., 1997)

Build in generalization or transfer procedures *(see below p. 335)*

PHASE III:
COGNITIVE RESTRUCTURING AND SOCIAL PROBLEM-SOLVING

Use cognitive restructuring or "rethinking" procedures -- focus on reappraisal and reframing; use evidence-based, alternatives, and implication questions; use Socratic questioning *(see below p. 299)* and a **two chair dialogue** to help the patient differentiate the two sides of a conflict.

Address the patients' beliefs about trust, fairness, injustice, entitlement (i.e., what they see as their "issues," values, convictions). View world as less conflict-oriented. *(See below p. 302)*

Use coping modeling procedures -- initially show videotapes of individuals losing control. Have patients analyze these scenes and then generate alternatives. Then show coping models handling the same situation. What is different between these two modeling films? Analyze and rehearse coping responses. Therapist can use think aloud and ask patients how angry they would feel if they were thinking in this manner. Consider alternative ways of thinking and behaving and possible benefits. Therapist can demonstrate and model anger coping responses in provocation situations that arise in therapy. *(See below p. 307)*

Problem-solving intervention (Goal, plan, do, check -- *see below p. 311*)

Social skills enhancement (listening, communicating, conflict resolution, assertiveness, bargaining to resolve a problem, parenting, supervisory skills.) Discuss what strategies to use at what phase of the de-escalation cycle (e.g., communication skills training -- *see below p. 317*).

Discuss the **"wisdom" of postponing discussion of conflictual issues** until a more opportune time

Use **humor as a way to vent anger**, but discuss when and how to use humor appropriately.

Use **application training** (imaginal role playing and behavioral rehearsal of simulated graduated exposure responses); apply coping skills under conditions of increased anger arousal, *"barb" techniques as described below*)

Train coping skills in conjunction with **progressive exposure** to graduated doses of provocation in a therapeutic setting and eventually in vivo.

Incorporate external prompts and **natural consequences** into the treatment program in **Generalization Guidelines** – *see below p. 339*.

Enlist peers and family members as "allies" in the treatment process. Encourage the patient to spend time with people who support the changes they are making.

PHASE IV:
REVIEW AND PLAN FOR THE FUTURE

Self-attribution procedures -- ensure that patients **"take credit"** and **"ownership"** for the changes they have implemented throughout the course of treatment *(see below p. 349)*

Relapse prevention procedures -- identify high-risk situations, early warning signs, and collaboratively develop plans and back-up plans of action; point out times of vulnerability to excess anger and examine and practice ways to handle lapses *(see below p. 355)*

Include a follow-through plan and booster sessions

TREATMENT FORMAT

The treatment should be applied in a **flexible manner,** <u>not</u> in a lock-step progression. **The length of treatment usually varies between 6 to 20 sessions.** The number and timing of the treatment sessions are individually tailored to the needs of the patient. In general, the sessions are:

(1) once a week and in more severe cases initially twice a week;

(2) eventually treatment is thinned out (every other week, once a month, once every 6 weeks, once every 2 months);

(3) supplemented with booster sessions - booster sessions can be conducted on an individual, group, couples, or family basis.

In some preventative programs, the trainers are individuals who previously have gone through the Cognitive behavioral training and who receive additional instructor's training. They are then employed to run groups of their colleagues. This intervention strategy has been used with such groups as police officers, marine drill instructors, veterans, and probation officers who work with adolescent offenders.

We will now consider some of the training procedures in more detail, namely, how therapists can:

1) **Develop a Therapeutic Alliance and Engage in Collaborative Goal-Setting**

2) **Educate About Anger**

3) **Teach Self-control Procedures such as Time -out Procedures**

4) **Conduct Self-instructional Training**

5) **Employ Cognitive Restructuring, "Rethinking", Letter Writing, Journaling and Problem-solving Interventions**

6) **Teach Communication Skills Training**

7) **Employ Application Training**

8) **Incorporate Self-Attribution Procedures**

9) **Conduct Relapse Prevention**

SUMMARY:
WHAT YOU SHOULD TAKE AWAY FROM SECTION IV

1. That the empirical basis for treatment of anger is limited, but promising. Secondly, that the treatment of anxiety and depression is more effective than anger.

2. That CBT interventions have been employed successfully with a variety of diverse populations both on a preventative and treatment basis.

3. That there are a set of :core tasks" that characterize all forms of psychotherapy (therapeutic alliance, self-attribution, relapse prevention and attending to the needs of traumatized patients).

4. That CBT are multifaceted and can be viewed as following four interdependent phases:

   (i)   initial education and conceptualization;
   (ii)   skills training and stress inoculation training;
   (iii)   cognitive restructuring and social problem-solving;
   (iv)   review and planning for the future, preparing for possible lapses.

TEST YOUR EXPERTISE: SECTION IV

1. A friend, relative, colleague comes to you and says, "I found a Website where you can take a course on anger management. Or at my workplace, church, they are giving a course on anger management. Just how effective are such anger management interventions?" How would you answer this question?

2. Relative to the treatment of other affective disorders (anxiety and depression), the treatment of patients with anger is <u>less effective</u>. Why do you think this is? What can be done to improve the treatment of patients with anger?

3. What percentage of your clientele has problems with anger-control? Does anger co-occur with other psychiatric disorders? How do you alter your assessment and treatment approaches when the issues of anger and aggression emerge?

4. What are the "core tasks" of conducting treatment with patients who have anger-control problems and who are aggressive? How can these "core tasks" be applied to the treatment of other comorbid disorders?

5. Outline the **4 phases** of cognitive-behavioral treatment of patients with anger-control problem. How are the "core tasks" of therapy incorporated within the treatment format?

SECTION V: INITIAL PHASE OF COGNITIVE BEHAVIORAL TREATMENT

This **SECTION** focuses on the **Initial Phase** of the cognitive behavioral intervention. The major task of this phase is to engage the patient in a **therapeutic alliance** and to **engender patient motivation to change**. Three specific procedures designed to achieve these objectives are reviewed, namely, how to:

(1) **develop a therapeutic alliance** even with patients who become **angry in therapy**;

(2) **collaboratively establish treatment goals**;

(3) **educate the patient**.

Although these therapeutic techniques are highlighted at the outset of therapy, they each play a critical role **throughout the entire therapy process**.

CONTENTS SECTION V

SPECIFIC COGNITIVE-BEHAVIORAL INTERVENTIONS: INITIAL PHASE

DEVELOPING A THERAPEUTIC ALLIANCE

(See Deffenbacher, 1998; Deffenbacher & McKay, 2000; DiGiuseppe et al., 1994; Meichenbaum, 1994)

"After approximately a half century of psychotherapy research, one of the most consistent findings is that the quality of the therapeutic alliance is the most predictive of treatment success. This finding has been evident across a wide range of treatment modalities." (Safran & Segal, 1990)

The finding that the quality of the therapeutic relationship has consistently been found to have the most significant impact on successful patient outcome presents a particular challenge to therapists who work with patients who have anger-control problems and who are aggressive. As Novaco and Chemtob (1998) observe, *"Angry people are often fiercely resistant to anger treatment."* (p. 171)

"Anger treatment requires great patience on the part of the therapist, which in part involves not fighting the client's resistance." (Robins & Novaco, 1999, p. 332)

People with severe anger problems are often very **resistant to change**. They believe their anger and aggression are justified, appropriate, and caused by other people or by external events. They tend to portray themselves as "helpless victims" who are overwhelmed by the "energy" of anger. They are often distrustful, suspicious, and combative. They view their anger as automatic and as being out of their control. They deny their responsibility for their actions and minimize the effects on others and on themselves. A major challenge for the therapist is how to develop a working therapeutic alliance with resistant patients who can be confrontative, if not threatening, and who may have engaged in aggressive behavior that is disturbing to the therapist.

There are no easy answers to these challenging questions. But in spite of any reservations (countertransference concerns) the task for the therapist, if he/she is to be successful, is to develop a **therapeutic working alliance**, a sense of "we-ness", instead of a "you versus me" attitude. The therapist needs to create a setting, in which the patient feels **safe**, **supported**, and **heard**. As Ornstein (1999, p. 291) observed:

"The therapist must listen as an ally to the subjective inner world of the patient."

The therapist needs to be **emotionally attuned** and **empathetically responsive** with their patients. The therapist needs to communicate an understanding of the patient's perspective and to provide patients with a **corrective emotional experience** that allows them to examine in depth, with emotion, their anger and aggressive behaviors. The focus is on what the patients can do to manage their anger. The therapist needs to draw a distinction between the unacceptable behaviors that the patient engaged in without considering the patient to be an unacceptable person. By means of conveying empathy, respect, understanding and being nonjudgmental, the therapist can nurture the patient's potential for change. As Strupp (1995, p. 5) has observed:

> *"Empathy is the single most important human and technical tool at the therapist's disposal."*

The therapist can accomplish these objectives by:

(1) <u>listening</u> in a <u>nonjudgmental respectful fashion</u> to the patient's account and **acknowledging the reasons** why the patient is coming to therapy;

(2) <u>conveying empathy</u> for the patient's sense of being treated unfairly (see the world through the patient's eyes, searching to understand the patient's developmental experiences and beliefs that contribute to anger problems); *"I can appreciate the anger and frustration that X creates when he does Y. That is a real hassle." "I would find it hard not to get angry if X occurred. So you have important reasons to ..."; "I understand that you find it really upsetting and frustrating when others do X."*;

(3) <u>conveying understanding</u> of the patient's sense of having been treated unfairly; being affectively attuned; *"As <u>we</u> have both noticed ..."; "As I know you are aware of ..."*;

(4) <u>acknowledging</u> the patient's anger by <u>validating the legitimacy</u> of the cause of his anger -- explore the nature of the provocations and the negative events that evoked anger. Indicate that the patient *has "every right" to feel angry, given what he experienced*;

(5) ask the patient <u>what he did with his anger</u>. As noted, it is useful to treat the patient's emotion of anger **as commodity or product** that he does something with (e.g., stuff it, suppress it, displace it, drink it away, act out. The therapist can thus acknowledge the patient's right to feel angry, but explore what is the impact of handling anger in such a fashion.). Over the course of therapy the patient can learn how to accept, tolerate and transform anger into a problem-to-be-solved, rather than view anger as an emotion resulting from a perceived provocation and personal threat.

(6) **exploring the consequences** of the patient's anger/aggression for self and for to others. *"What is the impact, the toll, the price of anger/aggression?"; (As noted previously, if the patient says, "I don't know", the therapist can say, "I don't know either. How can we go about finding out, and moreover, why would finding out be helpful to you in achieving your goals?")*;

(7) **assessing the patient's current goals** -- Why is the patient here now; Who is most bothered about the anger problem; What has the patient tried in the past; How will the current attempt to help differ from previous attempts?;

(8) **collaboratively generating** specific possible **treatment goals**;

(9) **developing a shared understanding** of the patient's problems and treatment goals and a jointly agreed upon means to achieve these goals; entering these "narrative text" of the patient, using the patient's generated metaphors and collaboratively "sculpting" new mutually-generated "healing metaphors";

(10) **developing a common language of concepts and terms** that provide the tools for practical application; use the language of a "personal scientist" … "explore, discover, predict, test out, monitor, evaluate" *(see pp. 313)*;

(11) conveying that the patient and therapist can work together **as a team**; the therapist can help **bolster the patient's self-confidence** as the therapist highlights and appreciates what the patient brings to therapy (i.e., a set of survival skills and other strengths);

(12) **continuously monitoring and checking** as to whether the therapist has understood the patient's aims correctly and is making progress;

(13) **addressing** any **"ruptures"** in the ongoing therapeutic relationship. The therapist is **persistent**, not give up in the face of the patient's failure or resistance.

Throughout this process, the therapist should try and help the patient put into words what he/she is experiencing. When the therapist paraphrases or summarizes what the patient said, the therapist's comments should be offered in a **tentative collaborative manner** in the form of **hypotheses worthy of testing**. The therapy process should be a two-way street, as patients are **given opportunities to ask questions and provide feedback.**

A **guided participation model** is used throughout treatment. (See Patterson & Chamberlain, 1994; Sanders & Lawton, 1993) The therapist's style is captured by the popular television character **Detective Columbo**, played by Peter Falk. Columbo-style questions are collaborative in nature, as the actor Peter Falk uses his bemusement and befuddlement and his desire to understand as a means of inquiry.

It sounds like ... Does that fit with your view of things?.

Can you help me understand .... ? Can you say more about ... ?

I'm puzzled about ... Are you saying ... ?

It makes me wonder if ... What occurs to me is ...

I can't help but think .... As I see it ...

It seems that (as if) ... My sense is that ...

I am wondering if maybe ... Any sense of what might be going on?

If I'm understanding you properly...

Am I reading you right? ... Am I correct in assuming that ... ?

Is this a good description of what you were saying?

Does it seem to you that I heard what you said correctly?

Have I understood how you see the situation?

Are these the main concerns, as you see them?

Where was I off track? See if I am understanding.

It seems like you are working on X, but Y seems to get in the way. Is this the way you see it?

Could it be that ... ? At the risk of simplifying, it sounds like ...

Let me put things a little differently and see what you think .... Is that about right?

How does that sound to you?

If I'm understanding you properly, what you are saying is ...

Bear with me. I'm struggling to hear you correctly. I want to understand where you are coming from.

The therapist can **nurture the collaborative** process by saying:

I am willing to follow your lead right now. Any sense of what would be a useful way of going about … ?

You have given me a good idea about how to …

What you are saying right now sounds very important to you. Can you tell me more about … ?

Are you open to exploring X a little more?

Do you think it would be useful to try … ?

Somehow the piece we have to figure out is how to help you decide to (develop, try out) …

What do you think of the idea … ?

Are you saying you need to try … ?

Are you aware of whether you … ? What choices do you have?

What might happen if …?

Do you have an awareness (appreciation) of doing anything to interfere with … ?

Is there any way you can make the situation much worse?

On the one hand you say (feel, think, do) X, but on the other hand you do Y. Help me see how these things go together.

Is this something (a project) you could work on?

Does that make sense?

Do you have any questions?

The therapist can **validate** the patient's experience and at the same time **move** the patient **along the change process**. For instance, the therapist can say:

> *I can see how you would feel ...*
>
> *I understand that it was really frustrating and inconvenient to ...*
>
> *It sounds like people at work (home) don't do things the way you like.*
>
> *What makes this important is ... Is that correct?*
>
> *I am __not__ suggesting that you don't have a right to feel hurt and upset about what happened to you. I am only suggesting that __we__ can work together so you can learn ways to control your anger and develop more effective ways to achieve your goals.*

The therapist can also help to **nurture hope**, by asking:

> *Are you saying that you have more resources to deal with him when you lower your anger?*
>
> *Based on your experience (disappointment, dissatisfaction) with previous therapy, how will our working together be different?*

The therapist can **"go public with the data"** and check out his/her observations in a tentative fashion, conveying a desire to understand the patient's experience. In this way the patient can have access to the therapist's reasoning. The therapist can share hypotheses, inferences, and his/her effort at understanding. As a key part of "going pubic with the data," the patient is given the opportunity to ask questions and provide feedback.

> *Let me see if I understand. You are X because he/she did Y. You seem to make a habit of doing Z.*
>
> *I am noticing that ... It seems to me that ... Have you noticed that as well?*
>
> *There is an expression on your face that makes me think you are feeling .... Help me out. Are you feeling that way or am I off base?*
>
> *I have a sense that I am starting to get you angry because I noticed ... Is that indeed the case?*

In **summary**, the purpose of each of these therapeutic strategies of

   a) actively listening;

   b) conveying empathy and understanding;

   c) validating the patient's experience;

   d) engaging the patient in the therapy goal-setting process;

   e) nurturing hope;

   f) prompting and modeling anger management strategies;

is to **foster a collaborative therapeutic alliance** and help motivate the patient to change. The need for these **engagement enhancing** therapeutic strategies was highlighted in the discussion of the high treatment nonadherence of batterers *(SECTION II, p. 104)*. The following list summarizes the behavioral features of **high** versus **low motivated** patients. Since **motivation to change** is such an important predictor of treatment involvement and treatment adherence, some investigators such as Prochaska and DiClemente (1986) and Levesque et al. (2000) have suggested that patients' go through so-called stages of change. Before embracing a transtheoretical model of such stages, the interested reader should consider the critical analysis of the Stage Models of Change offered by Bandura (1998), Davidson (1998) and Sutton (2000).

INDICATIONS OF <u>HIGH</u> MOTIVATION TO CHANGE

- Came to treatment on own initiative

- Conveys that he has a "problem" or acknowledges difficulties or perceives need for treatment

- Conveys interest and desire to change

- Collaborates in establishing treatment goals – is helpful

- Makes a commitment willingly to put out effort to work on treatment goals

- Responds favorably to notion that change "won't be easy"

- Views symptoms (problematic behaviors) as being psychologically-based and acknowledges own contribution to problems

- Expresses belief that therapy (training) can provide an opportunity for self-exploration and behavior change

- Has a past record of benefiting from treatment (training)

- Actively taking steps to address personal problems

- Expresses positive value in treatment and expresses belief (hope) in its efficacy

- Willing to make sacrifices for therapy (training) (e.g., investment of time of money)

- Performs "homework" assignments (e.g., self-monitoring)

- Views therapy (training) as "learning process" and views lapses as "learning opportunities"

- Has significant others who support and nurture change (e.g., willing to become involved in treatment, help with homework)

- Worries about lapsing and is willing to take steps to anticipate and address potential barriers to change

- Able to teach (share) "lessons" of what is learned in treatment with others

INDICATIONS OF <u>LOW</u> MOTIVATION TO CHANGE

- Treatment is mandated and treatment (training) is perceived as being imposed against one's will

- Expresses unwillingness to change

- View aggression (antisocial behavior) as part of definition of who they are and not see they have a problem

- Presence of rigid belief system that views aggression as central and instrumental to achieving personal goals (e.g., morbid jealousy, racial hatred, religions zealot, cultural norm of seeking revenge)

- Aggression part of cultural and community norms ("code of honor:, "code of the streets")

- Externalizes blame – denial and blame others

- Absence of guilt, shame, remorse, empathy (callous)

- Evidences cognitive deficits

- Lacks self-reflective skills (impulsive)

- Avoidant coping style

- Abuses substances

- Absence of helpful others or others who may undermine or interfere with treatment progress

- Past history of resisting help (history of treatment nonadherence)

- Not foresee any possible impediments (obstacles) or challenges to change

- Payoff for aggressive behaviors (e.g., valued by peer group, presence of "secondary gains")

COLLABORATIVE GOAL-SETTING

The ability of patients and therapists to agree on the treatment goals and the means by which such goals can be achieved has been seen as central to the development of a therapeutic alliance and to the nurturing of hope (Safran & Segal, 1990; Schaap et al., 1993). The purpose of this **SECTION** is to describe how therapists can:

1) **educate patients** about the nature of goal-setting and **provide guidelines** for effective goal-setting;

2) use the **"art of questioning"** as a means to help patients formulate and follow-through on goal-setting;

3) **nurture hope** as a result of goal-setting *(Snyder, 2000, has discussed <u>hope</u> as a form of <u>goal-directed thinking</u>).* (The chronic state of goal blockage leads to despair, depression which in turn can lead to anger and hostility. *"Hostility reflects the death of hope"* Crowson et al., 2001, p. 251);

4) help patients **use worksheets** to formulate, implement and evaluate their treatment goals.

Educating Patients About the Nature of Goal-Setting

In order for goal-setting to be effective it is important to educate patients about the importance of goal-setting and to provide guidelines of what features contribute to effective and ineffective goal-setting. The therapist can begin by asking patients whether (when) they have established goals for themselves and for others in the past and how successful were the patients in achieving their goals. For example, the therapist can ask the patients if he has ever set New Year's Resolutions. How effective were the patients in achieving their goals? What worked? What did not work? Why?

In the course of this discussion, the therapist can incorporate the following definition:

> *A <u>goal</u> is something someone wants to obtain or*
> *something someone wants to have happen and is willing*
> *to work to get it. Goals are behavioral objectives that can*
> *be measured.*

In this discussion draw a distinction between those things that can change and those things that cannot be changed because we do <u>not</u> have control over them.

The therapist can convey that in order for goals to be effective and achievable, the patients' goals should be:

(1) collaboratively set, clear positive goals that the patients value and that can be related back to overall treatment goals;

(2) specific and behaviorally-defined;

(3) doable (not too difficult to preclude success; refine goals into a series of sub-goals or steps); match goals to patient's abilities;

(4) manageable (3 to 5 goals to be worked on at any one time) and prioritized; break long-term goals into smaller substeps;

(5) stated in approach terms (i.e., what the patients wish to achieve, as compared to goals that are designed to avoid aversive or negative events);

(6) personally meaningful in order to motivate patients to put out the necessary effort and persist (i.e., underscore that it is the trying, the effort, that is crucial); as training progresses, include "we" goals as well as "me" goals;

(7) relevant, leading to desirable short-term, intermediate and long-term consequences;

(8) incorporate "stretch goals" – goals that increase and challenge the patients by building on abilities, talents and previous performance;

The therapist should:

(9) remind patients of other times when they summoned the motivation to achieve goals and handle roadblocks;

(10) help patients create a mental script of the chain of activities required to achieve goals;

(11) help patients view barriers as challenges and a normal part of life, rather than as failures -- barriers are normal and are to be expected; view failures as a result of ineffective strategies, lack of adequate practice, insufficient training, rather than as an occasion to blame oneself;

(12) encourage patients to focus on one goal at a time, monitor and record progress, and take credit for improvements; chart progress, not do upward comparisons;

(13) take time-outs from pursuing their goals.

The therapist can use **questions** *(See Table 10-19)* and a **Patient Handout / Worksheet** to help patients think about how they can achieve their treatment goals and reflect on their willingness to:

> *Find acceptable methods of <u>displaying</u> anger; learn ways*
> *to use and <u>transform</u> their anger, instead of suppressing*
> *their anger or acting out; <u>accept</u>, <u>tolerate</u> and <u>control</u>*
> *their anger so they do <u>not</u> behaviorally escalate to the*
> *point of aggression.*

The following set of **therapist questions** can be used to help patients collaboratively establish, plan and work toward achieving their treatment goals. The questions cover the following areas of how to:

Table 10	**(p. 230)**	**DEFINE TREATMENT GOALS**
Table 11	**(p. 230)**	**HIGHLIGHT THE SITUATIONAL VARIABILITY: WAYS OF NURTURING HOPE**
Table 12	**(p. 231)**	**PRIORITIZE GOALS**
Table 13	**(p. 231)**	**ENHANCE MOTIVATION**
Table 14	**(p. 232)**	**GET GOING**
Table 15	**(p. 232)**	**ASSESS AND BOLSTER CONFIDENCE**
Table 16	**(p. 233)**	**ELICIT COMMITMENT STATEMENTS**
Table 17	**(p. 234)**	**ELICIT SELF-MOTIVATIONAL STATEMENTS**
Table 18	**(p. 235)**	**NOTICE POSSIBLE CHANGES THAT THEY CAN BRING ABOUT IN THE FUTURE**
Table 19	**(p. 235)**	**ASSESS THEIR UNDERSTANDING AND COMPREHENSION OF THE TREATMENT RATIONALE**

Table 10
QUESTIONS TO HELP PATIENTS <u>DEFINE TREATMENT GOALS</u>

How would you like to change?

Exactly what changes would you most like to see?

What goals do you think <u>we</u> should be working on in treatment / training?

Does this goal involve changes about yourself, or involve changes in others, or both?

Do these goals involve things that are under your control?

Therapy is like <u>taking a trip</u>. It goes better if you have a good road map and you know where you are going. It would be helpful if you would put in your own words where you would like to go in therapy. Draw a map for both of us of what you would like to achieve in therapy.

Let's consider a few alternative goals before you settle on one or two goals to work on first.

Table 11
QUESTIONS DESIGNED TO HIGHLIGHT <u>SITUATIONAL VARIABILITY</u>: WAYS OF <u>NURTURING HOPE</u>

As you describe your problems, I am wondering whether they are always the same or do the problems change? (Sometimes, is it worse than at other times?)

Are there some times that you can handle your anger better than at other times?

What is different when things are <u>not</u> as bad or when you are <u>not</u> experiencing X ?

Are there small pieces of this desired behavior that are already occurring? What do you need to do to make it happen more? How can you build on what you already know and do?

Our discussing (exploring) the occasions or exceptions when your anger does <u>not</u> get out of hand (or is <u>not</u> as bad) may lead us to find some solutions. We want to learn what you are doing to control your anger.

For now don't change anything; just keep track (notice) when things are better (or when the exceptions occur).

Table 12
QUESTIONS DESIGNED TO HELP PATIENTS PRIORITIZE GOALS

Are there goals you should tackle right away?

Of the different aspects of your life that we have been discussing, what are the two or three things that you want to focus on in therapy?

Which goals would make the most improvement in your life?

I think I am getting a sense of what you want to work on in therapy, but I would like to make sure. Would you please list the goals that you have for therapy. Please be as specific as you can be.

Which of the many goals that you can work on is the most important to you at this time? ... Why?

Are there any subgoals we should be working on first?

How long do you think it will take to achieve each subgoal?

Are these goals "realistic," "doable" (potentially achievable)?

Table 13
QUESTIONS DESIGNED TO ENHANCE MOTIVATION TO CHANGE

What is different when the problem is absent or manageable?

How would you like for things to be different?

If you were completely successful in accomplishing what you want in therapy, what would be changed? What specifically would you like to feel or do differently?

How would things be different if you followed this idea and did X? ... or did not do Y? Or if you got support with ...?

What difference could it make to you (or others) if you were free of this problem?

If you succeed in achieving this goal, what else do you think might happen?

Have you asked yourself what will happen, what are the "risks", if things don't change? If that is the way you see it, then what do you think should be done?

How could we tell if our working together was successful? What would have to be accomplished?

At a minimum, what would you hope to have happen as a result of our working together?

What would you be doing differently if you reached this goal?

Can you imagine a time in the future when this problem is reduced (resolved)? What would that be like? How will your life be different?

Is it possible that you could look at this as a "project" you are taking on? How could you go about doing that?

What suggestions, if any, would you have on how we can improve the training program?

Table 14
QUESTIONS DESIGNED TO HELP PATIENTS <u>GET GOING</u>

What do you need to do first before this final goal is possible?
What are one or two things you should do first?
Is there anything else that you think is important to add to this list?
How can you break your goals into a smaller number of steps?
It sounds like what you'd like to do is ... Have I heard you correctly?
If this were a friend's goal, what would you advise him/her to do to get started?
People tend to recall their goals better if they know where they are and can specify
*   their goals clearly. As best you can, would you please describe your goals for*
*   therapy and describe how I can help you get there. .... Now we can consider how*
*   you can get going.*
Please share with me how you came to choose these treatment goals.

Table 15
QUESTIONS DESIGNED TO <u>ASSESS</u> AND <u>BOLSTER CONFIDENCE</u>

How confident do you feel you will be able to do X?
How sure are you, say on a 1 to 10 scale, that you can keep doing what you are doing?
What things might get in the way of your being able to follow through on this?
What can you do (or with the help of others) about this problem?
How sure do you think your family (friends) are that you can keep doing X ? What do
*   you think makes them confident? What would make them more confident about*
*   your doing Y ?*
You mentioned that you might forget to do X. How do you generally remember to do
*   something that is important? What kind of reminders have you been using to solve*
*   the problem so far?*
If you were to wake up tomorrow with complete confidence in your abilities to handle
*   X, what would you be able to do differently?*
It sounds like what you'd like to do is ... , but you're afraid that such and such will
*   happen. Is that the way you see it? If so, then what can <u>we</u> do to help you with*
*   that?*

Table 16
QUESTIONS DESIGNED TO <u>ELICIT COMMITMENT STATEMENTS</u>

What will it take in order for you to do Y ?
How would you know if the effort was worth it?
How long do you think it will take to accomplish this goal?
What would it take for you to do X ?
Would you be willing to do X?
So, are you saying that you are willing to try doing Y ? Is that what you are saying?
Are you saying, and I want to make sure that I get this straight, that you would
*   be able to: (Therapist chooses from this list.)*

  (1) notice when you are in that situation (or entering a high risk situation, or
  *   when you are beginning to work yourself up);*
  (2) catch yourself and interrupt the cycle before it gets out of hand;
  (3) follow your game plan and use your coping strategy, which consists of ... ;
  (4) put out the effort to try;
  (5) monitor or keep track of how it is going;
  (6) review how it went with ... ;
  (7) pat yourself on the back or reinforce yourself for having tried, having put
  *   out the effort, and having tried out your strategy (game plan).*

That is impressive! I look forward to seeing how it works. I expect you do, as well.

Table 17
QUESTIONS DESIGNED TO ELICIT SELF-MOTIVATIONAL STATEMENTS

I don't know if this would be too difficult for you, but ...
Maybe this is asking too much of you.
A training program like this one requires a lot of motivation and effort. I'm not sure if this is too much to ask at this time. We usually don't get to this point in this training program until much later, if at all.
Of the things we have discussed, which are the most important reasons to change?
How are you going to do that in spite of ... ?
Of these different options, which one would you choose? How did you choose to select that one? I would have guessed you would have chosen the easier option. You continually surprise me.
Are you saying, are you telling yourself, that in spite of X, you are willing to try (be able to do Y)? Is that what you are saying? How will you go about doing that?
If you are not ready then I don't think you should make a commitment (promise) to do Y. This is too important to decide now.
I respect your decision not to do X, but I want your decision to be as fully informed as possible. I want to make sure that you have taken into account all of the factors involved. Can we talk about (write out) the pros and cons of changing? What would be the short-term and long-term consequences? (Use a decisional balance sheet of pros and cons, short and long-term consequences.)
Note, that this will take considerable work on both of our parts, but it will be worth it. Are you up to committing yourself to this effort? It should prove to be a fascinating and worthwhile journey to take together.
Okay, let's look at where we can go from here.

Table 18
**QUESTIONS DESIGNED TO HELP PATIENTS <u>NOTICE POSSIBLE CHANGES</u>
THAT THEY CAN BRING ABOUT <u>IN THE FUTURE</u>**

What would be the first signs that you are making progress or improving?
What small steps would show you that you were inching toward your goal?
*What one change in your behavior (or other's behavior), even if it were a small
    change, would show you that you are on the right track?*
How will you know you are making progress? What will be different in your life?
*What changes would let you know that you (others) are trying and that things are
    moving in the right direction?*
*What would your (husband, wife, child) have to do, even one small thing, to show that
    he/she is willing to work things out with you?*
*Who else would notice such changes? How would they tell? What would they notice?
    How might they react to such changes? What would you do then?*
How would you feel about these changes?
How would you know when your subgoals and goals have been achieved?

Table 19
**QUESTIONS DESIGNED TO ASSESS PATIENT'S <u>UNDERSTANDING</u> AND
<u>COMPREHENSION</u> OF THE <u>TREATMENT RATIONALE</u>**

*Let me try to pull together what we have been discussing .... Does this capture what we
    agreed to as you see it?*
*Are you with me so far concerning what we are going to do and why? Any questions
    or comments?*
*Please take a moment and describe <u>in your own words</u> what we have agreed to work on
    and, most importantly, why.*
Do you have any ideas about how you might do that?
*Does this make sense and sound like something you would like to try (do)? Do you
    have any doubts or concerns about the treatment plan (about the conflict
    resolution skills you will be learning)?*

PATIENT HANDOUT:
GOAL STATEMENTS

A useful way to translate the patient-therapist discussion into a series of concrete steps is to have patients fill-out the following worksheet. The therapist can **use a portion** of these goal-statements, tailored to the specific patient.

GOAL STATEMENTS

My goal(s) is: *(Be specific and focus on goals pertaining to self.)*

Exactly what changes would I like to see?

The reason(s) I chose this goal is or why these goals are important is:

The evidence that my goal is "doable" or "realistic" is:

My specific game-plan to achieve this goals is:

Are there small pieces of my goals that are already occurring? What do I need to do to make it happen more?

The advice I would give someone else who wants to achieve this goal is:

How can I break my goals into a series of subgoals to work on one at a time?

How can I get started? What small change can I make to begin with?

What skills and strategies do I have for accomplishing this goal?

How hard am I willing to work to achieve my goals?

How would I know if I am making progress and if my goal was achieved? What specific changes would I observe?

Who else would notice the changes? What would he/she observe and likely say? How will I react?

What has kept me from accomplishing this goal until now?

What possible barriers or obstacles to progress can I anticipate?

What is my game-plan to anticipate, address, and avoid these potential barriers?

What things should I look out for, so if I encounter them then I can be prepared (Include in my goal statements "Lookout for", "If .. then" and "Whenever, … I will do, say" statements).

How can I build in reminders to follow through in carrying out my plans?

With whom can I share these goals and game plans so I can make a public commitment to change to someone who is important to me?

Let me review, once again, the reasons why I should work to achieve these goals (conduct a `cost-benefit analysis, pros and cons, short-term, long-term for working on these goals).

Whenever I feel myself losing confidence in myself or in my ability to achieve my goals what can I do?

How can I take credit for the changes I have made? What specifically have I done to bring about change?

How can I reward myself for having tried and for my efforts to change?

In order to <u>solicit</u> the patient's <u>commitment</u> to work on implementing his goals, the therapist can:

(1) <u>ask a series of questions</u> that increase the likelihood that the <u>patient</u> will <u>come up with the suggestions</u> of what should be done next *[N.B. As a therapist, I believe I am at my therapeutic best when the patients I see are one step ahead of me offering the advice I would otherwise offer.]*;

(2) provide a <u>rationale</u> of why it is important to set goals:

> *"It is important that we set goals for change so we know what we are working towards and establish a way to determine whether we are making progress."*

(3) have the patient indicate what he is <u>going to do</u> and <u>why</u>;

(4) have the patient <u>set rules</u> to follow in order to achieve their goals;

(5) have the patient <u>verbalize aloud</u> or <u>write out</u> in a decisional balance sheet (2 x 2 box of pros and cons, short-term and long-term gains) the possible consequences of achieving his goals;

(6) play "<u>devil's advocate</u>" and challenge the patient as to why he would want to change (patient self-generated reasons are much more powerful in nurturing commitment than the therapist directing the change process);

(7) use "<u>foot-in-the-door</u>" procedures before requiring bigger changes);

(8) give patient <u>choices</u> -- highlight the patient's freedom to choose;

(9) help the patient <u>connect</u> present commitments with prior commitments;

(10) have the patient make a <u>public commitment</u> to other members of the group, as well as to significant others in their lives;

(11) have the patient <u>reinforce himself</u> for following through.

(See Meichenbaum and Turk, 1987, for a discussion of various intervention strategies to facilitate treatment adherence.)

GOAL ATTAINMENT SCALING

As noted in the **Case Conceptualization Model**, a central feature of goal-setting is collaboratively formulating with patients a systematic way to prioritize and evaluate progress. Kiresuk (1990) has developed an evaluation procedure whereby progress toward individualized treatment goals can be assessed. Sanders and Ralph (2001) have adapted this procedure in the form of **Goal Achievement Scales** where the patient and therapist first negotiate and subsequently evaluate the rate of change for each target behavior or goal on a five point scale of 0% (no change), 25%, 50%, 75% and 100% (maximum change). Behavioral criteria for the level of change in the target behavior (e.g., reduction of aggressive behaviors, production of prosocial positive changes, emotional self-regulation) are specified and monitored on a weekly basis.

HOW THE THERAPIST CAN RESPOND WHEN THE PATIENT BECOMES ANGRY

(Adapted from APA Training Tape, 1998; Dalenberg, 2000 a, b; Deffenbacher, 1999; Matsakis, 1998; Meichenbaum, 1994)

Sometimes patients will express intense anger responses during therapy sessions. As Novaco and Chemtob (1998, p. 173) observe:

> *"Composure on the part of the therapist is <u>imperative</u> for enhancing the therapeutic relationship, as well as for clinical safety. Treatment of angry clients requires the mastery of anxiety about assaultive risk. This requires sharpened awareness, safe arrangement of physical surroundings, training in personal protection and having a security response to crisis."*

How can therapists respond to such angry outbursts?

1. The therapist needs to **maintain composure** in the context of a safe and secure environment. (See the list of **DO'S** and **DON'TS** about how to respond to angry and potentially violent patients.) *(p. 192)*

2. **Convey empathy** for the patient's situation without approving his use of aggression. For example, the therapist can say:.

> *"Given what you have experienced (gone through, had happen), I can well understand what would lead you to become so angry."*
>
> *"I can't say I know what it feels like to experience (suffer) X, but I can see how it would lead to ..."*
>
> *"Help me understand, of all the different things you could have done with your anger, how did you choose Y?"*

The therapist in a **nonjudgmental fashion** can **acknowledge** and **validate** the patient's anger.

3. **Assess** the level of the patient's current level of anger. For example, the therapist .

> *"Tell me what you are feeling right now."*

> *"Can you tell me how angry you are feeling right now?"*

> *"How much distress, 'emotional pain' are you in right now?"*

> *"Have you ever been this angry before? What happened? Are you feeling that same way now?"*

> *"You seem very tense and upset. Is there some way I can be of help?"*

> *"I feel like I am involved in a struggle with you and I am not sure what is going on. Does this connect with your experience?"*

> *"Apart from the anger, is there anything else you are concerned about?"*

4. The patient and the therapist need to consider the patient's **chain of thoughts, feelings and behaviors** and **resultant interpersonal consequences**. The therapist should take the **patient's perspective** of feeling harmed, being treated unjustly, feeling hurt, helpless and frustrated. The therapist can **say**:

> *"I am troubled by your anger. If we can talk about this problem then we may come up with a solution."*

> *"I really want to understand; I want us <u>both</u> to understand what got you so angry. Let's look at what happened, and the order in which the events occurred.*

> *"I haven't done anything to get you angry, as far as I know. Is that indeed the case? I wonder whom you are really mad at. Help me understand what got you so mad. What happened?*

5. The therapist can convey that the patient's current anger and outburst **provide** us with an **"opportunity"** to better understand what gets him so angry. **Commend the patient** for feeling safe enough in therapy to get in touch with his feelings and for feeling comfortable enough to express them. For example, the therapist can say:

> *"Do you think you can help us both by telling me specifically what you saw me do that was so X (upsetting, frustrating, etc.)?"*

> *"I would like to spend a little bit of time trying to understand what is going on between us right now. My hope is that this type of exploration will provide us with some clues as to what may go on for you in your relationships with other people."*

> *"How did that make you feel? I am wondering, does this happen when you are with ... ? What do others see when all this is going on? Is that always the case? Any exceptions?*

> *"Ok. Let's agree that X (the target of the patient's anger) probably should have behaved differently. Right now, though, you are too angry to think through what you'd like to do about it. Let's try using some of those self-calming exercises first and then we'll talk about X." (Dalenberg, 2000, p. 42)*

> *"I know that I (disappointed, upset, hurt) you and I hope we can try to work it out. That matters to me. But right now you are sending me a message that our whole relationship is in jeopardy, instead of just letting us be angry at each other for a short time. I end up being worried about your threat of destroying our relationship that I stop thinking about the thing I originally did wrong." (Dalenberg, 2000, p. 44)*

6. The therapist can even go one step further and **commend** the patient for being angry. I am reminded when I was a consultant to a Veterans' (VA) hospital and I was asked to meet with a group of belligerent patients. Immediately, the group of patients verbally attacked me and offered numerous complaints about the VA system. Imagine you were in my shoes. How would you have responded to this group of angry verbally assaultive patients? My reactions was to say:

> *"Whew, what a relief! You know, before I came in here I was told that each and everyone of you guys were 'emotional deadwood'. The fact that you can attack a stranger indicates just how much you are in touch with your feelings ..You hold onto your indignation, your sense of unfairness, and your desire to make things right. In fact, there are features of the system that may be much worse than you are considering."*

The task for the therapists is to help patients reframe their anger as a **call to constructive action**, to change or improve the situation.. This leads to a discussion of the patient's **goals** and various **means** (including aggression) to achieve them. (Note, the patients are not likely to give up their indignation anyway, so it is wise for the therapist to 'go with' and use the patients' reactions.)

These **Guidelines** are consistent with Miller and Rollnick's (1991) suggestion that therapists should view their patient's **resistance as ambivalence**. They encourage therapists to *"roll with the resistance",* rather than be confrontative. By means of using **open-ended questions** followed by **reflection** and **empathic understanding**, the therapist can formulate a therapeutic alliance. For example, the therapist can observe:

> *"You have talked about not reoffending. I can see that you are <u>not</u> happy with (be specific). Is that the way you see it? Can you tell me more about your concerns? What part of what you are now doing <u>does not make sense to you</u> and leads you to be <u>dissatisfied</u>?*

Instead of trying to persuade the patient and providing the reasons to change, the therapist should encourage the patient to present arguments for change. By starting with where the patient is and finding out the patient's position, the therapist can engage the patient in generating suggestions and reasons for change. As noted, the Socratic **"art of questioning"** (using "Columbo-like probes" instead of the therapist being a "surrogate frontal lobe") can be used to foster change and overcome patient resistance.

7. To reiterate, the therapist can help patients view their feelings of anger as a **"commodity"** or **"product"** and ask them what they do with their anger. Patients may indicate that they "stuff it, drink it away, explode, avoid, etc.".. Once again, the therapist can have patients **examine the short-term and long-term impact** (toll, price) of handling their anger in such a fashion.

> *"Is the anger and accompanying aggression getting the patients all that they want?"*

8. Yet, another way to have patients consider their personal goals is to conduct both a **chain analysis** and a **situational analysis** as to whether the anger evident in the therapy session is also evident in the patients' everyday experiences. The therapist can ask, *"What is common across these different situations?"* Consider common triggers, underlying hurts, common reactions of others, etc. Analyze the chain of feelings, thoughts, behaviors that contribute to the present anger and whether a similar **pattern** occurs outside of therapy.

9. Conduct a **developmental analysis** exploring, *"How long has this (be specific) been going on? What contributes and helps to maintain your anger?"* As in the case of the situational analysis, the developmental analysis provides an opportunity for the patients to consider the anger episode in terms of "triggers", "secondary emotions", and a "vicious cycle" of appraisal, feelings, thoughts, behaviors and reactions of others.

10. Use **humor** and **self-disclosure** appropriately. Help the patients to learn to laugh at themselves and their personal predicaments. The therapist can use self-disclosure, sharing **teaching stories** (often humorous) that provide a framework for change. My favorite teaching story is included below *(p. 247).*

11. Comment that later in treatment having the patients **re-experience their anger** in the session will prove very helpful. Such anger episodes indicate that the patients are **good candidates** for the treatment. The therapist can express particular concern for those individuals who are not in touch with their feelings and who suppress their anger. Help the patients view their anger expressions as a **favorable prognostic indicator**.

12. If the patient's anger is too intense and threatening to engage in these steps then the use of taking a "time out" should be considered. Another possibility is attempting to **defuse** the patient in "crisis" to help him become a better problem-solver. See **Appendix A** for a detailed description of **how to "defuse" an individual's anger**.

SUMMARY OF THE THERAPIST'S RESPONSE
TO THE PATIENT'S ANGER

1.   **Maintain composure.**

2.   **Convey empathy.**

3.   **Assess the patient's about his current level of anger.**

4.   **Take the patient's perspective.**

5.   **View the anger as an "opportunity" to learn.**

6.   **Commend the patient for becoming angry. Anger is a "call to constructive action" and an occasion to reassess treatment goals.**

7.   **Help the patient view anger as a "commodity" and/or a "product" and examine impact.**

8.   **Conduct a chain analysis and a situational analysis.**

9.   **Conduct a developmental analysis.**

10. **Use humor, self-disclosure and teaching stories.**

11. **View anger expression as a sign of being a "good candidate for treatment" (favorable prognostic indicator).**

12. **Defuse the patient's anger (See Appendix A).**

These various guidelines can be translated into a series of questions that can be asked of the patient. The therapist can sample from the following questions.

ASSESS THE PATIENT'S CURRENT LEVEL OF ANGER

Tell me how angry you are right now.

On a scale from 1 to 10, where 1 is feeling just annoyed and 10 feels like you are going to explode, where are you right now?

Can you stop and tell me how angry you are you right now?

Are you more angry or less angry then when we first began the session today?

Are you getting more angry as we discuss this?

Can you tell me more about your anger?

Am I correct in assuming that you don't want to talk about your anger or about any feelings related to your anger at this time?

EXPLORE THE PATIENT'S UNDERSTANDING OF THE CAUSE OR CONSEQUENCES OF HIS/HER ANGER

What happens that results in your becoming angry?

Is there something I am doing right now (or not doing) that is making you angry?

What is making you so angry?

You are really angry with me right now, perhaps like you are with other people. Can we take a moment and go back to the point when you got angry with me and walk me through what happened in slow motion. I want to understand what you were reacting to and how you were feeling.

A few minutes ago you were not angry. Then you became angry with me. Describe for me what angered you and what went on inside of you.

Let us go step by step through what is making you so mad.

Is anyone telling you to do something violent (toward someone else, toward yourself, toward property)?

ASSESS THE PATIENT'S LEVEL OF PERCEIVED CONTROL

Do you think your present anger will get out of control?

What happened the last time you felt this way?

How do you usually control your anger? Would any of these ways work now or are you feeling too upset (angry) to use those controls now?

Have you ever lost control of your anger? What happened? How do you feel about that now?

CONSIDER "TRANSFERENCE: FEATURES: DOES THE PATIENT REACT SIMILARLY IN OTHER SITUATIONS

Does what I said (or did) that resulted in you becoming angry with me remind you of any other times in your life? Please tell me about that.

What happened as a result of your expressing your anger in that way?

Is your anger getting you all of what you want?

What are some other ways of handling that situation?

How is becoming angry (aggressive) working for you?

THERAPIST PROVIDING SUPPORT

What can I do to help you find ways to improve your situation and to support you?

I can suggest some ways to handle your anger, but let's see if you can first think of some ways that might work for you.

What do you want the outcome of today's session to be?

Does any part of what I have said describe how you might be feeling right now and what you can do about it?

TEACHING STORY

One of my favorite teaching stories involves my four children, when they were growing up. I call it the **"garbage-can" story** and I share it with patients <u>after</u> they have described examples of what gets them angry. The story is designed to illustrate that I, the therapist, can also become angry. Moreover, we then analyze what got me so angry (using the component analysis conveyed in the anger-aggression cycle see Figure 6, p. 265).

Teaching stories, to be effective, should be short, humorous, eliciting patient affect and lend themselves to straightforward analysis. When patients are asked what they learn in therapy, they often tell me that they know how to look for "garbage cans" in their own lives – a metaphor for *"nurturing, catching, anticipating, interrupting, and altering"* their behavior.

The story is <u>simple</u>. I not only have four children, but I am also the proud possessor of three garbage cans. On each Tuesday morning, I put out the three garbage cans. I don't mind doing this. It gets me going in the morning. I have asked my four children on several occasions, to please bring in the garbage cans at the end of the day. I do <u>not</u> find this it be an unreasonable request, given all that I do for them.

On this one Tuesday I had a rough day at work with hassles from colleagues, graduate students, the computer service going down, and the like. Well, when I got home that evening what did I see, but the three garbage cans at the curbside. Not only the garbage cans, but the kids' bikes were all over the driveway. We have talked about the need for them to put away their bikes. Given this array of noncompliant behaviors, I entered the house in my <u>clinically sensitive fashion</u>. (I remind myself that repetitive noncompliance is the major reason parents seek professional help.)

Something had to change! So, I rounded up my four children and marched them down to the curb and had them encircle the three garbage cans. Now picture the following. The five of us encircling the three garbage cans holding hands, and conducting a SÉANCE to see what thoughts if any would emerge. I thought this might be an interesting way to get my request across to them.

At this point, my son said, "Can I say something important." To which I said, "Not now Dave, we are waiting for thoughts to emerge." He retorted, "But dad, this is really important." "It better be.", I responded.

> *"I don't know how to tell you this Dad, but these three garbage cans aren't ours. We brought in our garbage cans. These are Mark's. We just left them here to see how you would react."*

At this point, I turn to my patients and indicate that all of the lessons of therapy that we will work on <u>boil down</u> to how do I respond at this <u>critical moment in time</u>, when my *son tells me that these are not my garbage cans. Do I view this "trick" as a personal threat and provocation and escalate the situation or do I view this "trick" as a clever way to give me pause and teach me a lesson?*

Do I view it as a perceived provocation and say:

> *"What do you mean that they are not our garbage cans? Whose idea was this anyway?"*
>
> *"Does mom know about this? Was she in on this?"*
>
> *"Is this the first time you guys have done this to me, or are there other times that you have conspired against me?"*
>
> *"This is not about the garbage cans. What about the bikes? What about all the things I do for you and this is the way you treat me. What about the fighting that has been going on and … (I bring out a long list of parental grievances.)"*
>
> *"Do you have any idea what would happen if I had ever done this to my father?" (Now, where did he come from? My father is a readily available heuristic that I can call upon at any given time.) The examples I offer are in a mood-congruent fashion. My current feelings are like a flashlight or channel selector in the examples I offer.*
>
> *"Each of you will go up to your room and have your own personal SÉANCE, and when you get the message you check with me."*

In short, I ask patients should I appraise my children's prank as a provocation and react in a way that escalates the situation, or instead, should I view their efforts as a way to teach me a lesson and give me pause?

> *"What do you mean that they are not our garbage cans? I can't believe you did that." While chuckling to myself, "When you guys grow up you should write scripts for TV sitcoms. The stuff you pull on me are funnier than anything I see on TV."*
>
> *"If you guys did not do these things to me what would I have to tell my patients (or share with my colleagues)?"*

THAT IS THE STORY! At this point, I ask my patients:

> *"Why do you think I told you this story?"*

I always ask patients this question, because they often come up with better answers than I would otherwise offer. At this point we collaboratively analyze the **Garbage-can Story** in terms of what were the stimulus events (garbage cans, bikes) that triggered my going in the house in my "clinically sensitive fashion". What feelings and thoughts did I have? Feelings -- of irritation, anger; Pre-anger states – frustration fatigue, "fuse lit", before I got home; Automatic thoughts – "Oh shit, not again! I'll teach them a lesson; Secondary emotions – feel disrespected, "tricked", conspired against, my "losing control"; Behavior – what did I do and how did the kids respond and how did the cycle escalate.

I also examine with my patients, what choices did I have. How did I make the situations worse? What could I have done differently? The patients can now ask themselves and each other,

> *"Where are all the garbage cans in their lives?"*

Collaboratively, we work on analyzing what gets the patients so angry and how can we conduct a functional, behavioral chain, component analysis so they can come to see the interdependence between situational triggers, feelings (both primary and secondary), thoughts, behaviors and reactions from others. Can they learn to anticipate when they are going to become angry? What are the intra-and interpersonal warning signs?

We consider the adage:

> *"There is no situation so bad that we can't make it worse by the way we behave."*

How does my garbage can story illustrate this point? The therapist should remember that these are teaching stories and the therapist should model a coping style that patients can take away with them (i.e., "Taking the therapist's voice with them."). In **subsequent** sessions, I will say to patients:

> *"Remember, I mentioned the story about my four kids and the three garbage cans. Well, it happened again! I couldn't believe it, but I came home and saw the three garbage cans on the curb, once again. This, after I did the whole thing with the SÉANCE. But this time something different happened. I could see I was working myself up again. So I caught myself and interrupted my natural instincts. I drove up, stopped the car, and got out. I checked to see if they were my garbage cans. They are not going to fool me more than once. They were my garbage cans. You know what I am going to do? I'm going to buy garbage bags and not use the garbage cans. I have decided not to make this an issue."*

In the retelling of my story, I deliberately used **active transitive (metacognitive) verbs** – "see, caught, interrupt, checked, decided". One object of the teaching story is to model choices and convey a sense of personal agency. Anger just doesn't happen to people, but rather how they appraise situations and their abilities to handle (cope with) situations is critical. Insofar as patients can spontaneously incorporate such transitive verbs into their social discourse and behavioral repertoire, they will begin to change and exert control.

WHERE ARE ALL THE GARBAGE CANS IN YOUR LIFE? HOW DO YOU RESPOND? WHAT CHOICES DO YOU HAVE?

EDUCATION ABOUT ANGER: HOW TO CONDUCT THE PROCESS

The ways in which the education process is conducted is as important as the information that is covered. In cognitive-behavioral interventions, **education is an <u>ongoing, collaborative, discovery-based</u> Socratic process**. Throughout the discussion it is important to have the patients provide personal examples. The therapist may give patients materials to read or **Personalized Handouts**. The clinician can also use self-monitoring, imagery assessment, videotape modeling films, analysis of in vivo homework assignments, group feedback and the like, as a means of educating patients.

Whatever the educational format, the information should <u>not</u> be covered as a didactic lecture, but rather should be incorporated as part of the **social discourse of therapy**. The therapist can embed relevant information at various appropriate points in the therapy process. Several of the points such as helping the patient become more aware of the various components that contribute to the anger-cycle *(See Figure 5, p. 260)* and how to better understand the various reasons that individuals become angry can be **examined collaboratively over several sessions**.

The best format is to have the patient **inductively discover** how these conceptual frameworks apply to their own anger-aggression behaviors. For example, this can be achieved by having the therapist introduce the **vicious cycle framework** *(Figure 5, p. 260)* and then asking the patient to fill in their own examples. The therapist can provide the patient with a written copy of this material to be added to his personal diary (Workbook).

Another example of how the educational process can be collaboratively conducted is illustrated by the discussion of the various reasons that individuals become angry. The therapist can examine with groups of patients what gets them angry and then examine the common pattern or themes. The patients can generate examples of the various provocations such as interruption of plans, violation of expectations, goal blockage, and the like that get them angry and then develop intervention plans.

Yet another way to conduct the educational process is to have the patients **watch videotapes of individuals who become angry**. The patients can then analyze both the reasons why the characters in the videotape are becoming so angry and the various components of the cycle that contribute to their anger-aggression. The videotaped modeling film can also include the exact same scene with the characters now using their coping skills to handle the perceived provocations, as discussed below, p. 264.

Throughout the educational process, the therapist should use **simple, everyday language, analogies ,** and **avoid using jargon**. The therapist should solicit suggestions form the patient, encourage the patient to ask questions and give feedback.

Education is most effective when the patient is one step ahead of the therapist, providing suggestions that the therapist would otherwise offer. The name of the game is for the therapist to have the patient come up with what should be done next, thus anticipating the therapist. Why should the therapist adopt the strategy of having the patient come up with the idea and the accompanying reasons, rather than having the therapist be directive and didactic. Two reasons:

1. Patients are more likely to follow through and do things in vivo if they patients COME UP with the idea themselves and the accompanying reasons, than if the therapist gives the patients the suggestions.

2. If patients come up with the ideas or suggestions, they are more likely to feel **empowered and enabled, thus bolstering their sense of self-efficacy and self-confidence** that they will be able to generate possible solutions on their own. In fact, the therapist can ask the patient the following question:

   "Do you ever find yourself, in your day-to-day experience, asking yourself the kind of questions, that we ask each other right here?"

With this as introduction, we can now consider the various instructional formats and what are the key points that should be included in educating the patient about anger and its relationship to aggression.

DIFFERENT WAYS TO CONDUCT EDUCATION

The therapist can educate patients about the nature of anger and coping processes using a variety of procedure, including:

1. **Interviewing** the patients about current and developmental difficulties and strengths, using time lines to identify risk and protective factors;

2. **Assessing** the patients and providing feedback;

3. **Sharing a Case Conceptualization Model**;

4. Having the patient engage in **self-monitoring**;

5. **Discussing** with the patient the adaptive and maladaptive functions of anger, warning signs, conflict cycle, nature of provocations, cognitive distortions, relapse prevention, and defensive responses such as denial, minimization of severity, rationalization about how one is provoked (A, B, C analysis) and the tendency to blame others;

6. **Considering myths** concerning anger and aggression

7. Considering **cultural influences** - code of honor, street code, gender influences;

8. Incorporating within the education discourse **metaphors, analogies, journaling, letter-writing** (e.g., See Wexler, 2000, House of Abuse and House of Self-worth and Empowerment);

9. **Therapist modeling, using coping-oriented self-disclosure, story-telling**;

10. **Providing written materials**, handouts for the patient and spouse, refer to books and Websites on anger control;

11. Engaging the patient in **skills-training** procedures (e.g., relaxation, self-instructional training, communication skills) and providing individual and /or group with feedback;

12. Using **videotape modeling films, relaxation tapes**, etc.;

13. Having the patient engage in **graded experiments** (in therapy -- imagery-based, behavioral rehearsal and outside of therapy);

14. Putting the patient in a **consultative mode** (patients are asked to explain what to do and examine why and how they brought about change). Engage patients in **self-attributions** (have them "take credit" for change).

EDUCATION ABOUT ANGER: INCORPORATE IN DISCOURSE

(This is not a patient Handout, but rather a set of Guidelines of what information should be covered in treatment.)

1. Anger is a <u>complex emotion</u> which can be adaptive (emerge over the course of evolution) and can work for you. Anger acts like a <u>stimulus</u> to <u>alert</u> the person to a <u>threat</u>. Anger is a <u>prod to take action</u> and tells someone to <u>search</u> and <u>identify</u> the source of the problem so you can do something about it. Anger tells you to take <u>corrective action</u>. Anger acts like a <u>smoke detector</u> that something is wrong. It captures your attention and directs you to find the threatening agent. (Note sometimes there may be <u>false alarms</u> -- smoke detectors may go off even when there is no real threat. The same applies to people. Exactly when the alarm – smoke detector – goes off will vary from person to person. Need to <u>check it out</u>.) Anger is a <u>warning signal</u> or a cue that something needs to be changed. The key task is <u>knowing what to change</u> and <u>when and how to change</u> it. Sometimes when people are angry they use aggression (verbal or physical) to try and change things. Such aggression can result in negative consequences for self and others.

2. Consider the <u>adaptive</u> and <u>useful functions</u> anger serve. Anger is a state of <u>emotional arousal</u> and a <u>normal part of any relationship</u> that tells us that something is wrong. How can anger help? Anger has informational value, just like physical pain. Anger <u>communicates</u> the presence of a threat, a <u>warning</u> to protect oneself and others, a need to correct an <u>injustice</u> or inequity, or that there is a <u>problem</u> in need of a solution.

3. It is important <u>not</u> to <u>equate anger</u> with <u>aggression</u>. They are <u>not synonymous</u>. People often use other ways besides aggression to express anger. What are some adaptive ways people express anger? The therapist can convey:

    > *"Although anger and aggressive acts often go together, there is an important <u>difference</u> between feeling angry and acting out on that anger. Feeling anger and causing harm to others are related, but they are <u>not the same thing</u>. Anger is a feeling and aggression is an action. An individual can have angry thoughts and feelings and <u>not</u> have to act upon them. It is important to talk about feelings like anger, rather than act upon them. Some can have strong feelings, but can decide <u>not</u> to act upon those feelings. Does that make sense?"*

4. Anger <u>varies along a dimension</u> from mild irritation to annoyance to frustration to fury to rage. Help the patient to draw a distinction between feeling "bothered, irritated, upset, hassled, annoyed, frustrated" <u>versus</u> feeling "angry, burned-up, pissed off, irate, furious, boiling over, outraged".

5. Anger has different components that include feelings, physiological reactions, thoughts, and behaviors. Consider with the patient how these components can form a "vicious cycle" that escalates anger and how information-processing concepts apply to explaining anger. See Figure 5 (p. 260) for an example of the framework that the therapist can use to educate patients about the component processes that contribute to the anger-aggression cycle. Figure 5 provides an overview of the model and the accompanying Table 20 (p. 261) provides detailed examples of the component processes. Although the Boxes in Figure 5 are numbered sequentially, it is important to highlight for the patient the <u>dynamic interplay</u> between these processes (e.g., feelings can affect thoughts and vice versa).

    As part of their "homework" assignment patients can be asked to generate an individualized description of their own anger-aggression cycles. The therapist can then explore with the patients what they can do to "break their cycle". Where are all the entry points? What has proven successful in the past? What advice would they have for others who wish to break the anger-aggression cycle? What may get in the way of their breaking the cycle?

6. Why do people get angry -- <u>variety of reasons</u>. Most of the time individuals become angry in social situations and anger results from conflicts within relationships (with family members). <u>Anger serves several social functions</u> such as remedying a perceived injustice, altering or maintaining already existing power positions or ways of exerting control. Several investigators (e.g., Carpenter & Halberstadt, 2000) have attempted to categorize these special triggers. Table 21 (p. 264) provides a category system we developed (see Welch, 1988) to summarize what gets peoples angry in interpersonal situations. The categories are summarized under the mnemonic II CE HOPE. These categories can be supplemented by such additional perceived provocations as a desire to avenge insults, acquire prestige, reputation at stake, eliminate competition, out of loyalty to others, and life-long antagonisms against others.

    When we teach patients to identify and categorize provocations (what "sets them off"), we do so in an <u>inductive Socratic manner</u>. Rather than present them deductively with the category of social events that elicit anger (II CE HOPE), we have them describe the variety of situations in which they become angry and we <u>inductively</u> and <u>collaboratively</u> have them cluster the events into categories as violation of expectations or goal blockage. This inductive approach is especially effective when treatment is conducted on a group basis where the participants can collaboratively generate categories of provocations. We have the participants not only discuss and label their provocations, but we may also play videotapes of other individuals describing what gets them upset and angry, and have the participants use the mnemonic to categorize these videotape vignettes. Note, sometimes a specific provocative event <u>may elicit several features</u> (i.e., the event may occur in a public setting leading to embarrassment, violate the individual's expectations, occur when the individual is tired and stressed, and occur for the "hundredth time" – history repeats itself, and also puts the individual at risk for future difficulties. It is proposed that the more features that contribute to anger (as indicated in the mnemonic II CE HOPE enumerated in Table 20),the greater the likelihood of anger and of that anger escalating to the point of aggression.

The next time you get angry, pause and ask yourself, "What got me so angry?" Call upon your mnemonic II CE HOPE. Did you get angry because the event or behavior of others:

(1) interrupted your plan or blocked you from achieving a goal (<u>I</u>)

(2) had implications or raised concerns about the possible consequences (short term, and long-term) (<u>I</u>)

(3) raised concerns about possible injury (short term and long term) (<u>C</u>)

(4) violated your expectations of what should or should not have been done (<u>E</u>)

(5) reflected yet another occasion of noncompliance (<u>H</u>)

(6) was not tolerable given your present physical and emotional state (<u>O</u>)

(7) reflected a strongly held personal rule, vulnerability, belief (<u>P</u>)

(8) occurred in a social setting – not so much what was done, but where it was done – in front of others who you value (<u>E</u>)

(9) or some combination of these eight categories (II CE HOPE)

One step in teaching patients to self-regulate their emotions and behavior is to have them interrupt their automated anger scripts and to notice, label and deautomize, interrupt the behavioral sequence (see Fehr et al., 1999). The <u>therapist can self-disclose</u> what gets him/her angry and code the events aloud using the mnemonic II CE HOPE and then indicate how he/she learned to "notice", "catch", "interrupt", "use a game plan", "identify high risk situations", "take time out", "relax", and "change scripts". (When reflecting to the client, the therapist should sample from this array of self-control verbs.) Note, that by means of modeling the therapist is teaching the patients a language system to exert emotional and behavioral controls.

7. Consider <u>warning signs</u> (<u>Red flag</u> words, self-talk, situations that stir things up. Use concept of Anger Ladder or Red-Yellow-Green Safety Zones.) The therapist can note:

> *"Having some <u>early warning signs</u> of anger is like knowing how to read the sky to know <u>if a storm is coming</u>. We can learn the early warning signs of our anger by paying attention to physical cues inside of us and then we can get away from the emotional storm. The relaxation training will make it easier to recognize these signs. Simply by being aware of the physical cues can help us to take action to stop the escalation of anger turning into aggression."*
> *(Wexler, 2000, p.51)*

8. Discuss <u>physiological consequences</u> of prolonged anger and hostility on one's health. Also, consider the impact of suppressed anger on one's health. The therapist can give the patient books, use cartoons, and share personal anecdotes. Ask the patient to monitor blood pressure as a way to demonstrate what anger does to one's health. (See Williams and Williams 1993 book, <u>When anger kills</u>.)

9. Consider how <u>anger</u> can act as a <u>secondary emotion masking</u> other feelings such as shame, fear of rejection, humiliation, insecurity. Consider developmental factors that contribute to <u>hypersensitivity</u> -- "antennae", "radar." Anger can defend individuals against certain feelings. How can the patient learn to tolerate and regulate emotions without "shutting down" or "lashing out" at the source of the pain. The therapist can convey that sometimes anger is a "defense" against more painful and problematic feelings such as masking feelings of sadness, grief, powerlessness and shame. The therapist can observe:

> *"Often when we have one feeling – for example, anger – we may be feeling another feeling at the same time, such as sadness or disappointment or fear. That is why feeling our feelings is often so difficult, because we are not experiencing just one feeling, but many feelings. This can be both confusing and disorienting. It may be difficult to talk about your anger when it co-exists side by side with other strong feelings. It is not uncommon for example for people to feel full of rage toward people they love, or for people to feel protective or attached to people with whom they are furious.*
>
> *Perhaps, one reason you are having a hard time talking about your anger is because anger is not the only emotion you are experiencing right now." (Matsakis, 1998, p. 35)*

Stosny (1995) and Raab (2000) have described how anger and accompanying aggression can be viewed as a response to an underlying "core hurt". They describe a formula for <u>understanding "core hurts"</u> by which individuals with anger-control problems can <u>make bad feelings worse</u> (see Figure 6, p. 265).

Hanna and Hunt (1991) have offered an analogy of a <u>burning match</u> to convey the notion of an "underlying hurt" contributing to aggression.

> *"Anger is like a flame of a burning match. The match stick itself represents the hurt that fuels the anger and that gives it life. When a match head is struck through friction or force, the hurt is lit (ignited), just like the sulphur of the match. But the flame of the anger burns only if the hurt, that is the match stick is there to keep it going."*
> *(Hanna & Hunt, 1991, p. 64).*

Patients are taught how to identify and understand so-called "core hurts" and how to better cope with underlying and concurrent emotions and their causes. Patients are encouraged to address these causes and to put their "core hurts" off-limits -- ("Push them within yourselves so no-one can have access and work on them but you"). The patients are encouraged to view "core hurts" as problems-to-be-solved and <u>not</u> as personal and emotional "wounds" that need to contribute to anger and aggression. In order to accomplish these goals the therapist can teach the patients the formula in FIGURE 5 (p. 260) of how to understand "core hurts".

10. Consider <u>factors</u> that <u>influence anger</u> (role of substance abuse; distal setting events, such as job dissatisfaction, commuting; cultural factors such a "code of honor" and cultural and group norms, "code of the streets", neighborhood influences, gender differences). In particular, consider the impact and function of alcohol on behavior, cues for drinking, social pressure to drink, excuse-making, and the like.

11. Consider <u>illustrative myths concerning anger and aggression</u>

    A. MYTHS --The expression of anger results in a <u>decrease</u> in angry feelings through "catharsis." In fact, venting anger can increase anger intensity. Venting anger can generate and reinforce negative thinking and behavior.

    B. MYTHS --Women are less likely to experience anger. Men and women get angry with the same frequency and intensity and for the same reasons. (Rather, major gender differences appear in how anger is expressed: men tend to use more verbal and physical forms of anger; females tend to use more relationship forms of anger expression.) *(See discussion of gender differences, p. 71)*

C. **MYTHS --Depression is due to anger turned inwardly. (In fact, clinically depressed individuals have higher levels of anger then nondepressed individuals. Strong expression of anger are associated with increased levels of depressive symptoms. Depression is <u>not</u> anger turned on oneself.)**

12. **Consider <u>treatment options</u> and <u>goals</u>. The goals that the patient and therapist agree on should be concrete behaviorally specifiable, attainable goals stated in the first person, that reflect the patient's efforts at personal change and <u>not</u> merely expectations that others will change. The patient and therapist need to not only agree on the treatment goals, but they must also agree on the tasks or means by which these treatment goals can be achieved. (See the discussion of goal setting, *p. 227*.)**

13. **Another means to educate patients is to show them <u>videotapes</u> of individuals who become angry and who lose control. The patients are then asked to discuss whether they have had similar experiences and to analyze what is getting the individual in the video so angry. They than can discuss possible coping strategies and then be given an opportunity to watch the same scene with the main character (model) now coping with anger. Following this demonstration, patients discuss, practice, and try out the coping techniques in the clinic and then "in vivo".**

   Treatment programs using such videos, as well as accompanying workbooks and telephone consultations, have been employed successfully for various clinical problems such as anxiety, depression, preparation for surgery, coping with the aftermath of rape, as well as with controlling anger (see Meichenbaum, 1994; Steffen, 2000).

   For example, Steffen (2000) has developed a multicomponent anger-management video series, workbook and telephone consultation for individuals who have to handle the anger and stress of taking care of their family members who have dementia. Steffen's 8-week intervention included awareness training, tension-reduction strategies (relaxation, thought stoppage, distraction), cognitive change strategies (cognitive restructuring and self-instructional training) and assertive training. The need for such programs is underscored by the findings of community-based prevalence surveys that indicated that 4% to 6% of elderly are abused. A Canadian survey of family violence found 7% of older adults experience some form of emotional abuse; 1% financial abuse; 1% physical abuse or sexual abuse in the previous 5 years by adult children, caregivers, and parents (Podnieks, 1992). *(See Appendix B Websites on elder abuse.)*

14. <u>Use of psychoeducational videos.</u> When using videos as part of the psychoeducational process, the therapist can use the following questions in order to engage patients in a <u>guided discussion</u>:

> *Why do you think I chose to show you this video? (Note, patients often come up with better reasons than the therapist could have offered?)*
>
> *What do you think about what you just saw?*
>
> *Were the people and the situation in the video like what you are faced with in your daily life?*
>
> *What do you think is getting this person (in the video) so angry?*
>
> *What is the problem, as you see it?*
>
> *What led up to the problem?*
>
> *How is X (main character in videotape) feeling?*
>
> *How can you tell that he/she is feeling Y?*
>
> *What might he/she be thinking? (What angry thoughts might he/she be having?)*
>
> *What could he/she be telling himself/herself?*
>
> *What choices did he/she make? What were the consequences of the choices he/she made?*
>
> *Did he/she make a "smart" choice?*
>
> *How can he/she anticipate and handle the situation better?*
>
> *Which choices would have helped him/her control his/her anger?*
>
> *Has anything like that happened to you? What happened? How did you handle it?*
>
> *What advice would you have so he could handle the situation differently?*
>
> *How would you know if what he/she did worked?*
>
> *What would make it easier for him/her to do that?*
>
> *What might get in the way of him/her using that coping plan (engaging in the behaviors)?*

15. <u>Provide Handouts</u> (e.g., See Patient Handouts in this Handbook and the APA website on anger which is http://www.APA.org/pubinfo/anger.html) (See additional WEBSITES in Appendix B) The PATIENT HANDOUTS are on pages 236.

FIGURE 5
ANGER - AGGRESSION CYCLE

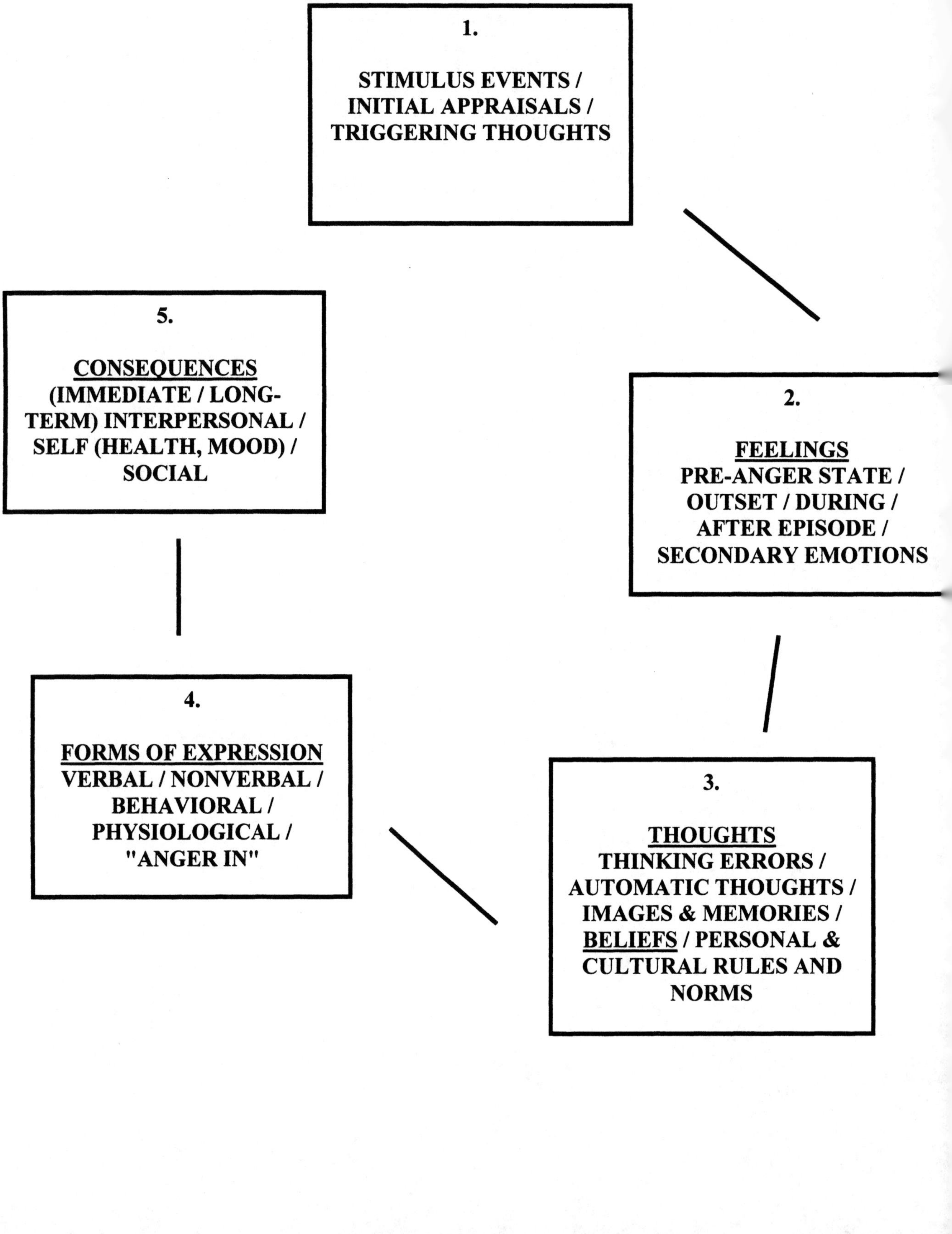

1.

**STIMULUS EVENTS /
INITIAL APPRAISALS /
TRIGGERING THOUGHTS**

5.

**CONSEQUENCES
(IMMEDIATE / LONG-
TERM) INTERPERSONAL /
SELF (HEALTH, MOOD) /
SOCIAL**

2.

**FEELINGS
PRE-ANGER STATE /
OUTSET / DURING /
AFTER EPISODE /
SECONDARY EMOTIONS**

4.

**FORMS OF EXPRESSION
VERBAL / NONVERBAL /
BEHAVIORAL /
PHYSIOLOGICAL /
"ANGER IN"**

3.

**THOUGHTS
THINKING ERRORS /
AUTOMATIC THOUGHTS /
IMAGES & MEMORIES /
BELIEFS / PERSONAL &
CULTURAL RULES AND
NORMS**

Table 20
ANGER - AGGRESSION CYCLE:
(USE WITH FIGURE 5)

BOX 1

STIMULUS EVENTS
   Events, People, Behaviors

INITIAL APPRAISALS	**TRIGGERING THOUGHTS**
Intentional	*"On purpose"*
Unjustified	*"No one has a right to"*
Undeserved / Unwarranted	*"No one has to put up with"*
Preventable / Controllable	*"Not have to happen"*
Unreasonable	*"Stupid rule", "Dumb system", "Asking for it", "Deserve punishment"*
Disrespectful	*"Dissed", "Dishonored" – cultural expectations violated*

BOX 2

FEELINGS – High arousal and tense state

PRE-ANGER STATE	**TRIGGERING FEELINGS**
Irritable	*"On edge, short fuse, keyed up. stressed, overwhelmed"*
Exhausted	*"Fatigued, wit's end, hungry, tired"*
Mood	*"Depressed, anxious, bored, jealous"*
Low frustration tolerance	*"Frustrated, disappointed, cynical, hostile"*
Trait features	*"Argumentative "*

FEELINGS AT OUTSET OF EPISODE
   Furious, enraged, pissed off

FEELINGS DURING THE EPISODE --- Can Exacerbate Anger
   Trapped, locked in, no other options

SECONDARY EMOTIONAL TRIGGERS / EXACERBATE ANGER
   Feel humiliated, scared, anxious, depressed, rejected, ashamed, embarrassed, hurt

BOX 3

THOUGHTS

THINKING ERRORS	AUTOMATIC THOUGHTS
Catastrophic interpretation	*Use dramatic terms: Awful, Can't stand it!*
Demanding and coercive language	*"Shoulds, oughts, have to, need to"*
Overgeneralization	*"Always, never, completely hopeless"*
Categorical thinking	*"Stupid, Nerd"*
Inflammatory thinking	*"SOB, Asshole"*
Misattribution	*"Did it on purpose"*
Mind reading	*"Should know how I feel"; "I know what you're up to"*
Black/White - either or thinking	*"Show love or punch him out"*

IMAGES AND MEMORIES

Memory of wrongdoing, images of getting even

BELIEFS

Justified, lack responsibility	*"Not my fault"*
Violate personal (narcissistic) rules of living	*"It's my home, you do it my way"*
Authority challenged	*"No lip from you"*
Disrespectful, dishonorable	
Unable to control anger	*"Once a fuse is lit, it blows", "Not able to stop it"*

BOX 4

FORMS OF EXPRESSION

Verbal	*Verbal assault, argue, relationship aggression, gossip, lie*
Non-Verbal	*Glares, dirty looks, gestures, threatening posture, threatening acts*
Behavioral	*Physical assault against people, objects; Follow cultural display rules*
Physiological	*Arousal. tenseness, biochemical changes*
"Anger In"	*Suppress anger, turn anger on self -- self injury, self-critical*

BOX 5

CONSEQUENCES (IMMEDIATE / LONG TERM)

INTERPERSONAL	*Elicit counter-aggression. alienate others, rejection, damaged relationships, self-destructive behaviors and leave problems unresolved*
SELF	**Feelings** -- *guilty, depressed, fearful, inadequate, puzzled, dismayed* **Health** -- *increased coronary heart disease, essential hypertension, dental problems like bruxism*

Table 21
WHAT KIND OF <u>SITUATIONS MAKE PEOPLE ANGRY</u>:
CODING PROVOCATIONS

<u>I I</u>   <u>C E</u>   <u>HOPE</u>

Interruption of planned activities and obstacles to goal-directed behaviors – the closer someone is to the achievement of his/her goal, the greater is the frustration and anger when interrupted

Implications of noncompliance (possible short and long-term consequences of the significant other not complying) – e.g., not only what others do, but the implications for the future as in the case of significant others engaging in unhealthy behavior

Concern about possible injury to others or to self and possible concern of what might have happened – e.g., other engaging in high-risk behaviors

Expectations violated – disruption of the flow of interpersonal interactions by breaking implicit shared rules. Something that significant other "should" or "should not" be doing that elicits anger

History repeats itself (over and over again) – pattern of annoying behaviors that can accumulate over time

Overload of the individual – fatigue or stress can lessen the tolerance level of the individual (i.e., it takes less to get someone angry – "straw that breaks the camel's back")

Personal peeve (violation of personal rules and values) – e.g., being "dissed" or disrespected in front of others

Embarrassment (noncompliant behavior occurs in public places in front of others)

FIGURE 6
UNDERSTANDING "CORE HURTS"

I am feeling

Name feelings

Frustrated
Disappointed
Sad
Lonely
Ashamed
Afraid

which means **that I am**

Unlovable
Defective
Unimportant
Useless
Abandoned
Powerless
Helpless

that leads to feelings of

Shame
Guilt
Rage
Panic
Depression
Jealousy

which leads to my behaving

Overt
Aggressively
Toward Others
Property
Self
——————
Passive /
Aggressively
Towards
Others
"Yes/ Buts"
Avoidance

with the result **that**

Elicit
Negative
  reactions
  from others
Negative
  feelings
Counter-
  aggressive
  behaviors

Thus, the "Cycle" Continues

THERAPISTS' USE OF METAPHORS AS PART OF THE EDUCATIONAL PROCESS

In the same way that patients may use metaphors to describe their experience with anger, the therapist may also use metaphors to convey the nature of anger and ways to control anger and aggression. The therapist should use the patients' metaphors to foster the change process. (See Meichenbaum, 1994 for a further discussion of how therapists can use metaphors). As noted in the **Section on Education,** the therapist should remind patients that there is nothing wrong with being angry per se, but rather highlight that how they react to anger or what they do with the anger that are the key issues. The following lists are examples of possible metaphors that therapists may use.

DESCRIPTIONS OF ANGER

Anger is an overkill and underthink

Anger functions like ice that you put on a wound so you won't feel pain, but it does <u>not</u> fix the basis of the sore.

Anger can numb "psychic pain".

Anger acts like an amphetamine – restorers depleted energy (provides a surge of energy).

Anger is a failure of compassion

Anger is a warning sign.

IMPACT OF ANGER

So mad you can't think straight.

Anger causes thought contraction.

Polarizes your thoughts.

Anger results in your misreading social cues.

Anger causes you to timeslide (lapse into your old anger habits).

Toxic blame

Back log of anger

Mindset (prejudiced - see hostility all over)

Contaminate yourself with anger

ANGER AS A MEANS OF DEFINING ONESELF

Reactaholic

Anger junkie

Puppet on a string. You are the puppet and those who get you angry are the puppeteers.

Robot who responds when your button is pushed.

SELF-CONTROL METAPHORS

Put brakes on

Internal choices

Empower yourself

Break cycle of abuse

Give yourself permission to ...

ANGER AS A PRODUCT OR COMMODITY

As highlighted previously, the therapist can also examine with the patient the notion that **anger can be viewed as a <u>product</u> or <u>commodity</u>** that one does something with. The therapist can ask:

"When you become angry, what do you do with your anger?"

The patient may indicate that he "stuffs the anger". The therapist can explore collaboratively with the patient when he "stuffs feelings"; how long this has been going on; when has stuffing feelings worked. The therapist can convey that the patient appears "<u>stuck</u>" using a coping strategy that worked in the past, but now takes a <u>toll</u>. What is the impact, the emotional price of 'stuffing feelings"? What are alternative ways of handling emotions? As noted, if the patient answers, "I don't know.", then the therapist can answer "I don't know either. How can we go about finding out? Moreover, why would our finding out be helpful?" (relate back to the patient's goals). The notion of considering anger as a "product" that the patient does something with, implies that there are more adaptive, less destructive ways to handle anger.

Another metaphor that the therapist may use with patients is the concept that there are different **"parts"** to the patient. *(Although I don't believe that there are different parts to the patient, the use of this metaphor is often helpful in nurturing patient self-control.)* The therapist can observe that:

> *"It seems to me, and correct me if I am wrong, that there is a <u>part of you</u> that ..., but <u>another part of you</u> that .... (Therapist can refer to evidence that the patient did exert control in the face of provocations on some occasions.)*

> *"Tell me about the <u>part of you</u> that disagrees with ... or that thinks ..."*

> *"Tell me about the <u>part of you</u> that thinks the idea that .... might make sense or might help you."*

> *"It sounds that there is a <u>part of you</u> who has not given up hope <u>in spite of</u> ... Is that indeed the case? Does that fit with your observations (experiences)?"*

SUMMARY:
WHAT YOU SHOULD TAKE AWAY FROM SECTION V

There are five major issues that were highlighted and that the "expert" therapist should have in his/her repertoire, namely, how to

1. develop a therapeutic alliance;

2. collaboratively conduct a goal-setting with patients;

3. address the challenge of working with patients who became angry in therapy;

4. educate patients about anger and coping processes;

5. motivate patients to want to change.

If you were asked to teach these clinical skills to a novice therapist, could you readily generate and model how to perform each of these "core tasks" of therapy? Consider the following set of questions and role playing activities as a way to further develop and **TEST YOUR EXPERTISE**.

TEST YOUR EXPERTISE: SECTION V

1. Research has repeatedly demonstrated that the development and maintenance of a therapeutic alliance is critical to treatment outcomes. What are the specific challenges of developing a therapeutic alliance with patients with anger-control problems and how can these be addressed?

2. Lists the steps involved in collaboratively setting goals with patients.

   A friend comes to you with a series of New Year's resolution. What specific guidelines would you provide to increase the likelihood that he/she would be able to achieve his/her goals?

3. **Role play** with colleagues how to work with a **low motivated patient**. (See examples of the features of low motivated patient on page 226.) How can the therapist motivate a patient to want to change?

4. **Role play** with colleagues the variety of ways of how to deal with a patient's anger. Once again, have one person play the role of the angry patient, the other the therapist, and the third can act as a coach following the suggestions offered in this **SECTION**.

5. What are the key concepts to include when educating patients about anger and aggression? In what ways can anger be an adaptive emotion? What are the variety of different ways you can conduct this educational process?

6. As part of your education efforts, how can you use metaphors, videos, written materials, figures, and the like?

7. Research indicates that <u>what gets people angry</u> can be summarized under the acronym **II CE HOPE**. Monitor when you become angry and attempt to determine what triggers your anger. Was it that your plans were Interrupted (**I**), or Implications (**I**), Concerns (**C**) were raised, or your Expectations (**E**) were violated, or that History (**H**) repeated itself, especially when you feel overload (**O**), or the provocation may derive from a personal peeve (**P**) that occurs in public leading to embarrassment (**E**). It is proposed that if you become angry it is due to one of these 8 reasons or some combination therein. Can you use this model with patients to help them understand what gets them angry?

8. Finally, what were your goals in reading the **HANDBOOK**? How well are your goals being achieved? How would you know that you are making any changes in your behavior?

SECTION VI: SKILLS TRAINING PHASE

"Regardless of the root cause of violence, the immediate cause is often a breakdown of self-control" **(Baumeister, 1996, p.14)**

This **SECTION** reviews in detail the procedural steps designed to teach patients a variety of cognitive, affect-regulating, behavioral and interpersonal skills to reduce anger and to develop adaptive intra- and interpersonal coping skills. Supplemental **Patient Handouts** are included.

Also included in the description of each skill is a discussion of the clinical techniques required to engage patients in the acquisition, practice and application of the skills. It is not enough to have patients receive information and learn skills. They must be "challenged" to apply skills in new settings. The high incidence of patient noncompliance underscores that much clinical skill is required in conducting training.

The patients need to be taught to :

      (1) lengthen their reaction time between triggering events and their responses;

      (2) stop and calm down;

      (3) identify the problem and their feelings;

      (4) become aware of their thought patterns that foster anger and aggression and resultant consequences and learn alternative coping responses;

      (5) practice "cognitive scripts" for engaging in positive prosocial behaviors;

      (6) accept and tolerate angry feelings;

      (7) engage in effective communication skills;

      (8) empathize with others;

      (9) evaluate their efforts and use back-up plans accordingly.

In this **SECTION VI** we will consider how therapists can help patients acquire and implement these skills.

CONTENTS SECTION VI

SECTION VI highlights that a variety of interventions are required to teach patients **anger management** and **violence prevention** skills. These include **emotion-regulation activities** such as learning to take a time-out, learning to control arousal by means of relaxation and self-talk strategies, as well as **direct-action problem-solving** and interpersonal communication skills training. We will consider how each of these component skills can be taught and integrated into a treatment regimen. In the next **SECTION VII** we will consider what steps need to be taken to ensure the **generalization** and **maintenance** of these **skills**.

A good example of how these various skills have been implemented in an integrative fashion was offered by Weingardt and Zeiss (2000) who employed cognitive behavioral skills training on a psychiatric Intensive Care Unit. A brief review of their group treatment program will set the stage for the more detailed presentation. Their program consists of seven modules, implemented over the course of 10 days. These modules include:

I.   **Anger Management**

1. Group members discuss, *"What does it feel like when you are angry?"*

2. Group considers **"bad"** and **"good"** ways to **handle anger** and negative and positive **consequences** of each.

3. Group considers good ways to express anger and good ways of preventing anger.

II.   **Goal Setting**

1. Group discusses what **goals** they would like to accomplish when they leave the hospital.

2. For each patient, **work backwards** from goal to identify **subgoals** and **small steps** that need to be accomplished (**"get from here to there"**).

3. Create personal **time-line** and **game plan.**

III.   **Communication Skills**

1. Group discusses, *"How to get what you want from other people."*

2. Discuss what **communication means** (sender, receiver, message) and what is **effective communication** (verbal and nonverbal).

3. Teach, model, and practice skills.

IV.   **Drugs and Alcohol**

1. Group members consider **reasons** to use and not to use. Consider why do they use drugs. Why do drugs and anger go together.

2. Consider some of the **"bad" things** that have happened to them as a result of using alcohol and drugs.

3. Use **decisional balance sheet** to consider pros and cons; positive and negative consequences.

4. Consider **strategies** to stay clean and sober (e.g., avoid certain people, places get help, how to handle slips and view them as a "learning opportunity").

V.   **Relationships**

1. Consider what "relationships" mean and what makes for **"good"** relationship

2. Consider and practice skills designed to initiate and maintain relationships (e.g., use eye contact, personal distance, initiate conversation, identify common interests, listen and respond).

VI.   **Coping with Mental Illness**

1. Consider patients' understanding of "mental illness" and examine how to **cope with mental illness**.

2. What are positive and negative ways to cope.

VII.   **Relapse Prevention**

1. Consider strategies on *"how to stay out of the hospital"*.

2. Consider **early warning signs** that are unique to each individual.

3. Consider and practice **coping strategies** (e.g., call doctor or for help; talk to someone you trust; don't stop taking your medication; take care of yourself; don't use drugs and alcohol).

We will consider **in detail** each of these component skills, as well as other related skills. We begin with the skills of teaching patients how to use **time-out procedures**. While taking a time-out seems rather straightforward and simple, a fine-tune analysis indicates the complexity involved. **PATIENTS HANDOUTS** are included in this **SECTION** that are designed to foster skills training. **The reader has permission to copy, edit and use these HANDOUTS with his or her patients.**

LEARNING TO USE TIME OUT (TO) PROCEDURES

One of the most effective self-control techniques that patients who have anger-control problems can use is **learning how to take a time out**. Patients need to learn how to distance themselves from provocations in order to lower their anger and generate more effective behaviors. Taking time out, however is a **complex skill** that involves multiple behavioral components. These include the patient's ability to:

1)   **identify early and interruptible cues** (i.e., develop a personal profile of warning signs, learn emotional and social recognition skills)

2)   **view taking TO as a means of exerting personal control**-- patient is encouraged <u>not</u> to view taking time out as "rolling over," "giving in," or "selling out;" instead view taking a TO as an opportunity to exert control (use sports metaphor that taking TO is akin to taking an opportunity to create a game plan) and engage in self-control and self-soothing activities

3)   **remove self for a period of time** (the length of time depends on the situation)

4)   **rehearse and use exit lines** (no slamming doors). For example, patients can learn to say:

> *"I'm beginning to feel like things are getting out of control and I don't want to do anything that will mess up our relationship. So I need to take a time out."*
> *"I need some time to think it over." "I'll get back to you tomorrow."*
> *"I am getting angry now and I will say things I do not mean or that I will regret."*
> *"I need some time to calm down." (Provide an estimate of how long planning to be away.)*
> *"We both just need a break right now until things calm down."*
> *"I'm going out for a walk around the neighborhood. I'll be back in 15 minutes. Let's try talking about this when I get back. Okay?"*

5)   **handle others' possible negative reactions** to taking a time out

> *"Call me what you will, but I am <u>not</u> going to get caught up in this."*
> *"I need to get my act together."*
> *"I'm going for a walk, and when I get back, we can talk about it."*

6)   **give oneself permission** to take a time out

> *"I am getting pissed off. It is okay to take a time out."*
> *"Let my feet do the talking, not my hands."*
> *"I am going to use my thought-stopping and interrupt this cycle."*

7)   **role play and imaginally rehearse** the use of time out procedures

8)   **discuss and practice what to do during time out** (e.g., not brood, not think about retaliation, curse, use inflammatory language, but rather use anger reduction procedures). Include **implementation intention statements** such as *"Whenever situation X arises, I will do Y."*; *"If ... then statements," "When and where statements."* (See Gollwitzer, 1999, for a discussion of how to implement such goal statements.)

9)   once "calmed down" return to the scene and **call "time in"** (not avoid the situation)

10)   **solicit the patient's commitment statements** and the **reasons** for using the time out procedure; teach others -- put **patient in a consultative mode** where he can describe how to use time out and why doing so is important.

11)   **inform partner** in advance of the purpose and the steps involved in taking a TO. (See Wexler, 2000 pp. 55-56 for a Patient Handout sheet on TO that can be given to one's partner.)

12)   **follow through in using TO** – in order to accomplish this goal the therapist should follow procedural guidelines (as described on **p. 169**) for giving **"homework."** Check patient's comprehension, skills, commitment to using TO. Anticipate possible barriers *("What problems do you think you will have in using the TO?")*

13)   **summarize and describe the time out procedure.** The therapist should ensure that the following points are covered:

   a)   TO is "stop-gap" measure - it does <u>not</u> resolve the issue, but puts it on hold
   b)   TO is a way to avoid conflict, control anger, and a <u>sign of respect</u> for the relationship
   c)   TO should <u>not</u> be used as a weapon or as a controlling device against others
   d)   Learning to take TO is a "skill" that needs practice
   e)   Learn to anticipate high-risk situations and recognize early warning signs. Develop a **Responsible Game Plan.**
   f)   Learn to view a "provocation" as a "problem-to-be-solved" that is in need of a solution

14) In subsequent sessions the therapist should review **the patient's use of TO**. Ask the patient:

> *"Did you use the TO procedure?"*
> *"How did it work?"*
> *"Could you feel the anger being worked off when you took a TO?"*
> *"What difficulties, if any, did you have?" "How did you handle them?"*
> *"What surprised you most about using your TO plan?"*
> *"What problems do you anticipate in using the TO in the future? How will you handle these possible problems and potential obstacles to your using TO?"*

15) When the patient lapses the therapist should be supportive and non-accusatory. These lapses should be viewed as **learning opportunities**. Refer to the patient's problematic behavior as:

> *"Some of the old pattern"*
> *"Residual features"*
> *"Evidence of your still being stuck using old ways to solve a problem"*
> *"An instance of time sliding"*
> *"Even though you learned to be much more X, some of the old pattern of Y is still around sometimes. That is to be expected."*

LEARNING RELAXATION SKILLS

(See Bernstein & Borkovec, 1973; Deffenbacher & McKay, 2000; Deffenbacher & Suinn, 1988; Meichenbaum 1994; for a more detailed description on how to teach relaxation skills)

Before enumerating procedural guidelines concerning the teaching of relaxation skills, several points should be highlighted:

1. Research has indicated that the overall physiological pattern of arousal of angry and aggressive individuals is **increased muscle tension** and **elevated blood pressure**. Thus, interventions for this population should include a relaxation component with a focus on **progressive muscle relaxation exercises**.

2. As will be described, there are several different ways to teach relaxation skills and I do not know of any research that has evaluated the differential effectiveness of these various relaxation procedures with patients who have anger-control problems.

3. As Rachman (1977) has noted, it may be the **role of mental relaxation**, as much as physical relaxation responses that mediates behavioral change, as well as the **sense of psychological control** that is nurtured in patients.

4. The key to the effectiveness of the relaxation skills training is not the acquisition of the skills per se, but rather whether the patients **practice** their relaxation skills **daily** and whether they apply their **relaxation skills in vivo**. As Meichenbaum, and Turk (1987) have reported, the patients' treatment nonadherence with the request to practice and apply relaxation skills is the major challenge. Thus, much emphasis should be given to how the therapist needs to engage the patients and focus on the possibility of their noncompliance.

   The therapist needs to attend carefully to how the **treatment rationale for relaxation** is offered and on how the patients will **implement** the relaxation procedures, and possible barriers that might get in the way of their practicing.

RATIONALE THAT IS OFFERED TO LEARN RELAXATION SKILLS

1. Learning to relax is essential to anger management. Refer back to the **anger/aggression cycle that anger requires several components**, namely, triggers, physiological arousal and tension, anger-engendering and triggering thoughts, and accompanying aggressive behavior that "pulls for" counter-aggressive behavior. **(See Figure 5, p. 260)** There is a **need to break this cycle**. One way to do so is to learn to control physiological arousal by means of relaxing. *(The therapist can attempt to have the patient come up with the idea that relaxation is one way to break the cycle.)*

2. Highlight for the patient the research findings on what anger and aggression do to the body, underscoring the role of increased muscle tension and elevated blood pressure. Examine the long-term negative health consequences of engaging in angry behavior.

3. Being <u>both</u> relaxed and being keyed up at the same time is <u>not</u> possible. They are **incompatible responses**.

4. Relaxation is a **skill** that can help individuals calm down, think straight, stay in control. It is a skill and like any other skill requires daily practice with feedback and hard work and commitment.

5. Discuss with the patients how they now go about relaxing and any prior efforts to learn to relax. Also discuss how they go about learning any skills (e.g., computer proficiency, playing an instrument, driving, etc.). Draw parallels to the present task of learning the skill of relaxing. Underscore the importance of **commitment, effortful** and **deliberate practice** to achieve specific objectives. **There is a need to undertake practice with resolve.**

LEARN DIFFERENT TYPES OF RELAXATION SKILLS
(See Deffenbacher & McKay, 2000; for a detailed description)

1. **Progressive muscular relaxation training** -- tense and release various muscle groups. Focus on slow diaphragmatic breathing that directly lowers heart rate.

2. **Use cue-controlled relaxation** -- while relaxing, the patients practice saying relaxing statements such as "Relax", "Calm", "Let tension (anger) go".

3. **Use relaxing images** -- a clear easily visualized, relaxing image. This calming image should be filled with sensory detail and be a "snapshot relaxing memory."

Discuss How The Patient Can Apply Relaxation In Vivo

1. Discuss when the patient should practice relaxation procedures and possible barriers to practicing. The patient needs to make *"an appointment with oneself"* and plan ahead when and how to practice relaxation skills. The patient should be encouraged to practice at a specific time each day. Enter in his appointment book relaxation times. It takes practice to improve relaxation skills so they can become <u>automatic</u> and <u>second nature</u>.

2. Use relaxation audiotape with patient's own voice. Emphasize that the patient should **notice and relax** when he/she is getting upset. Model this in the therapy session.

3. Anticipate possible difficulties in applying relaxation skills in vivo. Encourage the patient to try the relaxation skills in less provocative situations at first.

4. Help the patient to alter his expectations for success. The patient is encouraged <u>not</u> to become despondent if the relaxation skills don't worry perfectly at the outset. It takes time. Use the metaphor of learning to downhill ski and highlight the need to practice on the right level hill (not too easy, not too hard). Once again, solicit the patient's commitment to practice, *"Are you willing to commit yourself to doing home practice?"*

5. Review with the patient the potential benefits of learning self-control procedures of relaxation (health, interpersonal, other benefits).

6. Have the patient keep a log of practice efforts.

7. As the patient develops relaxation skills , ask if he knows anyone who could benefit from such training. Put the patient in a **consultative mode**, explaining and teaching others the relaxation skills.

8. Teach significant others (e.g., frontline staff, parents) the relaxation skills at the same time that the patients are being taught and have them cue each other and practice using their relaxation skills together in vivo.

SELF-INSTRUCTIONAL TRAINING

Another important self-control skill is learning how to **use self-talk**. The therapist can indicate that:

> *"Self-talk is a way we talk silently to ourselves and how we go about figuring things out."*

The therapist can teach the value of using **self-talk** to figure out how to deal with problems. In preparing patients to use **self-talk coping self-statements** the therapist should go through the following steps:

1. help patients appreciate that their anger sequence consists of **<u>different phases</u>**

    a) preparing for stressful encounters and getting worked up (anticipating provocative event);
    b) having to deal with perceived provocations and confrontations;
    c) dealing with anger at its most intense point;
    d) reflecting back on how they handled the situation;

2. **review what thoughts and feelings the patients had at each phase** and their negative anger-inducing impact; help the patients identify thoughts and feelings that jack-up their anger and come up with calmer alternatives; explore how can the patients can identify triggering thoughts (e.g., use self-monitoring);

> *"How can what you say to yourself get you more or less angry."*

> *"How can 'expecting the worse' and 'taking the bait' set you up to get into fights?"*

> *There is a saying that there is "No situation so bad that you can't make it worse by how you react or by what you say to yourself." Can you give me an example of that from your life?*

3. **have patients <u>appreciate</u> that "anger" does <u>not</u> just happen**, but how the patients appraise situations, what patients say to themselves at each phase of a provocative situation influences the anger-aggression cycle. **(See Figure 5, p. 260)** Help patients to "notice", "catch" themselves and each other and to "produce" incompatible coping self-statements and behaviors;

4. consider what **different anger-reducing coping thoughts and feelings** that they might use instead at each phase;

5. collaborate with the patients in **generating a possible list of individualized coping self-statements**;

6. **share** the list of self-statements that other patients who have had problems controlling their anger have come up with;

7. **discuss where and how** the patient can use their anger-reducing self-statements;

8. discuss **how it would feel to say that to yourself in that situation**. *"Do you think you could say these things? What might get in the way?"*

The patient is taught how to **<u>rescript angry dialogues</u> and <u>images</u>**. Such **"rethinking"** exercises are **like writing scripts of internal plays in one's head**. In the rescripted version the patient alters the images and self-dialogue so the central character in the <u>**internal play**</u> he has in mind is calm and controlled, but <u>not</u> emotionally detached, nor withdrawn (Deffenbacher, 1999). For example, consider the following **anger control scripts** developed by one patient with the help of the therapist:

> *This is going to upset me, but I know how to deal with it. ... Try not to take this too seriously. ... Time for a few deep breaths of relaxation. ... Remember to keep my sense of humor. ... Just roll with the punches; don't get bent out of shape. ... There is no point in getting mad. ... I'm not going to let him get to me. ... Look for the positives. Don't assume the worst or jump to conclusions. ... There is no need to doubt myself. I'll let him blow off some steam and make a fool of himself. ... He is just angry. It is the anger speaking. Let's take the issues point by point. ... My anger is a signal of what I need to do. ... Try to reason it out. ... I can't expect people to act the way I want them to. ... Try to shake it off. Don't let it interfere with my job. ... Don't take it personally!*

In order to help patients develop such coping scripts, the therapist can collaboratively generate with the patient's assistance a compilation of possible coping self-statements, as noted below. As you consider the lists of possible coping self-statements that can be shared with the patient, it is important to recognize that the therapist does <u>not</u> give the patient a list of self-statements and ask them to memorize them. Instead, the list of possible coping strategies needs to be **collaboratively generated** and **individually tailored** to the patient's needs. For example, the therapist can say to the patient:

> *"I have been giving some thought to what we talked about last time concerning when you become angry. We discussed how your anger varied across different situations. We also examined the kind of feelings and thoughts you had at each phase of the situation. We came to see how your thoughts can make a bad situation worse. Our discussion led us to work together to generate a list of possible coping self-statements that you could say to yourself at each phase -- for example, when preparing for a possibly provocative situation, when confronting and handling your anger, and finally reflecting upon the situation.*

I have taken the liberty of summarizing our discussion by putting together a list of coping self-statements you offered, as well as some suggestions that have been offered by other folks like yourself who have had similar problems with anger control. I would like us to go over this list together and see how they might apply in your case. Remember, each person is unique and each person's situation is different. Thus, some of the suggestions included on this list may be useful for you in helping you handle your anger, while others may <u>not fit</u> your situation. Let's consider which do and do <u>not</u> apply in your case.

Once we have examined the pros and cons of this list, we can consider how you can use these coping strategies to control your anger and resolve conflicts."

Following the examination of possible coping self-statements, the patient is asked to put together an **anger control script** that he/she can use in provocative situations.

"You can think about this as a <u>mental</u> and <u>behavioral script</u> or as a <u>internal play</u> designed to reduce your anger. You can think of yourself as the main character in the play. Your character is someone who is committed to respond to anger in a <u>constructive manner</u>.

Let's look together at some of the things you can tell yourself:

a)   *before you enter a potentially provocative situation*
b)   *during the actual confrontation*
c)   *reflecting on how you handled the situation*

Let's go over the following list of possible self-statements together and consider which ones apply best in your situation.

Deffenbacher and McKay (2000) propose that the therapist highlight that the use of such self-statements will prove especially helpful and important <u>after the therapy program is over</u>. Using these coping self-statements will help the patient to stay <u>in control</u> as he learns to <u>talk back to his anger</u>. In this way, the patient can learn to <u>control the anger</u> and <u>internal scripts</u>, instead of having the anger control him. These alternative self-statements will be thoughts that <u>make sense to you</u> and that you <u>really believe in</u>, especially as you practice them over and over so they <u>become second nature</u>.

The following **Patient Handouts** can be given to patients. As noted, **much preparation and processing are needed before these Handouts are given to patients**. The following **Patient Handouts** have been adapted from Novaco 1975; Deffenbacher & McKay, 2000; Meichenbaum 1985, 1994.

PATIENT HANDOUT

EXAMPLES OF <u>SELF-STATEMENTS</u> TO CONTROL ANGER

WHAT CAN YOU SAY TO YOURSELF WHEN YOU ARE:

Preparing for provocation

I can tell I am starting to get mad and I want to be in control and not lose my temper. I think I'll do X and see how that works.

This could be one to those high-risk situations. I am going to use my game-plan, my coping self-statements. Stop and think. What should I do?

This is going to upset me, but I know how to deal with it.

I can work out a plan to handle this.

I have choices!

What is it that I have to do first?

If I find myself getting upset, I'll know what to do.

There won't be any need for an argument.

Try not to take this too seriously.

This could be a testy situation, but I believe in myself.

Time for a few deep breaths of relaxation. Stay in control, relaxed, and at ease.

Easy does it. Remember to keep your sense of humor.

He wants me to lose my cool. I won't let him control me. I'm in charge.

Dealing with confrontations

Stay calm. Just continue to relax.

As long as I keep my cool, I'm in control.

Just roll with the punches; don't get bent out of shape.

Think of what you want to get out of this.

You don't need to prove yourself.

There is no point in getting mad. Stay task-focused.

Don't make more out of this than you have to. No mountains out of molehills!

I'm not going to let him get to me.

I don't want to let them make me angry and lose my temper because then I might do something I'd be sorry for.

Look for the positives. Don't assume the worst or jump to conclusions.

It's really a shame that he has to act like this.

For someone to be that irritable, he must be awfully unhappy.

If I start to get mad, I'll just be banging my head against the wall. So I might as well just relax.

There is no need to doubt myself. What he says doesn't matter.

I'm on top of this situation and my anger is under my control, not under his control.

Fighting is <u>not</u> the only response to an insult or conflict.

Stay focused on the problem, not on the person.

It is possible for <u>both</u> parties in a conflict to win.

Dealing with anger at its most intense point

My muscles are starting to feel tight. Just relax!
Getting upset won't help.
It's just not worth it to get so angry.
I'll let him blow off some steam.
I have a right to be annoyed, but let me keep the lid on.
Time to take another deep breath.
Let me take the issues point by point.
My anger is a signal of what I need to do. Time to coach myself.
I'm not going to get pushed around, but I'm not going haywire either.
Is this situation important enough for me to have a "meltdown" and blow it?
Try to reason it out. Treat each other with respect
Let me try a more cooperative approach. Maybe we are both right.
Negatives lead to more negatives. Work constructively.
He'd probably like me to get really angry. Well I'm going to disappoint him.
I can't expect people to act the way I want them to.
Take it easy, don't get pushy.
Time to relax and slow things down.

Other self-controlling responses

I can see the roller coaster of my emotions starting and I can stop it.
I can see when I am getting into emotional overdrive.
I can notice (catch, interrupt, change, redirect) the vicious cycle.
Calm down so I don't spiral out of control.

Self-soothing self-statements

This too shall pass.
She's just doing her job.
I can accept people the way they are. I don't have to be the "fixer".
Hang in there. This is disturbing, but not dangerous.

Reflecting on the provocation and on how you handled it

a) When conflict is unresolved

Forget about the aggravation. Thinking about it only makes me more upset.
These are difficult situations, and they take time to straighten out
Try to shake it off. Don't let it interfere with your job.
I'll get better at this as I get more practice.
Remember relaxation. It's a lot better than anger.
Can I laugh about it? It's probably not so serious.
Don't take it personally.
Take a slow deep breath.
At least I tried. I can learn from this.

b) When conflict is resolved or coping was successful

I handled it pretty well. It worked!
That wasn't as hard as I thought.
It could have been a lot worse.
I could have gotten more upset than it was worth.
I actually got through that without losing control, getting angry, becoming aggressive, being physical.
My pride can sure get me into trouble, but when I don't take things too seriously, I'm better off.
I guess I've been getting upset for too long when it wasn't even necessary.
I'm doing better at this all the time.
I now know I always have a back-up plan.

This previous list of **coping anger-reducing self-statements** was clustered **according to the phases of dealing with anger episodes**, namely, preparing, confronting, handling intense reactions and reflecting upon how the episode was handled. Deffenbacher and McKay (2000, pp. 154-156) have proposed that the **coping thoughts** can be clustered according to their **psychological functions**. These include:

Cool Thoughts
> *Take a few deep breaths. Chill out.*
> *Getting pissed off won't help.*

Problem-solving Thoughts
> *It's not the end of the world, just a problem to be solved.*
> *Develop a plan.*

Escape Routes
> *I can always walk away, rather than totally lose it.*
> *Bottom line, I'll walk before I hit. I'll take a time out.*

Self-efficacy Thoughts
> *I can handle this. I've done it before.*
> *I have what it takes to get through this hassle.*

Reattribution
> *They are probably just overwhelmed.*
> *Don't take it personally*

See the Whole Picture
> *Look at the other side.*
> *Any exceptions?*

Getting Accurate
> *Just the facts. Tell me like it is.*
> *Keep it simple.*

Preferences, Not Shoulds
> *It doesn't have to be my way. I just prefer it that way.*
> *This is what I want, not a should. What I want and what has to be are two different things. Stay with my wants.*

People Doing Their Best
> **They are only doing what they know how to do.**
> **I don't like how they are behaving, but they are trying.**

They key in using self-statements is to have the patient <u>generate</u> and <u>apply</u> his own individual package of self-statements. *Remember, it is <u>not</u> enough for the patient to change, the therapist needs to ensure that the patient attributes the improvement to his own efforts. The therapist can ask, "How did using the coping self-statements help? How did it feel to say these things to yourself in that situation?"*

PATIENT HANDOUT

<u>SELF-THOUGHTS</u> TO CONTROL ANGER:
CORRECTING COGNITIVE ERRORS

(Adapted from Deffenbacher, 1988)

Our thoughts play a key part in our becoming angry and in increasing our anger. Below are listed several types of thoughts that can increase anger. Following each example are some helpful alternatives which can help you to manage anger more effectively and to deal more appropriately with frustrating, irritating, and disappointing situations.

A. <u>**Catastrophising Thoughts**</u> --This is the tendency to make things worse than they are, i.e., "terrible, awful, devastating", etc. You then respond angrily, and perhaps, attack as if these things were very bad.

Examples:
1. This is the worst thing that's ever happened.
2. I just can't stand the way that he/she is talking to me.
3. This is terrible!

Examples of <u>helpful self-thoughts</u> to be used instead of catastrophizing:
1. It's not the end of the world. It's just frustrating.
2. It's just not worth getting all angry about it.
3. I'll just make the best out of this situation that I can.
4. Hang in there. It'll be over soon.
5. Getting all bent out of shape doesn't help. Then I have two problems. What I am dealing with and being all angry.
6. Hang loose and cope. Don't let it get you down. It's not worth it.
7. Why should I get all upset? Who will know or care in a week anyway.
8. I'll do what I can. If it works, great. If not, well I did the best I can. No need to go crazy about it. Keep things in perspective.
9. So what if I don't get what I want? Sometimes I do and sometimes I don't. There's no guarantee. No reason to blow up about it.

B. <u>**Demanding/Coercive Thoughts**</u> -- This is the tendency to make your wants into demands for yourself or for the rest of the world. It is the tendency to think that things "should", "ought", "need to be", "have to be", "are expected to be", "must be", certain ways. When you demand that people or situations be a certain way, then you tend to become very angry and upset. You often feel justified in your anger when the demand is not met.

Examples:
1. He/she should have known that would hurt my feelings.
2. They should have done that.
3. It's not fair! (implying that it ought to be)

"Who appointed you a God who gets to tell others how to live or be?" Actually, only you did! Frankly, there is no absolute reason why things "should" be the way that you want, other than that you want it that way. Stay with your wants, desires, and preferences. It is frustrating, disappointing and inconvenient when you do not get what you want. Stay with that. You can cope with that.

Examples of helpful self-thoughts for demanding/coercing:
1. There's no one right way; we just have a difference of opinion.
2. Look, I want it this way and I am going to stick up for what I think, but they don't have to do it my way.
3. I can't expect people to always act the way I want them to.
4. I don't like this. It's not going my way. So what am I going to do about it? Getting all righteous won't help. How am I going to handle the hassle? That's it, focus on it as a problem to be solved, not as a personal threat.
5. I don't really know why he/she did that. Maybe I need to ask him/her.
6. So I don't get what I want. So what's the big deal. Sure, it's frustrating (disappointing, hurts, is a hassle, etc.), but I can cope.
7. Sure it's not "right" from my point of view, but they have "rights" too. Who says they've got to agree with me?

C. **Overgeneralized Thoughts** --This is the tendency to go way beyond the facts in our thinking, to make things far bigger than they really are. These thoughts take irritation or frustration and blow them out of proportion, making you more angry.

Examples:
1. That ruins the whole evening (time).
2. He/she is always inconsiderate.
3. This always happens to me when I am in a hurry.
4. I'm never going to get over this.

Rarely are things "always" or "never" a certain way, even though they may be negative in a given situation. Stay with that. You can cope with a specific situation. Big broad labels are rarely true, e.g., "worthless", "worst", "total junk", etc. Try to stay with the realistic negative feelings and cope with that, rather than blowing them out of proportion and going way beyond what is true.

Examples of <u>helpful self-thoughts</u> for overgeneralized thinking:
1.   What's really true? So it's frustrating. Stay cool and cope with that. It's only this hassle in this situation, nothing more.
2.   It's frustrating, but I don't need to make a federal case out of it.
3.   This irritates me, but that's all. I don't have to let it get to me.
4.   All things considered, this is pretty small issue.
5.   This is negative, but other things are going positive.
6.   Stay with the situation. I'm the one who really suffers when I get really angry and out of control.
7.   No big deal. No need to make myself all upset about this.

D. <u>Categorical Thinking</u> -- This is the tendency to label situations in very extreme, angering terms. For example, labeling some one a "jerk", "slob", "bastard", "an ass", "son of a bitch", "worthless", "no good", etc. just cranks your anger up. Many of these expressions tend to be obscenities and carry with them extra anger automatically.

Examples:
1. That jerk (slob, son of a bitch, ass, etc.)
2. God damn it.
3. That thing is just a worthless piece of crap!

These categorical labels and obscenities increase anger, but rarely are they true. Think for example of the two common meanings of the word "ass". One is a small horse-like animal and the other refers to buttocks. Now what has that got to do with the person or situation to which it has been applied? Try to replace these labels with realistic behavioral descriptions.

Examples of <u>helpful self-thoughts</u> for categorical thinking:
1. He/she is not an ass, just a person with whom I have a disagreement.
2. God damn it! No, it's just frustrating and not the way I want, but I can cope with that.
3. It's just broke, that's all.
4. There I go "helling again." It's not hell, just a hassle. Hassles I can deal with.

E. <u>One-Track Thinking</u> -- This is the tendency to think of things only one way, often tending to personalize the reasons, rather than thinking about multiple reasons for why things happened the way that they did. If you hold a negative interpretation that is not true, your anger will follow at a higher level.

Examples:
1. He/she is doing that to get to me.
2. They wouldn't have done that if they were my friends.
3. It's all my (their) fault.

Sometimes your interpretation may be true. Staying with reality, this would lead to frustration, disappointment, hurt, loss, etc. However, often there are other reasons or explanations you have not thought of. Your anger may be at an inappropriate or exaggerated level if you do not have all the facts.

Examples of helpful self-thoughts for one-track thinking:
1. Don't jump to conclusions. Check out the facts.
2. Maybe they didn't know. I better check it out first, before going off half-cocked.
3. I may not have all the facts.
4. Getting angry does not help me figure out what went wrong.
5. Where's my evidence that this is the only reason?
6. Maybe they're just "constipated" (or some other humorous explanation).

ADDITIONAL WAYS TO CHANGE
YOUR ANGRY SELF-DIALOGUE

Think about a situation in which you become angry and ask yourself:

WHAT DID I WANT THAT I WAS NOT GETTING?

WHAT WAS I GETTING THAT I DID NOT WANT?

Ask your self:

WAS THERE SOME WAY I COULD HAVE GOTTEN WHAT I WANTED, OR AVOIDED WHAT I DIDN'T WANT, WITHOUT BECOMING ANGRY?

**Make a copy of this and carry it with you
and refer to it when you become angry.**

PATIENT HANDOUT

WAYS TO COPE WITH ANGER AND AVOID AGGRESSIVE BEHAVIOR

Individuals who have problems controlling their anger or difficulty resolving conflicts in a nonaggressive fashion often feel that their **anger is immediate** and **out of control**. This **Patient's Handout** describes many ways individuals can better control their anger and avoid and reduce their aggressive behavior. The suggestions include ways individuals can:

    a) <u>Increase</u> <u>Awareness</u>: **Recognize**

    b) **Ways To <u>Prevent</u> Themselves From Becoming Angry And Aggressive**

    c) **Things To Do <u>During</u> Episodes When They Become Angry**

    d) **Things To Do <u>After</u> They Become Angry**

    e) **Behaviors To <u>Watch Out For</u>**

The therapist can use this **Patient Handout** in a number of ways:

    (1) The **Handout** is a quick reminder to determine if these points have been covered in training.

    (2) The **Handout** can be given to patients (<u>in portions</u> or in total) as a reminder of what has been covered in treatment. *(Don't give the entire Handout at one time since it can overwhelm some patients. Sample from each section to meet the needs and style of your patients.)*

    (3) The **Handout** can be used as a basis for discussion with groups of patients or with couples, parent-adolescent meetings, and the like.

PATIENT HANDOUT

SELF-CONTROL STRATEGY
INCREASE <u>AWARENESS</u> TRAINING

In order to control my anger, it is important to <u>first become aware</u> of <u>warning signs</u>, <u>high-risk situations</u> and <u>factors</u> that increase the likelihood of aggression. I should be <u>on the lookout for</u>:

Things that **set me off**

Triggers or **warning signs** that I am becoming angry

"High-risk" situations (settings where I usually get angry)

Types of **things that get me angry** (e.g., job dissatisfaction, stress at work, commuting, daily frustrations and hassles)

Role of **addictive substances** such as alcohol and other drugs

How my thoughts can become **"self-fulfilling prophecies"** (How I think influences how I behave.)

The influence of my **"should" statements** in contributing to my anger

That sometimes my feelings of anger and my acts of aggression help me to **compensate for, blot out, or distract myself from** other feelings of being afraid, anxious, ashamed, humiliated, insecure, vulnerable, betrayed, helpless and sad. *(Anger and aggression can provide a sense of power and control. There is a need for me to find more constructive ways of responding to these underlying feelings of shame, frustration, disappointment, and helplessness.)*

The **circumstances** and **feelings** I need to **protect myself against**.

Whether **anger is a "personal problem"** for me.

Ways to break my anger-aggression cycle into a **series of steps,** with each step representing a **choice point** for possible intervention.

That each time my **expectations are violated** or a **plan is interrupted**, this is an **"invitation to anger."** I may choose to accept the "invitation" or not. **I have a choice!**

The **pattern of events** that **trigger my anger**. I can ask myself, *"What is common across these situations? Is there a rule that you hold that is being violated?"*

The number of times you **say "no" to others**. Ask yourself, *"Which are the necessary "nos" (bottom-line)?"* I can ask myself, *"Are there any "nos" that can be eliminated or compromised and any responsibilities that can be shared?"*

Times in the past when I handled my anger or **prevented it** from getting out of hand. Ask myself, *"If there is anything I used in the past that I can use here?"*

My **"game-plan"** of how I can **remember to use my coping skills.**

That there is nothing wrong in becoming angry if I **use constructive ways** to express and handle my anger.

That anger can **serve a protective function** that signals the need to protect myself and others, to correct an injustice, to solve a problem.

WAYS TO <u>PREVENT</u> MYSELF FROM BECOMING ANGRY AND AGGRESSIVE

In order to control my anger, it is important to <u>prepare ahead of time</u> or <u>have a game plan</u>. My game plan includes how to:

Avoid using **alcohol** and other **addictive substances.**
Avoid "high risk" situations and **conflicts.**
Avoid anger-provoking events (e.g., agree not to discuss a hot issue at this time, rather wait until I cool down; walk away from tense situations).
Choose low-conflict situations.
Change internal cues (e.g., brooding, ruminating) and **distance myself from provocative external cues** (e.g., confrontations, frustrating situations) that trigger my anger.
Control my tendency to use **inflammatory language.**
Imaginally rehearse how I am going to handle a potential provocation scene **beforehand.**
Learn to distinguish between **various degrees of emotion** (e.g., what it takes to elicit feelings of being annoyed, irritated, frustrated, <u>versus</u> angry, furious, enraged).
Write out a script of how I can handle my anger and control myself. **Create an "internal play"** with me as a character who remains **calm** and **controlled**. As part of the script, **generate a list of alternative ways** I can handle anger situations and the reasons why (beneficial consequences to self and to others) if I control my anger.
Change my angry self-dialogue and **guide myself** through provocation events in a calmer task-focused manner.

When **provoked**, I can ask myself the following questions:

> *"Is this matter really important to me?"*
> *"Is what I'm feeling and thinking appropriate (helpful)? "*
> *"What should I do when I <u>notice</u> that I am starting to get angry?*
> *"How can I <u>avoid getting angry</u> in the first place? "*
> *"If I do get angry, how can I keep the anger at a <u>moderate level of intensity</u>? (Being annoyed and irritated and not becoming furious and enraged.) "*
> *"How can I <u>set limits</u> so my anger does <u>not spiral out of control</u>? "*
> *"What are the <u>costs</u> to me and to others when I get angry? "*
> *"Is my anger helping me <u>achieve all of my goals</u>? "*

Notice the cycle of anger developing and **interrupt** and **redirect** the cycle.
Make a commitment and **sign a behavioral contract** (witnessed and cosigned by someone special) <u>not</u> to use aggressive behaviors and what I can do instead.
Keep a list of the benefits (short-term, intermediate and long-term) for self and others of controlling my anger with me and refer to it regularly. Stay focused on **long-term goals.**
Keep busy and **task-oriented**. (Don't get sidetracked.)

THINGS TO DO <u>DURING</u> EPISODES WHEN I BECOME ANGRY

Check for my anger signals. Notice where in my body I feel anger.
Scan my body and mood.
Ask myself, *"What is my body telling me? What is my gut saying if it could speak?"*
Acknowledge my anger to others and to myself.
Use my self-control "game plan" and follow my **non-angry script.**
Use my **self-statements** to guide me through my angry feelings.
Challenge my **angry self-dialogue.**

Ask myself questions such as:

> *"What did I want, that I was <u>not</u> getting?"*
> *"What was I getting, that I did <u>not</u> want?"*
> *"Was there some way I could have gotten what I wanted , or awarded what I didn't want, without becoming angry?"*

Let go of my desires that are **impossible to satisfy.**
See provocations as a **"problems-to-be-solved"** and <u>not</u> take them personally. Define my problems-to-be-solved early enough to lend themselves to possible solutions. **Use self-imposed limits.**

> *"What is the problem to be solved?"*
> *"Is the situation modifiable?"*
> *"Is it worth taking action?"*
> *"What choices (options) do I have?"*

Turn my anger into a **positive reaction.** See my anger as energy for **constructive action.**
Try out my coping skills. Give myself permission to fail, but view such failures, should they occur, as **"learning opportunities."**

Ask myself questions such as:

> *"Can I <u>call attention to something that needs correction</u> without being accusatory or sarcastic?"*
> *"Can I <u>listen for</u> something that is said which I could <u>agree with</u>?"*
> *"Can I <u>see his/her viewpoint</u>?"*
> *"Can I <u>keep it current</u> and think into the future and leave out the past? <u>Not bring up 'old history'</u>?"*
> *"Can I talk in terms of my <u>own wishes and needs</u>, rather than about what is wrong?"*
> *"Can I <u>compromise</u> on this?"*

Take a time out. *(Tell someone, "I need a little time to think through the issue and tell him/her that I will get back to him/her.")*

Relax myself. *(Tell myself, "I can calm down and I don't have to spiral out of control.")*

Take slow deep breaths. (Use diaphragmatic breathing: 3 to 5 slow deep breaths, relaxing more and more with each exhalation.)

Reduce mental overactivity. Play a different CD in my head. Don't make things worse.

Relax my mind. (Use imagery and meditation procedures.) Relaxation is a way to intentionally turn down my "nerves" and lower my sympathetic arousal system.

Tame the feeling of anger by turning down the fight or flight response -- **lengthen my fuse.** Learn to **tolerate** painful emotions.

Delay anger responding by saying, *"Can I think about what I said and get back to you?" Not have to respond immediately. Can I defer the discussion until I calm down? "Can I put my emotions on the shelf for now?"*

Use **imagery and self-statements** to change the event from feeling furious and enraged, instead to feeling only irritated and annoyed.

Think of a time when I was really angry and I did <u>not</u> take it out on someone. Reflect and **learn from what I did** to handle that situation.

Use **perspective taking.** Take the role of another person.

Put myself in the other person's shoes and imagine what he/she is thinking and feeling.

Think of a time when someone got angry with me. How did that make me feel? Did I want to be his/her friend? Did I want to cooperate with that person? What can I learn from this reflection? **Share this reflection** with someone else.

Remind myself that I don't always do what others want. Why should I expect that others will do what I want all of the time? Ask myself, *"Who appointed me God to give commandments? I have wants and preferences; I don't issue commandments."* Talk in terms of my wishes, needs, rather than in terms of what is right and wrong.

Refocus attention away from my anger. **Use my distraction techniques.** For example, think of pleasant images.

Hide my reactions for the time being and **do something constructive** with these feelings later on (e.g., confide in others, engage in problem solving, engage in arousal-reducing activities).

Remind myself of the **costs** of being angry (personal, interpersonal, physical).

Think of consequences (costs) of becoming angry and aggressive for myself and for others.

Ask myself, *"If I use my anger, will anyone be hurt by it? Will I be hurt by the consequences?"*

Use a small tape recorder and **record my thoughts** and **feelings.** Fill out my **"hassle log."**

Ask myself, *"What do I want in the long run? What small steps can I take in that direction? Am I part of the solution and not part of the problem?"*

Use patience - *enduring the unwanted without aggression.*

Use humor appropriately - use silly humor (e.g., image literally "dumb asses").

Ask myself, *"How would <u>someone I know</u> who controls his or her anger <u>handle this situation?"</u>*

Write a letter (draw a picture) describing my feelings. (Don't mail the letter.)

Use **arousal-discharge outlets** (exercise, deep breathing relaxation procedures, imagery exercises, distraction procedures).

Use **communication skills.** (Tell someone how I feel, acknowledge my anger, and use it constructively to correct the situation, improve things.)

Confide in a friend. Talk about it with someone who understands; with someone I can trust; with the person I am angry at using "I feel" statements.

Become **appropriately assertive**. (Tell someone.)

Use **conflict management skills**.

Take responsibility for what happened; <u>not</u> blame anyone else or anything else.

Be flexible: *"I am willing to give up what I cannot have and accept what I cannot change."*

Accept that which I do not want, but cannot avoid.

Focus on one thing at a time. Try not to solve too many problems at one time.

Remind myself of the **Serenity Prayer**: *"Give me the courage to change what I can, the serenity to accept what I cannot change; and the wisdom to know the difference."*

THINGS TO DO <u>AFTER</u> I BECOME ANGRY

In order to <u>control my anger</u>, it is important to learn from what happened. I can do this by learning how to:

Figure out afterwards **how my anger arose** and what I can **learn** from this.

Visualize the situation in which my anger arose and ask myself, *"What did I want, that I wasn't getting? What was I getting, that I didn't want?"*

Reflect afterwards, by asking myself, *"Was there some way I could have gotten what I wanted or avoided what I didn't want, without becoming angry?"*

Ask myself, *"What other things could I have done? What are some other ways to handle the situation should it arise in the future?"*

Recognize my own contribution to repeated failure.

Repair the situation; make amends.

Take note of changes and **take credit** for what I did to bring about these changes.

Develop a **"game-plan" for future high-risk** anger-provoking **situations**. *Have a back-up plan.*

Know what is provoking and **act beforehand** in the future. **Be prepared!**

Praise myself for having tried (praising my efforts, not just considering the outcome).

Remind myself that *"One mistake doesn't spoil all of the work I have done."*

Reflect on what I have learned. *"What steps did I forget to do?" "How can I handle this better next time?" "I know how to do it I just need more practice." "I'll do better next time." "I'm learning from my errors." "Now I can move on."*

Praise (reward) yourself for having taken the effort to work on your coping efforts.

BEHAVIORS TO <u>WATCH OUT FOR</u>

In order to <u>control my anger</u>, it is important to keep in mind that I:

Don't look for slights.

Don't take it personally.

Don't take the "bait".

Don't rage against that which cannot be changed (e.g., Just like raging against bad weather.)

Don't expect the worst.

Don't become "infected" by other's gripes.

Don't sulk.

Don't use "silent anger" (isolation, suppress anger, get back at someone).

Don't use sarcasm, threats, and intimidation.

Don't ruminate, brood, blame others, and carry grudges.

Don't get stuck using "shoulds" and "coulds."

Don't bring up "old history."

Don't use indirect aggression (gossip, ostracize, be passive-aggressive).

COGNITIVE RESTRUCTURING ("RETHINKING") PROCEDURES

(See Meichenbaum, 1994 for more details)
(ALSO SEE PATIENT HANDOUT ON CORRECTING COGNITIVE SELF-THOUGHTS TO CONTROL ANGER, p.284)

The scripts or blueprints that we hold predispose or contribute to angry responses. These scripts and responses are informed by the display rules of the individual's culture.

The object of the **cognitive restructuring or "rethinking" procedures** is to help angry patients appreciate how their beliefs, appraisals, expectations, thinking patterns, self-statements, and developmental mental scripts, play a role in contributing to and exacerbating their angry response to the point of aggression. The **"rethinking" procedures** are designed to help patients appreciate how they "crank up" or "jack up" their anger as a result of how they think and to promote personal agency and ownership in order to enhance greater self-control. *(I have found it useful to use the phrase "rethinking" instead of cognitive restructuring with patients.)*

The examples offered earlier under **self-instructional training** illustrate ways that the therapist can help the patients develop a different more adaptive script. In addition, there is a need to help patients become aware of their **thinking habits**.

For example, the therapist can discuss with the patient his history of exposure to anger/aggression and its impact on self and others. The therapist can compare the concept of anger to that of a **learned blueprint** or **script**.

> *Anger is like an architect's blueprint. The availability of the blueprint does **not** cause a building to be constructed, but it does make the construction easier. Like an architect's blueprint is critical to building a house, anger makes aggression a lot easier. (Kassinove, 1995)*

> *Individuals learn "scripts" about how and when to become angry. For example, just like someone learns a restaurant script (MacDonald's, Japanese restaurant), people learn anger and aggression scripts. The scripts or implicit rules are culturally specific and are formed and accumulated by a group of people who share a particular lifestyle and values. (Nisbett, 1993)*

THINKING STYLE, HABITS, AND COGNITIVE DISTORTIONS

(See Katz, 1988; Yochelson & Samenow, 1976, 1977; Walters, 1990
for a discussion of "thinking errors" and personal ideology of angry and aggressive
individuals. Deffenbacher & McKay, 2000, provide a description of possible antidotes or
coping behaviors for each "thinking error.".)

The therapist can help patients understand and control their anger by teaching them to **recognize, label** and **challenge** their "thinking errors." **Cognitive restructuring or rethinking procedures** can be used to help patients focus attention on their thinking style, habits, and cognitive distortions and the ways they automatically appraise events and process information. The therapist can help patients appreciate how they deny, minimize, justify, excuse, and rationalize their aggressive behavior. Perpetrators often see themselves as "victims" (suffered, been mistreated, exploited, misunderstood, hurt). Perpetrators are often insensitive to victim's pain and fail to consider the consequences of their acts.

In order to help patients change these cognitive activities, the therapist helps patients become aware of and change their **thinking patterns** which may include:

    a)   **magnifying / catastrophizing thinking;**

    b)   **exaggerated overgeneralizing thinking;**

    c)   **dichotomous or black-white thinking;**

    d)   **demanding, commanding and coercive language and imposing perfectionistic standards on themselves and on others;**

    e)   **inflammatory and global language;**

    f)   **misattributions;**

    g)   **blaming, minimizing, justifying.**

The following list of **"thinking errors"** is not offered to the patient as a mini-lecture, but as the patient manifests them over the course of the therapy sessions. The therapist will introduce each concept and help patients recognize the impact and their relationship to anger and aggression. In turn, the patient will learn various antidotes to coping skills on how to "notice," "catch," and "correct" cognitive distortions and cognitive errors. It is helpful if the therapist waits for a number of examples of the patient's thinking errors and uses these as examples.

For instance, the therapist can reflect to the patient:

"You say you can show love or punch him out."
"You either love her or hate her."
"You said that they are in full support of you or they are out to get you."

Metaphorically, the therapist can hold a flashlight up to the patient's thinking style and ask him if he sees the same pattern of thoughts and reactions. With acknowledgment and elaboration, the therapist can in this case introduce the concept of dichotomous thinking (either-or, black-white thinking) and explore with the patient what the impact is on the patient and on significant others of engaging in such dichotomous thinking. If it has this impact, then what can be done? Collaboratively with the patient, a series of coping antidotes can be introduced and practiced. When treatment is conducted on a group basis, examples of the various cognitive errors/distortions can be introduced using examples from several patients. The therapy process is **inductive** and not deductive, **collaborative** and **Socratic** and not didactic.

DESCRIPTION OF "THINKING ERRORS" AND ANTIDOTES

1. **magnifying / catastrophizing ways of thinking** that make the problem **bigger** and **worse** than it really is. The angry patient tends to use such descriptive phrases such as ***"disgusting", "devastating". "terrible", "horrible", "sickening", "can't stand it"***.

   Antidote: Have the patient learn to **describe the situation accurately and specifically**. Change vocabulary to convey **gradation of distress** -- use such words as ***"annoyed", "frustrated", "disappointed", "a pain", "hassle", "loss", "perturbation"***.

2. **exaggerated overgeneralizing ways of thinking**. The patient tends to use language that goes beyond the details of a specific situation as reflected in such tip-off words as ***"always, all, every, never, everybody"***

   Antidote: Have the patient **use accurate and specific descriptions** and to be on the **lookout for exceptions**.

3. **dichotomous or black-white thinking**. The angry patient tends to use polarized, **either-or**, broad categorizations of events.

   Antidote: Have the patient **qualify his/her language** by using adjectives and adverbs such as ***"a little", "somewhat",***. Also, have the patient consider **multiple dimensions of the situation, *"On the one hand, ..., but on the other hand .... Bad in some respects, such as ..., but good in other respects such as ...***

4. **demanding, commanding and coercive language and use of perfectionist standards**. The angry patient tends to view and convey personal preferences and desires as dictates and commandments. This is evident in the patient using such phrases as ***"should, ought, have to, needs to"***. These reflect the often rigid absolutistic beliefs that events or people must be a certain way and that conditions such as success and approval are absolute necessities. The patient insists that things be a certain way conveying a **sense of entitlement**. For example, ***"They ought to be grateful for what I did."; "She should know what I need without my asking."; "He should have known that I was going to get angry."***

   Antidote: The patient needs to learn to **view demands and commands as preferences and wants**. ***"You should"*** statements can be conveyed to others as ***"I'd prefer that you X."*** The patient needs to learn to **question their rigid demands**. How would he/she like to be treated in such a fashion? Such **self-questioning** challenges the implicit set of rules that the patient holds about how other people should or should not behave.

As Deffenbacher and McKay (2000), convey to the patient:

> *"The key thing to remember about <u>shoulds</u> is that people do what they want to do <u>not</u> what you think they should do. Your needs are <u>not</u> their needs. Because you want something or believe in something, it <u>doesn't mean that</u> they have to agree with you. <u>Shoulds can push your anger out of control.</u> The best way to cope with should is to think of them as <u>personal preferences</u> or <u>wants.</u> It's better to think "<u>I'd prefer</u>", rather than "<u>He should</u>". (Adapted from page 99, emphasis added).*

Sometimes the patient may impose the notion of "shoulds" on themselves as they engage in implicit <u>perfectionistic standards</u>. The therapist can convey:

> *"I understand that you would become upset with yourself when you ... It sounds like you expect yourself to do everything perfectly. Is that indeed the case?"*

> *"It sounds like you don't need anyone else to be a critic. You do such a good job on yourself, you don't need help from others. What is the impact of holding such perfectionistic standards."*

5. **inflammatory and global language**. The angry patient tends to use highly obscene verbal labels filled with negative highly affectively-charged expressions (e.g., "asshole, SOB, jerk, idiot, total screw-up," and other obscene expressions). Such labels condemn the person and do not consider the specific distressing behavior. Such inflammatory language acts as *"mental gasoline to be added to already existing angry (seething) fuel"*. These inflammatory labels can *"shorten your fuse, blow things further out of proportion, prime your pump, get you more pissed off."*

   Antidote: Teach the patient to **notice** when he/she uses such inflammatory labels and ask helpful others to point out when the patient tends to use such labels. Instead, the patient needs to **provide accurate detailed descriptions** of offensive behavior. Be specific. *Who did <u>what</u> in <u>which situation</u> with <u>what effect</u> (reactions)?* The description should focus on what the person did, not who he is.

6. **misattributions**. The angry patient tends to **mind-read** others' intentions and behaviors by **jumping to conclusions** and **readily interpreting others' motives as hostile intentions**. *"They are out to get me. They did this on purpose."* Such **personalized appraisals** can escalate angry responses and contribute to aggressive behavior.

Antidote: Once again, the patient needs to become **more mindful and aware** of his/her tendency to engage in such misattributions. The patient needs to engage in **reality checks**. They have to learn to use **interpersonal phrases** such as:

"I have a feeling you are X when I do Y. Is that the way you see it?"

"It occurred to me that MAYBE you think I was X. Am I imagining things or is there some truth to this?"

Was there a reason that you did X?

Besides learning and practicing this form of interpersonal questioning **(reality checks),** the patient can be taught ways to consider alternative explanations. The therapist can set the stage for such interventions by encouraging patients **not to believe everything they say to themselves and to view their automatic thoughts as <u>hypotheses</u> worthy of testing, rather than as God-given truthful assertions.** *(In the same way that you don't believe everything you read in a newspaper, perhaps you should learn to question what you tell yourself.)*

The therapist can ask the patient:

Can you remember any time that you have made an assumption about someone else's behavior, motives, or feelings and that you learned later that you were way off base (wrong)? Have you ever caught yourself jumping to conclusions that you later found were wrong? I know I have. Let me give you an example.

7. <u>**blaming, minimizing and justifying**</u>. The angry patient tends to **externalize the problem** and conveys having been **victimized** and being **"helpless".** The patient conveys that he/she wants others to "fix" the problem and that he/she <u>cannot</u> do anything until others take action.

"I am not to blame. Factors beyond my control. I had no choice. I had to defend myself, defend my rights."

"It wasn't so bad."

"Everyone else joined in."

If they want me not to get angry, they know what they should do."

Antidote: The therapist can help the patient **recognize the interdependence and coercive nature of the anger/aggressive cycle**. The therapist can ask the patient to provide a detailed blow-by-blow account of what happens and wonder what is it about the patient's behavior that triggers (provokes) others? The therapist can provide **provisional hypotheses**:

"Maybe when you get X, she feels Y and does Z. Have you ever thought about her side of things and what she might feel? How could you check that out?"

Deffenbacher and McKay (2000) have summarized these antidotes to thinking errors as **Counter-response Plans**. These counter-response plans include the patient looking for:

> **EXCEPTIONS**
> **ALTERNATIVE EXPLANATIONS**
> **PREFERENCES, NOT SHOULDS**
> **BEING SPECIFIC AND ACCURATE**
> **LOOKING FOR THE BIGGER PICTURE**
> **BEING REALISTICALLY NEGATIVE**

The discussion of these thinking errors can be supplemented by having the patients generate specific examples of each category. Deffenbacher and McKay (2000, pp. 106-112) have developed an **Anger Distortions Handout** for patients that includes the name and definition of the thinking errors, examples, and coping efforts. (See their **Client Manual**)

Another way to have the patient become familiar and proficient in identifying *"thinking errors"* is to have the patient watch portions of films of anger episodes and have them identify the seven forms of cognitive errors and examine possible coping techniques and counter-response plans.

In order to help patients become aware of the nature and impact of their thinking processes, the therapist can ask the patient:

> *How does black-white thinking contribute to your anger?*
> *How can you become more aware of your pattern of thinking?*
> *When you thought X, did it seem to feed your anger? And did thinking he was X make you more pissed off?*
> *What happens to your anger when you think X?*
> *If you were going to change that thought, what could you say to yourself differently?*
> *What are some of the triggering thoughts associated with your anger? What is the "thinking error" that lies behind each triggering thought? Let's examine that together.*
> *What assumptions go with that triggering thought?*
> *If you were going to replace your label with a specific description of the problem, how would you do that?*
> *When you become angry, what happens to your thinking and to how you behave?*

Is there any other possible alternative explanation for why he behaved that way? Is there a way to open a door to an alternative explanation or interpretation?

In order to convey the information about "thinking errors" to the patient, the therapist can **use analogies**, brief to-the-point **teaching stories**, and self-disclosure of **anecdotal accounts**. For example, Deffenbacher (1999, p. 303) provides several examples to help patients reframe anger episodes.

Example 1:

Therapist: *It seems like you are becoming angry about things that are beyond your control. It is <u>like the weather</u>. For example, consider that you were planning to visit the beach or have a picnic on a warm sunny summer's day. Although the day started nice, the weather turned cold and rainy. Would you rant and rave at the weather? You don't have to like the weather, but you don't have to become enraged and try to attack it either. You accept it as unfavorable and go to plan B. I wonder if some of the situations you describe when you become angry and upset are <u>like the weather</u>.*

Example 2:

Therapist: *What are the differences between <u>preferences</u> and <u>commandments</u>? The reason I ask is that at times you sound like a God who issues commandments. Like mortals however, you only have a series of wants and preferences. Some of these preferences will be fulfilled and others won't. For example, do you always do what others want? Why not? Well, if you treat your wants and preferences as commandments, then what reactions are you likely to have?*

Example 3:

Therapist: *It sounds like people (at work, home) don't do the things the way you would like.*

Patient: *Yeah, they are really frustrating people.*

Therapist: *But why shouldn't you have to put up with frustrating people? Why shouldn't you have to put up with your share of frustration?*

These examples are designed to help patients **reframe and rethink how they handle provocations**. The following set of questions that focus on

    a) EVIDENCE-BASED QUESTIONS
    b) ALTERNATIVE-BASED QUESTIONS
    c) IMPLICATION-BASED QUESTIONS

are designed to help patients further reconsider the role that cognitions play in the experience and expression of anger and aggression.

By using **Socratic questioning**, the therapist can help patient's **question their automatic thoughts and consider their underlying beliefs or schemas**. For example, the therapist can ask <u>evidence-based</u> and <u>alternative-based questions</u>:

What led you to the conclusion that ...?
Can you think of an example of where you made a mountain out of a molehill?
How does that observation (conclusion, statement) fit with ...?
How does that follow from ...?
Help me understand how you decided ... .
Where is the evidence for ...?
What is another way of looking at that?
Do you know anyone who would look at it differently? In what way?
Can you think of a way to question that assumption?
I was wondering if there is a way to stand back and look at the whole picture.
What predictions are you making for yourself?

EXPLORE IMPLICATIONS: USE A DOWNWARD ARROW PROCEDURE

With a highly emotional event, help the patient **explore implications**

If indeed, what you describe is accurate, what are the implications for you (and others)?
How can you test that out?
What is it about X that makes you feel Y?
So what would happen if you were wrong?
What does this mean to you?
What does this mean about other people?
What does this say about other people?
What does this say about the world/your life/your future?
If this is true, then what might happen?
Is this what you want to happen?
If not, why not?
What have you been doing about this?
What can you do about this now?
Let me ask a related question. What would it mean if you tried X?
I am going to suggest a personal experiment, if this is okay?

TEST UNDERLYING BELIEFS: HELP THE PATIENT TO

Make specific predictions based on old and new beliefs.
Plan personal experiments (discuss possible problems and how to handle them).
Perform experiments.
Record outcomes (Check out the "data").
Repeat, as necessary.
Consider implications (Help patients take "data" as "evidence" to unfreeze their beliefs about self, others, and the world).
Consider self-definition and core beliefs.

Ask the patient:

> *What would you need to <u>believe</u> in order to be motivated to take these actions (change, use your coping skills)?*

There is also value in helping patients address such issues as jealousy, revenge (how to let go of past events) and anti-egalitarian attitudes toward women. (See Holbrook, 1995). One way to facilitate this process is to have patients use **letter-writing** and **journaling**. A second way is to have patients engage in **problem-solving**. We now turn our attention to these interventions.

LETTER-WRITING AND JOURNALING

As part of the **rethinking procedure**, the therapist can help the patient consider the developmental influences that contribute to his anger and rage. **Letter-writing** and **journaling** have been used to help patients better appreciate how early relationships (e.g., relationship with their father) influence their current behavior. There is a need to transform these "insights," or co-constructive narrative explanations, into the present by having patients consider what lingers from these early experiences. What are the conclusions they draw about themselves and about others as a result of these developmental influences? How do such experiences impact their current bouts of anger? What can patients do to combat these influences? One possibility is to have the patients engage in **"here and now" problem-solving training**.

Another means to address developmental influences is to increase patients' awareness by having them engage in **letter-writing** and **journaling**. **Letter-writing** and **journaling** have been used as a way to help individuals **"come to terms"** with their anger and let "bygones be bygones". Donovan and Pedin-Rivera (1999), as part of a 12 week partial hospitalization program with combat veterans who experience PTSD and substance abuse, include an experiential exercise of having participants write *"A letter to your father."* or to some other significant person(s). (In other instances, the patient may write a letter as an adult speaking back to a likely critical mother on behalf of the child.)

The **letter**, which is <u>not sent</u>, is written whether or not the father (person) is still alive. In the letter the patients may be asked to write about:

    a)   things their father did that they are <u>thankful for</u>;
    b)   things that made them <u>angry, embarrassed, humiliated, shamed</u> and/or <u>sad</u>;
    c)   things they <u>resent</u> or <u>regret</u>;
    d)   ways they <u>wish</u> their relationship with their father had been different.

These letters are read over several sessions to the group, during which the participants explore:

    a) what impact do such early experiences still have on their current behavior;
    b) what "lingers from"; what "conclusions", what "beliefs", what "attitudes and behaviors" derive from these early experiences;
    c) what understanding, what self-acceptance and self-forgiveness; what compassion toward oneself and toward others can be experienced.

In this way the group members can explore the nature and triggers of their "rage."
Writing can also be used by having patients describe their experiences in traumatic situations such as in combat. For example, one Vet was asked, "What he would say if his buddy who died in combat walked into the room right now?" The Vet was asked to write a letter to his friend in order to move emotionally from punishing himself for surviving to honoring the memory of his friend. In this way, the Vet came to view his <u>anger</u> as a <u>secondary emotion</u> designed to address "survivor guilt."

As a by-product of the letter-writing and journaling activities, participants may come to consider the potential benefits of **forgiveness** as a way to resolve past "hurts". Worthington (1998) and Meyer et al. (2000) have viewed forgiveness as a form of **positive risk-taking** and have summarized the steps involved with the acronym of **REACH** which stands for:

> **R**ecall and acknowledge the "hurt

> **E**mpathize (imagine the other person's perspective)

> **A**ltruistic gift (recall when you have been forgiven by another; What was that feeling like? Can you give it to another person?

> **C**ommit to your choices (formal action that includes letting go, positive feelings, and clarifying boundaries of the relationship in a way that is safe and good for you)

> **H**old onto your choices

The use of **forgiveness** should <u>not</u> be imposed on patients. Moreover, therapists should <u>not</u> convey to patients that they cannot "heal" from an "injustice" or "hurt" without forgiveness. The therapist can engage patients in a guided discussion of the pros and cons, the costs and benefits of forgiving. (See Enright & Fitzgibbons, 2000)

PROBLEM-SOLVING TRAINING (GOAL, PLAN, DO, CHECK)

The goal of **Problem-Solving Training (PST)** is to have the patients come to view personal threats and provocations as **problems-to-be-solved**. **PST** consists of teaching patients to engage in a series of steps, as follows:

1. Help the patients to view provocations and frustrations, and hassles as **problems-to-be-solved** and <u>not</u> as personal threats. Nurture a task-oriented problem-solving set. **Table 21 (p. 264)** provides an enumeration of provocative situations that can be summarized using the mnemonic **II CE HOPE**. This analysis will help the patients to appreciate that problems are made up of **goals** and **obstacles**.

2. **Problem identification** - encourage patients to think aloud to solve the problem and to use self-questioning in order to focus on issues and objectives and on desired outcomes of anger situations.

    "What is my <u>goal</u> in this situation?"
    "What is the <u>problem-to-be solved</u>?"
    "Is this a problem that I can change or influence or is this a <u>problem</u> that I have <u>no</u> power to change? This will determine which strategy I use."
    "What possible <u>obstacles</u> might I encounter and how will I deal with them?"

3. **Break the problem down into parts** or **chunk it** into manageable steps.

    "Break it down? I can handle little problems much better."
    "I feel ... when I ... and I need ... "

4. **Make a plan: Encourage patients to ask themselves:**

    "What is the source of the problem and how should I handle this?"
    "Have I encountered problems like this in the past?"
    "What are my resources to cope with this?"
    "Can I get anyone to help?"
    "What are my choices?"
    "Now that I thought this over, it looks like the best thing to try is ..."

5. **Solution implementation and evaluation** –

    "Okay let me try it out. If it works great. If not, I'll step back and figure something else out."
    "Just stay calm and focused, rather than get all twisted (pissed off, upset, etc.)."
    "So, my first step is ..."
    "What are my options?"
    "What will I do?"

"Should I take a time out?"
"If I can't handle it any other way, I will walk away."
"What will happen if ... ?"
"Bottom line is that I am in control."
"I can't seem to figure this out at this time. I'll come back to it later."
"I can always use my back-up plan."
"How did it turn out?"

6. **Reflection and taking credit for change**

   "Good job! I was angry and I expressed it, but I didn't do anything dumb."
   "I am getting better at this anger management. I was able to (notice, catch, interrupt, predict, stop, take a time out, relax, use my game plan, etc.)"

7. **Use problem-solving charts.** *(See Tables 22, 23 and 24, pp. 314, 315, 316, which were adapted from D'Zurilla & Maydeu-Olivares, 1995; D'Zurilla & Nezu, 1982; Wasik, 1997.)*

8. Work on **"happiness projects."** Laufer (1998) proposes that patients should be encouraged to develop **"happiness projects"** of their plans, hopes, and images of what would make then happy. Thus, the treatment should <u>not</u> only focus on anger reduction and conflict resolution, but on how patients can work constructively on fulfilling their **happiness projects**. These projects are selected so they are incompatible with the experience of anger and conflict (e.g., develop and strengthen relationship with others, succeed at work or school, teach anger management skills to others, etc.)

9. Have the patient **"take credit"** for change or improvements. The therapist can use the questions enumerated in **Table 25, p. 349.**

In order to nurture the patient's self-questioning, **the therapist can ask the patient** the following question:

To highlight once again: *Let me ask you a different type of questions. Do you ever find yourself, in your everyday experience, asking yourself the kind of questions <u>we</u> ask each other here in therapy?*

In this way patients are encouraged to learn to become their own therapist or trainer, asking themselves questions that are asked in the therapy sessions. **The patients are thus encouraged to "take their therapist's voice with them."**

The **Questions** that the therapist uses can both teach and model a <u>problem-solving style</u>. The therapist can say:

> *Please describe a recent example when you became angry (lost control). What happened? What started it? What happened next? How were you feeling by that time? Then what happened? How did the incident end?*

> *What do you want to have happen??*
> *What have you tried so far in dealing with X?*
> *What do you think would help in this situation?*
> *Do you recall what you did last time to handle this situation?*
> *Do you see any similarities between X and Y?*
> *How might you set up a routine in order to …*
> *Now that you have tried X, tell me <u>two things</u> that went well.*
> *Let's go over what you could do <u>next time</u>, if something like this happens again.*
> *You may already be using some of these strategies. Let's check it out.*
> *When do you think you will need to … ?*

The therapist's style of inquiry is to provide a **minimum number of prompts** so patients can become active participants in the change process as they implement specific action plans. The therapist can use the verbs and phrases below as a way to model the language of problem-solving. In time, patients will come to spontaneously use this language. *(See Appendix A for examples of this PST interventions.)*

Evidence that **patients** have **"internalized" the problem-solving process** is when they use (without prompts) problem-solving language. The therapist should listen for the patient using such terms and concepts as:

> *Break my cycle / Notice / Revise my goals / Plan ahead / Look out for early warning signs / Plan for unforeseen events / Trace events that contribute to*

> *Go into my safety zone / Choose / Have a back-up plan / Have options / Direct myself / rewrite my internal play*

> *Organize things so I am <u>not</u> forced to make a rushed decision / Fine-tune my plan / Gather data / Not go down that route*

> *Replace / Negotiate a middle path / Generate strategies (routines) / Check critical steps / Not pick a fight*

> *Evaluate / Know if it works / Two months ago I would have …*

> *Anticipate barriers / Going over my "stuck points" / Envisage possible difficulties*

Tables 22, 23 and 24 illustrate how the problem-solving format can be used with patients Adapted from Wasik).

Table 22 PROBLEM SOLVING STRATEGY		
Key Questions	**Situation 1**	**Situation 2**
1. What is the concern? • What is bothering me? • Why is it a problem? • What do I want to happen? • What is my goal?		
2. What could I do? • Write down all the possible solutions (even if they seem silly or impossible).		
3. Think it over? • What could happen with each solution? (Consider the time required, costs involved, effects on me personally, effects on other people.)		
4. Make a decision. • Pick a solution that is best for me (consider the consequences).		
5. Now do it. • What do I need to carry out my solution and do it?		
6. How did it work? • Am I satisfied? • If I am not satisfied, what else could I do?		

Table 23
PROBLEM SOLVING SKILLS

PROBLEM SOLVING STEPS

1.   WHAT IS THE CONCERN?

Say what is bothering me. Why is it a problem? Clearly say what I want to happen. What is my goal in this situation?

2.   WHAT COULD I DO?

Think of all of the possible solutions I can use for handling this concern, even if they seem silly or impossible at first.

3.   THINK IT OVER.

Think about what could happen with each solution. Think about the time required, the costs involved, any effects on me personally, and any effects on other people.

4.   MAKE A DECISION.

Pick the solution that's best for me, at this time. Consider the different consequences.

5.   NOW DO IT!

Think about what I need to carry out my solution, then do it.

6.   HOW DID IT WORK?

Am I satisfied with the way it worked? If I am not satisfied, what else could I do? If I am satisfied, think about other areas where I can use my idea.

Table 24
PROBLEM SOLVING STEPS

What is the problem?	**Problem Identification**
What am I feeling?	**Affect Recognition**
What are some possible solutions? What are my choices?	**Response Generation**

For each solution ask:
  Is it <u>safe</u>?
  How might <u>others feel</u>?
  Is it <u>fair</u>?
  Will it <u>work</u>?
	Means-End Thinking

What might happen?
  What is the <u>best</u> thing that could happen?
  What is the <u>worst</u> thing that could happen?
  What is <u>most likely</u> to happen?
	Consequential Thinking

What will I do ?	**Decision Making**

What did I do? Is it working?
  If not, what can I do now?
	**Self-evaluation, self-praise and
	    self-coaching for next time**

Why was I angry?
  What did I do?
  What worked?
  What didn't work?
  What would I do differently?
  Am I improving how I handle
    these situations?
  Did I do a good job?
	Reflection

COMMUNICATION SKILLS TRAINING

(Adapted from Gottman et al., 1976; Wexler, 1991)
(See Felson & Tedeschi, 1983, for an Interactionist view of aggression and violence)

The treatment outcome research on anger-control procedures indicated that anger reduction interventions were effective in reducing aggressive behavior, but they were less effective in nurturing prosocial interpersonal skills. Thus, work with angry and aggressive individuals needs to focus on ways to nurture social skills, especially communication and negotiation skills. How individuals can assert themselves effectively without becoming aggressive, how they can perspective-take and develop more egalitarian (less controlling) attitudes are critical features of treatment. In order to achieve these goals, patients are taught how to recognize confrontational situations and how to communicate more effectively by means of skills training that include group discussion, observation (videotape modeling films, role playing), rehearsal of new skills in the session and application (in vivo "homework"). In order to illustrate how such interpersonal skills can be taught, the following list of training activities that were used with **distressed couples** who had problems with anger and aggression is offered. These procedures and concepts can be employed with any clinical population where there is interpersonal conflict (e.g., parent-adolescent conflict). The goals of these interventions is to help participants explore the triggers and their reactions and to understand how exchanges unfold and escalate from feeling angry to becoming violent.

The research on **distressed couples** whose arguments escalate to the point of violence indicates that their communication pattern is marked by sarcasm, cross-complaining, destructive criticism, use of threats (Gottman, 1979, 1994). They evidence few positive behaviors with each other and engage in demandingness and withdrawal, an absence of validating each other's position and engage in more "summarizing self" than summarizing the other's position. These high frequency conflictual behaviors generally last a long period of time. Interestingly, there are no major differences between maritally distressed and non-distressed couples when they interact with strangers. The major differences between distressed and non-distressed couples emerge mainly when interacting with their partners (Bornstein & Borstein, 1986). This suggests that a certain level of communication skills are in the distressed couple's repertoire. Somehow, interacting with their spouse results in a "set of buttons" being pushed that are in their repertoire. Gottman et al. (1976) provided a useful model of how to teach distressed couples to **recognize** the pattern of their negative communication and to learn how to **interrupt** ("catch") themselves and to **produce** more prosocial interactions.

The communication skills training begins with a general discussion of what is effective communication and incorporates the concepts of sender, message and receiver and the factors that may get in the way of this transmission and reception process (see Fincham & Bradbury, 1988, 1992; Fincham et al., 1999, Wile, 1981). The treatment goals are to have distressed couples reduce their aversive conflict styles of interacting, to increase their constructive conflict resolution skills and to enhance social supports and intimacy in their relationship.

Finally, as noted in **Figure 6**, the treatment also focused on the patients' secondary emotions (feelings of hurt, shame, fear, humiliation) that were part of the behavioral chain from anger to aggression. Part of what may contribute to couples' not communicating more effectively are the "primary" emotions that each partner brings to their interactions that often go unaddressed. As Fruzzetti and Levensky (2000) observe that treatment would be enhanced if it **"focused on emotions other than anger which may allow other skills to be learned"** (p. 44).

1.   Gottman et al. (1976) provide a description of the types of conflicts that distressed couples experience:

Kitchen sinking	*(Bringing into the argument everything, but the kitchen sink. Bring up past annoyances.)*
Cross-complaining	*(Criticize others with more fervor with each complaint.)*
Mind reading	*(Expecting others to mind read your feelings; you're mind reading other's feelings. Telling others what they think and feel.)*
Off-beaming	*(Switching the topic and not coming to a resolution. Cutting off the conversation and exiting. "It's fine, I'll do it your way." "Whatever!" "So what.")*
Character Assassination	*(Making "you" statements that refer to other's personality flaws and not refer to specific behavior or issues.) ("You always", "You never")*
Yes / But	*(Seemingly agree, but highlight possible obstacles that preclude implementation.)*
Put downs	*(Criticisms, challenges. "You're doing it again." "You "should have" statements)*

In a discovery fashion the participants gave examples of the types of conflicts they had with their partners and inductively came to describe them according to these categories. How communication breakdowns contributed to the escalating conflicts was highlighted and the following **communication skills** were taught.

2.   Make sure that your partner **gets the message that was sent**

   Actively Listen:

   Don't interrupt
   Allow the other person to finish speaking
   Draw partner out

   Paraphrase:

   "I think you are saying"
   "So what you are saying is"
   "What you said so far is"
   "What I understand you to be saying is"
   "Is that correct?"

   Validate other's feelings:

   "That must of hurt your feelings."
   "That would have made me mad too."
   "I think I know what you are going through."
   *"I can see how you can think and feel that way, even if I don't see it the way
   you do."*

   Keep the listener from slipping away. Shift back to the issue and <u>calmly repeat</u> your
   point. Indicate how important this is you to and why.

3.   **Take the other's perspective**. Try to see the problem through the other person's eyes and
   develop empathy. Put yourself in his/her shoes. The other person's viewpoint can make
   sense even if you don't agree.

   "I know you have had a tough day. Let's talk about this later."
   *"Can you help me see this from your perspective? I am having some trouble
   doing that."*

   If you want someone to treat you in a certain way, you should treat them the way you want
   to be treated. Ask about the other person's specific complaints so you can understand and
   attempt to solve the problem.

4. **Check it out**.

   "What do you understand about what I said?"

5.   **Give good feedback.** Say how you feel. Communicate clearly. Don't store up grievances. Change complaints into suggestions. **Be assertive.**[12]

   Use X, Y, and Z communication

   When you do X in situation Y it makes me feel Z.

   For example: Instead of saying - "You are a rotten driver."
   Say - *"When you drive so fast, when we are coming home from work, I feel scared."*

   "When you don't praise me after I work so hard to please you I feel hurt."

   Use "I" statements instead of "you" statements

   "I felt upset when you" (be specific)
   "I feel bad when you"
   "I disagree with you when you say"
   "I felt uncomfortable when you"
   "I would like to X. What will it take to get your trust?"
   "How can I show you that I'm ready to handle this?"

6.   **Use stop action. Talk about the discussion process.**

   "I think we are getting off track, let's start the discussion over. Now then, what do you feel is the problem?"
   "What we are trying to do is …"
   "Let's stay in the here and now, no 'kitchen sinking' (i.e., in an argument bringing in everything, but the kitchen sink). What is the problem?"
   "The way I see the problem is …, do you see the problem that way?"

---

[12] Wolpow et al. (2000) have noted that for many patients being assertive has been associated with a familial history of conflict and patients have learned to avoid expressing their feelings and asserting their rights in a non-confrontational manner. Skills training need to address these emotional barriers to engaging in a prosocial assertive, but nonconfrontational manner.

7. **Convey willingness to accept responsibility** for how your partner feels. **Use "I"** **statements.**

> *"I was wrong for saying that."*
> *"I can understand why you would be upset when I do ..."*
>
> *Ask - "What can <u>we</u> do to make things better? "Well, here is what I am* *going to do to make things better. Do you have any thoughts about that?"*

Admit past errors. Avoid letting the other person sidetrack you with accusations about the past. Admit that you may have made some errors in the past, but this is now and you are trying to handle things better.

8. Tell your spouse about your **"filter" (i.e., feelings that are getting in the way of your** **communicating effectively).**

> *"I had a long day at work and I need a little time to just cool down."*
> *"I am feeling particularly shaky at this time. I need some tender loving care* *(TLC)."*

9. Find something **positive** to say. Edit what you say and consider how you say it. State things positively. Find something to praise in others. **Use "<u>I</u>" instead of "<u>You</u>"** **statements.**

> Instead of saying: "You never pay any attention to me."
> Say *"I would like you to find some time when we could talk."*
>
> Instead of saying: "You never ask me how my day was.
> Say: *"I would feel really appreciated if you would share with me how your* *day went and I could do the same with you."*

10. **Don't put yourself down, nor make excuses, nor appear helpless.** For example, <u>avoid</u> <u>saying</u>:

> *"I can't help it because I am just not that way, because that is not how I was* *raised."*

11. **Relax and take a Time Out**. Keep your cool. Use your self-talk. Catch yourself when you "catastrophize", when you use categorical, coercive, demanding, one-track, generalizing forms of thinking. Instead say:

> *"I am in a cooling off period. (Take a break, go for a walk, talk to a friend.)"*

Take a Time Out: Suggest to the other person that you both wait for a less tense time to discuss the problem. Delay responding until people have calmed down and can be more reasonable.

12. **Use problem-solving: <u>Goal</u>, <u>Plan</u>, <u>Do</u>, <u>Check!</u>**

> *What is my goal? What is the problem? Be specific. Stay realistic. Ask my partner what he/she sees as the problem. Focus on the present. Don't bring up old business. State my problems in behavioral terms (XYZ). Generate alternative possible solutions. Help others solve problems. Use the "art of questioning." -- "Who , what, where, how" questions.*

Use a suggestion box in the home, at work.

Ask my partner (co-worker) what can be done to resolve the problem.

Ask my partner - *"What do I say or do that makes you feel bad?" "That makes you feel good?" "What do you wish I would say to you?"*

When you feel you are stuck, talk to someone you trust. Be creative, try something different

Evaluate the pros and cons of the alternatives, both short-term and long-term. How will each alternative help you achieve your goal?

Things to consider:

> *When is the best time and place to do my problem solving? Build an agenda for the discussion, a game plan so I and my partner can work on the problem.*

> *"If we try it and it doesn't work that doesn't mean we have to give up. We can learn from our mistakes. Let us try something else."*

> *"What will get in the way of our following through on our plan? (Consider barriers)*

> *"Let us have a follow-up conversation to see how our solution is working. We don't want to let problems simmer."*

"What are high risk situations we should consider for the future?"
(Interruption of plans, overload, history repeats itself, violation of
expectations, pet peeves, personal goals.)

13.   Engage in **negotiation** and **form mutual agreements**. Make **joint commitment** to make it work. Focus on specific behaviors. *"What can we do to work this out?"*

14.   **Compromise**. Give and take. Be generous, as well as polite. Keep reminding yourself about your goal(s). What is really important? Don't get bent out of shape by making mountains out of molehills. Express willingness to collaborate.

"I can't ... but I am willing to ..."

"I said (did) ..., What can I do instead?"

15.   **Use humor**. Consider how silly we sometimes can be. Be careful with sarcasm.

16.   **Have fun**. Remember we often fight most with the people we love. People can learn. People can change.

These Guidelines are given to patients and their partners (family members) as a summary of the communication skills training.

SELF-MANAGEMENT AND INTERPERSONAL SKILLS TRAINING

The use of anger and aggression have been viewed as a reflection of a **skills deficit**. The developmental research reviewed in **Section II** underscores the role of skills deficit. For example, clinicians who work with patients who are diagnosed with Borderline Personality Disorder have focused on teaching skill in the areas of emotional dysregulation, anger control and interpersonal assertiveness. As part of such a skills training program, Linehan (1993) has taught patients how to conduct a **CHAIN ANALYSIS** of problematic behaviors. They teach patients to engage in self-questioning and provide worksheets as reminders. The following **Patient Handouts** provide patients with reminders of questions that they can ask themselves when conducting a **CHAIN ANALYSIS** and when working on controlling their anger in the form of a mnemonic **DEAR MAN** (Linehan, 1993).

A number of cognitive-behavioral trainers have developed **acronyms** to summarize the coping skills that can be taught. For example, Meyer et al. (2000) has offered the following mnemonics to help patients recall and guide their behavior.

RAID – <u>use to avoid conflicts</u>

Resolve   -- talk through the problem or seek assistance of others (e.g., peer mediation, if available)

Avoid   -- avoid each other

Ignore   -- use positive self-talk *("She must be having a bad day.")*

Defuse   -- decrease tense situations (e.g., imagine what it felt like to be in other's shoes; not "expect the worst"; "take the bait")

SCIDDLE – <u>use to make responsible decisions</u>

Stop

Calm down

Identify the problem and your feelings about it

Decide among your options

Do it

Look back

Evaluate

RSLV – <u>how to resolve conflicts</u>

Respect others	-- listen to what they have to say
Speak clearly	- how else can they understand what you mean (Use "I" statements; "X-Y-Z" statements)
Listen to yourself	-- calm down, and listen to yourself. Ask yourself, ***"What do I want?"*** Use calming self-talk.
Value the relationship	-- show respect

PATIENT HANDOUT
CHAIN ANALYSIS

What exactly is the major problem I am analyzing?

What prompting events ("triggers") in the environment started me on the chain to my problem behaviors?

What things in myself and in my environment made me vulnerable?

What are some of the possible "links"?

What have I done to make my bad feelings worse?

How have I contributed to my "vicious cycle"? How can I break this "cycle"?

What are the consequences of this behavior for me and for others?

Immediate consequences ….

Delayed consequences …

What are the ways to reduce my vulnerability?

What are ways to prevent the prompting event ("triggers") from happening again?

My plans to notice, interrupt and alter the chain are:

What might get in the way of this plan and how do I intend to deal with this?

Should this plan not work, my backup plan is:

Why is it important for me to do X (stop and calm down, use self-talk, etc.) before I act?

What are three ways I can do X?

In addition to teaching patients how to conduct a CHAIN ANALYSIS, Linehan (1993) has developed a variety of skills packages[13] that are summarized under a series of mnemonics. For example, she uses the mnemonic DEAR MAN to summarize self-control and interpersonal skills that patients can use when they become angry and which they can employ to avoid aggression.

PATIENT HANDOUT
DEAR MAN: SELF-CONTROL PROCEDURES

Describe the current situation

Express feelings and opinions

Assert by asking or saying "no"

Reinforce the person ahead of time

Mindful of objectives without distraction

Appear effective and competent

Negotiate alternative solutions

---

[13] Linehan's Dialectical Behavior Therapy (DBT) includes 4 sets of skills that are interrelated with one another. **Core Mindfulness Skills** which focus on increasing the patient's ability to be present in the moment in a nonjudgmental manner; **Interpersonal Effectiveness Skills** highlighting assertive skills; **Emotional Regulation Skills** that increase the patient's ability to identify, describe, reduce vulnerability to negative emotions and that increase positive emotions; and **Distress Tolerance Skills** that teach patients how to manage difficult feelings when they are unable to change them.

Wexler (1991) has proposed a **Freeze-Frame Technique** where individuals are trained to view their angry and aggressive behavior **as a movie** and they are trained to freeze the frame in which the "uncontrollable" behavior occurs and to analyze and change it. The steps in the **Freeze-Frame Technique** include having the patient:

1. Identify the angry/aggressive behavior

2. Recall the scene as if in a movie (as vividly as possible)

3. Slow time down and freeze the frame when the aggressive behavior is about to occur

4. Scan for physical sensations, feelings, thoughts and the behaviors of self and others

5. Identify the central needs or goals

    "What was your goal(s) in this situation?"
    "What was the need you were trying to fill?"

6. Generate a list of creative options for satisfying your needs, for achieving your goals.

7. Choose the options that have the highest satisfaction and the lowest negative side-effects.

8. Redirect the movie with the new ending and observe the effects, both internally and externally.

9. Rehearse the options you have chosen.

10. Plan specifically how these skills can be implemented and consider what barriers might get in the way and how these can be anticipated and addressed.

ROLE-PLAYING

In order to help patients translate the information they receive in treatment into specific action plans, the therapist can use role-playing. Sanders and Ralph (2001) have outlined the steps involved in **role-playing**. These include:

1) The therapist and patients develop a **shared understanding** of the skills to be worked on, and moreover, how learning these skills will help patients <u>achieve their treatment goals</u>;

2) **Label skills** to be taught and **describe** the role-playing procedure

> *"For the fist run through, I will show you how to use strategy X. I would like you to pretend to be Y and I will pretend to be you. Are there any questions before we start?"*

3) The therapist **models** the desired behavior (e.g., communication skills of using "I" versus "you" statements). Signals the beginning and end of each role-play episode by saying:

> *"Let's start the practice now."*
> *"Let's stop right there."*
> *"Can I stop you there, so we can discuss it?"*

This is followed by a **discussion** of the role-play. The therapist provides a think aloud commentary using the organizational framework: *"First, I used ... then this was followed by my ... I wanted to ... so I ... When you responded I decided to ... "*

4) **Check the patient's reactions**

> *"What do you think about the way I carried out the strategy of ... ?"*

5) The therapist and patient **swap roles**

> *"Ok, let's swap roles. This time I would like you to play yourself and I'll play Y. We will use the same situation. Try to implement the strategy in your own way, using your own words."*

6) Have the patient **evaluate** the role-play. Initially, ask the patient to identify <u>two strengths</u> in the way he implemented the strategy. This can be followed by having the patient identify <u>one weakness</u> or one area that requires further work. The therapist can use prompts:

> *"How did that go?"*
> *"Tell me two things that you did well."*
> *"Is there anything you would do differently next time?"*
> *"Let's think about Step 1 where you ... You did X. What did you do next?"*
> *"What do you think could be improved?"*

It is important for the therapist <u>not</u> to get <u>sidetracked</u>.

> *"Can I stop you there? You said / did X. Let's see how that helped you achieve your goal of ... "*

7) <u>Discuss</u> how the patients can <u>apply</u> role-play in vivo. Solicit the patients' **commitment** statements and their **intent** to implement the strategies.

8) Discuss **possible obstacles** that might get in the way of practicing skills. How can the patients plan ahead for these barriers and formulate back-up plans? Remind the patients that implementing new skills may initially feel unnatural and somewhat demanding at first, but with practice patients would feel more and more comfortable and that the patients will be "<u>surprised</u>" by how they comes to apply their strategies in new situations.

9) Encourage **generalization (transfer)** of skills.

SECTION VII examines the specific steps trainers should follow in order to **increase the likelihood of generalization**.

SUMMARY:
WHAT YOU SHOULD TAKE AWAY FROM SECTION VI

Given the multifaceted nature of anger and aggression and the variety of factors that influence their developmental and maintenance, it is <u>not surprising</u> that a variety of cognitive behavioral interventions have been developed to address the patient's multiple needs and deficits. **SECTION VI** focused on the "how to" features of skills training. As noted in the **TEST YOUR EXPERTISE** section, the reader should come away with specific treatment guidelines on how to conduct a variety of skills training components that range form emotional regulation to cognitive rescripting to interpersonal skills development.

What the reader will <u>not take away</u> from this **HANDBOOK** is how to treat various comorbid disorders (e.g., substance abuse, depression, PTSD, anxiety, guilt), each of which complicate the treatment of patients with anger control problems. To cover these treatment objectives would make this book twice the size. The interested readers should see my **<u>Clinical Handbook on Treating PTSD and Related Disorders</u>**.

TEST YOUR EXPERTISE: SECTION VI

1. This section includes a number of coping skills that can be employed with patients. They include:

    a) **Taking Time Out**

    b) **Relaxation Skills**

    c) **Self-instructional Training**

    d) **Cognitive Restructuring ("Rethinking")**

    e) **Stress Inoculation Training**

    f) **Communication Skills Training**

    g) **Self-management Training**

    h) **Role playing**

    Consider each of these skills. Which ones do you feel confident in employing in therapy? Which ones need more work?

2. With colleagues, practice these skills. Try them with your patients.

3. How can you use **Patient Handouts**?

4. Knowing how to teach skills is only one part of the task for clinicians. There are two key additional features, namely, how does the therapist increase the likelihood that patients will indeed follow-through **(be treatment adherent),** and moreover, apply skills across settings and over time **(generalize).** What specific treatment strategies can the therapist employ to address these critical issues? *(See if you can anticipate SECTION VII.)*

SECTION VII: GENERALIZATION GUIDELINES AND APPLICATION TRAINING

This **SECTION** highlights that it is <u>not</u> enough to train patients on skills and hope that the skills will transfer. There is a need to **explicitly train for generalization** and to explicitly implement procedures to increase the likelihood that the training effects **will be maintained** and **improved over time**, without the support of the therapist. The focus of this **SECTION** is on spelling out a series of procedural steps that the therapist should implement to **increase the likelihood of transfer** and to **assure generalization to the natural environment**. This **Generalization Checklist** provides the basis for evaluating treatment programs.

It is <u>not</u> enough to have patients change. In order to ensure maintenance of the behavioral change process, there is a need for patients to **take credit** for the changes they have brought about. The therapist should ensure that such **self-attributional processes** occur. How this can be achieved is described below.

Finally, given that there is a high likelihood that patients will have lapses (setbacks), it is critical to include **relapse prevention procedures in treatment**. While the discussion of the procedures of **generalization, self-attribution** and **relapse prevention** have been saved for the end of this **Clinical Handbook**, the "expert" therapist will have embedded them throughout the course of the treatment.

CONTENTS SECTION VII

GUIDELINES FOR IMPROVING GENERALIZATION (TRANSFER)

"Treatment is not only about change, it is about the generalization of that change." (Larson & Lochman, in press)

The training and treatment literatures are replete with examples of intervention programs that sound encouraging, but they often fail to evidence generalization or transfer across settings, across response domains, and over time. As Stokes and Baer (1979) have observed, trainers should not "train and hope" for generalization, but instead they should **explicitly train for transfer**. The following **Checklist** of items enumerates what trainers should do at the **outset**, **during** and **following** training in order to increase the likelihood of generalization. This set of guidelines operationalizes the "implicit technology" that is required to foster transfer. The Reader is encouraged to assess his/her training programs and determine how many of these features have been incorporated. It is proposed that the more of these training features that have been included, the greater the likelihood of generalization. While these training guidelines are listed sequentially, in effective intervention programs they will be implemented in a recursive and highly interdependent fashion. A **Guided Participation Model** is used to engage the patient in the transfer process.

Bodine and Crawford (1978) have proposed that the learning and transfer of skills goes through a series of phases and for skills to transfer sufficient training has to be conducted to move participants through the four phases. The Phases include:

(1) Have no knowledge of what skills are needed (Unconsciously unskilled)

(2) Recognize the need for certain skills (Consciously unskilled)

(3) Learn to perform the skills in a rote, rehearsed manner (Consciously skilled)

(4) Being able to generalize and perform skills automatically in a variety of settings (Unconsciously skilled)

Meichenbaum and Biemiller (1998) have proposed that a **fifth consultative stage** needs to be added to the skill acquisition process if generalization is to occur. They offer a **three dimensional model of learning that highlights the critical role of placing trainees in a consultative role** where they need to mentally represent and **communicate either to others or to themselves** what they have learned. This mental representation may be in a verbal or diagrammatic form (e.g., procedural flow-chart), or by means of a demonstration (e.g., teaching others what they have learned), or in the form of self-coaching (e.g., think aloud, mentally rehearse). Insofar as trainees can learn to "take ownership" and apply what they have learned, there is a greater likelihood of transfer.

As individuals move back and forth through these various phases in a circular manner, they will develop and hone their skills and moreover, be able to describe the learning process using their "metacognitive skills." **Teaching at the metacognitive level** (i.e., using executive skills of monitoring, planning, self-interrogating, problem-solving, and the like) **increase the likelihood of transfer**. (See Meichenbaum & Biemiller, 1998 for a review of the literature.)

In short, generalization training should <u>not</u> be an afterthought or an add on to training. They must be integrated into the structure of the intervention <u>from the outset</u>. The following **Procedural Checklist** provides guidelines on how to enhance transfer **before**, **during** and at the **completion of training**.

PROCEDURAL CHECKLIST ON WAYS TO IMPROVE GENERALIZATION

AT THE <u>OUTSET</u> OF THE TRAINING

1. Engage the participants in **explicit goal-setting**. Highlight that the treatment is not only about changing, but the training program focuses heavily on having participants transfer (extend) these skills (changes) to new situations / settings.

2. **Discuss** the **challenge** for participants to generalize or transfer skills. Lead participants to view generalization as an **attitude**, rather than just as a set of transferable skills. Participants need to find (search out) opportunities to practice what was learned.

3. **Raise concerns** for transfer **from the outset** of training. Have participants examine how learning such skills will help them achieve their short-term and long-term goals. Discuss **why** learning these skills is **of value**. Relate skills and homework tasks to treatment goals.

4. Provide participants with opportunities to **come up with suggestions** of what should be done to transfer skills. Use collaborative Socratic questioning and **discovery learning**.

5. **Name** and **describe** what it is being taught. **Label** and **refer** to transfer strategies and convey that generalization is the goal of treatment. Help them understand how similar skills can be applied across multiple settings (e.g., self-talk, problem-solving). Trainers should discuss, model, and label metacognitive strategies.

6. **Tell** participants **explicitly** that transfer is **expected**. **Encourage** and **challenge** patients to **apply** and **adapt** skills and strategies to varied and novel situations, rather than learn to apply specific skills to discrete behaviors and settings.

7. Solicit **public commitment statements** of what they are going to do and **why**. Write out on a decisional balance sheet, the pros and cons of making changes. Use **behavioral contracts** that include transfer activities.

8. **Tailor instructions** to the **developmental needs** of the participants and be sensitive to **gender** and **cultural differences** and train skills that are **ecologically valid**. Training should **build upon** the trainees' **strengths** and **abilities**.

9. Throughout the course of therapy **anticipate** and **discuss possible barriers** and obstacles to implementing homework (both external and internal barriers). Include in the training program skills designed to handle potential barriers.

10. Help participants **select training and transfer tasks carefully** - where there is a high likelihood of similarity. The more similar the features of the training and the real life setting, the greater the likelihood of generalization (e.g., use exposure-based training and provocation challenge procedures in training that are ecologically valid and similar to real life.)

11. Nurture and help develop a "**community of learners**" -- where participants can help each other (e.g., an Alumni club of graduates, other trainees, prosocial peers).

DURING THE TRAINING ACTIVITIES

12. Ensure that **training tasks** are tailored to the trainees' level of competence, namely: **slightly above current ability levels** ("teachable window" or work within the "zone of proximal development"). Skills to be taught should be broken down into identifiable parts. Trainers should use minimal prompts and fade supports (**scaffold instruction**), as trainees gain competence.

13. Keep training simple by using **acronyms** to summarize teaching skills (e.g., RAID, SCIDDLE, RSVL, DEAR MAN), so they come to be readily retrievable **mnemonics**. Use **reminders**. Have trainees keep a **Training Folder** and refer back to it often.

14. Provide **prolonged, in-depth training** to the point of proficiency in order to **ensure conceptual understanding**. Facilitate skill practice and provide constructive feedback. The length of training should be performance-based, rather than time-based. Provide extended individual and group training where indicated, so participants can **develop mastery** of skills and strategies. Provide help and coaching to complete homework assignments.

15. **Promote awareness** of skills and teach **problem-solving metacognitive executive skills** and **strategies** (self-monitoring, planning and freeze-frame procedures) that can be applied across settings. Use overt and covert **rehearsal** and **self-monitoring**.

16.   Begin by **accessing participants' knowledge**. Provide **advance organizers** ("big picture", remind of goals) and **informed instruction** (how the content of this session relates to previous sessions; *"Where we have been?" and "Where we are headed?"*).

17.   **Explicitly instruct** on **how to transfer**. Use direct instruction, discovery-oriented instruction and scaffolded assistance (fade support and reduce prompts as patients' performances improve). Employ videotape coping **modeling films** as training material.

18.   Conduct training **across response domains** and **settings**. **Training** is conducted **"loosely".** This involves varying the stimulus context for training. In training use diverse examples to illustrate the application of skills to different behaviors and to different situations. Use **multiple trainers**. Work on skills development and maintenance in **real world settings** using **environmental modification** and **supports** (e.g., trainer maintains close contact with classroom teachers and provides them and parents with training).

19.   Use **cognitive modeling** and **think aloud - diaries, journals**. Have an **Alumni Club** of recent graduates who act as teaching models.

20.   Use the **"art of questioning"** – "what" and "how" questions.

21.   Have participants **repeat reasons** why they should engage in transfer activities; have participants reconfirm **public commitment statements**; review **goal statements** with **"If ... then"** and **"Whenever ...."**rules.

22.   Use **relapse prevention** training procedures throughout training. Have students analyze and learn from transfer failures and successes.

AT THE **CONCLUSION** OF TRAINING ACTIVITIES

23.   Put participants in **consulting reflective** roles. Following an experiential activity have participants **reflect on the activity** (i.e., think about what they just did and what it meant, how can they use these skills in future situations). Have participants **teach** (demonstrate, coach) and **explain** verbally or diagrammatically (alone or with others) their acquired skills and transfer strategies. Have participants be in a position of **responsibility**, giving presentations to and consult with other beginning participants, younger individuals. Have them make **teaching videotapes** for others.

24.   Ensure that participants **directly experience** the **benefits** ("pay offs")of choosing new (nonaggressive) options. Receives naturally occurring rewards.

25. **Label** and **reinforce** participants' transfer activities. Talk about **maintaining** and **building upon change**.

26. **Provide between session coaching**. Access to ongoing counseling (computer chat lines, telephone counseling and hotlines).

27. Have the patient develop an explicit written **relapse prevention plan** and "trouble shoot" possible solutions to potential obstacles, barriers and responses to possible lapses. Encourage trainees to view "failures" as a reflection of a lack of skills, not enough practice, the training program not being sensitive to trainees' needs and skill levels, and not as a sign of being a "sick", "bad", or an "incompetent" person.

28. Provide active **aftercare case management supervision**. Use Websites and ongoing computer chat-lines. Fade supports and "scaffold" assistance throughout training.

29. **Review progress** and ensure that participants **take credit** (make self-attributions) and **declare ownership** for performance gains and transfer efforts. Have participants talk about what they learned and take "personal ownership" of coping skills. (Trainers use "how" and "what" questions.) Nurture patient's sense of **personal agency**.

30. Encourage participants to **design personal transfer activities**. Enlist participants in a **mutual search** for situations in which the coping skills can be employed, discussed and practiced. Ask the patients to **discuss** and **identify** the variety of situations where they could apply new skills and strategies. **Prompt** the patients to set goals for implementing these skills over the next week. **Provide monitoring forms** to map progress. Have the patient adopt a *"personal scientist's"* approach.

31. **Involve significant others** in training. Keep in touch with significant others (peers, parents, teachers, administrators, family members) **from the outset** of training through follow-up. Use a **primary prevention program** school-wide intervention for peers or a peer mediation program to supplement training for the targeted group.

32. Provide **booster sessions** and ongoing follow-up group meetings. Have patients enter group training if they fail to handle lapses successfully. (Use General Practitioner – analogy that going for ongoing "checkups" and "fine-tuning" is a smart thing to do.)

33. Use a **graduation ceremony**, involving significant others and include certificates of completion and appreciation.

REPORT CARD ON HOW WELL YOUR TRAINING PROGRAMS FOSTER GENERALIZATION

How many of these 23 features are included in your training program?
What grade would you give to your Intervention Program to foster generalization?

In order to foster transfer at the <u>OUTSET OF TRAINING</u>, my program:

1. Uses explicit <u>collaborative goal-setting</u> when discussing the <u>reasons</u> and <u>value</u> of transfer and relates training tasks to <u>treatment goals</u>.

2. Explicitly <u>instructs</u>, <u>challenges</u> and <u>conveys an "expectant attitude"</u> about transfer.

3. Uses <u>discovery learning</u>, <u>labeling</u> transfer skills and strategies.

4. Solicits participants' <u>public commitment</u> and uses <u>behavioral contracts</u>.

5. Anticipates and discusses <u>possible</u> barriers to transfer.

6. <u>Chooses</u> training and transfer tasks <u>carefully</u> (build in similarities and use ecologically-valued training tasks).

7. Develops a "<u>community of learners</u>" (e.g., Alumni Club).

In order to foster transfer <u>DURING TRAINING</u>, my training program:

8. Keeps training <u>simple</u> – uses <u>acronyms</u> and <u>reminders</u>.

9. Uses <u>performance-based</u> training to the <u>point of mastery</u>.

10. Teaches <u>metacognitive skills</u> – involving self-monitoring, planning, etc.

11. <u>Accesses prior knowledge</u> and skills, uses <u>advance organizers</u> and <u>scaffolded instruction</u>.

12. Conducts training <u>across settings</u>, using <u>multiple trainers</u> and <u>environmental supports</u>.

13. Uses <u>cognitive modeling</u>, <u>think alouds</u>, <u>journaling</u>.

14. Includes <u>relapse prevention</u> activities <u>throughout training</u>.

In order to foster transfer at the <u>CONCLUSION</u> of training, my program:

15. Puts trainees in a <u>consultative role</u> (uses reflection, opportunity to teach others, puts trainee in a position of responsibility).

16. Ensures participants <u>directly</u> benefit and <u>receive reinforcement</u> for using and <u>describing</u> transfer skills.

17. Provides <u>between sessions coaching</u>.

18. Provides <u>active aftercare supervision</u> – fade supports and "scaffold" assistance.

19. Ensures participants <u>take credit</u> and <u>ownership</u> for change (self-attributions). Nurtures <u>personal agency</u>.

20. Ensures participants design <u>personal transfer activities</u>.

21. Involves <u>significant others</u>.

22. Provides <u>booster sessions</u>.

23. Conducts a <u>graduation ceremony</u>.

APPLICATION TRAINING

Once individuals learn the various anger management skills, they can be given opportunities to rehearse and practice using their coping skills in the form of **exposure training**. This type of **rehearsal** can be done by means of:

a)   **imaginal rehearsal**

b)   **behavioral rehearsal**

c)   **graded in-vivo exposure**

We will consider each form of Application Training in turn. First, let us consider **Imaginal Training**.

Imaginal rehearsal - employs a **coping imagery technique**. For example, a patient may be asked to generate a hierarchy of anger-provoking scenes and then incorporate within the scene the ability to "notice, catch, interrupt" the anger cycle and to employ various coping techniques ala the new "script" that has been developed in treatment.

IMAGERY-BASED REHEARSAL TECHNIQUES

When the **imagery rehearsal technique** is used, the following **procedural steps** should be included:

1. various provocations that the patient experience should be put along a dimension from the least to the most provocative, or most anger-engendering (where 0 is <u>not</u> angry at all and 100 is the most furious possible);

2. initially, the patient should be asked to visualize scenes that fall in the 40 to 60 range on a 0 - 100 scale. In subsequent sessions, the level of intensity of the provocation scenes to be imaginally rehearsed should be increased so they fall in the range of 75 to 100;

3. the generation of the scene to be imagined should be collaboratively established with the patient;

4. the visualized scenes should be vivid, full of details and include sensory stimuli, making them as real as possible;

5. the image should be in the first person and in the here and now, and the patient should become involved as if it were happening now. *"Let yourself really be there. Put yourself right into it, like it was happening at this very moment."*;

6. the patient should describe the scene to the therapist. Initially, the therapist can guide the patient in the telling of the scene by asking questions about the context, details of what happened, physical sensations;

7. ensure that the patient shares his feelings and thoughts that precede, accompany and follow the specific situations;

8. have the patient focus on triggering events (both external and internal triggers). Include a consideration of the patient's pre-anger state. Ask the patient to *tell the main things he is aware of*. Can the patient notice any **anticipatory upset** or feelings of preparing for the provocation? Could the patient predict that he would become angry in this situation? **Encourage the patient to stay in the scene and report what thoughts are most provocative**;

9. have the patient share **any other feelings** he might be experiencing (e.g., feel humiliated, afraid, sad);

10. encourage the patient to use the language of **"thinking errors"** to notice how he is making himself more angry (e.g., use of black-white thinking);

11. encourage the patient to stay in the scene and focus on his experience, paying particular attention to internal cues;

12. encourage the patient to incorporate into the image various **coping efforts** including relaxation, self-instructional procedures, taking time-out, and other anger-reduction procedures. At first, the therapist can provide explicit assistance and guidance, but as the patient develops proficiency, the therapist can fade support sand scaffold guidance;

13. initially, the patient is asked to image for a very brief period (some 30 seconds) and asked to focus on a specific coping skill such as identifying triggers or engaging in slow-deep breathing. As the therapy progresses, the patient can be asked to extend the image into several minutes during which he can combine various anger-reduction procedures into a developed **game plan** or **coping script**;

14. the patient can be asked to repeat the same scene for several trials (4 to 6) until the level of anger is significantly reduced (below 40 on the scale 0 to 100 scale);

15. the patient describes the scenes aloud to the therapist so the therapist can provide guidance on how to cope with the provocations. For example, the therapist can encourage the patient to take a slow deep breath, while saying, *"Relax. I can control this."* Or the therapist can ask the patient to choose three coping self-

statements to say to himself in order to reduce his anger. *"Remember your coping self-statements. Go ahead, talk back and take charge of your anger."*

16. the therapist can provide general guidance as the patient **develops imagery coping skills**. Deffenbacher and McKay (2000) offer the following suggestions that the therapist can use with patients:

> *"Tell yourself to focus on the situation as a problem-to-be-solved and start developing a plan for dealing with it."*
>
> *"Remember your coping efforts. Use whatever relaxation procedure that works best for you. Go ahead and cope using whatever relaxation and rethinking methods that work best for you. Use whatever anger-management tools that work best in this situation."*
>
> *"Go ahead and decide how best to handle and control your anger. You can decide what works best for you. As you practice, you will notice that you are getting better and better at this."*
>
> *"Take a moment to feel good and satisfied with your being in control, relaxing away the anger and rethinking the situation in a calmer, more clear-headed way, letting the anger go."*

17. the patient can be asked to raise his hand at the outset of visualizing the anger provocation scene and to lower it when the anger is reduced to an agreed upon level (e.g., go from 90 to 70 on the 0 to 100 scale);

18. following the imagery rehearsal, the therapist and patient should discuss in detail what the patient did to control his anger. In the image rehearsal, what thoughts worked best in controlling your anger? Examine how and when the patient can use these same coping procedures in his day to day experience; how can the patient remind himself to use coping procedures;

19. the therapist should follow the steps outlined in the **Section on Self-monitoring / Homework** (p. 260) in order to have the patient engage in the extra-therapy activities (e.g., solicit commitment statements, check comprehension, anticipate possible barriers, ensure practice, etc.);

20. finally, the way in which imagery rehearsal is conducted has varied. Deffenbacher and McKay (2000) suggest that the patient view the image and then learn to stop it. Meichenbaum (1994) has taken a more narrative collaborative approach employing a coping imagery format where patients incorporate coping procedures to handle their anger in provocative situations.

BEHAVIORAL REHEARSAL TECHNIQUES

The **behavioral rehearsal procedures** include exposing patients to provoking stimuli that would elicit anger. In collaboration with the patient, the therapist can generate a list of specific expressions and behaviors that *"light the patient's fuse"* and then use these provocations as part of the **"barb" challenge task**. The use of these planned provocations by the therapist provides patients with an opportunity to practice their skills in a safe supportive environment. This procedure can be used effectively with group training. The patients can be encouraged to instruct the therapist on how best to role play these provocations as patients practice their coping skills.

A major concern in implementing the **application phase** of treatment is whether the therapist may put him/herself at risk. Tafrate (1994) has reported that exposing 45 angry patients to over 500 provocations did <u>not</u> elicit any verbal or physical attacks on the therapist, but instead elicited a strong therapeutic bond and alliance. The patients eagerly engaged in the provocation exercises, even instructing the therapist as to how he/she could convey the provocations more effectively. While great caution and preparation are required when conducting such coping skills training with provocations, such exposure practice can prove invaluable to the therapy process. **The more similar the features of the training and the real life setting, the greater the likelihood of generalization or transfer** (Tafrate & Kassinove, 1998).

Each time that the provocation practice trials are used, there is a need to remind the patient about the reasons why these exercises have been included in training. The patient's **collaborative involvement** in the formulation of the provocative triggers and in the rehearsal of coping techniques increases the likelihood that patients will be able to maintain appropriate distance and controls and employ effective coping techniques.

Use of "Barb" Provocation Challenge Procedures

These **challenge practice exercises** can be conducted in the form of **in vivo role-playing** or by means of **imaginal role playing**, either in individual treatment, or more effectively, on a group basis. For example, see Brondolo et al., (1997) for a description of how these procedures were used in training city traffic agents and Meichenbaum and Novaco (1977) on how these procedures were used with policemen to help them learn to cope more effectively with anger-aggressive behavior. Gunderson at al. (1997) have developed a similar psychoeducational approach with families of Borderline patients. One aspect of the treatment is teaching parents how to deal with confrontational situations with their children. For example, the parents practice how when subjected to prolonged abusive tirades they can exit (take time out) and take up the perceived injustice or concern at a time when their child is not as angry and when they are not feeling upset about it. They are encouraged to talk about it with somebody else before addressing the issue with their son or daughter. Using such a **provocation "barb" procedure**, family members can practice their coping skills.

PROCEDURAL STEPS IN USING PROVOCATION SCENES

1. Engage patients in a **collaborative process** in understanding the purpose and importance of practicing their coping skills in arousing and tension-producing situations. Have the patients contribute specific examples of provocation situations. Use the patient's **Anger Logs (p. 175)** and the conceptualization of provocation situations (*II CE HOPE*) **(p. 264)** to generate examples of provocations.

   a) **Highlight that it is important to learn how to experience anger without reflexively acting out.**

   b) **How to tolerate anger without immediate retaliation.**

   c) **How to learn not to be afraid of angry feelings.**

2. **Involve the patients** in generating specific verbal and nonverbal provocations that elicit anger and aggressive behavior. Ask them to consider the full range of emotions. What would it take to make them feel only annoyed, irritated, bothered, frustrated <u>versus</u> feeling really angry to the point of acting out? Help patients identify the key words and behaviors that trigger their anger (e.g., when someone refers to the patient as, "You people!").

3. **Coping imagery procedures** can also be used as a form of cognitive rehearsal. The patient can be asked to visualize an anger-provoking scene and signal (raise finger) when anger is being experienced. The patient is told to pay attention to the anger and let it build. After 20 to 30 seconds of arousal, the patient is encouraged to generate a coping image (seeing himself using his coping repertoire). The patient can be asked to see himself as being extremely angry (75 on a 0 to 100 scale) and then to change the image so that he is only annoyed and irritated (<40 on 0 to 100 scale). What changed in the scene to reduce his anger?

4. Use group members to **provide "barbs" (challenges).** Have the targeted patient and the therapist sit in the middle of a circle and practice coping with these provocations. The therapist can coach the patient by whispering suggestions:

   "Keep calm. Use your breathing control procedures. Remind yourself <u>not</u> to take it personally. You have choices! See it as a problem-to-be-solved and <u>not</u> as a personal threat."

5. Afterwards ask the group members for **constructive feedback** on how the patient handled the challenges. Note that learning to handle **anger is a skill that takes time and practice**. (Ask for examples of other skills training that patients have learned – computer, driving.) As part of the feedback, the patient or the group of patients can be asked"

> *"What did the patient do well? What were the first signs of tension that they saw? What were the emotional messages sent by the patient's different kinds of body language? What else could the patient have done to improve how he coped?"*

6. When using the barb technique, **<u>graduate</u> the exposure** from low to higher provocation situations. Slow down and pace the challenges to meet and extend the patient's coping skills. Such exposure trials usually **last about 10 minutes**.

7. Review with the patients how they can use their coping responses in **real-life situations**. What might get in the way of their using their coping skills?

8. As patients develop anger management skills, they can be encouraged to practice them **in vivo, in a graduated fashion**, beginning with the least challenging situation. The patient can rate situations along a dimension of Subjective Units of Distress (SUDS). The patient can begin with situations that fall at the 50 SUDS level on a 100 SUDS scale. The therapist should build in **back-up plans** and **relapse prevention procedures**, in case the coping procedures (e.g., assertive skills) do not work. *(See below page 355)*

9. Such **barb procedures** should **<u>not</u> be used** when patients evidence alcohol or drug influences during treatment or when they evidence schizophrenia, especially when there is evidence of intrusive ideation of personal threats of harm from others.

SELF-ATTRIBUTION PROCEDURES

It is _not_ enough for patients to change. In order for the **improvement to persist over time** and to generalize across situations, it is critical that patients **"take credit"** for these changes. Such **personal attributions** or **"positive blame,"** where patients note the changes and the connections to their instrumental efforts foster a sense of **personal agency** and **self-efficacy**.

As noted, throughout the therapy process, and especially at the end of the treatment, the therapist should ensure that the patient **"takes credit"** and **"ownership"** for any changes. The therapist should routinely ask patients a series of questions that pull for **self-attributions**. For example, the following sequence of questions can be asked:

1.   **How have you (the patient) handled the situation _now_ compared to how you handled it in the past?**

     "What exactly did you do to help you achieve your goals?"

     "How did you use your self-control strategies?"

2.   **Where else did you do this?**

3.   **How did that make you feel?**

     (Emotions have been characterized as the "glue" between attributions and behavior.)

4.   **Are you telling me, are you saying to yourself, that you can now _notice_ when you are getting worked up, that you were able to use your _game plan_ and take a _time out_, that you viewed this provocative situation as a _problem-to-be-solved_, etc.?** *(The therapist should select from this list of self-control verbs.)*

5.   **What does this mean about you as a person? (Help the patient appreciate how developing coping skills constitutes a real achievement and underscore how these coping skills will keep helping the patient in the future.) Use praise and encouragement to help patients build their confidence in their abilities.**

     "What do these changes you made tell you about yourself?"

     "It sounds as if there were so many things you know how to do, but you didn't know that you knew them."

6.   Other questions that can be raised throughout the course of treatment include the following: (Note that they are mainly *"what"*, *"how"*, and *"even though"* and *"in spite of"* questions.)

What were your angry thoughts in that situation? How did you neutralize (control) them?

Listen to what you just said. Is there a different way to look at the situation?

How did you remind yourself to relax, (take a time out, use your game plan)?

What were you thinking or saying to yourself in order to ... ?

What are you now saying to yourself (doing) that is different?

Are you walking away from some provocative situations, even though ... ?

How did you use your problem-solving plan?

In spite of the fact that 'old habits die hard" you were able to ... How did you accomplish that?

7.   The therapist should explore with the patient throughout the treatment the **consequences and outcomes of their coping efforts** at developing anger-control skills. The therapist can ask the patient such questions as:

Since you have been applying what you learned in treatment, what changes have you noticed in yourself and in those who are close to you?

Have you noticed any changes in your relationships?

Has anyone commented on the changes they have seen in you?

What changes that you have made have surprised you the most? Namely, that at the outset of treatment you didn't think you could change and you surprised yourself? ... I can see how you can find that to be an impressive change.

If I understand you correctly, all your hard work and practice, your effort and commitments are beginning to pay-off. How can you continue to use your new skills to achieve your goals?

Table 25 provides further examples of the kinds of questions therapists can use to foster **patient ownership** and **self-attributions**.

Table 25
**QUESTIONS DESIGNED TO HELP THE PATIENTS <u>TAKE CREDIT</u> FOR
<u>CHANGE</u> OR <u>IMPROVEMENTS</u>**

How did it go? ... What has changed?

How did you get from point A to point B?

Are you saying that ... you exploded but you did <u>not</u> hit her? You were provoked, but walked away ... You kept your cool and took a time out <u>in spite of</u> your feeling humiliated? How did you accomplish this?... This is a big step. This shows growth on your part.

How were things different this time as compared to the last time?

What do you think accounts for the change?

What, if anything, did you do differently this time?

Were you able to follow your "game plan"? How did your "game plan" work?

What surprises, if any, were there? How did you handle them?

How did the present success differ from previous times when it did <u>not</u> work?

Where else did this improvement show up?

Are certain coping strategies working more effectively than others? Which ones?

Are you telling me, saying to yourself, that you can "notice", "catch yourself", "be aware of warning signs", "interrupt the cycle", "check things out", "back-off", "take time out", etc. (The interviewer can select from this list.)

Where else have you been able to use these skills?

How do you remember to use your coping strategies?

What does it feel like to be able to do ...?

How did you manage to do ...?

What you have shown yourself is that you can use words to tell someone how angry you are instead of hitting them.

What you have shown is that you let your feet do the walking <u>instead of</u> ... What you have shown is that you are in control and you won't let others just get you into trouble, nor "take the bait". Is that indeed the case?

Why <u>not</u> just put up with ... or why <u>not</u> just give in (trainer plays "devil's advocate")?

What does this mean about you as a person? ... What does this tell us?

Do I have <u>your permission</u> to share how you handled this with other of my patients and my colleagues, without using your name. I won't violate any privacy. I just want others to benefit from the changes you made, to learn from your example of how "in spite of provocations" you were able to maintain your cool and use your coping skills. Would that be okay?. (Help patients make a gift of their coping efforts.)

THERAPIST/STAFF FEEDBACK TO PATIENTS

In order to help patients further **reflect** on the changes they have made and possible future options, the therapist can provide feedback and praise. The therapists' feedback should be descriptive and <u>not</u> evaluative, so the patients can "take credit" for the changes they are bringing about. The therapist can praise what the patients are **doing** and **<u>not</u> doing** to achieve their therapy goals. The following list provides examples of the type of feedback statements that the therapist can use. The true test of how well therapy is working is <u>not</u> only how much the patients' behaviors are changing, but the **explanations that patients offer for these changes**. One goal of therapy is to have patients <u>on their own initiative</u> spontaneously use expressions like those on the following list as a way to describe their behavioral changes. How many of the following descriptive statements are your patients likely to offer on their initiative (with minimal prompts)? In order to foster this "internalization" process so patients can metaphorically come to **take the therapist's voice with them**, the therapist can provide feedback to patients. The therapist can help patient identify specific examples of their behavior that illustrate their abilities to:

> (1) **Engage in behavioral self-management skills**
> (2) **Tolerate and control their emotions**
> (3) **Use interpersonal strategies**
> (4) **Nurture a "possible self" as a non-aggressive individual**

In order to nurture and foster these skills, the therapist can provide feedback using the following list. The therapist can say, *"I can see that when you did X, you were ..."*; *"Are you saying that when you did Y, you were ...?"*

<u>Engage in Behavioral Self-Management Skills</u>

> *Read warning signs*
> *Identified in advance*
> *Notice / Catch / Interrupt your behavior*
> *Kept a cool head*
> *Walked away*
> *Took time-out*
> *Slowed everything down so it was manageable*
> *Used your freeze-frame technique*
> *Interrupted the vicious cycle (anger-aggression cycle)*
> *Recognized options / Made smart "choices"*
> *Used your "game plans" / Think through options*
> *Prioritize and alter your goals / Establish reasonable goals*
> *Break your goals into a series of do-able sub-goals*
> *Used self-control strategies / Shift gears*
> *Played a different CD in your head / Controlled your thoughts*
> *Edit what you said*
> *Refocus your attention*

Keep your sights on your long-term goals
See multiple pathways
Become an "intention" detective
Learn from these episodes

Tolerate and Control Emotions

Manage your anger
Control your moods
Ride out your emotional storms, ride your emotional wave and tolerate your anger
Soothe yourself
Tolerate / Accept your anger
Move toward acceptance of your anger and the anger of others
Learn to cope with your anger, not master it
Vent your anger in more appropriate ways
Put your emotions on the shelf (back burner) for now

Use Interpersonal Strategies

Defuse the situation
Stake out a middle ground
Short-circuit the conflict
Distance yourself
Talk to them differently
Talk them out of ...
Find an acceptable way to express your anger
Redirected the conversation
Helped others
Seek help
Share your feelings without jeopardizing your relationship
Negotiate / Compromise
Take the perspective of others / See things through their eyes
Show compassion
Forgive others, as well as forgive yourself
Put people first

Nurture "Possible self" as Non-aggressive Individual

Become a take-charge person
Be "street smart" / Make wise choices
Act as your own coach, as your own therapist
Use what you learned without reminders
Put things in perspective
Helps you focus on a particular issue. Look at it as a problem and find a solution.
Acknowledge that by doing X you were avoiding feeling Y and doing so only made things worse. You could see this happening and do something about it.
Empower yourself
Use your "new me" skills and not use your "old me" thinking
Do right
Give yourself permission to …
Engage in life-style changes
Live a life without violence
Keep promises to yourself (and to others)
Promote previously unrecognized strengths
You must be proud of the positive changes you are making

THINGS PATIENTS LEARN <u>NOT</u> TO <u>DO</u>

Not suppress your anger, but <u>transform</u> and use your anger
Avoid risky situations
Not take the "bait", so you get sucked right in
Not give in …
<u>In spite of</u> provocations (being "dissed"), you were able to …
Handle yourself without …
Not fall into the same behavioral rut of …
Not let someone else dictate how you will feel and how you should behave
Choose <u>not</u> to let someone else get you into trouble

The therapist can convey:

That's an idea that sounds worth trying.
That is a big step.
You are able to "walk the walk and <u>not</u> just talk the talk."

When patients spontaneously use expressions that reflect that they are becoming an "observer" of their behaviors, the therapist can "pluck" and "reflect" the patients' expressions and ask for further clarification and examples. Asking patients to provide examples of such metacognitive activities fosters personal agency and self-efficacy. The therapist can observe to the patient, *You mentioned that you always seem to run into a gate that blocks you. It sounds like you have learned to become the gate-keeper. How did you accomplish this?:*

"Isn't that interesting."
"You are more aware."
"You are beginning to pull back and taking charge."
"You are <u>now</u> seeing."
"You are giving yourself permission to say no."
"Not expecting the worst."

By asking patients to provide detailed examples of these activities, the **therapist can foster generalization and self-attributions, foster hope** and **overcome patient resistance.**

PROGRAM SATISFACTION QUESTIONNAIRE

Yet another way to have patients **take credit for changes** is to have them fill in a **Program Satisfaction Questionnaire**. For example, see Deffenbacher and McKay (2000, p. 164). Patients are asked to evaluate the treatment program on a 1 to 7 scale covering such areas as **how effective, helpful, useful, level of improvement, do it again, recommend program to others**.

The therapist can review the **Program Satisfaction Questionnaire** have the patient indicate:

> *What aspects of the training program were most useful and why?*
>
> *What features of the training program did <u>not</u> work particularly well for him?*
>
> *What aspects of the program did he find easiest and most enjoyable to learn?*
>
> *Which skills were most difficult to learn and to apply?*
>
> *What could have been done to make the learning easier?*
>
> *What suggestions, if any, would he have to improve the training program?*
>
> *What aspects of the training program will stick with him the longest?*
>
> *What factors might get in the way of him continuing to use his anger control coping skills?*

With the latter question, the therapist begins the process of considering **RELAPSE PREVENTION PROCEDURES**.

Eyeberg (1993) has summarized a number of **consumer satisfaction** measures. These questionnaires usually cover three areas:

1) the quality of the services received;

2) whether the treatment met the patients' needs and helped them achieve their goals;

3) would the patients recommend the treatment program to others.

RELAPSE PREVENTION PROCEDURES

Relapse Prevention (PR) is designed to **address eventual setbacks** and any **backsliding** or possible **newly arisen difficulties** that may get in the way of continued improvements. The steps in **RP** include the therapist helping the patients:

1. by <u>thinning out the schedule</u> of appointments – increasing the time intervals between sessions so the patients can apply and become more self-confident about the coping skills they have acquired;

2. <u>discuss</u> what they have <u>learned</u> and how they will use this information and skills training <u>in the future</u>;

3. <u>review</u> the steps involved in the <u>anger-aggression-offense</u> chain and the associated thoughts, feelings and behaviors;

4. <u>discuss high-risk factors</u> that may contribute to lapses and escalate from such lapses into full-fledged relapses (i.e., situations, feelings, thoughts and behaviors);

5. <u>keep a "risk" diary</u> so they can come to recognize high-risk situations beforehand and the accompanying warning signs;

6. <u>conduct a decisional chain analysis</u> (i.e., anger does <u>not</u> just occur, but rather it should be viewed more like a comic strip with boxes of individualized risk factors and reactions; move away from a "victim," blaming others stance);

7. <u>discuss and practice intra- and interpersonal coping strategies</u> of avoidance, escape, self-control, acceptance and tolerance skills (e.g., use self-talk, distraction, urge management, social supports, etc.);

8. <u>examine ways to guard against relapse</u> by not using well-worn cognitive and behavioral scripts. The therapist can have participants consider

    "What would keep you from using your coping skills? ... from coming to booster sessions? ... from taking your medication?"

    "Have there been times <u>in the past</u> when it was difficult to always take your meds or when you changed the way you took your meds? What led to that? Are these likely to reoccur?"

    "How can you learn to anticipate and address these potential obstacles?"

    "How can you plan ahead for high-risk situations? How can you avoid any potential difficulties <u>before</u> any trouble starts?"

9. <u>**learn to use the language of RP**</u> by including RP metaphors and concepts *(see examples below, p. 359)*;

10. <u>**review difficulties**</u> that patients have had in the latter stages of treatment in controlling anger and aggression

   "What can be learned from these episodes?"

11. view <u>**lapses as "learning opportunities"**</u>, rather than as occasions for *"catastrophising"* that trigger full-blown relapses. The patient can be encouraged to :

   a) view lapses as a normal part of life and as part of the learning process;

   "What could I have done differently?"
   "What lessons can I learn?"

   b) employ a problem-solving coping set and strategies. Examine how patients managed lapses in the past. Have patients consider what they already know;

   c) nurture persistence and deliberate practice (keep treatment goals in mind).

12. <u>**rehearse for possible lapses**</u> and <u>**practice coping skills**</u> (use imaginal, behavioral and in-vivo procedures). Develop new strategies and routines so you can act quickly when lapses occur and apply these coping skills to new settings.;

13. <u>**continue**</u> to <u>**self-monitor**</u> and <u>**review**</u> coping efforts on a regular basis and <u>**engage in self-reinforcement**</u> for coping efforts;

14. <u>**set up a behavioral contract**</u> about how to maintain changes. (See Deffenbacher and McKay, 2000, p. 166 for examples of **Anger Plan Handouts** that include possible anger thoughts, coping thoughts, coping behaviors and ways to monitor progress.);

15. appreciate that <u>**anger management**</u> is an <u>**ongoing life-time project**</u> that requires commitment and social supports and there will be "unfinished business" that requires work and effortful practice;

16. <u>**enlist new social supports**</u> who abide by nonviolent norms (prosocial peer group) who will place the patient in a "safe" niche where the risk for relapse is lower;

17. <u>**nurture**</u> a new <u>**"possible nonviolent self."**</u> For example, Haaven et al. (1990) have the patient describe or put together a collage of self as an offender and label it the *"Old me"*. They then have patients collaborate in writing scenarios of *"New me"* behaviors that are future-oriented. Patients are encouraged to use <u>**"New me" skills**</u> <u>versus</u> employing *"Old me" thinking*. Patients can be asked to use "New me" skills and to monitor progress. The patients are challenged to **envision a future without violence** and to think about their future nonviolent life-style.

18. **maintain ongoing contact with the therapist**. For example, arrangements can be made for follow-up phone contacts, email exchanges, the patient mailing in Anger Logs, and the like;

19. participate in **follow-up and refresher booster sessions**;

20. conduct relapse prevention **throughout the course of treatment**, not only at the end of training.

NURTURE THE USE OF THE CONCEPTS AND LANGUAGE
OF RELAPSE PREVENTION

USE METAPHORS

Journey metaphor

-- by analogy highlight that a driver is free to explore any route, but such journeys often require planning and anticipation of possible road hazards. The driver must be relaxed, but vigilant, aware of warning signs of fatigue and of other drivers. Issue of transfer (e.g., drive in England – other side of road.) Apply this metaphor to the concept of choosing nonaggressive route and what to be on the lookout for, road map, etc.

Driver's education metaphor

-- learn to be a responsible driver. Initially mindful (conscious), with practice newly acquired skills become more automatic. Skills acquisition requires deliberate practice with specific goals. Learn from mistakes. Build-up subroutines for different hazards on the road(i.e., slippery slopes, back on track). Highlight the need to be "mindful."

Wave metaphor

-- like a surfer who rides a wave that builds, peaks and subsides (wave comparable to riding out emotions and urges). Talk self through an urge. Use acceptance and tolerance. For example, the therapist can ask:

"Describe the circumstances where you will
<u>not</u> give into your urge to … ?"
"What could you do or what could you say to
yourself during an urge to help you get
through it without offending?"

Fishing metaphor

-- like a fish, the individual takes the bait and is pulled into an "angry frame of mind." Recognize hooks (irritating injustice, perceived incompetencies, use mnemonic **II CE HOPE**) *(p. 264).* Learn to swim past the hooks ("Shoulds", "Frustrations") that lure you into angry waters.

"New me" Behaviors
  <u>versus</u> "Old me" Thinking

-- Haaven et al. (1990) have patients construct a narrative that represent "new (nonviolent) me." For example, have individuals produce a collage; keep a daily log of "new me" goals, subgoals, activities, accompanying feelings; have other patients role play voice of "old me" and refute it; play Lifestyle Challenge Game representing "new me".

RELAPSE PREVENTION TERMINOLOGY

As part of **Relapse Prevention**, the patient is taught related concepts and terms. How many of the following terms and concepts do your patients spontaneously employ?

> **Lapses / Relapses**
> **High-risk situations**
> **Individualized risk factors**
> **Decrease my vulnerability**
> **Plan of action**
> **Decisional chain analysis**
> **Seemingly unimportant decisions**
> **Early warning signs**
> **Set-ups**
> **Problems of immediate gratification**
> **Coping strategies (Self-talk, Rethinking, Self-questioning, Time-Out, Relaxation, Assertive "I" Statements)**
> **Envisage sub-goals as steps in a long journey, steps on a ladder**
> **Time sliding /Slippery slope**
> **"Old me" thinking / "New me" behaviors**
> **Manage set-backs**
> **Ride out urges**
> **Learning opportunities / Challenges**

Whatever the set of relapse-prevention procedures employed, the therapist should convey to the patient that anger-reduction efforts are a **life-long learning process. Moreover, once learned, these skills can never be unlearned.** It is like learning to ride a bicycle. If not used, skills may get rusty, but they don't disappear. Some things may get in the way of patients using what they have learned. But what they have gone through is **"just irreversible!"**

As part of the **RELAPSE PREVENTION PLAN** the patient can be given a **CHECKLIST** that summarizes the various therapeutic activities that the patient can use following treatment *(see p. 360)*. The therapist can review these with the patient and develop an **individualized treatment plan**. The **TREATMENT CHECKLIST** can be collaboratively generated with the patient. A specific plan of how the patient can use the combination of these coping strategies should be included in the final phase of treatment. Remember, it is important for the patient to indicate the "reasons" why using these strategies are important, possible barriers and the strategies on how these obstacles can be anticipated and addressed should they occur.

Finally, a **Therapist Checklist** is included that summarizes the various steps involved in **relapse prevention** *(see p. 361)*.

PATIENT HANDOUT:
TREATMENT CHECKLIST

Skills I will use:

- **Know Early Warning Signs**
- **Analyze the Source(s) of my Anger (II CE HOPE)**
- **Conduct a Chain Analysis of my Anger Behaviors**
- **Consider whether there are any "Core Hurts" that I should address**
- **Not make my feelings or the situation worse**
- **Break my "Vicious Cycle" Anger-Aggression-Acting Out Behaviors**
- **Take Time-Out**
- **Use Coping Self-talk**
- **Use Relaxation Procedures**
- **Catch my "Thinking Errors"**
- **Challenge my beliefs**
- **View provocations as "Problems-to-be-Solved"**
- **Use my problem-solving skills**
- **Mentally and behaviorally rehearse how to handle difficult situations**
- **Feel compassion (Perspective-Take) and where appropriate use Forgiveness**
- **Use assertive, but respectful communication skills**
- **Use "I" statements, not "You" statements**
- **Control alcohol and other substance abuse**
- **Anticipate any possible obstacles to change**
  - ➤ **Blaming others**
  - ➤ **"Minimizing" -- justifying anger and aggression**
  - ➤ **Use denial**
  - ➤ **Brood / Hold grudges <u>vs</u>. "Let it go." "Let bygones be bygones."**
- **Have confidence that "I will be able to change."**
- **Use my Relapse Prevention Plan**
  - ➤ **Identify High-Risk Situations and Use my Coping Skills**
- **"Take Credit" for change**
- **Be the "New ME"**

SUMMARY OF THERAPIST ACTIVITIES WITH THE PATIENT WHEN CONDUCTING RELAPSE PREVENTION (RP)

1. Thin out treatment schedule

2. Discuss what the patient has learned and how to it apply to the future

3. Review steps anger-aggression-offense chain

4. Discuss high-risk factors and high risk situations

5. Have the patient keep a "risk" diary

6. Conduct decisional chain analysis

7. Practice coping strategies

8. Consider ways to guard against lapses – anticipate and address possible obstacles

9. Teach the language and concepts of RP – use metaphors

10. Review past difficulties with lapses

11. View lapses as "learning opportunities"

12. Rehearse for possible lapses and relapses

13. Continue to self-monitor, review and self-reinforce effort

14. Use behavioral contract

15. View anger management as an ongoing life-time project

16. Enlist new social supports

17. Nurture new "possible non-violent self" – "New me"

18. Maintain ongoing therapist contact

19. Use booster sessions

20. Conduct relapse prevention throughout training

SUMMARY:
WHAT YOU SHOULD TAKE AWAY FROM SECTION VII

I have been in the business of training clinicians and giving workshops for 30 years. All too often the attendees are preoccupied with learning specific techniques. What they often fail to appreciate is that the actual training procedures account for a small percentage of the variance on predicting treatment outcome (approximately less then 20% and that is being generous). Most variance in treatment outcome is due to patient characteristics (motivation and abilities to change), the quality of the therapeutic alliance, and to characteristics of the therapist. The specific treatment procedures contribute much less to the therapeutic outcomes.

SECTION VII (and other **SECTIONS**) is designed to highlight the **strategies** and **procedural steps** that therapists need to follow in order to :

(1) Enhance patient's motivation to participate and to follow-through

(2) Increase the likelihood of generalization

(3) Address the challenging and recurrent problems of relapse

The Reader should come away from **SECTION VII** with a specific "game plan" on how to achieve these three objectives and ways to evaluate <u>all</u> training programs in light of these Procedural Guidelines. This will take not only knowledge, but also practice as the **TEST YOUR EXPERTISE** page highlights.

TEST YOUR EXPERTISE: SECTION VII

1. The major focus of this **SECTION** is on the issues of **generalization** and **maintenance of treatment effects**. Generate a list of what trainers should do at the <u>outset of training</u>, <u>during training</u> and at the <u>conclusion of training</u> in order to enhance the likelihood of generalization. (***There are some 33 features included on the Generalization Procedural Checklist, p. 335).***

2. Select a training program that you are familiar with or read an article about skills training. How many items on the **Report Card (p. 339)** are included in the training program? What grade, from A to F, would you give this skills training program in terms of ensuring generalization? An alternative challenge is to plan a skills training program with colleagues and build into your training manual explicit guidelines for generalization.

3. Other treatment components designed to enhance transfer include:

   a) **Imagery and behavioral rehearsal techniques (e.g., inclusion of provocation scenes);**

   b) **Self-attribution procedures;**

   c) **Relapse prevention procedures;**

   d) **Providing patients with feedback;**

   e) **Putting the patients in a reflective consultative role (e.g., Ask them to fill out A Program Satisfaction Questionnaire)**

   This **SECTION** highlights just how complex each of these therapy activities are (e.g., Imagery-based rehearsal procedures entail some 20 components; Behavioral rehearsal techniques – 9 steps; Self-attribution procedures – 7 steps; Relapse prevention procedures – 20 steps).

   While this level of detail may feel overwhelming, with practice and mastery they flow together in an effortless fashion. The therapist does <u>not</u> have to include every element from each intervention strategy. Instead, if someone asked you how you help your patients "take credit for change", or "prevent relapse", you should readily have a "game plan" in mind. The challenge is what will it take for you to translate your "game plan" or "informational script" into clinical action? What are the <u>potential barriers</u> that will get in the way of you trying any of the ideas offered in this **Handbook**? How can these obstacles be anticipated and addressed?

4. Practice each of these treatment interventions *(a through e)* with your colleagues. Once again, one plays the patient, the other the therapist, and the third the coach. Try these procedures with your patients.

THANK YOU FOR YOUR INTEREST.

HOPEFULLY, THIS HANDBOOK WILL REDUCE VIOLENCE.

PLEASE SHARE YOUR REACTIONS TO THIS HANDBOOK WITH ME.

ENJOY!

(dmeich@watarts.uwaterloo.ca)

SECTION VIII

CONTENTS SECTION VIII

REFERENCES

Abe, J. L., Jones, S. M., Brown, J. L., Chaudry, M., & Samples, F. (1998). Resolving conflict creatively. Development and Psychopathology, 10, 187-213.

Abe, J. L., Zane, N., & Chan, K. (1994). Differential responses to trauma: Migration-related discriminants of post-traumatic stress disorder among Southeast Asian refugees. Journal of Community Psychology, 22, 121-135.

Acton, R. G., & During, S. M. (1992). Preliminary results of aggression management training for aggressive parents. Journal of Interpersonal Violence, 7, 410-417.

Adams, K. A. (1974). The child who murders: A review of theory and research. Criminal Justice and Behavior, 1, 51-61.

Adams, R., & Laursen, R. (2001). The organization and dynamics of adolescent conflict with parents and friends. Journal of marriage and Family, 63, 97-110.

Aguilar, B., Sroufe, L., Egeland, B., & Carlson, E. (2000). Distinguishing the early-onset/persistent and adolescent-onset antisocial behavior types: From birth to 16 years. Development and Psychopathology, 12, 109-132.

Allen, D., & Tynan, H. (2000). Responding to aggressive behavior: Impact of training on staff members' knowledge and confidence. Mental Rehabilitation, 38, 97-104.

American Psychological Association. (1996). Violence and the family. Washington, DC: American Psychological Association.

American Psychological Association. (1998). Responding therapeutically to patient anger: A stimulus training tape. Washington, D.C.: American Psychological Association.

Anderson, E. (1994). The code of the streets. Atlantic Monthly, May, 81-92.

Anderson, E. (1997). Violence and the inner-city street code. In J. McCord (Ed.), Violence in childhood in the inner city. Cambridge, MA: Cambridge University Press.

Anderson-Malico, R. (1994). Anger management using cognitive group therapy. Perspectives in Psychiatric Care, 30, 17-20.

Andreasen, N. C., Endicott, J., Spitzer, R. L. et al. (1977). The family history method using diagnostic criteria: Inter-rater reliability and validity. Archives of General Psychiatry, 34, 1229-1235.

Andrews, D. A., & Bonta, J. (1994). The psychology of criminal conduct. Cincinnati, OH: Anderson.

Andrews, D. A., & Bonta, J. (1995). The Level of Services Inventory-Revised. Toronto Multi-Health Systems.

Andrews, D. A., Zingler, I., et al. (1990). Does correctional treatment work? A clinically-relevant and psychologically-informed meta-analysis. Criminology, 28, 365-404.

Annis, G., M. Kaplan, M. L., et al. (1997). Violence and homicidal behavior in psychiatric disorder. Psychiatric Clinics of North America, 20, 405-425.

Appel, A., & Holden, G. W. (1998). The co-occurrence of spouse and physical child abuse: A review and appraisal. Journal of Family Psychology, 12, 578-599.

Applebaum, P. S., Robbins, P. C., & Monahan, J. (2000). Violence and delusions: Data from the MacArthur Violence Risk Assessment study. American Journal of Psychiatry, 157, 566-672.

Appelbaum, P. S., Robbins, P. C., & Roth, L. H. (1999). Dimensional approach to delusions: Comparison across types and diagnosis. American Journal of Psychiatry, 156, 1938-1973.

Arboleda-Floren, J., Holley, H., Crisanti, A. (1998). Understanding causal pathways between mental illness and violence. Social Psychiatry and Psychiatric Epidemiology, 33, 38-46.

Archer, J. (2000). Sex difference in aggression between heterosexual partners: A meta-analytic review., Psychological Bulletin, 126, 651-680.

Arias, I. (2000). Special series: Intimate partner violence. Behavior Therapy, 31, 399-602. (See entire issue; pages 599-694).

Arnett, J. J., Offer, D., & Fine, M. A. (1997). Reckless driving in adolescence: "State" and "trait" factors. Accident Analysis and Prevention, 29, 57-63.

Arnold, M. E., & Hughes, J. N. (1999). First do not harm: Adverse effects of grouping deviant youth for skills training. Journal of School Psychology, 37, 99-115.

Arsenault, L., Moffitt, T. E., et al. (2000). Mental disorders and violence in a total birth cohort. Archives of General Psychiatry, 57, 979-986.

Artz, S. (1998). Where have all the school girls gone? Violent girls in the school yard. Child and Youth Care Forum, 27, 77-109.

Ary, D. V., Duncan, T. E., Duncan, S. C., & Hops, H. (1999). Adolescent problem behavior: The influence of parents and peers. Behavior Research and Therapy, 37, 219-230.

Asceltine, R. H., Gore, S., & Gordon, J. (2000). Life stress, anger and anxiety, and delinquency: An empirical test of General Strain Theory. Journal of Health and Social Behavior, 41, 256-272.

Ashford, J. B., Sales, B. D., & Reid, W. H. (2001). Treating adult and juvenile offenders with special needs. Washington, DC: American Psychological Association Press.

Augimeri, L., Webster, C., et al. (1998). Early Assessment Risk List of Boys: EARL-20B. Toronto: Earlscourt Child and Family Center.

Averill, J. R. (1982). Anger and aggression. New York: Springer Verlag.

Averill, J. R. (1983). Studies on anger and aggression: Implication for theories of emotion. American Psychologist, 38, 1145-1160.

Awalt, R. M., Reilly, P. M., & Shopshire, M. S. (1997). The angry patient: An intervention for managing anger in substance abuse treatment. Journal of Psychoactive Drugs, 29, 353-358.

Babcock, J. C., & Steiner, R. (1999). The relationship between treatment, incarceration, and recidivism of battering. Journal of Family Psychology, 13, 46-59.

Baldwin, M. W. (1992). Relational schemas and the processing of social information. Psychological Bulletin, 112, 461-484.

Bandura, A. (1973). Aggression: A social learning analysis. Englewood Cliffs, NJ: Prentice-Hall.

Bandura, A. (1998). Health promotion for the perspective of social cognitive theory. Psychology and Health, 13, 623-649.

Bandura, A., Underwood, B., & Fromson, M. E. (1975). Disinhibition of aggression through diffusion of responsibility and dehumanization of victims. Journal of Research in Personality, 9, 253-269.

Barbour, K. A., Eckhardt, C. I., et al. (1998). The experience and expression of anger in martially violent and martially discordant-nonviolent men. Behavior Therapy, 29, 173-191.

Barkley, R. A. (1995). ADHD Behavior Checklist for Adults. The ADHD Report 3(3).

Baron, R. A., & Richardson, D. R. (1997). Human aggression. (Second Edition.). New York: Plenum Press.

Barratt, E. S. (1993). The use of anticonvulsants in aggression and violence. Psychopharmacology Bulletin, 29, 75-81.

Barratt, E. S. (1994). Impulsiveness and aggression. In J. Monahan & H. Steadman (Eds.), Violence and mental disorder. (pp. 61-79). Chicago: University of Chicago Press.

Barratt, E. S., Stanford, M. S., et al. (1999). Impulsive and premeditated aggression: A factor analysis of self-reported acts. Psychiatric Research, 86, 163-173.

Batsche, G. M., & Knoff, H. M. (1994). Bullies and their victims: Understanding a persuasive problem in the schools. School Psychology Review, 23, 165-174.

Battle, C. L., Zlotnick, C., Najavits, L. M., et al. (in press). Posttraumatic stress disorder and substance use disorder among incarcerated women. In P. C. Oimette and P. J. Brown (Eds.). PTSD and substance use disorder comorbidity. Washington, DC: American Psychological Association.

Baumeister, R. F. (1990). Suicide as escape from self. Psychological Review, 97, 90-113.

Baumeister, R. F. (1996). Evil: Inside human violence and cruelty. New York: W. H. Freeman.

Baumeister, R. F., Smart, L., & Boden, J. M. (1996). Relation of threatened egotism to violence and aggression: The dark side of high self-esteem. Psychological Review, 103, 5-33.

Beauford, J. E., McNeil, D. E., & Binder, R. L. (1997). Utility of the initial therapeutic alliance in evaluating patient's risk of violence. American Journal of Psychiatry, 154, 1272-1276.

Beck, A. T. (1999). Prisoners of hate: The cognitive basis of anger, hostility, and violence. New York: Harper Collins.

Beck, A. T., Steer, R. A., & Garbon, M. G. (1998). Psychometric properties of the Beck Depression Inventory: Twenty-five years of evaluation. Clinical Psychology Review, 8, 77-100.

Beck, R., & Fernandez, E. (1998a). Cognitive-behavioral self-regulation of the frequency, duration, and intensity of anger. Journal of Psychopathology and Behavioral Assessment, 20, 217-229.

Beck, R., & Fernandez, E. (1998b). Cognitive-behavioral therapy in the treatment of anger: A meta-analysis. Cognitive Therapy and Research, 22, 63-74.

Beckham, J. C., Feldman, M. E., et al. (1997). Interpersonal violence and its correlates in Vietnam veterans with chronic posttraumatic stress disorder. Journal of Clinical Psychology, 53, 859-869.

Beckham, J. C., Moore, S. D., & Reynolds, V. (2000). Interpersonal hostility and violence in Vietnam combat veterans with chronic posttraumatic stress disorder: A review of theoretical models and empirical evidence. Aggression and Violent Behavior, 5, 451-466.

Beeman, S. K., & Edelson, J. L. (2000). Collaborating on family safety: Challenges for children's and women's advocates. Journal of Aggression, Maltreatment and Trauma, 3, 345-358.

Bennett, P., Wallace, L., et al. (1991). Treating Type A behaviors and mild hypertension in middle-aged men. Journal of Psychosomatic Research, 35, 209-223.

Bensley, L., Nelson, N., Kaufman, J., Silverstein, B, & Shields, J. (1995). Patient and staff view of factors influencing assaults on psychiatric hospital employees. Issues in Mental Health, 16, 433-446.

Bensley, L., Nelson, N., Kaufman, J., Silverstein, B, Kalat, J., & Shields, J. (1997). Injuries due to assaults on psychiatric hospital employees in Washington sate. American Journal of Industrial Medicine, 31, 92-99.

Benson, B. (1994). Anger management training: A self-control program for people with mild mental retardation. In N. Bouras (Ed), Mental health in mental retardation. (pp. 224-232). Cambridge: Cambridge University Press.

Benson, B., Johnson-Rice, C., & Miranti, S. V. (1986). Effects of anger management training with mentally retarded adults in group treatment. Journal of Consulting and Clinical Psychology, 54, 728-729.

Benson, P. L., Galbraith, J., & Espeland, P. (1995). What kids need to succeed. Minneapolis, MN: Free Spirit.

Berkowitz, L. (1993). Aggression: Its causes. consequences and control. New York: McGraw Hill.

Berman, M. E., Tracy, J. I., & Coccaro, E. M. (1997). The serotonin hypothesis of aggression revisited. Clinical Psychology Review, 17, 651-665.

Berns, S. B., Jacobson, N. S., & Gottman, J. M. (1997). Demand-withdraw interaction in couples with a violent husband. Journal of Consulting and Clinical Psychology, 67, 666-674.

Bernstein, D. A., Borkovec, T. D. (1973). Progressive relaxation training: A manual for the helping professions. Champaigne, IL: Research Press.

Bernstein, H. (1981). Survey of threats and assaults directed toward psychotherapists. American Journal of Psychotherapy, 35, 542-549.

Bernstein, N. (1996). Treating the unmanageable adolescent. Northvale, NJ: Jason Aronson.

Biaggio, M. K. (1987). Therapeutic management of anger. Clinical Psychology Review, 7, 663-675.

Biaggio, M. K., & Macuro, R. (1985). Recent advances in anger assessment. In D. C. Spielberger & J. N. Butcher (Eds.), Advances in personality assessment, Vol. 5. Hillsdale, NJ: Lawrence Erlbaum Associates.

Biaggio, M. K., Supplee, K., & Curtis, N. (1981). Reliability and validity of four anger scales. Journal of Personality Assessment, 45, 639-648.

Binder, R. L. (1999). Are the mentally ill dangerous? Journal of American Academy of Psychiatry and Law, 27, 189-200.

Birkett, D. L. (1997). Violence in geropsychiatry. Psychiatric Annals, 27, 752-756.

Bishop, D. M., Frazier, C. E. (1996). The transfer of juvenile to criminal court: Does it make a difference? Crime and Delinquency, 42, 171-191.

Blackburn, R., & Lee-Evans, J. N. (1985). Reactions of primary and secondary psychopaths to anger-provoking situations. British Journal of Clinical Psychology, 24, 53-100.

Blake, D. D., Weathers, et al. (1990). A clinician rating scale for assessing current and lifetime PTSD: The CAPS-1. Behavior Therapy, 18, 187-188.

Blanchard, E. B., Barton, K. A., & Malta, L. (2000). Psychometric properties of a measure of aggressive driving: The Larson Drivers Stress Profile. Psychological Reports, 87, 881-892.

Blechman, E. A., Cohen, W. M., et al. (1999). Preventing violence via a Constitutional Standard of Care for at-risk youth. Unpublished manuscript, University of Colorado, Boulder.

Blechman, E. A., Prinz, R. J., & Dumas, J. (1995) Coping, competence and aggression prevention: Part 1. Developmental Model. Applied and Preventive Psychology, 4, 211-232.

Boer, D. P., Hart, S. D., Kropp, P. R., et al. (1997). Manual for the Sexual Violence risk – 20: Professional Guidelines for Assessing the Role of Sexual Violence. Vancouver, BC: British Columbia Institute on Family Violence.

Bogg, R. A. (1999). Dostoevsky's enigmas: An analysis of violent men. Aggression and Violent Behavior, 4, 371-386.

Bongar, B. (Ed.). (1992). Suicide: Guidelines for assessment, management and treatment. New York: Oxford university Press.

Bonta, J., Law, M., & Hanson, K. (1998). The prediction of criminal and violent recidivism among mentally disordered offenders: A meta-analysis. Psychological Bulletin, 123, 123-142.

Booth-Kewley, S., & Friedman, H. (1987). Psychological predictors of heart disease: A quantitative review. Psychological Bulletin, 201, 343-362.

Borduin, C. (1999). Multisystemic treatment of criminality and violence in adolescents. Journal of American Academy of Child and Adolescent Psychiatry, 38, 242-249.

Bornstein, P. H., & Bornstein, M. T. (1986). Marital Therapy: A behavioral-communication approach. New York: Pergamon Press.

Borum, R. (1996). Improving the clinical practice of violence risk assessment: Technology, guidelines, and training. American Psychologist, 51, 945-956.

Borum, R. (2000). Assessing violence risk among youth. Journal of Clinical Psychology, 56, 1263-1280.

Borum, R., Bartel, P., & Forth, A. (2000). Manual for the Structural Assessment for Violence Risk in Youth (SAVRY). Tampa, FL: University of South Florida.

Borum, R., Fein, R., et al. (1999). Threat assessment: defining an approach for evaluating risk of targeted violence. Behavioral Sciences and the Law, 17, 323-337.

Borum, R., Swartz, M., & Swanson, J. (1996). Assessing and managing violence risk in clinical practice. Journal of Practical Psychiatry and Behavioral Health., 2, 205-215.

Bowlby, J. (1997). The making and breaking of affectional bonds. British Journal of Psychiatry, 130, 201-210.

Bowman Edmundson, C., & Cohen Conger, J. (1996). A review of treatment efficacy for individuals with anger problems: Conceptual assessment and methodological issues. Clinical Psychology Review, 16, 251-275.

Boyanowsky, E. (1999). Violence and aggression in the heat of passion and in cold blood. International Journal of Law and Psychiatry, 22, 257-271.

Bradbury, T. N., & Fincham, F. D. (1990). Attributions in marriage: Review and critique. Psychological Bulletin, 107, 3-33.

Brannen, S. J., & Rubin, A. (1996). Comparing the effectiveness of gender-specific and couples groups in a court-mandated-spouse-abuse treatment program. Research and Social Work Practice, 6, 405-424.

Brennan, P. A., Mednick, S. A., & Hodgins, S. (2000). Major mental disorders and criminal violence in a Danish birth cohort. Archives of General Psychiatry, 57, 494-500.

Brestan, E. V., & Eyberg, S. M. (1998). Effective psychosocial treatment of conduct-disordered children and adolescents: 29 years, 82 studies, 5,275 children. Journal of Clinical Child Psychology, 27, 180-189.

Briggs, R. (1999). Transforming anxiety, transcending shame. Deerfield Beach, FL: Health Communications.

Brondolo, E., Baruch, C., et al. (1994). Aggression among inner city youth: A biopsychosocial model for school-based evaluation and treatment. Journal of Social Distress and the Homeless, 3, 53-80.

Brondolo, E., DiGiuseppe, R., & Tafrate, D. C. (1997). Exposure-based treatment for anger problems: Focus on the feeling. Cognitive and Behavioral Practice, 4, 75-98.

Brondolo, E., Masheb, R. et al. (1998). Anger-related traits and response to interpersonal conflict among New York City traffic agents. Journal of Applied Social Psychology, 28, 2089-2118.

Browne, K., Saunders, D., & Staeker, K. (1997). Process-psychodynamic groups for men who batter: A brief treatment model. Families in society: The Journal of Contemporary Human Services, May/June, 265-271.

Brummett, B. H., & Williams, R. B. (1998). Hostility and risk for disease. Current Opinion in Psychiatry, 11, 607-613.

Budlong, M. J., Holden, M. J., & Mooney, A. J. (1993). The National Residential Child Care Project: Therapeutic Crisis Intervention. Ithaca, NY: Cornell University Press.

Bullard, H. (1994). Management of violent patients. In J. Shepherd (Ed.), Violence health care: A practical guide to coping with violence and caring for victims. Oxford, England: Oxford University Press.

Burke, L. F., & Follingstad, D. R. (1999). Violence in lesbian and gay relationships: Theory, prevalence and correlational factors. Clinical Psychology Review, 19, 487-512.

Burtle, V. (1985). Therapeutic anger in women. In I. Rosewater and L. Walker (Eds.), Handbook of Feminist Therapy: Women's Issues in Psychotherapy. New York: Springer Publishing.

Busby, D. M., Christensen, C., Crane, D. R., & Larson, J. H. (1995). A revision of the Dyadic Adjustment Scale with distressed and nondistressed couples. Journal of Marital and Family Therapy, 21, 289-308.

Bush, J. (1995). Teaching self-risk management to violent offenders. In J. McGuire (Ed.), What works: Reducing re-offending. Chichester, England: Wiley.

Bushman, B. J., & Anderson, C. (2001). Media Violence and the American public: Scientific facts versus media misinformation. American Psychologist, 56, 477-489.

Bushman, B. J., & Cooper, H. M. (1990). Effects of alcohol on human aggression: An integrative research review. Psychological Bulletin, 107, 341-354.

Buss, A. H., & Durkee, A. (1975). Aggression-hostility Scale. Journal of Consulting Psychology, 21, 343-349.

Buss, A. H., & Perry, M. (1992). The Aggression Questionnaire. Journal of Personality and Social Psychology, 63, 452-459.

Buss, A. H., & Warren, W. L. (2000). Aggression Questionnaire. Los Angeles: Western Psychological Services.

Butterfield, F. (1995). All God's Children: The Bosket family and the American tradition of violence. New York: Avon Books.

Byrne, C. A., & Riggs, D. S. (1996). The cycle of trauma: Relationship aggression in male Vietnam veterans with symptom of posttraumatic stress disorder. Violence Victims, 11, 213-225.

Caeser, P. L., & Hamberger, L. K. (Eds.). (1989). Treating men who batter: Theory, practice and programs. New York: Springer.

Carden, A. D. (1994). Wife abuse and the wife abuser: Review and recommendations. The Counseling Psychologist, 22, 539-582.

Carll, E. K. (1999). Violence in our lives: Impact on workplace, home and community. Des Moines, IA: Allyn Bacon.

Carlson, E. B. (1997). Trauma assessments. New York: Guilford Press.

Carmel, H., & Hunter, M. (1990). Compliance with training in managing assaultive behavior and injuries from inpatient violence. Hospital and Community Psychiatry, 41, 558-560.

Carpenter, S. C., & Halberstadt, A. G. (1996). What makes people mad? Laypersons' and psychologists' categorization of anger in the family. Cognition and Emotion , 10, 627-656.

Carpenter, S. C., & Halberstadt, A. G. (2000). Mothers' reports of events causing anger differ across family relationships. Social Development, 9, 458-477.

Carr, E. G., & Newsom, C. (1985). Reducing behavior problems through functional communication training. Journal of Applied Behavioral Analysis, 18, 111-126.

Carrillo, R., & Tello, J. (Eds.). (1998). Family violence and men of color: Healing the wounded male spirit. New York: Springer.

Carroll, E., Rieger, D. D., et al. (1985). Vietnam combat veterans with PTSD. Journal of Abnormal Psychology, 94, 329-337.

Carroll, K. (1998). A cognitive-behavioral approach: Treating cocaine addiction. NIDA Therapy Manual of Drug Addiction Monograph Series (Vol. 1). Washington, DC: DHHS Pub. No. 98-4308.

Catalano, R. P., Berglund, M. L., et al. (1998). Positive youth development in the U.S.: Research findings. *(Available online at http://www.aspe.hhs.gov/hsp/positiveyouthdev99)*

Cauffman, R., et al. (1998). Posttraumatic stress disorder among female juvenile offenders. Journal of American Academy of Child and Adolescent Psychiatry, 37, 1209-1216.

Chamberlain, P., & Reid, J. B. (1998). Comparison of two community alternatives to incarceration for chronic juvenile offenders. Journal of Consulting and Clinical Psychology, 66, 624-633.

Chambless, D. L., & Ollendick, T. H. (2001). Empirically supported psychological interventions: Controversies and evidence. Annual Review of Psychology, 52, 685-716.

Chemtob, C. M., Hamada, R. S., et al. (1994). Anger, impulsivity and anger control in combat-related posttraumatic stress disorder. Journal of Consulting and Clinical Psychology, 61, 827-832.

Chemtob, C. M., Novaco, R. W., et al. (1997a). Anger regulation deficits in combat-related posttraumatic stress disorder. Journal of Traumatic Stress. 10, 17-36.

Chemtob, C. M., Novaco, R. W., Hamada, R. S., & Gross, D. M. (1997b). Cognitive-behavioral treatment for severe anger in post-traumatic stress disorder. Journal of Consulting and Clinical Psychology, 65 184-189.

Chermack, S. J., & Giancola, P. R. (1997). The relation between alcohol and aggression: An integrated biopsychosocial conceptualization. Clinical Psychology Review, 17, 621-649.

Chermack, S. J., & Taylor, S. (1995). Alcohol and human physical aggression: Pharmacological versus expectancy effects. Journal of Studies on Alcohol, 56, 449-456.

Chesney, M. A., & Rosenman, R. H. (1985). Anger and hostility in cardiovascular and behavioral disorders. Washington, DC: Hemisphere.

Chesney-Lind, M., & Brown, M. (1999). Girls and violence. In D. Flannery & R. Huff (Eds.), Youth violence prevention, interventions and social policy. Washington, DC: American Psychological Association. pp. 171-199.

Christensen, A., & Heavey, C. L. (1990). Gender and social structure in the demand/withdraw pattern of marital conflict. Journal of Personality and Social Psychology, 59, 73-81.

Christensen, A., & Sullaway, M. (1984). Communication Patterns Questionnaire. Unpublished manuscript, UCLA.

Citrome, L., & Volavka, J. (1997). Psychopharmacology of violence. Psychiatric Annals, 27, 691-703 (Parts I and II).

Clancy, J. (1990). Anger and addiction: Breaking the relapse cycle. Madison, WI: Psychological Press.

Coccaro, E. F. (1998). Impulsive aggression: A behavior in search of clinical definition. Harvard Review of Psychiatry, 5, 336-339.

Coccaro, E. F., & Kavoussi, R. J. (1997). Fluoxetine and impulsive aggressive behavior on personality-disordered subjects. Archives of General Psychiatry, 54, 1081-1088.

Coccaro, E. F., Kavoussi, R. J., et al. (1998). Intermittent explosive disorder-revised" Development, reliability and validity of research criteria. Comprehensive Psychiatry, 39, 368-376.

Coffey, S. F., Dansky, B. S., Falsetti, S. A., et al. (1998). Screening for PTSD in a substance abuse sample. Journal of Traumatic Stress, 11, 393-399.

Cohen, C. (1980). Crime among mental patients: A critical analysis. Psychiatric Quarterly, 52, 100-107.

Cohen, D. (2001). Cultural variation: Considerations and implications. Psychological Bulletin, 127, 451-471.

Cohen, D., & Nisbett, R. E. (1997). Field experiments examining the culture of honor: The role of institutions in perpetuating norms about violence. Personality and Social Psychology Bulletin, 23, 1188-1199.

Cohen, D., Nisbett, R. E., Bowdle, D. K., & Schwarz, N. (1996). Insult, aggression and Southern culture of honor: An "experimental ethnography". Journal of Personality and Social Psychology, 70, 945-960.

Cohn, E. (1990). The effect of temperature on crime. British Journal of Criminology, 32, 340-351.

Compas, B. E., Davis, J. E., & Forsythe, J. (1985). Characteristics of life events during adolescence. American Journal of Community Psychology, 13, 677-691.

Conduct Problems Prevention Research Group (1999a). Initial impact of the FAST Track prevention trial for conduct problems. I Journal of Consulting and Clinical Psychology, 67, 631-647.

Conduct Problems Prevention Research Group (1999b). Initial impact of the FAST Track prevention trial for conduct problems. II Journal of Consulting and Clinical Psychology, 67, 648-657.

Conduct Problems Prevention Research Group (2000). Merging universal and indicated prevention programs: The FAST Track Model. Addictive Behaviors, 25, 913-927.

Convit, A., Isay, D., Otis, D., & Volavka, J. (1990). Characteristics of repeatedly assaultive inpatients. Hospital and Community Psychiatry, 41, 1112-1115.

Cook, W. W., & Medley, D. M. (1994). Proposed hostility scales for the MMPI. Journal of Applied Psychology, 38, 414-418.

Cornell, D. G. (1989). Causes of juvenile homicide: A review of the literature. In E. L. Benedek & D. G. Cornell (Eds.), Juvenile Homicide. Washington, DC: American Psychiatric Press (pp. 3-36).

Cornell, D. G., Peterson, C. S., & Richards, H. (1999). Anger as a predictor of aggression in incarcerated adolescents. Journal of Consulting and Clinical Psychology, 67, 108-115.

Corrigan, P. W., Yudofsky, S. C., & Silver, J. M. (1993). Pharmacological and behavioral treatments of aggressive psychiatric inpatients. Hospital and Community Psychiatry, 44, 125-133.

Cotterell, N. (1999). Applying cognitive therapy: Seven steps to anger management. Cognitive Therapy Today, 4, 2-5.

Cox, M., Klinger, E., & Blant, J. P. (1991). Alcohol use and goal hierarchies: Systematic motivational counseling for alcoholics. In W. R. Miller & S. Rollnick (Eds.), Motivational interviewing: Preparing people to change addictive behavior. (pp. 200-271). New York: Guilford.

Crane, D. R., Allgood, S. M., et al. (1990). Assessing marital quality with distressed and non-distressed couples: A comparison and equivalency table for three frequently used measures. Journal of Marriage and the Family, 52, 87-93.

Creamer, M. (2000). Posttraumatic stress disorder following violence and aggression. Aggression and Violent Behavior, 5, 431-449.

Crick, N. R. (1997). Engagement in gender normative versus non-normative forms of aggression: Links to social-psychological adjustment. Developmental Psychology, 33, 610-617.

Crick, N. R., & Dodge, K. A. (1994). A review and reformulation of social information-processing mechanisms in children's social adjustment. Psychological Bulletin, 115, 74-101.

Crick, N. R., Werner, N. E., et al. (1999). Childhood aggression and gender: A new look at an old problem. In D. Bernstein (Ed.), Gender and Motivation: Vol. 45 of the Nebraska Symposium on Motivation (pp. 75-141). Lincoln: University of Nebraska Press.

Crowson, J. J., Frueh, B. C., & Snyder, C. R. (2001). Hostility and hope in combat-related posttraumatic stress disorder: A look back at combat compared to today. Cognitive Therapy and Research, 25, 149-166.

D'Zurilla, T. J., & Maydeu-Olivares, A. (1995). Conceptual and methodological issues in social problem solving assessment. Behavior Therapy, 26, 415-438.

D'Zurilla, T. J., & Nezu, A. M. (1982). Social problem solving in adults. In P. C. Kendall (Ed.), Advances in cognitive behavioral research and therapy. (Vol. 1, pp. 201-274). New York: Academic Press.

Dahlberg, L. L. (1998). Youth violence in the United States: Major trends, risk factors, and prevention approaches. American Journal of Preventive Medicine, 14, 259-272.

Dahlen, E. R., & Deffenbacher, J. L. (in press). A partial component analysis of Beck's cognitive therapy for the treatment of general anger. Journal of Cognitive Therapy and Research.

Dalenberg, C. J. (2000a). Countertransference and the management of anger in trauma therapy. National Center – PTSD. Clinical Quarterly, 9, 42-45.

Dalenberg, C. J. (2000b). Countertransference and the treatment of trauma. Washington, D.C.: American Psychological Association Press.

Daly, M., & Wilson, M. (1988). Homicide. Hawthorne, NY: Aldine de Gruyter.

David, W., Kollmar, K., & McCall, S. (1998). Safe without sight: Crime prevention and self-defense strategies for people who are blind. Boston, MA: National Braille Press.

Davidson, R. (1998). The transtheoretical model:A critical overview. In W. R. Miller & N. Heather (Eds.), Treating addictive behaviors (2nd ed.), (pp. 25-38). New York: Plenum.

Davis, D., & Boster, L. (1992). Cognitive-behavioral-expressive interventions with aggressive and resistant youths. Child welfare League of America, 71, 557-578.

Davis, D., & Boster, L. (1998). Multifaceted therapeutic interventions with the violent psychiatric inpatients. Hospital and Community Psychiatry, 39, 867-869.

Davis, T. C., Byrd, R. S., et al. (1999). Low literacy and violence among adolescents in a summer sports program. Journal of Adolescent Health, 24, 403-411.

Davison, G. C., Robins, C., & Johnson, M. K. (1983). Articulated thoughts during simulated situations: A paradigm for studying cognition in emotion and behavior. Cognitive Therapy and Research, 7, 17-40.

Davison, G. C., Williams, M. E., et al. (1991). Relaxation, reduction in angry articulated thoughts, and improvement in borderline hypertension and heart rate. Journal of Behavioral Medicine, 14, 453-468.

Dean, P. J., & Kange, L. M. (1999). Testing the escape theory of suicide in an outpatient clinical population. Cognitive Therapy and Research, 23, 561-572.

DeBaryshe, B. D., Smith, D. C., Salzman, M., & Larson, J. D. (2001). A meta-analysis of anger management programs for children and youth. Paper presented at the meeting of the Society for Research in Child Development.

Deffenbacher, J. L. (1988). A cognitive-relaxation approach to anger reduction. Ft. Collins, CO: Colorado State University.

Deffenbacher, J. L. (1994). Anger reduction: Issues assessment, and intervention strategies. In A. W. Siegman, & T. W. Smith (Eds.), Anger, hostility, and the heart. Hillside, NJ:Erlbaum.

Deffenbacher, J. L. (1995a). Ideal treatment package for adults with anger disorders. . In H. Kassinove (Ed.), Anger disorders: Definition, diagnosis and treatment. Washington, DC: Taylor & Francis.

Deffenbacher, J. L. (1995b). Assessing Forms of Anger Expression. (Unpublished manuscript, Colorado State University, Dept. Psychology, Ft. Collins, CO 80523)

Deffenbacher, J. L. (1999). Cognitive-behavioral conceptualization and treatment of anger. In Session: Psychotherapy in Practice, 55, 295-309.

Deffenbacher, J. L., Demm, P. M., & Brandon, D. (1986). High general anger: Correlates and treatment. Behavior Research and Therapy, 24, 481-489.

Deffenbacher, J. L., & Hahloser, R. (1981). Cognitive and relaxation skills in stress inoculation training. Cognitive Therapy and Research, 53, 211-215.

Deffenbacher, J. L., Huff, M., Lynch, R., Oetting, E., & Salvature, E. (2000). Characteristics and treatment of high-anger drivers. Journal of Counseling Psychology, 47, 5-17.

Deffenbacher, J. L., Lynch, E. R., et al. (1996). Anger reduction in early adolescents. Journal of Counseling Psychology, 43, 149-157.

Deffenbacher, J. L., Lynch, E. R., et al. (in press). High anger drivers: Characteristic and cognitive-behavioral treatment.

Deffenbacher, J. L., & McKay, M. (2000). Overcoming situational and general anger. Oakland, CA: New Harbinger (Also see accompanying patient manual)

Deffenbacher, J. L., & McNamara, K. (1990). A comparison of cognitive-behavioral and process-oriented group counseling for general anger reduction. Journal of Counseling and Development, 69, 167-172.

Deffenbacher, J. L., Oetting, E. R., et al. (1990). The expression of anger and its consequences. Unpublished Manuscript, Colorado State University.

Deffenbacher, J. L., Oetting, E. R., & Di Giuseppe, R. (in press). Principles of empirically supported interventions applied to anger management.

Deffenbacher, J. L., Oetting, E. R., et al. (1996a). State-trait Anger Theory and the utility of the Trait Anger Scale. Journal of Counseling Psychology, 43, 131-148.

Deffenbacher, J. L., Oetting, E. R., et al. (1996b). Evaluation of two cognitive behavioral approaches to general anger reduction. Cognitive Therapy and Research, 20 551-573.

Deffenbacher, J. L., Oetting, E. R., & Lynch, R. S. (1994). Development of a driving anger scale. Psychological Reports, 74, 83-91.

Deffenbacher, J. L., Oetting, E. R., Lynch, R. S., & Morris, C. D. (1996). The expression of anger and its consequences. Behavior Research and Therapy, 34, 575-590.

Deffenbacher, J. L., & Stark, R. (1992). Relaxation and cognitive-relaxation treatments of general anger. Journal of Counseling Psychology, 39, 158-167.

Dent, N. (2000). 'Anger is a short madness': Dealing with anger in Emile's education. Journal of Philosophy of Education, 34, 313-325.

Derogatis, L. R. (1994). SCL-90R: Administration, scoring and procedures manual. Minneapolis, MN. National Computer Systems.

Derzon, J. H. (2001). Antisocial behavior and the predictions of violence: A meta-analysis. Psychology in the Schools, 38, 93-106.

deShazer, S. (1988). Clues: Investigating solutions in brief therapy. New York: Norton.

Detweiler, J. B., & Whisman, M. A. (1999). The role of homework assignments in cognitive therapy for depression: Potential methods for enhancing adherence. Clinical Psychology, 6, 267-282.

Diamond, E. (1982). The role of anger and hostility in essential hypertension and coronary heart disease. Psychological Bulletin, 92, 410-433.

DiGiuseppe, R. (1995). Developing the therapeutic alliance with angry clients. . In H. Kassinove (Ed.), Anger disorders. Washington, DC: Taylor & Francis.

DiGiuseppe, R. (1999). End Piece: Reflections on the treatment of anger. In Session: Psychotherapy in Practice, 55, 365-370.

DiGiuseppe, R., Eckhardt, C., et al. (1994). The development of self-report and structured interview for anger. Unpublished manuscripts (Ray DiGiuseppe, Department of Psychology, St. John's University, 8000 Utopia Parkway, Jamaica, New York, 11439)

DiGiuseppe, R., & Tafrate, R. C. (2001). Anger treatment for adults: A meta-analytic review: Unpublished manuscript.

DiGiuseppe, R., Tafrate, R. C., & Eckhardt, C. F. (1994). Critical issues in the treatment of anger. Cognitive and Behavioral Practice, 1, 111-132.

Dishion, T. J., Andrews, D. W., Kavanaugh, K., & Soberman, L. H. (1996). Preventive interventions for high risk youth: The Adolescent Transitions Program. In R. DeV. Peters & R. McMahon (Eds.), Preventing childhood disorders, substance abuse and delinquency. (pp. 184-214). Thousand Oaks, CA: Sage.

Dishion, T. J., McCord, J., & Poulin, F. (1999). When interventions harm: Peer groups and problems. American Psychologist, 9, 755-764.

Dishion, T. J., Patterson, G. R. (1993). Antisocial behavior: Using a multiple gating strategy. In M. I. Singer (Ed.), Handbook for screening adolescents at psychological risk. (pp. 375-399). New York: Lexington Books.

Dodge, F., Pettit, G. S., et al. (1995). Social-information processing patterns partially mediate the effect of early physical abuse in later conduct problems. Journal of Abnormal Psychology, 104, 632-643.

Dodge, K. A. (1993). Social cognitive mechanisms in the development of conduct disorder and depression. Annual Review of Psychology, 44, 559-584.

Dodge, K. A., & Crick, N. R. (1990). Social information-processing bases of aggressive behavior in children. Personality and Social Psychology Bulletin, 16, 8-22.

Dolan, M., & Doyle, M. (2000). Violence risk prediction. British Journal of Psychiatry, 177, 303-311.

Donker, F. J., Breteler, M. H., & Van der Staak, C. P. (2000). Assessment of hostility of patients with coronary heart disease. Journal of Personality Assessment, 75, 158-177.

Douglas, K. S., Cox, D. N., & Webster, C. D. (1999). Violence risk assessment: Science and practice. Legal and Criminological Psychology, 4, 149-184.

Douglas, K. S., Ogloff, J. R., & et al. (in press).Assessing risk for violence among psychiatric patients: The HCR-20 Violence Risk Assessment Scheme and the Psychopathy Checklist-Screening Version. Journal of Consulting and Clinical Psychology.

Douglas, K. S., & Webster, C. D. (1999). Predicting violence in mentally and personality disorder individuals. In R. Roesch, S. D. Hart, & J. R. Ogloff (Eds.), Psychology and Law: The state of the discipline. (pp. 175-239). New York: Plenum.

Douglass, F. M., & Douglass, R. (1995). The Marital Problems Questionnaire. Family Relations, 44, 238-244.

Dryden, W. (1990). Dealing with anger problems: Rational-emotive therapeutic interventions. Sarasota, FL: Practitioner's Resource Exchange.

Dua, J. K., & Swinden, M. L. (1992). Effectiveness of negative thought reduction, meditation, and placebo treatment in reducing anger. Scandinavian Journal of Psychology, 33, 135-146.

Dubin, W. (1981). Evaluating and managing the violent patient. Annals of Emergency Medicine, 10, 481-484.

Duncan, R. D., Saunders, B. E., et al. (1996). Childhood physical assault as a risk factor for PTSD, depression, and substance abuse: Findings from a national survey. American Journal of Orthopsychiatry, 66, 437-449.

Dunford, F. W. (2000). The San Diego Navy experiment: An assessment of interventions for men who assault their wives. Journal Consulting and Clinical Psychology, 68, 468-476.

Dunlop, B. D., Rothman, M. B., et al. (2000). Elder abuse: Risk factors and use of case data to improve policy and practice. Journal of Elder Abuse and Neglect, 12, 95-122.

Dutton, D. G. (1994). Patriarchy and wife assault: The ecological fallacy. Violence and Victims, 9, 167-182.

Dutton, D. G. (1995). Intimate abusiveness. Clinical Psychology: Science and Practice, 2, 207-224.

Dutton, D. G. (1995b). Male abusiveness in intimate relationships. Clinical Psychology Review, 15, 567-5891.

Dutton, D. G. (1998). The abusive personality: Violence and control in intimate relationships. New York: Guilford Press.

Dutton, D. G. (1999). Traumatic origins of intimate rage. Aggression and Violent Behavior, 4, 4341-447.

Dutton, D. G., & Golant, S. (1995). The batterer: Violence and control in intimate relationships. New York: Basic Books.

Dutton, D. G., Landolt, M. A., Starzowski, A., & Bodnarchuk, M. (2001). Validation of the Propensity for Abusiveness Scale in diverse male populations. Journal of Family Violence, 16, 59-73.

Dutton, D. G., Van Ginkel, C., & Strazomski, A. (1995b). The role of shame and guilt in the intergenerational transmission in abusiveness. Violence and Victims, 10, 121-131.

Dvoskin, J. A., & Steadman, H. J. (1994). Using intensive case management to reduce violence by mentally ill persons in the community. Hospital and community Psychiatry, 45, 679-684.

Dwyer, K., Osher, D., et al. (1998). Early warning, timely response: A guide to safe schools. Washington, DC: American Institute for Research.

Eckhardt, C. I. (1994). Assessment of anger/hostility disorders by structured interview. Unpublished manuscript, University of North Carolina, Wilmington.

Eckhardt, C. I., Barbour, K. A., & Davison, G. C. (1998). Articulated thoughts of maritally violent and nonviolent men during anger arousal. Journal of Consulting and Clinical Psychology, 66, 259-269.

Eckhardt, C. I., Barbour, K. A., & Stuart, G. L. (1997). Anger and hostility in maritally violent men: Conceptual distortions, measurement issue, and literature review. Clinical Psychology Review, 17, 333-358.

Eckhardt, C. I., & Deffenbacher, J. L. (1998). Diagnosis of anger disorders. In H. Kassinove (Ed.), Anger disorders. Washington, DC: Taylor & Francis.

Ecton, R. B., & Feindler, E. L. (1990). Anger control training for temper control disorders. In E. L. Feindler & G. R. Kalfus (Eds.), Adolescent behavior therapy handbook. (pp. 351-371). New York: Springer.

Edari, B. (1998). Risk and resiliency factors for violence. Pediatric Clinics of North America, 45, 293-305.

Eddy, J. M., Leve, L. D., & Fagot, B. I. (2001). Coercive family process: A replication and extension of Patterson's Coercion Model. Aggressive Behavior, 27, 14-25.

Edelson, J. L. (Eds.). (1999). Interventions and issues in the co-occurrence of child abuse and domestic violence. [Special Issue] Child Maltreatment, 4, 91-182.

Edelson, J. L., & Tolman, R. N. (1992). Intervention for men who batter. Thousand Oaks, CA: Sage.

Eichelman, B. S. (1995). Strategies for clinician safety. In B. Eichelman & A. C. Hatwig (Eds.), Patient violence and the clinician (pp. 139-154). Washington, DC: American Psychiatric Press.

Eichelman, B. S., & Hartwig, A. (Eds.). (1995). Patient violence and the clinician. Washington, DC: American Psychiatric Press.

Elkind, D. (1981) Children and adolescents. (3rd ed.) New York: Oxford University Press.

Elliott, D., Hamburg, B., & Williams, K. (Eds.). (1998). Violence in American schools. New York: Cambridge.

Ellis, A. (1977). Anger: How to live with and without it. New York: Reader's Digest Press.

Engebretson, T. O., Sirota, A. D., et al. (1999). A simple laboratory method for inducing anger: A preliminary investigation. Journal of Psychosomatic Research, 47, 13-26.

Engebretson, T. O., & Stoney, C. M. (1995). Anger expression and lipid concentrations. International Journal of Behavioral Medicine, 2, 281-298.

Enright, R. D., & Fitzgibbons, R. P. (2000). Helping clients forgive: An empirical guide for resolving anger and restoring hope. Washington, DC: American Psychological Association Press.

Epps, J., & Kendall, P. C. (1995). Hostile attributional bias in adults. Cognitive Therapy and Research, 19, 159-178.

Epstein, N., & Baucom, D. H. (1989). Cognitive-behavioral marital therapy. In A. Freeman, K. M. Simon, L. E. Beutler, & H. Arkowitz (Eds.), Comprehensive handbook of cognitive therapy. New York: Plenum Press.

Eronen, M., Angermeyer, M. C., & Schulze, B. (1998). The psychiatric epidemiology of violent behavior. Social Psychiatry and Psychiatric Epidemiology, 33, 813-823.

Evans, D. R., & Strangeland, M. (1971). Development of the Reaction Inventory to measure anger. Psychological Reports, 29, 412-414.

Ewing, C. P. (1990). When children kill. Lexington Books: Lexington, MA.

Fabiano, E. A., & Ross, R. R. (1985). Time to think. Ottawa: T3 Associate Training and Consulting.

Falsetti, S. A., Resnick, H. S., et al. (1993). The modified PTSD Symptom Scale: A brief self-report measure of posttraumatic stress disorder. The Behavior Therapist, 16, 161-162.

Fava, M. (1997). Psychopharmacologic treatment of pathological aggression. Psychiatric Clinics of North America, 20, 427-451.

Fava, M. (1998). Depression with anger attacks. Journal of Clinical Psychiatry, 59, 18-22.

Fava, M., Anderson, K., & Rosenbaum, J. (1990). "Anger attacks.": Possible variants of panic and major depressive disorder. American Journal of Psychiatry, 147, 867-870.

Fava, M.,. Rosenbaum, J. F., et al. (1991). Anger attacks in depressed outpatients in response to fluoxetine. Psychopharmacology Bulletin, 27, 275-279.

Fava, M., Rosenbaum, J. F., et al. (1993). Anger attacks in unipolar depression: Part I. Clinical correlates and response to fluoxetine treatment. American Journal of Psychiatry, 150, 1158-1163.

Favci, G. A., Grandi, S., et al. (1993). Hostility and irritable mood in panic disorder with agoraphobia. Journal of Affective Disorders, 29, 213-217.

Feeny, N., Zoellner, L., & Foa, E. (2000). Anger, dissociation, and posttraumatic stress disorder among female assault victims. Journal of Traumatic Stress, 13, 89-100.

Fehr, B., Baldwin, M., et al. (1999). Anger in close relationships: An interpersonal script analysis. Personality and Social Psychology Bulletin, 25, 229-312.

Fehrenbach, P. A., Thelen, M. H. (1981). Assertive skills-training for inappropriately aggressive college males: Effects on assertive and aggressive behaviors. Behavior Therapy and Experimental Psychiatry, 12, 213-217.

Feindler, E. L. (1995). Ideal treatment for children and adolescents with anger disorders. In H. Kassinove (Ed.), Anger disorders. Washington, DC: Taylor & Francis.

Feindler, E. L., & Ecton, R. (1986). Adolescent anger control: Cognitive-behavioral techniques. New York: Pergamon.

Feindler, E. L., & Guttman, J. (1994). Cognitive-behavioral anger control training for groups of adolescents. In C. W. LeCroy (Ed.), Handbook of child and adolescent treatment manual. (pp. 170-199). New York: Lexington books.

Feindler, E. L., & Scalley, M. (1999). Adolescent anger-management groups for violence reduction. In T. Kratochwill & K. Soiber (Eds.), Handbook of group interventions for children and families. New York: Allyn & Bacon.

Feldman, C. M., & Ridley, C. A. (1995). The etiology and treatment of domestic violence between adult partners. Clinical Psychology: Science and Practice, 2, 317-348.

Felson, R. B., & Tedeschi, J. T. (Eds.). (1993). Aggression and violence: Social interactionist perspective. Washington, DC: American Psychological Association.

Fernandez, E., & Turk, D. C. (1995). The scope and significance of anger in the expression of pain. Pain, 61, 166-175.

Fernandez, Y. M., & Marshall, N. L. (2000). Contextual issues in relapse prevention treatment. In D. R. Laws, S. M. Hudson, & T. Ward (Eds.). Remaking relapse prevention with sex offenders. (pp. 225 - 235). Thousand Oaks, CA: Sage Publication.

Feshbach, N., Feshbach, M., Fauvre, M., & Bullard-Cambell, M. (1983). Learning to care: Classroom activities for affective and social development. Glenview, IL: Scott, Foresman.

Feshbach, S. (1986). Reconceptualization of anger: Some research perspectives. Journal of Social and Clinical Psychology, 4, 123-132.

Feshbach, S., & Zagrodzka, J. (Eds.). (1997). Aggression: Biological, developmental and social perspectives. New York: Plenum Press.

Fincham, F. D., & Bradbury, T. N. (1988). The impact of attributions in marriage: Empirical and conceptual foundations. British Journal of Clinical Psychology, 27, 77-90.

Fincham, F. D., & Bradbury, T. N. (1992). Assessing attributions in marriage: The relationship attribution measure. Journal of Personality and Social Psychology, 62, 457-468.

Fincham, F. D., Bradbury, T. N., & Grych, J. H. (1999). Conflict in close relationships: The role of interpersonal phenomenon. In S. Graham & V. Folkes (Eds.). Attribution theory: Applications to achievement, mental health and interpersonal conflict. (pp. 161-184). Hillsdale, NJ: Erlbaum.

Findlater, J. E., & Kelly, S. (1999). Reframing child safety in Michigan: Building collaboration among domestic violence, family preservation, and child protective series. Child Maltreatment, 4, 167-174.

First, M. B., Spitzer, R. L., et al. (1997). Structural Clinical Interview for DSM-IV Axis I Disorders: Clinician Version. Washington, DC: American Psychiatric Association.

Flannery, D. J., Singer, M. I., & Wester, K. (2001). Violence exposure, psychological trauma, and suicide risk in a community sample of dangerously violent adolescents. Journal of American Academy of Child and Adolescent Psychiatry, 40, 435-442.

Flannery, R. B. (1995). Violence in the workplace. New York: Crossroad Press.

Flannery, R. B. (1998). The Assaulted Staff Action Program: Coping with the psychological aftermath of violence. Ellicott City, MD: Chevron Publishing.

Flannery, R. B. (1999). Critical Incident Stress Management and the assaulted staff action program. International Journal of Emergency Mental Health, 1, 103-108.

Flannery, R. B., Anderson, E., et al. (2000). The Assaulted Staff Action Program (ASAP) and declines in rates of assault: Mixed replicated findings. Psychiatric Quarterly, 71, 165-175.

Flannery, R. B., Fulton, P., Tausch, J., & DeLoffi, A. (1991). A program to help staff cope with the psychological sequelae of assaults by patients. Hospital and Community Psychiatry, 42, 935-938.

Flannery, R. B., Hanson, M. A., et al. (1998). Replicated declines in assault rates after the implementation of the Assaulted Staff Action Program. Psychiatric Service, 49, 241-243.

Flannery, R. B., Hanson, M. A.., & Penk, W. (1994). Risk factors for psychiatric inpatient assaults on staff. Journal of Mental Health Administration, 21, 24-31.

Flannery, R. B., Hanson, M. A., Penk, W., Flanagan, G. J., & Gallagher, C. (1995). The Assaulted Staff Action Program: An approach to coping with the aftermath of violence in the workplace. In L. Murphy, R. Hurrell, S. Sauter, & G. Keita (Eds.), Job stress intervention (pp. 199-212). Washington, DC: American Psychological Association.

Flannery, R. B., & Penk, W. (1996). Program evaluation of an intervention approach for staff assaulted by patients: Preliminary inquiry. Journal of Traumatic Stress, 9, 317-324.

Flannery, R. B., Penk, W., & Corrigan, M. (1999). Assaulted Staff Action Program (ASAP) and declines in the prevalence of assaults: Community based replication. International Journal of Emergency Mental Health, 1, 19-22.

Foa, E. B. (1995). Posttraumatic Stress Diagnostic Scale. Minneapolis, MN: National Computer Systems, Inc.

Foa, E. B., Cashman, L., et al. (1997). The validation of a self-report measure of posttraumatic stress disorder. Psychological Assessment, 9, 445-451.

Foa, E. B., Riggs, D. S., Massie, E. D., & Yorezower, M. (1995). The impact of fear activation and anger on the efficacy of exposure treatment for posttraumatic stress disorder. Behavior Therapy, 26, 487-499.

Forbes, M. R., Pratsinak, G. J., et al. (1992). Effects of group prosocial skills training n anger control in prison inmates. Psychological Reports, 70. 60-66.

Forehand, R., & McMahon, R. J. (1981). Helping the noncompliant child: A clinician's guide to parent training. New York: Guilford Press.

Forgatch, M. S., & DeGarmo, D. S. (1999). Parenting through change: An effective prevention program for single mothers. Journal of Consulting and Clinical Psychology, 67, 711-724.

Forgays, D. G., Forgays, D. K., & Spielberger, C. D. (1997). Factor structure of the State-Trait Anger Expression Inventory. Journal of Personality Assessment, 69, 497-507.

Forth, A., & Burke, H. (1998). Psychopathy in adolescence. In D. Cooke, A. Forth, & R. Hare (Eds.), Psychopathy: Theory, research and implications for society. (pp. 205-229). Boston: Klawer Academic Press.

Fraser, M. W. (1996). Aggressive behavior in childhood and early adolescence: An ecological-developmental perspective on youth violence. Social Work, 41, 347-361.

Frey, K. S., Hirschstein, M.,. & Guzzo, B. A. (2000). Second step: Preventing aggression by promoting social competence. Journal of Emotional and Behavioral Disorders, 8, 102-112.

Frick, P. J. (1998). Conduct disorders and severe antisocial behavior. New York: Plenum .

Friedman, A. S., Glassman, K., & Terras, A. (2001). Violent behavior as related to use of marijuana and other drugs. Journal of Addictive Diseases, 20, 49-72.

Frueh, B. C., Henning, K. R., et al. (1997). Relationship between scores on anger measures of PTSD symptomatology, employment, and compensation-seeking status in combat veterans. Journal of Clinical Psychology, 53, 871-878.

Fruzzetti, A. E., & Levensky, E. R. (2000). Dialectical behavior therapy for domestic violence: Rationale and procedures. Cognitive and Behavioral Practice, 7, 435-446.

Fruzzetti, A. E., Saedi, N. et al. (1999). Domestic Violence Interview Manual. Reno: University of Nevada.

Furlong, M. J., King Ery, P. M., & Bates, M. P. (Eds.), (2001). Special issue: Appraisal and prediction of school violence. Psychology in the Schools, 38.

Furlong, M. J., & Smith D. C. (1994). Anger, hostility and aggression: Assessment, prevention and intervention strategies for youth. New York: Guilford.

Gabriel, R. Hopson, M., & Powell, K. (1996). Youth violence prevention. American Journal of Preventive Medicine, 12, 48-55.

Gallagher, C. A., Wilson, D. B., et al. (1999). The effects of sex offender treatment on sexual reoffending. Corrections Management Quarterly, 9, 19-29.

Gallagher-Thompson, D., Rose, J., et al. (1992). Controlling your frustration: A class for caregivers. Palo Alto, CA: Dept. of Veterans Affairs Medical Center.

Gardner, W. I., & Cole , C. L. (1993). Aggression and related conduct disorders: Definition, assessment and treatment. In J. L. Matson & R. P. Barrett (Eds.), Psychopathology in the mentally retarded (pp. 213-252). Needham Heights, MA: Allyn & Bacon.

Garity, C., Jens, K., et al. (1997). "Bully-proofing your school": Creating a positive climate. Intervention in School and the Clinic, 32, 235-243.

Garmezy, N. (1987). Stress, competence and development. American Journal of Orthopsychiatry, 57, 159-174.

Geffner, R. A. (with Mantooth, C.) (2000). Ending spouse-partner abuse: A psychoeducational approach for individuals and couples. New York: Springer.

Geffner, R. A., Jaffe, P. G., & Sundermann, M. (2000). Children exposed to domestic violence: Current issues in research, intervention, prevention and policy development. Binghamton, NY: Hawthorn Press.

Gelles, R. J., Lackner, R., & Wolfner, G. D. (1994). Men who batter: The risk markers. Violence Update, 4, 1-2.

Gendreau, P. Little, T., & Goggin, C. (1996). A meta-analysis of the predictors of adult, offender recidivism: What works! Criminology, 34, 575-607.

George, D. T., Anderson, P., et al. (1989). Aggressive thoughts and behavior: Another symptom of panic disorder. Acta Psychiatric Scandinavia, 79, 500-502.

Gerlock, H. A. (1990). An anger management intervention model for veterans with PTSD. NC-PTSD Clinical Quarterly, 6, 61-64.

Gerlock, H. A. (1996). Veteran's response to anger management intervention. Issue in Mental Health Nursing, 15, 393-408.

Gest, S. D., Reed, M. G., Masten, A. S. (1999). Measuring developmental changes in exposure to adversity: A Life Chart and rating scale approach. Development and Psychopathology, 11, 171-192.

Gladue, B., A. (1991). Qualitative and quantitative sex differences in self-reported aggressive behavioral characteristics. Psychological Reports, 68, 675-684.

Gleason, W. J. (1997). Psychological and social dysfunctions in battering men: A review. Aggression and Violent Behavior, 2, 43-52.

Goldfried, M. (2000). Integrating gay, lesbian and bisexual issues into mainstream psychotherapy research and practice. Paper presented at the Mid-Atlantic Meting of the Society for Psychotherapy Research, Bethlehem, PA.

Goldstein, A. P. (1988). The Prepare Curricula: Teaching prosocial competencies. Champaign, IL: Research Press.

Goldstein, A. P. (1990). Delinquents on delinquency. Illinois: Research Press.

Goldstein, A. P. (1999). Physical maltreatment: Low level aggression. Champaign, IL: Research Press.

Goldstein, A. P., Glick, B., Gibbs, J. C. (1998). Aggression replacement training: A comprehensive intervention for aggressive youth. Champaign, IL: Research Press.

Goldstein, A. P., Glick, B., Zimmerman, D., & Reiner, L. (1987). Aggression replacement training: A comprehensive intervention for the acting out delinquent. Champaign, IL: Research Press.

Goldstein, H., Edelberg, R., Meier, C., & Davis, L. (1988). Relationship of resting blood pressure and heart rate to experienced anger and expressed anger. Psychosomatic Medicine, 50, 321-329.

Gollwitzer, P. M. (1999). Implementation intentions: Strong effects of simple plans. American Psychologist, 54, 493-503.

Gondolf, F. W. (1997). Patterns of reassault in batterers programs. Journal of Family Violence, 12, 373-387.

Gondolf, F. W., & Foster, R. A. (1991). Pre-program attrition on batterer's programs.. Journal of Family Violence, 6, 337-349.

Gondolf, E. W., & Russell, D. M. (1986). The case against anger-control treatment programs for batterers. Victimization of Women and Children, 9, 2-5.

Gondolf, E. W., & Russell, D. M. (1987). Man to man: A guide for men in abusive relationships. Bradenton, FL: Human Services Institute.

Goodenough, F. (1931). Anger in young children. Minneapolis: University of Minnesota Press.

Gottfredson, G. D. (1987). Peer group interventions to reduce the risk of delinquent behavior: A selective review and a new evaluation. Criminology, 25, 671-714.

Gottman, J. M. (1979). Marital interaction: Experimental investigations. New York: Academic Press.

Gottman, J. M. (1994). Why marriages succeed and fail. New York: Simon & Schuster.

Gottman, J. M., Jacobson, N. S., et al. (1995). The relationship between heart rate reactivity, emotionally aggressive behavior, and general violence in batterers. Journal of Family Psychology, 9, 227-248.

Gottman, J. M., Katz, L. F., & Hooven, C. (1996). Parental meta-emotion philosophy and the emotional life of families: Theoretical models and preliminary data. Journal of Family Psychology, 10, 243-268.

Gottman, J. M., & Krokoff, L. J. (1989). Marital interaction and satisfaction: A longitudinal view. Journal of Consulting and Clinical Psychology, 57, 47-52.

Gottman, J. M., Markman, H., Notarius, C., Gonso, J. (1976). A couple's guide to communication. Champaign, IL: Research Press

Gould, M. S., Shaffer, D., & Davies, M. (1990). Truncated pathways from childhood to adulthood: Attrition in follow-up studies due to death. In L. N. Robins & M. Rutter, (Eds.), Straight and devious pathways from childhood to adulthood. Cambridge: Cambridge University Press.

Green, B. L. (1996). Trauma History Questionnaire. In B. H. Strauss (Eds.). Measurement of stress, trauma and adaptation. (pp. 366 – 369). Lutherville, MD: Sidran Press.

Green, B. L., Lindy, J. D., & Grace, M. C. (1994). Psychological effects of toxic contamination. In R. Ursano et al. (Eds.), Trauma and disaster. New York: Cambridge University Press.

Greenberg, L. S., & Paivio, S. C. (1997). Working with emotion in psychotherapy. New York: Guilford.

Greenberg, M., Domitrovich, C., & Bumbarger, B. (2001). The prevention of mental disorders in school aged children: Current state of the field. Prevention and Treatment. Article (Available online at http://journals.apa.prg/prevention/volume4/pre0040001a.html)

Greenwald, D. J., Reznikoff, M., & Plutchik, R. (1994). Suicide risk and violence risk in alcoholism: Predictors of aggressive risk. Journal of Nervous and Mental Disorders, 182, 3-8.

Griffin, W. A., & Margan, A. R. (1988). Conflict in maritally distressed couples. American Journal of Family Therapy, 16, 14-22.

Grisso, T. (1998). Forensic evaluation of juveniles. Sarasota, FL: Professional Resource Press.

Grisso, T., & Appelbaum, P. S. (1998a). MacArthur Competence Assessment Tool for Treatment (MacCAT-T). Sarasota, FL: Professional Resource Press.

Grisso, T., & Appelbaum, P. S. (1998b). Assessing competence to consent to treatment: A guide for physicians and other health professionals. New York: Oxford University Press.

Grisso, T., Davis, T., et al. (2000). Violent thoughts and violent behavior following hospitalization for mental disorder. Journal of Consulting and Clinical Psychology, 68, 388-398.

Grossman, D. C. (1995). On killing: The psychological cost of learning to kill in war and society. Borton: Little Brown.

Grossman, D. C., Neckerman, H. J., et al. (1997).Effectiveness of a violence prevention curriculum among children in elementary school.. Journal of the American Medical Association, 277, 1605-1611.

Grych, J. H., & Fincham. F.D. (Eds.). (in press). Child developmental and interparental conflict. Cambridge: Cambridge University Press.

Gunderson, J. G., Berkowitz, C., & Ruiz-Sandi, A. (1997). Families of borderline patients: A psychoeducational approach. Bulletin of Menniger Clinic, 61, 440-457.

Haaga, D. A.., Davison, G. C., et al. (1994). Mode–specific impact of relaxation training for hypertensive men with Type A behavior pattern. Behavior Therapy, 25, 209-223.

Haaven, J., Little, R., & Petre-Miller, D. (1990). Treating intellectually disabled sex offenders: A model residential program. Orwell, VT: Safer Society.

Hackett, T. (1997). Management of the violent patient. Annals of Emergency Medicine, 10(9).

Hall, G. S. (1998-1899). A study of anger. American Journal of Psychology, 19, 516-591.

Haller, R., & Deluty, R. (1988). Assaults on staff by psychiatric in-patients: A critical review. British Journal of Psychiatry, 152, 174-179.

Hallock, D. (1998). Hell, healing and resistance. Farmington, PA: The Plough Publishing House.

Hamberger, L. K. (1996). Group treatment of men who batter their female partners. In Session: Psychotherapy in Practice, 2, 49-62.

Hamberger, L. K., & Hastings, J. E. (1993). Court-mandated treatment of men who batter their partners: Issues, controversies, and outcomes. In Z. Hilton (Ed.), Legal response to assault. (pp. 188-229). Newbury Park, CA: Sage.

Hamberger, L. K., & Lohr, J., et al. (1996). A large sample empirical typology of male spouse abusers and its relationship to dimensions of abuse. Violence and Victims, 11, 277-292.

Hamberger, L. K., & Lohr, J., & Gottlieb, M.. (2000). Predictors of treatment dropout from a spouse abuse abatement program. Behavior Modification, 24, 528-552.

Hammond, L., & Yung, B. (1991). Dealing with anger: A violence prevention program for African American youth. Champaign, IL: Research Press.

Hanna, F. J., Hanna, C. A., & Keys, S. G. (1999). Fifty strategies for counseling defiant, aggressive adolescents: Reaching, accepting and relating. Journal of Counseling and Development, 77, 395-403.

Hanna, F. J., & Hunt, W. P. (1999). Techniques for psychotherapy with defiant, aggressive adolescents. Psychotherapy, 36, 56-68.

Hansen, B. (1996). Workplace violence in the hospital psychiatric setting. American Association of Occupational Heath Nurses Journal, 44, 575-580.

Hanson, R. K. (1998). What do we know about sex offender risk assessment? Psychology, Public Policy & Law, 2, 293-323.

Harburg, E., Gleiberman, L., et al. (1991). Anger coping styles and blood pressure in black and white males. Psychosomatic Medicine, 53, 153-164.

Hare, R. D. (1991). Manual for the Hare Psychopathy Checklist-Revised. Toronto, Ontario: Canada Multi-Health System.

Hare, R. D. (1998). Psychopaths and their nature: Implications for the mental health and criminal justice systems. In T. Millon, E. Simonsen, et al. (Eds.), Psychopathology: Antisocial, criminal, and violent behavior. (pp. 188-212). New York: Guilford Press.

Hare, R. D. (1998). The Hare PCL-R: Some issues concerning its use and misuse. Legal and Criminological Psychology, 3, 99-119.

Harper, G. W., & Iwamasa, G. Y. (2000). Cognitive-behavioral therapy with ethnic minority adolescents: Therapist perspective. Cognitive and Behavior Practice, 7, 37-53.

Harris, D., & Morrison, E. (1995). Managing violence without coercion. Archives of Psychiatric Nursing, 9, 203-210.

Harris, G. T., & Rice, M. E. (1997). Risk appraisal and management of violent behavior. Psychiatric Services, 48, 1168-1176.

Harris, G. T., Rice, M. E., & Quinsey, V. L. (1993). Violent recidivism of mentally disordered offenders: The development of a statistical prediction instrument. Criminal Justice and Behavior, 20, 315-335.

Harris, J. A. (1997). A further evaluation of the Aggression Questionnaire: Issues of validity and reliability. Behavior Research and Therapy, 11, 1047-1053.

Harrison, P. A., & Hoffman, N. G. (1985). SUDS: Substance Use Disorder Diagnosis Schedule. St. Paul, MN: Ramery Clinic.

Hart, K. E. (1984). Anxiety management training and anger control for Type A individuals. Journal of Behavior Therapy and Experimental Psychiatry, 15, 133-139.

Hart, S. D., Cox, D., & Hare, R. D. (1995). Manual for the Screening Version of the Hare Psychopathy Checklist-revised. Toronto, ON: Multi-Health Systems.

Hart, S. D., Cox, D., & Hare, R. D. (1995). The Hare Psychopathy Checklist: Screening Version (PCL:SV). Toronto, ON: Multi-Health Systems.

Harway, M., & Evans, K. (1996). Working in groups with men who batter. In M. Andronico (Ed)., Men in groups: Insights, interventions and psychoeducational work. (pp. 357-375).

Hawkins, J. D., Catalano, R. F., et al. (1992). Preventing health-risk behavior by strengthening protection during childhood. Archives of Pediatrics and Adolescent Medicine, 153, 226-234.

Hawkins, J. D., Herrenkohl, T., et al. (1998). A review of predictors of youth violence. In R. Loeber & D. Farrington (Eds.), Serious and violent juvenile offenders: Risk factors and successful interventions. (pp. 106-146). Thousand Oaks, CA: Sage.

Hawkins, J. D., & Weins, J. G. (1985). The Social Development Model: An integrated approach to delinquency prevention. Journal of Primary Prevention, 6, 73-75.

Haynes, S. N., Chavez, R. E., & Samuel, V. (1984). Assessment of marital communications and distress. Behavioral Assessment, 6, 315-322.

Hazaleus, S. L., & Deffenbacher, J. L. (1986). Relaxation and cognitive treatment of anger. Journal of Consulting and Clinical Psychology, 54, 222-226.

Healey, K., Smith, C., & O'Sullivan, C. (1998). Batterer intervention: Program approaches and criminal justice strategies. Washington, DC: National Institute of Justice.

Heide, K. M. (1999). Young killers: The challenge of juvenile homicide. Thousand Oaks, CA: Sage.

Heide, K. M. (2000). Six concentrated areas to reduce juvenile violence in the 21st Century. Barry Law Review, 1, 143-158.

Heide, K. M., Spencer, E., et al. (2001). Who's in, who's out, and who's back: Follow-up data on 59 juveniles incarcerated in adult prison for murder or attempted murder in the early 1980s. Behavioral Sciences and the Law, 19, 97-108.

Heilbrun, K. (1997). Prediction versus management models relevant to risk assessment: The importance of legal decision-making context. Law and Human Behavior, 21, 347-359.

Heilbrun, K., Brock, W., et al. (2000). Risk factors for juvenile criminal recidivism. Criminal Justice and Behavior, 27, 275-291.

Hemphill, J. F., Hare, R. D., & Wong, S. (1998). Psychopathy and recidivism: A review. Legal and Criminological Psychology, 3, 139-170.

Hendin, H., & Haas, A. P. (1984). Wounds of war: The psychosocial aftermath of combat in Vietnam. New York: Basic books.

Henggeler, S. W., Schoenwald, S. K., et al. (1999). Multisystemic treatment of antisocial behavior in children and adolescents. New York: Guilford Press.

Henning, K. R., & Frueh, B. C. (1996). Cognitive-behavioral treatment of incarcerated offenders: An evaluation of the Vermont department of Corrections' Self-Change Program. Criminal Justice Behavior, 23, 523-541.

Henry, W., Schacht, T., & Strupp, H. (1990). Patient and therapist interject, interpersonal process, and differential psychotherapy outcome. Journal of Consulting and Clinical Psychology, 58, 768-774.

Hersch, K., & Borum, R. (1998). Command hallucinations, compliance and risk assessment. Journal of the American Academy of Psychiatry and Law, 26, 353-359.

Heyman, R. E., & Neidig, P. H. (1997). Physical aggression couples treatment. In W. K. Halford & H. J. Markman (Eds.), Clinical handbook of marriage and couples intervention. (pp. 589-617). New York: Wiley.

Heyman, R. E., & Slep, A. M. (2001). Risk factors for family violence. Aggression and Violent Behavior, Vol. 6, No. 23 (See entire issue.).

Heyman, R. E., & Vivian, D. (1993). Rapid Marital Interaction Coding System (RMICS): Training manual for coders. Stony Brook: NY. (http://www.psy.sunsb.edu/marital)

Heyman, R. E., Weiss, R. L., & Eddy, J. M. (1995). Marital Interaction Coding System: Revision and empirical evaluation. Behavior Research and Therapy, 33, 737-746.

Hiday, V. A. (1997). Understanding the connection between mental illness and violence. International Journal of Law and Psychiatry, 20, 399-417.

Hillerbrand, M. (1995). Aggression against self and aggression against others in violent psychiatric patients. Journal of Consulting and Clinical Psychology, 63, 668-671.

Hoagwood, K., & Erwin, H. (1997). Effectiveness of school-based mental health services for children: A 10-year research review. Journal Child and Family Studies, 6, 435-451.

Hoaken, P., Giancola, P. R., Pihl, R. O. (1998). Executive cognitive functions as mediators of alcohol-related aggression. Alcohol and Alcoholism, 33, 47-54.

Hodgins, S. (1998). Epidemiological investigations of the association between major mental disorders and crime: Methodological limitations and validity of the conclusions. Social Psychiatry and Psychiatric Epidemiology, 33, 29-37.

Hodgins, S., & Muller-Isberner, R. (2000). Violence crime and mentally disordered offenders: Concepts and methods for effective treatment and prevention. New York: John Wiley.

Hoge, R., & Andrews, D. (1996). Assessing the youthful offender. New York: Plenum.

Holbrook, M. I. (1995). Anger: Don't let it break you up. (Available from author, 124-G Saddleback Ridge, Motgomery, AL, 36117).

Holbrook, M. I. (1997). Anger management training in prison inmates. Psychological Reports, 81, 623-626.

Hollin, C. R. (1994). Treatment programs for offenders: Meta-analysis, "What works," and beyond. International Journal of Law and Psychiatry, 22, 361-372.

Hollin, C. R. (1999). Treatment programs for offenders: Meta-analysis, "What works,: and beyond. International Journal of Law and Psychotherapy, 22, 361-372.

Holtzworth-Munroe, A. (1992). Social skills deficit in maritally violent men: Interpreting the data using a social information processing model. Clinical Psychology Review, 12, 605-618.

Holtzworth-Munroe, A. (2000). Special Issue on domestic violence. Cognitive Therapy and Research, 24, 135-249.

Holtzworth-Munroe, A. (2000). A typology of men who are violent toward their female partners: Making sense of the heterogeneity of husband violence. Current Directions in Psychological Science, 9, 160-170.

Holtzworth-Munroe, A., Bates, L., et. al. (1997). A brief review of research on husband violence: Aggression and Violent Behavior, 2, 65-99 (Part I); 179-213 (Part II); 285-307 (Part III).

Holtzworth-Munroe, A., & Hutchinson, G. (1993). Attributing negative intent to wife behavior: The attributions of maritally violent versus nonviolent men. Journal of Abnormal Psychology, 102, 206-211.

Holtzworth-Munroe, A., Meehan, J. C., et al. (2000). Testing for the Holtzworth-Munroe and Stuart (1994) batterer typology. Journal of Consulting and Clinical Psychology, 68, 1000-1019.

Holtzworth-Munroe, A., Rehman, U., & Herron, K. (2000). General and spouse-specific anger and hostility in subtypes of maritally violent men and non-violent men. Behavior Therapy, 31, 603-630.

Holtzworth-Munroe, A., Smutzler, N., Bates, L., & Sandin, E. (1990). An overview of research on couple violence: What do we know about male batterers, their partners and their children. In Session: Psychotherapy in Practice, 2, 7-23.

Holtzworth-Munroe, A., Smutzler, N., & Stuart, G. L. (1998). Demand and withdraw communications among couples experiencing husband violence. Journal of Consulting and Clinical Psychology, 66, 731-743.

Holtzworth-Munroe, A., & Stuart, G. L. (1994). Typologies of male batterers: Three subtypes and the differences among them. Psychological Bulletin, 116, 476-497.

Holtzworth-Munroe, A., Stuart, G. L., & Hutchinson, G. (1997). Violent versus nonviolent husbands: Differences in attachment patterns, depending on jealousy, Journal of Family Psychology, 11, 314-331.

Horesh, N., Zalsam, G., & Apter, A. (2000). Internalized anger, self-control, and mastery experience in inpatient anorexic adolescents. Journal of Psychomatic Research, 49, 247-253.

Horne, M., & Lindley, S. E. (1995). Divalproex sodium in the treatment of aggressive behavior and dysphoria in patients with organic brain syndrome. Journal of Clinical Psychiatry, 56, 430-431.

Howard, K. A., Flora, J., & Griffin, M. (1999). Violence-prevention programs in schools: State of the science and implications for future research. Applied and Preventive Psychology, 8, 197-215.

Howells, K., & Hollin, C. R. (Eds.). (1989). Clinical approaches to violence. Chechester: Wiley.

Hoyt, S., & Scherer, G. (1998). Female juvenile delinquency: Misunderstood by the juvenile justice system, neglected by social science. Law and Human Behavior, 22, 81-107.

Huesmann, L. R. (1998). The role of social information processing and cognitive schema in the acquisition and maintenance of habitual aggressive behavior. In R. Geen & E. Donnerstein (Eds.), Human aggression: Theories, research and implication for social policy. (pp. 73-109). New York: Academic Press.

Huessmann, L. R. (Ed.). (1994). Aggressive behavior: Current perspectives. New York: Plenum.

Huessmann, L. R., Eron, L. D., et al. (1984). Stability of aggression over time and generations. Developmental Psychology, 20, 1120-1134.

Hufford, M. R. (2001). Alcohol and suicidal behavior. Clinical Psychology Review, 21, 797-811.

Ingram, R. E., & Wisnicki, K. S. (1988). Assessment of positive automatic cognition. Journal of Consulting and Clinical Psychology, 56, 898-902.

Irons, R., & Schneider, J. P. (1997). When is domestic violence a hidden face of addiction. Journal of Psychoactive Drugs, 29, 337-344.

Jacobson, N. S., & Gottman, J. M. (1998). When men batter women. New York: Simon & Schuster.

Jacobson, N. S., Gottman, J. M., et al. (1994). Affect, verbal content and psychophysiology in the arguments of couple with a violent husband. Journal of Consulting and Clinical Psychology, 62, 982-988.

Jacobson, N. S., Gottman, J. M. et al (1996). Psychological factors in the longitudinal course of battering: When do the couples split up? When does the abuse decrease? Violence and Victims, 11, 371-392.

Jacobson, N. S., & Margolin, G. (1979). Marital therapy: Strategies based on social learning and behavior exchange principles. New York: Brunner/Mazel.

Jenkins, P. J., & Davidson, B. P. (2001). Stopping domestic violence: How a community can prevent spousal abuse. New York: Kluvner/Plenum Publishers.

Johnson, W. Y., & Wilburn, B. (1991). Group counseling as an intervention in anger expression and depression in older adults. The Journal of Specialists in Group Work, 16, 133-142.

Johnson-Reid, M. (1998). Youth violence and exposure to violence in childhood: An ecological review. Aggression and Violent Behavior, 3, 159-179.

Jones, E. E. (1996). Introduction to the special section of attachment and psychopathology. Part I. Journal of Clinical and Consulting Psychology, 64, 5-7.

Kadden, R., Carroll, et al. (1994). Cognitive-behavioral coping skills manual with individuals with alcohol abuse and dependence. NIAAA Project Match Monograph Series, (Vol. 3), Washington, DC: DHHS Pub. No. 94-3724.

Karr-Morse, R., & Wiley, M. S. (1997). Ghosts from the nursery: Tracing the roots of violence. New York: Atlantic Monthly Press.

Kassinove, H. (Ed.), (1995). Anger disorders: Definition, diagnosis and treatment. Washington, DC: Taylor & Francis.

Katz, J. (1988). Seductions of crime. New York: Basic Books.

Kaufman, J., & Zigler, E. F. (1987). Do abused children become abusive parents. American Journal of Orthopsychiatry, 57, 186-192.

Kauppinen, N. R., & Keltikangas-Jarvinen, L. (2000). Relationships between hostility and physiological coronary heart disease risk factors in young adults: The moderating influence of depressive tendencies. Psychological Medicine, 30, 381-393.

Kazdin, A. E. (1985). Treatment of antisocial behavior in children and adolescents. Homewood, IL: Dorsey.

Kazdin, A. E. (1997). Parent management training: Evidence, outcomes, and issues. Journal of the American Academy of Child and Adolescent Psychiatry, 36, 1249-1356.

Kazdin, A. E. (2000). Psychotherapy for children and adolescents: Directions for research and practice. New York: Oxford University Press.

Kazdin, A. E., & Esveldt Dawson, K. (1986). The interview for antisocial behavior: Psychometric characteristics and concurrent validity with child psychiatric inpatients. Journal of Psychopathology and Behavioral Assessment, 8, 289-303.

Kazdin, A. E., Holland, L. et al., (1997). Barriers to treatment participation scale. Journal of Child Psychology and Psychiatry, 38, 1051-1062.

Kazdin, A. E., Wassell, G. (1999). Barriers to treatment participation and therapeutic change among children referred for conduct disorder. Journal of Clinical Child Psychology, 28, 160-172.

Kazdin, A. E., Weisz, J. R. (1998). Identifying and developing empirically supported child and adolescent treatment. Journal of Consulting and Clinical Psychology, 66, 19-36.

Kellner, R. A. (1987). A symptom questionnaire. Journal of Clinical Psychiatry, 48, 268-274.

Kemp, S., & Strongman, K. (1995). Anger theory and management: A historical analysis. American Journal of Psychology, 108, 397-497.

Kessler, R. C., Bromit, E., Hughes, E., & Nelson, C. B. (1995). Posttraumatic stress disorder in the National Comorbidity study. Archives of General Psychiatry, 5, 1048-1060.

Kessler, R. C., McGonagle, K. A., Zhao, S., et al. (1994). Lifetime and 12-month prevalence of DSM-III-R psychiatric disorders in the United States. Archives of General Psychiatry, 51, 8-19.

Kidd, B., & Stark, C. (1995). Management of violence and aggression in health care. Washington, DC: American Psychiatric Press.

Kirker, B., Tenenbaum, G., & Mattson, J. (1999). An investigation of the dynamics of aggression: Direct observations in ice hockey and basketball. Research Quarterly for Exercise and Sport, 71, 373-386.

Kirman, J. H.. (1995). Working with anger in groups. International Journal of Group Psychotherapy, 45, 303-329.

Kivel, P. (1992). Men's work: How to stop violence that tears our lives apart. New York: Ballantine.

Kleespies, P. M. (1998). Emergencies in mental health practice: Evaluation and management. New York: Guilford Press.

Kleespies, P. M., Deleppo, J. D., et al. (1999). Managing suicidal emergencies: Recommendations for the practitioner. Professional Psychology, 30, 454-463.

Knott, C. (1995). The STOP Programme: Reasoning and rehabilitation in a British setting. In J. McGuire (Ed.), What works: Reducing reoffending. (pp. 115-126). Chichester, UK: John Wiley & Sons.

Knox, D. (1997). Marriage happiness: A behavioral approach to counseling. Champaign, IL: Research Press.

Koerner, K., & Dimeff, L. (2000). Further data on dialectical behavior therapy. Clinical Psychology: Science and Practice, 7, 104-112.

Kopel, D. B. (2000). Guns, gangs and preschools: Moving beyond conventional solutions to confront juvenile violence. Barry Law Review, 1, 63-108.

Koss, M. P. (2000). Blame, shame and community: Justice response to violence against women. American Psychologist, Nov., 3-14.

Koss, M. P., Giduez, C. A., & Wisinewski, N. (1987). The scope of rape. Journal of Consulting and Clinical Psychology, 55, 162-170.

Kropp, P. R., Hart, S. D., Webster, C. W., et al. (1995). Manual for the Spousal Assault Risk Assessment Guide. 2nd Edition. Vancouver, BC: British Columbia Institute on Family Violence.

Kubany, E. S. (1994). A cognitive model of guilt typology in combat-related PTSD. Journal of Traumatic Stress, 7, 3-19.

Kubany, E. S., Gino, A., Denny, N., & Torigoe, R. (1994). Relationship of cyclical hostility and PTSD among Vietnam combat veterans. Journal of Traumatic Stress, 7, 21-32.

Kubany, E. S., Leisen, M. B., et al. (2000). Development and preliminary validation of a brief broad-spectrum measure of trauma exposure: The Traumatic Life Events Questionnaire. Psychological Assessment, 12, 210-224.

Kulka, R. A., Schlenger, W. E., et al. (1990). Trauma and the Vietnam war generation. New York: Brunner/Mazel.

Kurdek, L. A. (1994). Conflict resolution styles in gay, lesbian, heterosexual nonparent, and heterosexual parent couples. Journal of Marriage and the Family, 56, 705-722.

Kusche, C. A., & Greenberg, M. T. (1995). The PATHS Curriculum. Seattle, WA: Developmental Research and Programs.

Lahey, B. B., Waldman, I. D., & McBurnett, K. (2000). The development of antisocial behavior: An integrative causal model. Journal of Child Psychology and Psychiatry, 40, 669-682.

Laie, M. A., Pihl, R. O., & Peterson, B. (1995). Provocation, acute alcohol intoxication, cognitive performance, and aggression. Journal of Abnormal Psychology, 104, 150-155.

Lakoff, G. (1987). Women, fire and dangerous things: What categories reveal about the mind. Chicago: University of Chicago Press.

Lam, J., McNeil, D. E., & Binder, R. L. (2000). The relationship between patients' gender and violence leading to staff injuries. Psychiatric Services, 51, 1167-1170.

Langhirichsen-Rohling, J., Huss, M. T., & Ramsey, S. (2000). The clinical utility of batterer typologies. Journal of Family Violence, 15, 37-53.

Lanzi, M. (1991). Nursing staff characteristics related to patient assault. Issues in Mental Health Nursing, 12, 253-265.

Lanzi, M. (1992). Nurses as patient assault victims: an update, synthesis, and recommendations. Archives of Psychiatric Nursing, 16, 1653-171.

Larkin, K. T., & Zayfert, C. (1996). Anger management training with essential hypertension. In V. B. Van Hasselt & M. Hersen (Eds.). Sourcebook of psychological treatment manuals for adult disorders. New York: Plenum.

Larson, J. A. (1996). Driver's Stress Profile. In J. A. Larson (Ed.), Steering clear of highway madness. (pp. 25-28). Wilsonville, OR: Bookpartners.

Larson, J., & Lochman, J. E. (in press). Anger coping program: A cognitive-behavioral intervention with aggressive children in the school setting. New York: Guilford Press.

Lasko, N. B., Gurvits, T. V., et al. (1994). Aggression and its correlates in Vietnam veterans with and without chronic posttraumatic stress disorder. Comprehensive Psychiatry, 35, 373-381.

Lavine, R. (1997). Psychopharmacological treatment of aggression and violence in the substance using population. Journal of Psychoactive Drugs, 29, 321-329.

Laws, D. R., Hudson, S. M., & Ward, T. (Eds.) (2000). Remaking relapse prevention with sex offenders: A sourcebook. Thousand Oaks, CA: Sage Publications.

Leadley, K., Clark, C., & Caetano, R. (2000). Couples' drinking patterns, intimate partner violence and alcohol-related partnership problems. Journal of Substance Abuse, 11, 253-263.

Lederman, C. S., & Brown, E. N. (2000). Entangled in the shadows: Girls in the juvenile justice system. Buffalo Law Review, 48, 908-925.

Lehmann, P. (1997). The development of PTSD in a sample of child witnesses to mother assault. Journal of Family Violence, 12, 241-257.

Leifer, R. (in press). Healing anger, aggression and violence: A Western Buddhist view. Journal of Clinical Psychology.

Lemerise, E. A., & Dodge, K. A. (2000). The development of anger and hostile interactions. In M. Lewis and J. Haviland-Jones (Eds.), Handbook of emotions, Second Edition. New York: Guilford Press.

Leonard, K. E., & Senchak, M. (1996). Prospective prediction of husband marital aggression within newly wed couples. Journal of Abnormal Psychology, 105, 369-380.

Lerner, H. (1989). The dance of anger. New York: Harper Collins.

Lesch, K. P., Merschdorf, U. (2000). Impulsivity, aggression and serotonin. A molecular psychosocial perspective. Behavioral Sciences and the Law, 18, 581-604.

Lescheid, A. W., Cummings, A. L., et al. (2001). Aggression in adolescent girls: Implications for policy, prevention and treatment. Canadian Psychology, 42, 200-215.

Letellier, P. (1994). Gay and bisexual male domestic violence victimization: Challenges to feminist theory and response to violence. Violence and Victims, 9, 95-106.

Leventhal, T., & Brooks-Gunn, J. (2000). The neighborhoods they live in: The effects of neighborhood residence on child and adolescent outcomes. Psychological Bulletin, 126, 309-317.

Levesque, D. A., Gelles, R. J., & Velicer, W. F. (2000). Development and validation of a stages of change measure for men in batterer treatment. Cognitive Therapy and Research, 24, 175-199.

Levinson, D. (1989). Family violence in cross-cultural perspective. Newbury Park, CA: Sage.

Levy, F., Hay, D., et al. (1997). Attention-deficit hyperactivity disorder: A category or a continuum? Genetic analysis of a large-scale twin study. Journal of the American Academy of Child and Adolescent Psychiatry, 36, 737-744.

Levy, S. & Howells, K. (1990). Anger and its management. Journal of Forensic Psychiatry, 1, 305-327.

Lewis, S. F., & Fremouw, W. (2001). Dating violence: A critical review of the literature. Clinical Psychology Review, 21, 105-128.

Limber, S. P., & Nation, M. (1998). Bullying among school children. Washington, DC: Office of Juvenile Justice and Delinquency Prevention.

Lindsey, M., McBride, R. W., & Platt, C. M. (1993). Amend: Philosophy and curriculum for treating batterers. Littleton, CO: Gylantic Publishing.

Linehan, M. M. (1993). Cognitive-behavioral treatment of borderline personality disorder. New York: Guilford Press.

Linehan, M. M., Schmidt, H. et al. (1999). Dialectical behavior therapy for patients with borderline personality disorder and drug dependence. American Journal of Addictions, 8, 279-292.

Link, B. G., Stueve, A., & Phelan, J. (1998). Psychotic symptoms and violent behaviors: Probing the components of "threat/control override" symptoms. Social Psychiatry and Psychiatric Epidemiology, 33, 55-60.

Lipsey, M. W. (1992). Juvenile delinquency treatment: A meta-analytic inquiry into the variability of effects. In T. D. Cook et al. (Eds.), Meta-analysis for explanation: A casebook. (pp. 83-128) New York: Russell sage.

Lipsey, M. W., & Wilson, D. B. (1993). The efficacy of psychological, educational and behavioral treatment: Confirmation from meta-analysis. American Psychologist, 48, 1181-1209.

Lipsey, M. W., & Wilson, D. B. (1998). Effective intervention for serious juvenile offenders. In R. Loeber & D. Farrington (Eds.), Serious and violent juvenile offenders. (pp. 313-345). Thousand Oaks, CA: Sage.

Liskow, B., Campbell, J., & Nickel, B. (1995). Validity of the CAGE questionnaire in screening for alcohol dependence in a walk-in (triage) clinic. Journal of Studies in Alcohol, 156, 277-281.

Lochman, J. E., Coie, J. D., et al. (1993). Effectiveness of asocial relations intervention program for aggressive and nonaggressive rejected children. Journal of Consulting and Clinical Psychology, 61, 1053-1058.

Lochman, J. E., & Lenhart, L. A. (1993). Anger coping intervention for aggressive children: Conceptual models and outcome effects. Clinical Psychology Review, 13, 785-805.

Locke, H. J., & Wallace, K. M. (1959). Short marital adjustment and prediction tests: The reliability and validity. Marriage and Family Living, 21, 251-255.

Loeber, R. (1982). The stability of antisocial and delinquent child behavior: A review. Child Development, 53, 1431-1446.

Loeber, R. (1990). Development and risk factors of juvenile antisocial behavior and delinquency. Clinical Psychology Review, 10, 1-42.

Loeber, R., Burke, J. D., Lahey, B. B., Winters, S., & Zera, M. (2000). Oppositional defiant and conduct disorder: A review of the past 10 years, Part I. Journal of the American Academy of Child and Adolescent Psychiatry, 39, 1-17.

Loeber, R., Burke, J. D., Lahey, B. B., et al. (in press). Oppositional defiant and conduct disorder: A review of the past 10 years. Part II. Journal of the American Academy of Child and Adolescent Psychiatry.

Loeber, R., & Farrington, D. P. (2000). Young children who commit crime: Epidemiology, developmental origins, risk factors, early interventions, and policy implications. Development and Psychopathology, 12, 737-762.

Loeber, R., & Stouthamer-Loeber, M. (1998). Development of juvenile aggression and violence: Some common misconceptions and controversies. American Psychologist, 53, 242-259.

Long, N. J., & Dorf, R. (1994). The tip of the iceberg:: A red-flag carry -in incident. Journal of Emotional and Behavioral Problems, 3, 23-34.

Long, N. J., & Morse, W. (1996). Conflict in the classroom: The education of at risk and troubled students. Austin, TX: Pro-ed.

Lonigan, C. J., & Elbert, J. C. (Eds.). (1998). Special issue on empirically supported psychosocial interventions for children. Child Psychology, 27, 138-226.

Lynam, D. R. (1997). Pursuing the psychopath: Capturing the fledgling psychopath in a nomological net. Journal of Abnormal Psychology, 106, 425-438.

Lyons, J. S., Uziel-Miller, N., Reyes, F., & Sokol, P. (2000). Strengths of children and adolescents in residential settings. Journal of the American Academy of Child and Adolescent Psychiatry, 37, 176-181.

Mace, F. C., Page, T. J., et al. (1986). Analysis of environmental determinants of aggression and disruption in mentally retarded children. Applied Research in Mental Retardation, 7, 203-271.

MacKenzie, D. L. (2000). Evidence-based corrections: Identifying what works. Crime and Delinquency, 46, 457-471.

MacMillan, H. L. (2000). Child maltreatment: What we know in the year 2000. Canadian Journal of Psychiatry, 45, 702-709.

Madden, D., Lion, J., & Penna, M. (1976). Assaults on psychiatrists by patient. American Journal of Psychiatry, 133, 422-425.

Maier, G. J. (1993). Management approaches for the repetitively aggressive patient. In W. H. Sledge and S. Tasman (Eds.), Clinical challenges in psychiatry. Washington, DC: American Psychiatric Press.

Maiuro, R. D., et al. (1987). A brief measure for the assessment of anger and aggression. Journal of Interpersonal Violence, 2, 166-178.

Malmquist, C. (1996). Homicide: A psychiatric perspective. Washington, DC: American Psychiatric Press.

Malta, L. S., Blanchard, E. B., et al. (2001). Psychophysiological reactivity of aggressive drivers: An exploratory study. Applied Psychophysiology and Biofeedback, 26, 95-116.

Mammen, O. K., Shear, M. K., et al. (1999). Anger attacks: Correlates and significance of an underrecognized symptom. Journal of Clinical Psychiatry, 60, 633-642.

Mandler, G. (1980). The generation of emotion: A psychological theory. In R. Plitchik & H. Kellerman (Eds.), Emotion: Theory, research and experience. (pp. 219-243). New York: Academic Press.

Mann, R. E. (2000). Managing resistance and rebellion in relapse prevention intervention. In D. R. Laws, S. M. Hudson, & T. Ward (Eds.), Remaking relapse prevention with sex offenders. (pp. 187 - 200). Thousand Oaks, CA: Sage Publication.

Mann, R. E., & Rollnick, S. (1996). Motivational interviewing with a sex offender who believed he was innocent. Behavior and Cognitive Psychotherapy, 24, 127-134.

Mann, R. E., Wheatley, M. P. & Irons, D. (1999). The lifestyle challenge: A relapse prevention board game for sexual offenders. London: H. M. Prison Service.

Mantooth, C. M., Geffner, R., Franks, D., & Patrick, J. (1987). Family preservation: A treatment manual for reducing couple violence. Tyler, TX: Family Violence Research Program.

Margolies, L., & Leeder, E. (1995). Violence at the door: Treatment of lesbian batterers. Violence Against Women, 1, 139-157.

Margolin, G. (1988). Marital conflict is not marital conflict is not marital conflict. In R. D. Peters and R. J. McMahon (Eds.), Social learning and systems approaches to marriage and the family. New York: Brunner/Mazel.

Margolin, G., Burman, B. et al. (1990). The Domestic Conflict Index. Unpublished manuscript, University of Southern California.

Margolin, G., John, R. S., & Foo, L. (1998). Interactive and unique risk factors for husbands' emotional and physical abuse of their wives. Journal l of Family Violence, 13, 315-344.

Margolin, R., et al. (2000). The effects of family and community violence on children. Annual Review of Psychology, 51, 445-479.

Marques, J. F., Nelson, C., Alarcan, J. M., & Day, D. M. (2000). Preventing relapse in sex offenders. In D. R. Laws, S. M. Hudson, & T. Ward (Eds.). Remaking relapse prevention with sex offenders. (pp. 321 - 340). Thousand Oaks, CA: Sage Publication.

Marshall, W. L., Anderson, D., & Fernandez, Y. (1999). Cognitive-behavioral treatment of sexual offenders. London: Wiley.

Maruna, S. (1997). Going straight: Desistance from crime and life narratives of reform. In A. Lieblich & R. Josselson (Eds.), The narrative study of lives. (Vol. 5, pp. 59-93). Thousand Oaks, CA: Sage.

Maruna, S. (2001). Making good: How ex-convicts reform and rebuild their lives. Washington, DC: American Psychological Association.

Masten, A. S. (2001). Ordinary magic: Resilience processes in development. American Psychologist, 56, 227-238.

Masten, A. S., Hubbard, J. J., et al. (1999). Competence in the context of adversity: Pathways to resilience and maladaptation from childhood to late adolescence. Development and Psychopathology, 11, 143-169.

Mataskis, A. (1996). I Can't Get Over It: A Handbook for Trauma Survivors. Oakland, CA: New Harbinger Publications.

Mataskis, A. (1997). Vietnam Wives: Women and Children Surviving the Challenge of Living with Veterans with Post-Traumatic Stress Disorder. Lutherville, MD: The Sidran Foundation.

Mataskis, A. (1998). Managing client anger. Oakland, CA: New Harbinger Publications.

Matson, J. L., Bambury, J. W., et al. (1999). A validity study on the Question About Behavioral Function (QABF) scale: Predicting treatment success for self-injury, aggression and stereotypes. Research in Developmental Disabilities, 20, 163-176.

Matson, J. L., & Mayville, E. A. (2001). The relationship of functional variable and psychopathology to aggressive behavior in persons with severe and profound mental retardation. Journal of Psychopathology and Behavioral Assessment, 23, 3-9.

Matson, J. L., & Vollmer, T. (1995). Question About Behavioral Function (QABF). Baton Rouge, LA: Scientific Publications.

Maugh, B., Pickles, A., et al. (1996). Reading problems and antisocial behavior: Developmental trends in comorbidity. Journal of Child Psychology and Psychiatry, 37, 405-418.

Maugh, B., & Rutter, M. (1998). Continuities and discontinuities in antisocial behavior from childhood to adult life. In F. H. Ollendick, R. J. Prinz (Eds.), Advances in Clinical Child Psychology, Vol. 20 New York: Plenum.

Mayne, T. J., & Ambrose, T. K. (1999). Research review on anger in psychotherapy. In Session: Psychotherapy in Practice, 55, 353-364.

McAdams, D. P. (2001). The psychology of life stories. Review of General Psychology, 5, 100-122.

McClellan, A. C., & Kellen, M. R. (2000). Attachment theory and violence toward women by male intimate partners. Journal of Nursing Scholarship, Fourth Quarter, 353-360.

McClosky, L. A., & Walker, M. (2000). Posttraumatic stress in children exposed to family violence and single event trauma. Journal of the American Academy of Child and Adolescent Psychiatry, 39, 108-115.

McConnell, W. A., & Catalano, R. (2001). A challenge for the field: The association between violence and mental illness. Behavioral Healthcare Tomorrow, June, 16-19.

McCormick, R. A., & Smith, M. (1995). Aggression and hostility in substance abusers: The relationship to abuse patterns, coping style, and relapse triggers, Addictive Behaviors, 20, 555-562.

McCullough, L. E., McNeil, D. E., Binder, R., & Hatcher, C. (1986). Effects of a weapon screening procedure in a psychiatric emergency room. Hospital and Community Psychiatry, 37, 837-838.

McElroy, S. L. (1999). Recognition and treatment of DSM-IV intermittent explosive disorder. Journal of Clinical Psychiatry, 60, 12-16.

McElroy, S. L., Soutollo, C. A., Beckman, D. A., Taylor, P., & Keck, P. E. (1998). DSM-IV Intermittent Explosive Disorder: A report of 27 cases. Journal of Clinical Psychiatry, 59, 203-210.

McFall, M., Fantana, A., et al. (1999). Analysis of violent behavior in Vietnam combat veteran psychiatric inpatients with PTSD. Journal of Traumatic Stress, 12, 501-519.

McFall, M., Wright, P. W., et al. (1999). Multidimensional assessment of anger in Vietnam veterans with PTSD. Comprehensive Psychiatry, 40, 216-220.

McGee, J., & DeBernardo, K. (1999). The classroom avenger: Behavior profile of school-based shooting. Journal of American College Forensic Examiner, 8, 16-20.

McKay, M. (1992). Anger control groups. In M. McKay & K. Paley (Eds.), Focal group psychotherapy. Oakland, CA: New Harbinger, pp. 163-194.

McKay, M., & Rogers, P. D. (2000). The anger control workbook. Oakland, CA: New Harbinger.

McKay, M., Rogers, P. D., & McKay, J. (1989). When anger hurts: Quieting the storm within. Oakland, CA: New Harbinger Publications.

McLellan, A. T., Kushner, H., et al. (1992). The fifth edition of the Addition Severity Index. Journal of Substance Abuse Treatment, 9, 199-213.

McMahon, R. J., Slough, N., & Conduct Problems Research Group. (1996). Family-based intervention in the Fast Track Program. In R. De V. Peters & RE. J. McMahon (Eds.), Preventing childhood disorders, substance abuse, and delinquency. (pp. 90-100). Thousand Oaks, CA: Sage.

McMain, S., Korman, L. M., Dimeff, L. (2001). Dialectical behavior therapy and the treatment of emotion dysregulation. In Session: Psychotherapy in Practice, 59, 183-196.

McMillan, H. L. (2000). Child maltreatment: What we know in the year 2000. Canadian Journal of Psychiatry, 45, 702-709.

McNeil, D. E. (1998). Empirically-based clinical evaluation and management of the potentially violent patient. In P. M. Kleespies (Ed.), Emergencies in mental health practice: Evaluation and management. (pp. 95-116). New York: Guilford Press.

McNeil, D. E., & Binder, R. (1991). Clinical assessment of the risk of violence among psychiatric inpatients. American Journal of Psychiatry, 148, 1317-1321.

Medina, A. M., Margolin, G., & Wilcox, R. R. (2000). Family hostility and children's cognitive processes. Behavior Therapy, 31, 667-684.

Mednick, S. A., & Kandel, E. (1988). Genetic and perinatal factors in violence. In T. E. Moffitt & S. A. Mednick, (Eds.), Biological contribution to crime causation. Dordecht, North Hilliord: Maretinus Neghoff.

Meehan, J. C., Holtzworth-Munroe, A., & Herron, K. (in press). Maritally violent men's heart rate reacting to marital interactions: A failure to replicate the Gottman et al. (1995) topology. Journal of Family Psychology.

Mehrabian, A. (1996). Manual for the risk of Eruptive Violence Scale (Available from Albert Mehrabian, 1130 Alta Misa Road, Monterey, CA. 93940).

Mehrabian, A. (1997). Relations among personality scales of aggression, violence and empathy. Aggressive Behavior, 23, 433-445.

Meichenbaum, D. (1985). Stress inoculation training: A practitioner's guidebook. New York: Allyn & Bacon.

Meichenbaum, D. (1993). Stress inoculation training: A twenty year update. In R. L. Woolfolk & P. M. Lehrer (Eds.), Principles and practices of stress management. New York: Guilford Press.

Meichenbaum, D. (1994). Treating adults with PTSD. Waterloo: Ontario. Institute Press. (Contact author)

Meichenbaum, D., & Biemiller, A. (1998). Nurturing independent learners. Boston: Brookline Books.

Meichenbaum, D., & Deffenbacher, J. L. (1988). Stress inoculation training. The Counseling Psychologist, 16, 69-90.

Meichenbaum, D., & Fong, G. (1993). How individuals control their own minds: A constructive narrative perspective. In D. M. & J. W. Pennebaker (Eds.), Handbook of mental control. New York: Plenum Press.

Meichenbaum, D., & Jaremko, M. (1983). Stress reduction and prevention. New York: Plenum.

Meichenbaum, D., & Novaco, R. (1977). Stress inoculation: A preventative approach. In C. Spielberger & I. Saranson (Eds.), Stress and anxiety, Vol. 5. New York: Halstead Press.

Meichenbaum, D., & Novaco, R. (1985). Stress inoculation: A preventative approach. Issues in Mental Health Nursing, 7, 419-435.

Meichenbaum, D., & Turk, D. (1987). Facilitating treatment adherence: A practitioner's guidebook. New York: Plenum Press.

Melton, G. B., Petrila, J., Poythress, N., & Slobogin, C. (1997). Psychological evaluations of the courts: A handbook for mental health professionals and lawyers. New York: Guilford.

Menzies, R., Webster, C. D., et al. (1994). The dimensions of dangerousness revisited. Law and Human Behavior, 18, 1-28.

Menzies, R. J., Webster, C. D., & Sepejak, D. S. (1985). The dimension of dangerousness: Evaluating the accuracy of psychometric predictions of violence among forensic patients. Law and Human Behavior, 9, 35-56.

Mercer, D., Carpenter, G., et al. (1994). Addiction Recovery Manual (Vol. 2). Philadelphia: University of Pennsylvania: Treatment Research Unit.

Messer, S. B. (1999). Coping with the angry patient. Journal of Psychotherapy Integration, 9, 151-156.

Meyer, A. L., Farrell, A. D., et al. (2000). Promoting nonviolence in early adolescence. New York: Kluvner Academia / Plenum Publishers.

Miller, C. (2001). Childhood animal cruelty and interpersonal violence. Clinical Psychology Review, 21, 735-750.

Miller, T. Q., Smith, T. W., et al. (1996). A meta-analytic review of research on hostility and physical health. Psychological Bulletin, 119, 322-348.

Miller, W. R., & Rollnick, S. (1991). Motivational interviewing: Preparing people to change addictive behavior. New York: Guilford.

Millon, T. (1987). Manual for the Millon Clinical Multiaxial Inventory-II. Minneapolis, MN: National Computer Systems.

Millon, T. (1997). Millon Clinical Multiaxial Inventory (MCMI) Manual (3rd ed.). Minneapolis, MN: National Computer Systems.

Mills, J. F., Kroener, D. G., & Forth, A. E. (1998). Novaco's Anger Scale: Reliability and validity within an adult criminal sample. Assessment, 5, 237-248.

Milner, J. S. (1989a). The Child Abuse Potential Inventory: Manual (2nd Ed.). Webster, NC: Psytec Corporation.

Milner, J. S. (1989b). Additional cross-validation of the Child Abuse Potential Inventory. Psychological Assessment, 1, 219-223. *(Also see www.nnfr.org/eval/bcb-ins/Milner.html)*

Moffitt, T. E. (1993). Adolescence-limited and life-course-persistent antisocial behavior: A developmental taxonomy. Psychological Review, 100, 674-701.

Moffitt, T. E. (1993). The neuropsychology of conduct disorder. Developmental Psychopathology, 5, 135-151.

Moffitt, T. E. (1996). Measuring children's antisocial behaviors. JAMA, 275, 403-404.

Monahan, J. (1981). The clinical prediction of violent behavior. Rockville, MD: National Institute of Mental Health.

Monahan, J. (1984). The prediction of violent behavior: Towards a second generation of theory and policy. American Journal of Psychiatry, 141, 10-15.

Monahan, J. (1996). Violence predictions: The last 20 years and the next 20 years. Criminal Justice and Behavior, 23, 107-120.

Monahan, J., & Steadman, H. J. (Eds.). (1994). Violence and mental disorder: Development in risk assessment. Chicago: University of Chicago Press.

Monahan, J., Steadman, H. J., Applebaum, P., et al. (2000). Developing a clinically useful actuarial tool for assessing violence risk. British Journal of Psychiatry, 176, 312-320.

Moon, J. R.., & Eisler, R. M. (1983). Anger control: An experimental comparison of three behavioral treatments. Behavior Therapy, 14, 494-505.

Moore, E., Adams, R., et al. (1997). An anger management group for people with a learning disability. British Journal of Learning Disabilities, 25, 53-57.

Morey, L. C. (1991). The Personality Assessment Inventory Professional Manual. Odessa, FL: Psychological; Assessment Resource.

Morrison, G. M., & Skiba, R. (2001). Predicating violence from school misbehavior. Psychology in the Schools, 38, 173-184.

Morrison, J. (1997). When Psychological Problems Mask Medical Disorder: A Guide for Psychotherapists. New York: Guilford Press.

Moss, H. B., & Tarter, R. B. (1993). Substance abuse, aggression and violence: What are the connections? American Journal of Addictions, 2, 149-160.

Mossman, D. (1994). Assessing predictions of violence: Being accurate about accuracy. Journal of Consulting and Clinical Psychology, 62, 783-792.

Mossman, D. (2000). Commentary: Assessing the risk of violence – Are 'accurate" predictions useful. Journal of the American Academy of Psychiatry and Law, 28., 272-281.

Mueser, K. T., Bond, Y. R., et al. (1998). Model of community care for severe mental illness: A review of research on case management. Schizophrenia Bulletin, 24, 37-74.

Mulvey, E. P. (1994). Assessing the evidence of a link between mental illness and violence. Hospital and Community Psychiatry, 45, 663-668.

Murphy, C. M., & Baxter, V. (1997). Motivating batterers to change in the treatment context. Journal of Interpersonal Violence, 12, 607-619.

Murphy, C. M., & O'Farrell, T. J. (1996). Marital violence among alcoholics. Current Directions in Psychological Science, 5, 183-186.

Murphy, M. D., & Page, I. J. (2000). Relapse prevention with adolescent sex offenders. In D. R. Laws, S. M. Hudson, & T. Ward (Eds.). Remaking relapse prevention with sex offenders. (pp. 353 - 368). Thousand Oaks, CA: Sage Publication.

Najavits, L. M., & Weiss, R. D. (2000). Seeking Safety and Exposure Therapy for Men with PTSD and Substance Abuse 3. Falk Foundation.

Najavits, L. M., Weiss, R. D., et al., (1998). "Seeking safety": Outcome of a new cognitive-behavioral psychotherapy for women with posttraumatic stress disorder and substance dependence. Journal of Traumatic Stress, 11, 437-456.

Nakano, K. (1990). Effects of two self-control procedures in modifying Type A behavior. Journal of Clinical Psychology, 14, 495-505.

National Research Council and Institute of Medicine. (1998). In R. Chalk & P. A. King (Eds.), Violence in families: Assessing prevention and treatment programs. Washington, EC: National Academy Press.

Neidig, P. H., & Friedman, D. (1984). Spouse abuse: A treatment program. Champaign, IL: Research Press.

Neidig, P. H., Heyman, R. E., & Slep, A. M. (1995). Domestic conflict containment, Phase II: Parenting workbook. Strong Brook, NY: Behavioral Science Associates.

Nemeroff, C. B., Schatzberg, A. F. (1999). Phenomenology and treatment of aggression across psychiatric illnesses: Special issue. Journal of Clinical Psychiatry, 60, Suppl. 15, 3-50.

Nisbett, R. E. (1993). Violence and U.S. regional culture. American Psychologist, 48, 441-449.

Nisbett, R. E., & Cohen, D. (1996). Culture of honor: The psychology of violence in the south. Boulder, CO: Westview.

Nomenelli, S., & Katz, R. C. (1993). Effects of anger control training on abusive parents. Cognitive Therapy and Research, 7, 57-67.

Norcross, J. C., Frank-McNee, J., et al. (1999). Responding therapeutically to patient anger: A stimulus training tape. Washington, DC: American Psychological Association. (34 minute videotape and booklet).

Norcross, J. C., & Kobayashi, M. (1999). Treating anger in psychotherapy: Introduction and cases. In Session: Psychotherapy in Practice, 55, 275-282. *(See the entire issue which is on Treating Anger in Psychotherapy.)*

Normand, P., & Robert, M. (1990). Modeling of anger/hostility control with preadolescent Type A girls. Child Study Journal, 20, 237-262.

Norris, F. H. (1990). Screening for traumatic stress: A scale for use in the general population. Journal of Applied Social Psychology, 20, 1704-1718.

Norris, F. H., & Rind, J. K. (1997). Standardized self-report measures of civilian trauma and post-traumatic stress disorder. In J. P. Wilson and T. M. Keane (Eds.). Assessing psychological trauma and PTSD. (pp. 7 – 42). New York: Guilford Press.

Novaco, R. W. (1975). Anger control: The development and evaluation of an experimental treatment. Lexington, MA: Heath.

Novaco, R. W. (1976). Treatment of chronic anger through cognitive and relaxation controls. Journal of Consulting and Clinical Psychology, 4, 681-687.

Novaco, R. W. (1977). A stress inoculation approach to anger management in training of law enforcement officers. American Journal of Community Psychology, 5, 327-346.

Novaco, R. W. (1980). The training of probation counselors for anger problems. Journal of Counseling Psychiatry, 27, 385-390.

Novaco, R. W. (1990). Novaco Anger Scale. Irvine, CA: University of California.

Novaco, R. W. (1993). Clinicians ought to view anger contextually. Behavior Change, 10, 208-218.

Novaco, R. W. (1994). Anger as a risk factor for violence among the mentally disordered. In J. Monahan and H. J. Steadman (Eds.), Violence and mental disorder: Development in risk assessment. (pp. 21-60). Chicago: University of Chicago Press.

Novaco, R. W. (1996). Anger treatment and its special challenges. National Center for PTSD Quarterly, 6, 56-68.

Novaco, R. W. (1997a). Remediating anger and aggression with violent offenders. Legal and Criminal Psychology, 2, 77-88.

Novaco, R. W. (1997b). A stress inoculation approach to anger management in the training of law enforcement officers. American Journal of Community Psychology, 5, 327-346.

Novaco, R. W. (1997c). Stress inoculation: A cognitive therapy for anger and its application to a case of depression. Journal of Consulting and Clinical Psychology, 45, 600-608.

Novaco, R. W., Kliewer, W., & Broquet, A. (1991). Home environment consequences of commute travel impedance. American Journal of Community Psychology, 19, 881-909.

Novaco, R. W., Ramm, M., & Black, L. (in press). Anger treatment with offenders. In C. Hollin (Ed.), Handbook of offender assessment and treatment.

Nugent, W. R. (1991). An experimental and qualitative analysis of a cognitive behavioral intervention for anger. Social Work Research and Abstract, 27, 3-8.

O'Connor, D. B., Archer, J., & Wu, F. W. (2001). Measuring aggression: Self-reports, partner reports, and responses to promoting scenarios. Aggressive Behavior, 20, 79-100.

O'Donnell, C. R., & Worell, L. (1993). Motor and cognitive relaxation in the desensitization of anger. Behavioral Research and Therapy, 11, 473-481.

O'Farrell, T. G., VanHutton, V., & Murphy, C. M. (1999). Domestic violence before and after alcoholism treatment: A two-year longitudinal study. Journal of Studies in Alcoholism, 60, 317-321.

Office of Juvenile Justice and Delinquency Prevention (1995). Guide for implementing the comprehensive strategy for serious, violent and chronic juvenile offenders. Washington, DC: department of Justice.

O'Hanlon, W., & Weiner-Davis, M. (1989). In search of solutions. New York: Norton.

O'Keefe, M. (1998). Factors mediating the link between witnessing interparental violence and dating violence. Journal of Family Violence, 13, 39-57.

Oldham, J., Clarkin, J., et al. (1985). A self-report instrument for borderline personality organization. In T. H. McGlashon (Ed.), The borderline: Current empirical research. Washington, DC: American Psychological Association.

Olds, D. C., Henderson, C. R., et al. (1999). Prenatal and infancy home visitation by nurses: Recent findings. Future of Children, 9, 44-65.

O'Leary, C. A. (2000). Reducing aggression in adults with brain injuries. Behavioral Interactions, 15, 205-216.

O'Leary, K. D. (1996). Physical aggression in intimate relationships can be treated within a marital context under certain circumstances. Journal of Interpersonal Violence, 11, 450-452.

O'Leary, K. D. (1999a). Psychological abuse: A variable deserving critical attention in domestic violence. Violence and Victims, 14, 25-35.

O'Leary, K. D. (1999b). Developmental and affective issues in assessing and treating partner aggression. Clinical Psychology: Science and Practice, 6, 400-414.

O'Leary, K. D., & Arias, I. (1988). Prevalence, correlates and development of spouse abuse. In R. D. Peters and R. J. McMahon (Eds.), Social learning and systems approaches to marriage and the family. New York: Brunner/Mazel.

O'Leary, K. D., & Curley, A. D. (1986). Assertion and family violence: Correlates of spouse abuse. Journal of Marital and Family Therapy, 12, 281-289.

O'Leary, K. D., Heyman, R. E., & Neidig, P. H. (1999). Treatments of wife abuse: A comparison of gender-specific and co-joint approaches. Behavior Therapy, 30, 475-506.

O'Leary, K. D.,. & Maiuro, R. D. (Eds.). (1999). Psychological abuse in domestically violent relationships [Special Issue] Violence and Victims, 14(1).

O'Leary, K. D., Smith-Slep, A. M., & O'Leary, S. G. (2000). Co-occurrence of partner and parent aggression: Research and treatment implications. Behavior Therapy, 31, 631-648.

Olweus, D. (1979). Stability of aggressive reaction patterns in males: A review. Psychological Bulletin, 86, 852-875.

Olweus, D. (1993). Bullying at school: What we know and what we can do. Cambridge, MA: Blackwell.

Ornstein, P. H. (1999). Conceptualization and treatment of rage in self psychology. In Session: Psychotherapy in Practice, 55, 283-294.

Orwin, R. G., Maranda, M., & Ellis, B. (2000). The effectiveness of substance abuse treatment in reducing violent behavior. Journal of Psychopathology and Behavioral Assessment, 22, 309-324.

Osofsky, J. D. (Ed.). (1997). Children in a violent society. New York: Guilford Press.

Otto, R. K. (2000). Assessing and managing violence risk in outpatient settings. Journal of Clinical Psychology, 56, 1239-1262.

Overall, J. (1988). The Brief Psychiatric Rating Scale (BPRS). Psychopharmacology Bulletin, 24, 97-99.

Overholser, J. (1993). Elements of Socratic method 1: Systematic questioning. Psychotherapy, 30, 67-74.

Paivio, S. C. (1999). Experimental conceptualization and treatment of anger. In Session: Psychotherapy in Practice, 55, 311-324.

Paivio, S. C., & Greenberg, L. S. (1995). Resolving "unfinished business": Efficacy of experiential therapy using empty-chair dialogue. Journal of Consulting and Clinical Psychology, 63, 419-425.

Pajer, K. A. (1998). What happens to bad girls? A review of the adult outcomes of antisocial adolescent girls. American Journal of Psychiatry, 155, 862-870.

Pan, H., Neidig, P., & O'Leary, D. (1994). Predicting mild and severe husband to wife physical aggression. Journal of Consulting and Clinical Psychology, 62, 975-981.

Parson, E. R. (1994). Inner city children of trauma: Urban violence traumatic stress syndrome (U-VTS) and therapist's responses. In J. P. Wilson & J. D. Lindy (Eds.), Countertransference in the treatment of PTSD. New York: Guilford Press.

Patterson, G. R., & Chamberlain, P. (1994). A functional analysis of resistance during parent training therapy. Clinical Psychology: Science and Practice, 1, 53-70.

Patterson, G. R., Degarmo, D. S., & Knutson, N. (2000). Hyperactive and antisocial behavior: Comorbid or two points in the same process? Developmental and Psychopathology, 12, 91-106.

Patterson, G. R., Reid, J. B., & Dishion, T. J. (1992). Antisocial boys. Eugene, OR: Castalia.

Patton, J. H., Stanford, M. S., & Barratt, E. S. (1995). Factor structure of the Barratt Impulsiveness Scale. Journal of Clinical Psychology, 51, 768-774.

Paulhaus, D. L., & Christie, R. (1980). Spheres of control. In H. Lefcourt (Ed.), Advances and innovations in locus of control research. New York: Academic Press.

Pence, E., & Paymer, M. (1993). Education groups for men who batter: The Duluth Model. New York: Springer.

Pennebaker, W. (1992). Inhibition as the help in health. In H. S. Friedman, (Ed.), Hostility, coping and health. (pp. 127-139). Washington, DC: American Psychological Association.

Pepler, D. J., Craig, W. M., et al., (1994). An evaluation of an antibullying intervention in Toronto schools. Canadian Journal of Community Mental Health, 13, 95-110.

Pepler, D., & Rubin, K. (Eds.), (1991). The development and treatment of childhood aggression. Hillsdale, NJ: Erlbaum.

Permnanen, K. (1991). Alcohol in human violence. New York: Guilford Press.

Perry, B. D., & Pollard, R. (1998). Homeostasis, stress, trauma adaptation: A neurological view of childhood trauma. Child and Adolescent Psychiatric Clinics of North America, 7, 33-51.

Pillemer, K., & Suitor, J. J. (1992). Violence and violent feelings: What causes them among family caregivers? Journal of Gerontology, 47, 165-172.

Pittel, E. M. (1998). How to take a weapons history: Interviewing children at risk for violence at school. Journal of American Academy of Child and Adolescent Psychiatry, 37, 1100-1102.

Plutchnik, R., & VanPraag, H. M. (1990). A self-report measure of violence risk, II. Comprehensive Psychiarty, 31, 450-456.

Podnieks, E. (1992). National survey on abuse of the elderly in Canada. Journal of Elder Abuse and Neglect, 4, 5-58.

Pokorny, A. D., Miller, B. A., & Kaplan, H. B. (1992). The brief MAST, a shortened version of the Michigan Alcoholism Screening Test. American Journal of Psychiatry, 129, 342-348.

Polizzi, D. M., MacKenzie, D. C., & Hickman, L. (1999). What works in adult sex offender treatment? International Journal of Offender Therapy and Comparative Criminology, 43, 351-374.

Powell, K. E., Dahlberg, L., et al. (1996). Prevention of youth violence:Rationale and characteristics of 15 evaluation projects. American Journal of Preventive Medicine, 12, 3-12.

Preston, J. (1997). Shorter Term Treatment for Borderline Personality Disorders. Oakland, CA: New Harbinger Publications.

Prochaska, J. O., & DiClemente, C. C. (1986). Toward a comprehensive model of behavior change. In W. R. Miller & N. Heather (Eds.), Treating addictive behaviors: Processes of change. (pp. 3-27). New York: Plenum Press.

Pynoos, R. S. (1994). Post traumatic stress disorder: A clinical review. Lutherville, MD: Sidron.

Pynoos, R. S., & Eth, S. (1986). Witness to violence: The child interview. Journal of American Academy of Child Psychiatry, 12, 306-319.

Quinsey, V. L., Harris, G. T., Rice, M. E., & Cormier, C. A. (1998). Violent offenders: Appraising and managing risk. Washington, DC: American Psychological Association.

Raab, S. (2000). Men who explode: A special report on men and rage. Esquire, September, 247-255.

Rachman, S. (1977). Systematic desensitization. Psychological Bulletin, 67, 93-103.

Ramirez, C. A., Rosen, L. A., Deffenbacher, J. L., Hurts, H., Nicoletta, C., Rosencranz, T., & Smith, K. (1997). Anger and anger expression in adults with high ADHD symptoms. Journal of Attention Disorders, 2, 115-128.

Raynor, P., & Wanstone, M. (1996). Reasoning and rehabilitation in Britain: The results of the Straight Thinking on Probation (STOP) Program. International Journal of Offender Therapy and Comparative Criminology, 40, 272-284.

Reddy, M., Borum, R., et al. (2001). Evaluating risk for targeted violence in school: Comparing risk assessment, threat assessment, and other approaches. Psychology in the Schools, 38, 157-172.

Redl, F., & Wineman, D. (1952). Controls from within: Techniques for the treatment of the aggressive child. New York: The Free Press.

Reilly, P., Westley, C., Shopshire, M., Lewis, E., & Sorenson, D. (1994). Anger management and temper control: Critical components of posttraumatic stress disorder and substance abuse treatment. Journal of Psychoactive Drugs, 26, 401-407.

Renwick, S. J., Black, L., Ramm, M., & Novaco, R. (1997). Anger treatment with forensic hospital patients. Legal and Criminal Psychology, 2, 103-116.

Renzetti, C. (1992). Violent betrayal: Partner abuse in lesbian relationships. Newbury Park, CA: Sage.

Resick, M. D., et al. (1997). Protecting adolescents from harm: Findings from the National Longitudinal Study on Adolescent Health. Journal of the American Medical Association, 278, 823-830.

Rice, M. E. (1997). Violent offender research and implications for the criminal justice system. American Psychologist, 52, 414-423.

Rich, J., & Stone, D. A. (1996). The experience of a violent injury for young African-American men: The meaning of being a "sucker". Journal of General Internal Medicine, 11, 77-82.

Richardson, R. F. (1998). The psychology and pedagogy of anger. Baltimore: Warwick & York.

Rimm, D. C., Hill, G. A., et al. (1974). Group assertive training in treatment of expression of inappropriate anger. Psychological Reports, 34, 791-798.

Robins, S., & Novaco, R. W. (1999). Systems conceptualization and treatment of anger. In Session: Psychotherapy in Practice, 55, 325-337.

Rose, J. (1996). Anger management: A group treatment for people with mental retardation. Journal of Developmental and Psychical Disabilities, 8, 133-150.

Rose, J., West, C., & Clifford D. (2000). Group interventions for anger in people with intellectual disabilities. Research in Developmental Disabilities, 21, 171-181.

Rosenbaum, A., & O'Leary, K. D. (1986). The treatment of marital violence. In N. S. Jacobson & A. S. Garman (Eds.), Clinical handbook of marital therapy. New York: Guilford Press.

Rosenberg, M., O'Carroll, P., & Powell, K. (1992). Let's be clear, violence is a public health problem. Journal of the American Medical Association, 267, 3071-3072.

Rosenfeld, B. D. (1992). Court-ordered treatment of spouse-abuse. Clinical Psychology Review, 12, 205-226.

Roskes, E., Feldman, R., Arrington, S., & Leisher, M. (1999). A model program for the treatment of mentally ill offenders in the community. Community Mental Health Journal, 35, 461-472.

Roskies, E. (1983). Stress management of Type A individual. In D. Meichenbaum & M. E. Jaremko (Eds.), Stress reduction and prevention. New York: Plenum Press.

Ross, D. M. (1996). Childhood bullying and teasing: What school personnel, other professionals and parents can do. Alexandria, VA: ACA Publishers.

Ross, R. R., & Fabiano, E. A. (1985). Time to think: A cognitive model of delinquency prevention and offender rehabilitation. Johnson City, TN: Institute of Social Science.

Rossi, A. M., Jacobs, M. et al. (1999). Characteristics of patients who engage in assaultive or other fear-inducing behavior. Journal of Nervous and Mental Disease, 174, 154-160.

Royal College of Psychiatrists (1998). Management of Imminent Violence: Clinical Practice Guidelines to Support Mental Health Services. Royal College of Psychiatrists Paper OP41: London, England.

Russell, M. N., & Frohberg, J. (1995). Confronting abusive beliefs: Group treatments for abusive men. Thousand Oaks, CA: Sage.

Rusting, C. L., & Nolen-Hoeksema, S. (1998). Regulating responses to anger: Effects of rumination and distraction on angry mood. Journal of Personality and Social Psychology, 74, 790-803.

Rutter, M., Giller, H., & Hagell, A. (1998). Antisocial behavior by young people. New York: Cambridge.

Rutter, M., Maughan, B., et al. (1979). Fifteen thousand hours: Secondary schools and their effects on children. Cambridge, MA: Harvard University Press.

Rutter, M., Pickles, A., Murray, R., & Eaves, L. (2001). Testing hypothesis on specific environmental causal effects on behavior. Psychological Bulletin, 127, 291-324.

Safran, J. D., & Segal, Z. V. (1990). Interpersonal process in cognitive therapy. New York: Basic Books.

Salekin, R. T., Rogers, R., & Sewell, K. W. (1996). A review and meta-analysis of the Psychopathology Checklist and Psychopathy Checklist-Revised: Predictive validity of dangerousness. Clinical Psychology: Science and Practice, 3, 203-2145.

Sampson, R. J., & Lauritsen, J. L. (1994). Violent victimization and offending: Individual, situational, and community-level risk factors. In A. J. Riess, & J. A. Roth (Eds.), Understanding and preventing violence: Social influences. (p. 1-115). Washington, DC: National Academy Press.

Sampson, R.. J., Raudenbash, S., & Earls, F. (1997). Neighbors and violent crime: A multilevel study of collective efficacy. Science, 277, 918-924.

Sana Loue (2001). Intimate partner violence. . New York: Kluvner/Plenum Publishers.

Sanders, M. R., & Lawton, J. M. (1993). Discussing assessment findings with families: A guided participation model of information transfer. Child and Family Behavior Therapy, 15, 5-35.

Sanders,, M. R., & Ralph, A. (2001). Practitioner's manual for primary teen care: Triple P. Families Internal Publishing: Queensland.

Sapolsky, R. (1996). Why stress is bad for your brain. Science, 273, 749-750.

Sarason, I. G., Johnson, J. H., et al. (1979). Helping police officers to cope with stress: A cognitive-behavioral approach. American Journal of Community Psychology, 17, 593-603.

Saunders, D. G. (1996a). Intervention for men who batter: Do we know what works. In Session: Psychotherapy in Practice, 2, 81-93.

Saunders, D. G. (1996b). Feminist-cognitive-behavioral and process-psychodynamic treatment for men who batter. Interaction of abuser traits and treatment models. Violence and Victims, 11, 393-413.

Saunders, D. G. (1999). Feminist, cognitive and behavioral interventions for men who batter: An overview of rationale and methods. In D. Wexler (Ed.), Domestic violence 2000: An integrated skills program for men (pp. 21-31). New York: Norton.

Sayette, M. A., Wilson, G. T., & Elias, M. J. (1993). Alcohol and aggression: A social information processing analysis. Journal of Studies on Alcohol, 54, 399-407.

Scarpa, A. (1998). Aggression in physically abused children: The interactive role of emotion regulation. In A. Raine, D. Farrington, D. Brennan, & P. Mednick (Eds.), Unlocking crime: The biosocial key. New York: Plenum.

Scarpa, A., & Raine, A. (1997a). Psychophysiology of anger and violent behavior. Psychiatric Clinics of North America, 20, 375-394.

Scarpa, A., & Raine, A. (1997b). The biology of wickedness. Psychiatric Annals, 27, 624-629.

Schaap, C. Bennum, I., Schindler, K., & Hoogduun, K. (1993). The therapeutic relationship in behavioral psychotherapy. New York: John Wiley.

Schaefer, M. T. & Olson, D. H. (1981). Assessing intimacy: The PAIR Inventory. Journal of Marital and Family Therapy, 7, 47-60.

Schafer, J. (1996). Measuring spousal violence with the Conflict Tactics Scale. Journal of Interpersonal Violence, 11, 572-585.

Schank, R., & Abelson, R. (1977). Scripts, plans, goals and understanding. Hillsdale, NJ: Erlbaum.

Schechter, S., & Ganley, A. (1995). Domestic violence: A national curriculum for family preservation practitioners. San Francisco: Family Violence Prevention Fund.

Schilit, R., Lie, Y. Y., & Montagne, M. (1990). Substance use as a correlation of violence in intimate lesbian relationships. Journal of Homosexuality, 19, 51-65.

Schlee, K. A., Heyman, R. E., & O'Leary, K. D. (1998). Group treatment for spouse abuse: Are women with PTSD appropriate participants? Journal of Family Violence, 13, 1-20.

Schlesinger, L. B. (2001). Serial offenders: Current thought, recent findings. Boca Raton, FL: CRC Press.

Schlichter, K. J., & Horan, J. J. (1981). Effects of stress inoculation on the anger and aggression management skills of institutionalized juvenile delinquents. Cognitive Therapy and Research, 5, 359-365.

Schloss, P., Smith, M., et al. (1989). A respondent conditioning approach to reducing anger responses of a dually diagnosed man with mild mental retardation. Behavior Therapy, 20, 459-464.

Schoenwald, S. K., Brown, T. L., & Henggeler, S. W. (2000). Inside multisystemic therapy: Therapist supervisory and program practices. Journal of Emotional and Behavioral Disorders, 8, 113-127.

Schumacher, J. A., Slep, A. M., & Heyman, R. E. (2001). Risk factors for male-to-female partner psychological abuse. Aggression and Violent Behavior, 6, 255-268.

Schweinhardt, L. J., Barnes, H. V., Weinkart, D. P., et al. (1993). Significant benefits of the High/Scope Perry Preschool study through age 27. Ypsilanti, MI: High/Scope Press.

Sege, R., & Licenziato, V. G. (2001). Recognizing and preventing youth violence: A guide for physicians and other health care professionals. Massachusetts Medical Society: Waltham, MA.

Sege, R., Stringham, P., Short, S., & Griffith, J. (1999). Ten years after: Examination of adolescent screening questions that predict future violence-related injury. Journal of Adolescent Health, 24, 395-402.

Serin, R., & Kuriychuk, M. (1994). Social and cognitive processing deficits in violent offenders: Implications for treatment. International Journal of Law and Psychiatry, 17, 431-441.

Shapiro, D., Hui, K. K., et al. (1997). Reduction in drug requirements for hypertension by means of a cognitive-behavioral intervention. American Journal of Hypertension, 10, 9-17.

Sharkin, B. S. (1988). The measurement and treatment of client anger in counseling. Journal of Counseling and Development, 66, 361-365.

Shay, J. (1992). Fluxotine reduces explosiveness and elevates mood of Vietnam vets with PTSD. Journal of Traumatic Stress, 5, 97-101.

Shay, J. (1994). Achilles in Vietnam: Combat Trauma and the undoing of character. Toronto: Maxwell MacMillan.

Sheldrick, C. (1999). Practitioner Review: the assessment and management of risk in adolescents. Journal of Child Psychology and Psychiatry, 40, 507-518.

Sherman, L. W. (1999). Evidence-based policing. Washington, DC: The Police Foundation.

Sherman, L. W., Gotfredson, D., et al. (1997). Preventing crime: What works, what doesn't, what's promising. Washington, DC: National Institute of Justice.

Shophire, M. S., & Reilly, P. M. (1996). Manual for the assaultive behavior survey. Unpublished manuscript. University of California, San Francisco.

Siegal, J. M. (1986). The Multidimensional Anger Inventory. Journal of Personality and Social Psychology, 51, 151-200.

Siegal, J. M. (1992). Anger and cardiovascular health. In H. S. Friedman (Ed.), Hostility, coping and health. (pp. 49-64). Washington, DC: American Psychological Association.

Siegman, A., & Smith, T. (Eds.). (1994). Anger, hostility and the heart. Hillsdale, NJ: Lawrence Erlbaum Associates.

Silve, J. A., Ferrari, M. M. et al. (1998). The dangerousness of persons with delusional jealousy. Journal of American Academy of Psychiatry and Law, 26, 607-623.

Silver, E., Mulvey, E. P., & Monahan, J. (1999). Assessing violence risk among discharged psychiatric patients: Toward an ecological approach. Law and Human Behavior, 23, 237-255.

Simourd, D. G., & Mamuza, J. M. (2000). The Hostile Interpretations Questionnaire. Criminal Justice and Behavior, 27, 645-663.

Singer, J. A. (1997). Message in a bottle: Stories of men and addiction. New York: Free Press.

Singer, M. I., Anglin, T. M., et al. (1995). Adolescents' exposure to violence and associated symptoms of psychological trauma. JAMA, 273, 477-482.

Singer, M. I., Miller, D. B., et al. (1999). Contributors to violent behavior among elementary and middle school children. Pediatrics, 104, 878-884.

Skinner, H. A., & Allen, B. S. (1982). Alcohol dependence syndrome: Measurement and validation. Journal of Abnormal Psychology, 91, 199-209.

Smith, P. K., & Sharp, S. (1994). School bullying: Insights and perspectives. London: Routledge.

Snaith, R. P., Constantopoulous, A. A., et al. (1978). A clinical scale for the self-assessment of irritability, anxiety and depression. British Journal of Psychology, 132, 164-171.

Snell, U. W., McDonald, K., & Koch, W. R. (1991). Anger provoking experiences: A multidimensional scaling analysis. Personality and Individual Differences, 12, 1095-1104.

Snyder, C. R. (1994). The psychology of hope: You can get there from here. New York: Free Press.

Snyder, C. R., Crowson, Jr. J. J., et al. (1997). Assessing hostile automatic thoughts: Development and validation of the HAT scale. Cognitive Therapy and Research, 21, 477-492.

Snyder, C. R., Harris, C., et al. (1991). The will and the ways: Development and validation of individual differences measure of hope. Journal of Personality and Social Psychology, 60, 570-585.

Snyder, C. R., Ilardi, S. S., et al. (2000). The role of hope in cognitive-behavioral therapies. Cognitive Therapy and Research, 24, 747-762.

Snyder, C. R., McDermoth, D. et al. (1997). Hope for the journey: Helping children through good times and bad. Boulder, CO: Westview.

Snyder, C. R., Tran, T., Schroeber, L. L., et al. (2000). Teaching the Hope recipe: Setting goals, finding pathways to those goals and getting motivated. Reaching Today's Youth, Summer, p. 46-50.

Snyder, D. K. (1979). Multidimensional assessment of marital satisfaction. Journal of Marriage and the Family, 141, 813-823.

Snyder, D. K. (1981). Manual for the Martial Satisfaction Inventory. Los Angeles: Western Psychological Services.

Snyder, K. V., Kymissis, P., & Kessler, K. (1999). Anger management for adolescents: Efficacy of brief group therapy. Journal of American Academy of Child and Adolescent Psychiatry, 38, 1409-1416.

Sobell, L. C., & Sobell, M. B. (1992). Timeline follow-back: A technique for assessing self-reported alcohol consumption. In R. Z. Litten and J. P. Allen (Eds.). Measuring of alcohol consumption: Psychological and biomedical methods. (pp. 41-72). New Jersey: Human Press.

Solomon, P. (1992). The efficacy of case management services for severely mentally disabled clients. Community Mental Health, 28, 163-180.

Sonkin, D. J., & Durphy, M. (1984). Learning to live without violence: A handbook for men. Volcano, CA: Volcano Press.

Spanier, G. B. (1976).Measuring dyadic adjustment: New scales for assessing the quality of marriage and similar dyads. Journal of Marriage and the Family, 38, 15-28.

Spence, D. P. (1982). Narrative truth and historical truth: Meaning and interpretation in psychoanalysis. New York: Norton.

Spielberger, C. D. (1988). State-trait Anger Expression Inventory. Odessa, FL. Psychological Assessment Resources.

Spielberger, C. D. (1999). Manual for the State-Trait Anger Expression Inventory-Revised. Orlando, FL: Psychological Assessment Resources.

Spielberger, C. D., Jacobs, G., Russell, S., & Crome, R. (1983). Assessment of anger: The State-Trait Anger Scale. In J. N. Butcher & C. D. Spielberger (Eds.), Advances in personality assessment, Vol. 2 (pp. 159-187). Hillsdale, NJ: Lawrence Erlbaum Associates.

Spielberger, C. D., Johnson, E. H., et al. (1985). The experience and expression of anger: Construction and validation of an anger expression scale. In M. A. Chesney, & R. H. Rosenman (Eds.). Anger and hostility in cardiovascular and behavioral disorders. (pp.5-30). New York: Hemisphere.

Spielberger, C. D., Reheiser, E. C., & Sydeman, S. J. (1995). Measuring the experience, expression and control of anger. . In H. Kassinove (Ed.), Anger disorders. Washington, DC: Taylor & Francis.

Spitzer, R. L., Williams, J. B., et al. (1992). The Structured Clinical Interview for DSM-III R (SCID) I: History, rationale and description. Archives of General Psychiatry, 49, 624-629.

Sprague, J., Walker, H., et al. (2001). Predicting violence and delinquency using school and community data sources. Psychology in the Schools, 38, 197-206.

Stage, S. A., & Quiroz, E. R. (1997). A meta-analysis of interventions to decrease disruptive classroom behavior in public education settings. School Psychology Review, 26, 333-368.

Staub, E. (1989). The roots of evil: The origins of genocide and other group violence. New York: Cambridge University Press.

Steadman, H. J. (2000). From dangerousness to risk assessment of community violence: Taking stock of the turn of the century. Journal of the American Academy of Psychiatry and Law, 28, 265-271.

Steadman, H. J., Monahan, J., et al. (1994). Designing new generation of risk assessment research. In J. Monahan & H. Steadman (Eds.), Violence and mental disorder. (pp. 297-318). Chicago: University of Chicago.

Steadman, H. J., Mulvey, E. P., Monahan, J., et al. (1998). Violence by people discharged from acute psychiatric inpatient facilities and by others in the same neighborhoods. Archives of General Psychiatry, 55, 393-401.

Steadman, H. J., Silver, E., Monahan, J., et al. (2000). A classification tree approach to the development of actuarial violence risk assessment tools. Law and Human Behavior, 24, 83-100.

Steele, C. M., & Josephs, R. A. (1990). Alcohol myopia: Its prized and dangerous effects. American Psychologist, 455, 921-933.

Steffen, A. M. (2000). Anger management for dementia caregivers: A preliminary study using video and telephone interventions. Behavior Therapy, 31, 281-299.

Steffen, A. M., & Berger, S. (in press). Relationship differences in anger intensity during care-giving-related situations. Clinical Gerontologist.

Steinberg, L. (2001). We know some things: Parent-adolescent relationships in retrospect and prospect. Journal of Research on Adolescence, 11, 1-19.

Steiner, H., et al. (1997). Posttraumatic stress disorder in vulnerable juvenile delinquents. Journal Of American Academy of Child and Adolescent Psychiatry, 36, 357-365.

Steinert, T., Wolfe, M., & Gebhardt, R. P. (2000). Measurement of violence during in-patient treatment and association with psychopathology. Acta Psychiatrica Scandinavia, 102, 107-112.

Steinfeld, J. J. (1986). Spouse abuse: Clinical implications of research on the control of aggression. Journal of Family Violence, 2, 197-208.

Stenfert-Kroese, B., Dagnan, D., & Loumidis, K. (1997). Cognitive behavior therapy for people with learning disabilities. London: Routledge.

Stermac, L. E. (1987). Anger control treatment for forensic patients. Journal of Interpersonal Violence, 1, 446-457.

Stevenson, S. (1991). Heading off violence with verbal de-escalation. Journal of Psychosocial Nursing. 29, 8-10.

Stoff, D. M., Breiling, J., & Maser, J. D. (Eds.). (1997). Handbook of antisocial behavior. New York: Wiley.

Stokes, T. F., & Baer, D. M. (1979). An implicit technology of generalization. Journal of Applied Behavior Analysis, 10, 345-367.

Stordeur, R. A., & Stille, R. (1989). Ending men's violence against their partners. Thousand Oaks, CA; Sage.

Stosny, S. (1995). Treating attachment abuse: A compassionate approach. New York: Springer Publishing.

Straus, M. A. (1979). Measuring intrafamily conflict and violence: The Conflict Tactics (CT) Scale. Journal of Marriage and the Family, 41, 75-88.

Straus, M. A. (1994). Beating the devil out of them: Corporal punishment in American families. Lexington, MA: Lexington/MacMillan Books.

Straus, M. A., & Gelles, R. J. (1990). How violent are American families? Estimates from the national family violence survey and other studies. In M. A. Straus & L. J. Gelles (Eds.), Physical violent in American families. (pp. 95-112). New Brunswick, NJ: Transaction.

Straus, M. A., Gelles, R. J., & Steinmetz, S. (1980). Behind closed doors: Violence in the American family. Garden City, NY: Doubleday.

Straus, M. A., Hamby, S. L., et al. (1996). The Revised Conflict Factors Scale (CTS2): Development and preliminary data. Journal of Family Issues, 17, 283-316.

Strupp, H. H. (1995). Lasting lessons from psychotherapy practice and research. Paper presented at the meeting of the American Psychological Association, New York, August.

Stuart, R. B. (1980). Helping couples change: A social learning approach to marital therapy. New York: Guilford Press.

Stuckless, N.., & Goranson, R. (1992). The Vengeance Scale: Development of a measure of attitudes toward revenge. Journal of Social Behavior and Personality, 7, 25-42.

Sugarman, D. B., & Frankel, S. L. (1996). Patriarchal ideology and wife assault: A metacognitive-analytical review. Journal of Family Violence, 11, 13-40.

Suinn, R. M. (2001). The terrible twos - anger and anxiety. American Psychologist, 56, 27-36.

Suinn, R. M., & Deffenbacher, J. L. (1988). Anxiety management training. Counseling Psychologist, 16, 31-49.

Suls, J., & Wan, C. K. (1993). The relationship between trait hostility and cardiovascular reactivity: A quantitative review and analysis. Psychophysiology, 30, 615-626.

Sutton, S. (2000). A critical review of the transtheoretical model applied to smoking cessation. In P. Norman, C. Abraham, & M Conner (Ed.), Understanding and changing health behavior: From health beliefs to self-regulation, Reading Harwood Academic Press.

Swaffer, T., & Hollin, C. R. (1997). Adolescents' experiences of anger in a residential setting. Journal of Adolescence, 20, 567-575.

Swets, J. A., Dawes, R. M., & Monahan, J. (2000). Psychological science can improve diagnostic decisions. Psychological Science in the Public Interest, 1, 1-26.

Szapocznik, J., & Kurtines, W. (1980). Bicultural involvement and adjustment in Hispanic American youth. International Journal of Intercultural Relations, 4, 353-365.

Szapocznik, J., & Williams, R. A. (2000). Brief strategic family therapy: Twenty five years of interplay among theory, research and practice in adolescent behavior problems and drug-abuse. Clinical Child and Family Psychology Review, 3, 117-135.

Tafrate, R. C. (1995). Evaluation of treatment strategies for adult anger disorders. In H. Kassinove (Ed.), Anger disorders: Definitions, diagnosis and treatment. Washington, DC: Taylor & Francis.

Tafrate, R. C., & Kassinove, H. (1998). Anger control in men: Barb exposure with rational, irrational and irrelevant self-statements. Journal of Cognitive Psychology, 12, 187-211.

Talbot, M. (2000). The maximum security adolescent. The New York Times Magazine, Sept. 10, 41-58.

Tangey, A., Wagner, P., et al. (1992). Shamed into anger? The relation of shame and guilt to anger and self-reported aggression. Journal of Personality and Social Psychology, 62, 669-675.

Tangey, J., Wagner, P., et al. (1996). Relation of shame and guilt to constructive versus destructive responses to anger across the lifespan. Journal of Personality and Social Psychology, 70, 797-809.

Tardiff, K. (1992). The current state of psychiatry in the treatment of violent patients. Archives of General Psychiatry, 49, 493-499.

Tardiff, K. (1994). Violence. In R. E. Hales S. C. Yadofsky & J. A. Talbott (Eds.), The American Psychiatric Press Textbook of Psychiatry. Washington, D. C.: American Psychiatric Press.

Tardiff, K. (1996). Concise guide to assessment and management of violent patients. (2nd ed.)

Tarvis, C. (1989). Anger: The misunderstood emotion. (2nd Ed.). New York: Touchstone.

Tate, D. C., Repucci, N. D., & Mulvey, E. P. (1995). Violent juvenile delinquents: Treatment effectiveness and implications for future action. American Psychologist, 50, 777-781.

Taylor, P. J., & Gunn, J. (1999). Homicides by people with mental illness: Myth and reality. British Journal of Psychiatry, 174, 9-14.

Temple, C. (1994). Managing psychosocial assault in a healthcare setting. Rehabilitation Nursing, 19, 271-286.

Tescott, L. H., & Barondes, S. H. (1996). Genes and aggressiveness: Behavioral genetics. Current Biology, 6, 238-240.

Texas Youth Commission (1997). Specialized Treatment Recidivism Effectiveness Summary. Austin, Texas.

Thackery, M., & Bobbitt, R. (1990). Patient aggression against clinical and non-clinical staff in a VA medical center. Hospital and Community Psychiatry, 41, 195-197.

Thapar, A., Holmes, J., et al. (1999). Genetic basis of attention deficit and hyperactivity. British Journal of Psychiatry, 174, 105-111.

Thomas, S. P. (1993). Women and anger. New York: Springer.

Thomas, S. P. (1997a). Women's anger: Relationship of suppression to blood pressure. Nursing Research, 46, 324-330.

Thomas, S. P. (1997b). Angry? Let's talk about it! Applied Nursing Research, 10, 80-85.

Thomas, S. P. (1998). Assessing and interviewing individuals with anger disorders. Nursing Clinics of North America, 33, 121-133.

Thomas, S. P., & Jefferson, C. (1996). Use your anger: A woman's guide to empowerment. New York: Pocket Books.

Thorton, T., Craft, C., Dahlberg, L. L., Lynch, B., & Baer, K. (2000). Best practices of Youth Violence Prevention: A sourcebook for community action. Atlanta: Ccenters for Disease Control and Prevention.

Thurman, C. W. (1985). Effectiveness of cognitive-behavioral treatment in reducing Type A behavior among university faculty. Journal of Counseling Psychology, 32, 74-83.

Tishler, C. L., Gordon, L. B., & Landry-Meyer, C. (2000). Managing the violent patient: A guide for psychologists and other mental health professionals. Professional Psychology: Research and Practice, 31, 34-41.

Tjaden, P., & Thoennes, N. (1998, November). Prevalence, incidence and consequences of violence against women: Findings from the National Violence Against Women Survey. National Institute of Justice Centers for Disease Control and Prevention Research in Brief, 1-16.

Tobin, T., & Sprague, J. (2000). Alternative educational strategies: Reducing violence in school and the community. Journal of the Emotional and Behavioral Disorders, 8, 129-200.

Toch, H. (1973/1969). Violent men: An inquiry into the psychology of violence. Washington, DC: American Psychological Association.

Tolman, R. M. (1989). The development of a measure of psychological maltreatment of women by their male partners. Violence and Victims, 7, 159-177.

Tolman, R. M. (1996). Expanding sanctions for batterers: What can we do besides jailing and counseling them? In J. L. Edelson & Z. C. Eisikovits (Eds.), Future interventions with battered women and their families. Thousand Oakes, CA: Sage.

Tolman, R. M. (1999). The validation of the psychological maltreatment of women inventory. Violence and Victims, 14, 25-35.

Tolman, R. M., & Edelson, J. L. (1989). Cognitive-behavioral intervention with men who batter. In B. Thyer (Ed.), Behavioral family treatment. Springfield, IL: C. Thomas and Sons.

Tolman, R. M., & Edelson, J. L. (1995). Intervention for men who batter: A review of research. In S. Stith & M. A. Straus (Eds.), Understanding partner violence. (pp. 262 – 2724). Minneapolis: National Council of Family Relations.

Tonry, M. (1995). Malign neglect: Race, crime and punishment in America. New York: Oxford University Press.

Trestman, R. L. (1997). Clinical correlates and predictors of violence in patients with personality disorders. Psychiatric Annals, 27, 741-744.

Trezza, G. R., & Popp, S. M. (2000). The substance user at risk of harm to self or others: Assessment and treatment issues. Journal of Clinical Psychology, 56, 1193-1205.

Triffelman, E., Carroll, K., & Kellogg, S. (199). Substance dependence posttraumatic stress disorder: An integrated cognitive-behavioral approach. Journal of Substance Treatment, 17, 3-14.

Tsytsarev, S. V., & Grodnitzky, G. R. (1995). Anger and criminality. In H. Kassinove (Ed.), Anger disorders. Washington, DC: Taylor & Francis.

Tweed, R. G., & Dutton, D. G. (1998). A comparison of impulsive and instrumental subgroups of batterers. Violence and Victims, 13, 217-230.

Twemlow, S. W. (2000). The roots of violence: Converging psychoanalytic explanatory models for power strategies and violence in schools. The Psychoanalytic Quarterly,. 69, 741-785.

Twemlow, S. W., & Sacco, F. C. (1996). Peacekeeping and peacemaking: The conceptual foundations of a plan to reduce violence and improve the quality of life in a midsized community in Jamaica. Psychiatry, 59, 156-174.

Twemlow, S. W., Sacco, F. C., & Twemlow, S. (1999). Creating a peaceful school learning environment: A training program for elementary schools. Agawom, MA: T & S Publishing.

Tyron, G. (1986). Abuse of therapists by patients: A national survey. Professional Psychology Research and Practice, 17, 357-363.

U.S. Department of Justice (1991). Uniform Crime Report, 1990. Washington, DC: U.S. Government Printing Office.

U.S. Department of Justice (1997). Privacy and Juvenile Justice Records: A Mid-Decade Status Report. Washington, DC: U.S. Department of Justice, Office of Justice Programs.

U.S. Department of Justice (1998). Violence by intimates. (NCG Publication No. NCJ167237). Washington, DC: Author.

Uomoto, I., & Brockway, I. (1992). Anger management of brain injured patients and their family members. Archives of Physical Medicine Rehabilitation, 73, 674-679.

VandeCreek, L., Bennett, B. E., & Bricklin, P. M. (1994). Risk management with potentially dangerous patients: A self-study guide. Washington, DC: American Psychological Association.

VandeCreek, L., & Knapp, S. (2000). Risk management and life-threatening patient behaviors. Journal of Clinical Psychology, 56, 1335-1351.

Vandenbos, G., & Bulatao, E. (1996). Violence on the job: Identifying risks and developing solutions. Washington, DC: American Psychological Association.

VanElderen, T., Maes, S., Komproe, I. (1997). The development of anger expression and control scale. British Journal of Health Psychology, 2, 269-281.

VanGoozen, S. H., Fryda, P. H., et al. (1994). Anger process in women: Development and validation of the Anger Situation Questionnaire. Aggressive Behavior, 20, 79-100.

VanHasselt, V. B., & Hersen, M. (2000). Aggression and violence. Des Moines, IA: Allyn and Bacon.

Vaughn, C., & Leff, J. (1976). The measurement of expressed emotion in the families of psychiatric patients. British Journal of Social and Clinical Psychology, 15, 151-165.

Verlinden, S., Hersen, M., & Thomas, J. (2000). School shooters: An analysis. Clinical Psychology Review, 20, 3-56.

Villani, S. (2001). Impact of media on children and adolescents: A 10-year review of the research. Journal of the American Academy of Child and Adolescent Psychiatry, 40, 392-401.

Visalli, H., McNasser, G., Johnston, L., & Lazarro, C. (1996). Reducing high-risk interventions for managing aggression in psychiatric settings. Journal of Nursing Care Quality, 11, 54-61.

Vitiello, B., & Stoff, D. M. (1997). Subtypes of aggression and their relevance to child psychiatry. Journal American Academy of Child and Adolescent Psychiatry, 36, 307-318.

Vivian, D., & Malone, J. (1997). Relationship factors and depressive symptomatology associated with mild and severe husband-to-wife physical aggression. Violence and Victims, 12, 3-18.

Volavka, J. (1995). Neurobiology of violence. Washington, DC: American Psychiatric Association.

Wachtel, P. (1993). Therapeutic communication. New York: Guilford Press.

Wachtel, P. (1999). Race in the mind of America: Breaking the vicious circle between black and whites. New York: Routledge.

Wack, R. C. (1993). The ongoing risk assessment in the treatment of forensic patients on conditional release status. Psychiatric Quarterly, 64, 275-293.

Waldman, F. (1999). Violence or discipline? Working with multicultural court-ordered clients. Journal of Marital and Family Therapy, 25, 503-515.

Waldner-Haugrud, L. K., Gratch, L. V., & Magruder, B. (1997). Victimization and perpetration rates of violence in gay and lesbian relationships: Gender issues explored. Violence and Victims, 12, 173-184.

Walker, H. M., Colvin, G., & Ramsey, E. (1995). Antisocial behavior in school: Strategies and best practices. Pacific Grove, CA: Brooks/Cole.

Walker, H. M., & Epstein, M. (Eds.). (2000). Making schools safer and violence free: Critical issues, solutions and recommended practices. Austin, TX: PRO-ED.

Walker, H. M., & Sprague, J. R. (1999). The path to school failure delinquency and violence: Causal factors and some potential solutions. Interventions in School and Clinic, 35, 67-73.

Walker, L. (1984). The battered woman syndrome. New York: Springer.

Wallace, H. (1999). Family violence: Legal, medical and social perspectives. (2nd ed.). Needham Heights, MA: Allyn & Bacon.

Walters, G. D. (1990). The criminal lifestyle. Newbury Park, CA: Sage.

Wang, E. W., & Diamond, P. M. (1999). Empirically identifying factors related to violence risk in corrections. Behavior Sciences and the Law, 17, 377-389.

Wang, E. W., Owens, R. M., Long, S. A., Diamond, P. M.,. & Smith, J. L. (1999). The efficacy of intensive intervention for aggressive male prisoners. Unpublished manuscript, Lubbock, TX.

Ward, T., Hudson, S. M., Johnston, L., & Marshall, W. L. (1997). Cognitive distortions in sex offenders: An integrative review. Clinical Psychology Review, 17, 479-507.

Warren, R., & McLellarn, R. W. (1982). Systematic desensitization as a treatment for maladaptive anger and aggression: A review . Psychological Reports, 50, 1095-1102.

Webster, C. D., Douglas, K. S., Eaves, D., & Hart, S. D. (1997). HCR-20: Assessing risk for violence. (Version 2). Burnaby, BC: Mental Health, Law and Policy Institute, Simon Fraser University.

Webster, C. D., & Jackson, M. A. (Eds.). (1997). Impulsivity: Theory, assessment and treatment. New York: Guilford.

Webster-Stratton, C. (1989). The parents and children series. Eugene, OR: Castalia.

Webster-Stratton, C. (1991). Strategies for helping families with conduct disordered children. Journal of Child Psychology and Psychiatry, 32, 1047-1062.

Weeks, R., & Widom, C. S. (1998). Self-reports of early childhood victimization among incarcerated adult male felons. Journal of Interpersonal Violence, 13, 346-361.

Weingardt, K. R., & Zeiss, R. A. (2000). Skills training groups on a psychiatric intensive care unit: A guide for group leaders. Cognitive and Behavioral Practice, 7, 385-394.

Weiss, D. S., & Marmar, C. R. (1997). The Impact of Event Scale-Revised. In J. P. Wilson and T. M. Keane (Eds.), Assessing psychological trauma and PTSD. (pp. 399 – 411). New York: Guilford Press.

Weissman, M. M., & Bothwell, S. (1976). Assessment of social adjustment by patient self-report. Archives of General Psychiatry, 33, 1111-1115.

Welch, C. M. (1988). Stress and disciplinary behavior: A study of mothers' reactions to their preschoolers. Doctoral Dissertation at the University of Waterloo.

West, C. M. (1998). Leaving a second closet: Partner violence in same-sex couples. In J. L. Jasenski & L. M. Williams (Eds.), Partner violence: A comprehensive review of 20 years of research. (pp. 163-183). Thousand Oaks, CA: Sage.

Wexler, D. B. (1991). The adolescent self: Strategies for self-management, self-soothing and self-esteem in adolescence. New York: Norton.

Wexler, D. B. (2000). Domestic violence 2000: An integrated skills program for men. New York: W. W. Norton.

Wheeler, E., & Baron, S. (1994). Violence in our schools, hospitals and public places: A prevention and management guide. Venturay, CA: Pathfinder.

Whitaker, S. (1993). The reduction of aggression in people with learning difficulties: A review of psychological methods. British Journal of Clinical Psychology, 32, 1-37.

White, J. W., Smith, P. H., Koss, M. P., & Figueredo, S. J. (2000). Intimate partner aggression. What have we learned? Comment on Archer (2000). Psychological Bulletin, 126, 690-696.

Whitehouse, A. (1994). Anger control training with head injury clients. Journal of Cognitive Psychotherapy, 8, 140-160.

Whiteman, M., Fanshel, D., & Grundy, J. (1987). Cognitive-behavioral intervention aimed at anger of parents at risk of child abuse. Social Work, 32, 469-474.

Whittington, R., Shuttleworth, S., & Hill, L. (1996). Violence to staff in a general hospital setting. Journal of Advanced Nursing, 24, 326-333.

Whittington, R., & Wykes, T. (1991). Violence in psychiatric hospitals: Are certain staff prone to being assaulted? Journal of Advanced Nursing, 19, 215-225.

Wickless, C., & Kirsch, I. (1988). Cognitive correlates of anger, anxiety and sadness. Cognitive Therapy and Research, 12, 367-377.

Widom, C. S. (1989). Does violence beget violence? A critical examination of the literature. Psychological Bulletin, 106, 3-28.

Wilcox, D., & Dorwick, P. W. (1992). Anger management with adolescents. Residential Treatment for Children and Youth, 9, 29-39.

Wile, D. B. (1981). Couples therapy: A nontraditional approach. New York: Wiley.

Wilens, T. E., & Spencer, T. J. (2000). The stimulants revisited. Child and Adolescent Psychiatric Clinics of North America, 9, 573-603.

Williams, O. J. (1995). Treatment for African American men who batter. CURA Reporter, 25, 6-10.

Williams, O. J., & Becker, R. L. (1994). Domestic partner abuse treatment program and cultural competence: The results of a national survey. Violence and Victims, 9, 287-296.

Williams, R., & Williams, V. (1993). Anger skills. New York: Harper.

Wilson, D. B., Gallagher, C. A., et al. (1999). Corrections-based education, vocation, and work programs. Corrections Management Quarterly, 3, 8-18.

Winerip, M. (1998). Bedlam on the streets. New York Times Magazine, May 23. pp. 42-50.

Winner, L., Lanza-Kaduce, L., et al. (1997). The transfer of juveniles to criminal court: Re-examining recidivism over the long-term. Crime and Delinquency, 43, 548-563.

Wise, A., & Bowman, S. (1997). Comparison of beginning counselor's responses to lesbian vs. heterosexual partner abuse. Violence and Victims, 12, 127-135.

Witt, P. H. (2000). Book review: A practitioner's view of risk assessment: The HCR-20 and SVR-20. Behavioral Sciences and the Law, 18, 791-798.

Wolfe, D. A. (1999). Child abuse. (2nd E.). New York: Sage.

Wolfe, J., Kimmerling, R., et al. (1996). The Life Stress Checklist Revised. In B. H. Stamm (Ed.), Instrumentation in stress, trauma and adaptation. Northbrook, IL: Sidran Press.

Wolpow, S., Porter, M., & Hermonos, E. (2000). Adapting Dialectical Behavior Therapy (DBT) group for use in a residential program. Psychiatric Rehabilitation Journal, 24, 135-142.

Wondrak, R. (1989). Dealing with verbal abuse. Nurse Education Today, 9, 276-280.

Wood, M. M., & Long, N. J. (1991). Life space intervention: Talking with children and youth in crisis. Austin, TX: Pro-ed.

Wyatt, J., & Wyatt, M. (1995). Violence towards junior doctors in accident and emergency departments. Journal of Accident and Emergency Medicine, 12, 40-42.

Wyer, R. S. Jr., & Srull, T. K. (1993). Perspectives on anger and emotional: Vol. 6. Advances in social cognition. Hillsdale, NJ: Erlbaum.

Yassi, A. (1994). Assault and abuse of health care workers in a large teaching hospital. Canadian Medical Association Journal, 15, 1273-1279.

Yehuda, R. (1999). Managing anger and aggression in patients with PTSD. Journal of Clinical Psychiatry, 60, 33-37.

Yochelson, S., & Samenow, S. (1976). The criminal personality. I. New York: Jason Aronson.

Yochelson, S., & Samenow, S. (1977). The criminal personality. II. New York: Jason Aronson.

Youth Treatment Service (1994). The management of aggression and violence: A training package. (Youth Treatment Service, Glenthorne Center, Kingsbury Road, Erdington, Birmingham, B24 9SA, England).

Yudofsky, S. C., Silver, J. M., et al. (1986). The Overt Aggression Scale for the objective rating of verbal and physical aggression. American Journal of Psychiatry, 143, 35-39.

Zeanah, C. H., & Zeanah, P. D. (1989). Intergenerational transmission of maltreatment: Insights from attachment theory and research. Psychiatry, 52, 177-196.

Zelin, M. I., Adler, G., & Myerson, P. G. (1972). Anger self-report: An objective questionnaire for the measurement of aggression. Journal of Consulting and Clinical Psychology, 39, 340.

Zillman, D. (1971). Excitation transfer in communication-mediated aggressive behavior. Journal of Experimental Social Psychology, 7, 419-434.

Zillman, D. (1988). Cognition-excitation interdependencies in aggressive behavior. Aggressive Behavior, 14, 51-64.

Zillman, D., & Bryant, J. (1994). Effects of residual excitation on the emotional response and delayed aggressive behavior. Journal of Personality and Social Psychology, 30, 782-791.

Zimmerman, P. (1996). Assault support team. Journal of Emergency Nursing, 21, 42-43.

Zimring, F. (1998). American youth violence. New York: Oxford. University Press.

Zoccolillo, M. (1993). Gender and the development of conduct disorder. Developmental Psychopathology, 5, 65-97.

APPENDIX A

HOW HEALTH CARE PROVIDERS CAN HELP INDIVIDUALS IN "CRISIS" BECOME BETTER PROBLEM-SOLVERS

As part of my many consultations, I have been-asked to train frontline staff at psychiatric and residential facilities, correctional institutions, school counselors and principals and psychotherapists on ways to work with clients and students who are distressed, angry and aggressive. This **Appendix** includes the **Training Manual** that I developed for the staff training. Following a general introduction and group discussion on the nature of angry and aggressive behavior, the staff members studied the **Training Manual** and then practiced the **Phase-oriented Problem-Solving Skills** in **groups of three**. One staff member would role play a distressed client/student, the second would play the role of the helper, and the third staff member would act as a "coach" using the **Training Manual** as a guide. They would then take turns playing the different roles. They worked on one PHASE at a time to the point of proficiency before moving on to the NEXT PHASE (e.g., work on generating a Timeline before moving onto Generating Alternatives). The training included videotape feedback, group discussions and homework assignments where the staff could practice their problem-solving discourse with feedback from designated supervisors. The staff members came to use each other as observers, coaches and debriefers, as they created a milieu where problem-solving was the major mode of social discourse and where trainers could help trainees learn how to translate their problem-solving thinking into action.

HOW HEALTH CARE PROVIDERS CAN HELP INDIVIDUAL IN "CRISIS" BECOME BETTER PROBLEM SOLVERS[14]

This **Training Manual** is designed to help adults who work with distressed and angry, youth and adults. The goals of this **Training Manual** are to:

1. provide an **instructional framework for conducting problem-solving social discourse** that helps distressed individuals become better problem-solvers;

2. **educate** distressed individuals by means of **discovery-training** about the nature of anger and aggression;

3. **teach** staff a **variety of coping skills** and the **accompanying concepts and terms** (problem-solving vocabulary);

4. **ensure** that participants **apply** what they learn in their everyday settings.

In order to achieve these objectives a **THREE PHASE INTERVENTION MODEL** is outlined. The **THREE PHASES** include:

      I.   **PREPARATION PHASE**

      II.   **PROBLEM-SOLVING PHASE**

      III.   **IMPLEMENTATION PHASE**

PHASE I - PREPARATION -- focuses on establishing a **collaborative alliance** with distressed individuals by means of active listening, reflection, empathy, and reframing. It begins with eliciting the individual's (youth's) view of the problem-situation by asking for the sequence of what happened (developing a Timeline). The helper also probes about the individual's feelings and thoughts that preceded, accompanied and followed the precipitating event. Conduct a **behavioral chain analysis**.

PHASE II - PROBLEM-SOLVING -- focuses on developing a **collaborative problem-solving approach** that sensitizes the distressed individuals to **warning signs** and helps them generate **alternative solutions**. It helps them view provocations as problems-to-be-solved and turns "crisis" into "learning opportunities". **PHASE II** helps individuals generate a **step-by-step plan** and engage in **means-end** and **consequential thinking**. It also helps distressed individuals assume **more responsibility**, as it offers the proposed interventions as a set of **personal "challenges."**

---

[14] **I greatly appreciate the suggestions of Dr. Joan Asarnow (UCLA) in formulating this Training Manual.**

PHASE III - IMPLEMENTATION – focuses on the ways helpers can aide distressed individuals to practice, master and apply (**transfer**) what they are learning to their everyday life experiences. This is accomplished by helping individuals **formulate specific action plans**, including ways to anticipate consequences and address potential barriers. By means of **praising** the individuals for their efforts, placing them in "consultative" role of **explaining how** and **why** such changes are worth engaging in and by having them take credit for the changes they have made, the helper **increases the likelihood of generalization.**

The format of this **Training Manual** is to provide a way of talking to distressed and angry individuals who are in "crisis." The format has been laid out for one-on-one contact, but it can be readily adapted to group application. The **Training Manual** begins with a set of **Training Guidelines** of the **Do's** and **Dont's**. It is not only what is said, but how it is said that is important. Reading and rereading these **Guidelines** and following them will increase the effectiveness of the **Training Manual.**

The variety of suggested questions and statements in the **Training Manual should not be memorized**, but rather they are offered as a way to have helpers think through the steps and tasks required to move individuals from behaving in a "crisis" mode to functioning in a collaborative problem-solving mode.

Finally, the present **Training Manual** has benefited and incorporated the sage advice and experience of a number of pioneers. A number of clinicians writing from diverse theoretical perspectives have offered suggestions on how to help distressed, angry, aggressive individuals deescalate and engage in emotional and behavioral self-regulation. For example, Bernstein (1991), Redl and Wineman (1992), and Wood and Long (1991) offer creative solutions to achieve these goals. These suggestions have been combined with the research findings of cognitive-behavioral therapists (e.g., Deffenbacher & McKay, 2000; Di Giuseppe, 1999; Meichenbaum, 1994; Novaco, 1980) to develop the present **THREE PHASE INTERVENTION MANUAL.** While these **PHASES** are outlined sequentially, helpers should feel free to sample and integrate these various **PHASES** in a recursive and integrated fashion.

GUIDELINES FOR CONDUCTING PROBLEM-SOLVING DISCOURSE (PSD)

DO'S	DON'TS
Look for "right" time and place to conduct PSD	Insist that the youth talk NOW
Remove the youth from the group to do PSD	Embarrass and shame the youth in front of others
Listen attentively *(Use nonverbal signs to convey interest)*	Convey disinterest and a sense of being in a hurry
Follow the youth's lead *(Look for "openings" and use the youth's words – reflect)*	Put words in the youth's mouth. Tell youth what to do. *(Be a "Surrogate Frontal Lobe")*
Be brief. Use simple sentences and "What" and "How" Questions *(Use discovery learning and model a style of thinking)*	Lecture. Be judgmental. Use "should" and "should have" statements.
Give choices	Engage in "power" struggles. Force your explanations and impose your solutions.
Be supportive, collaborative and convey hope	Use put downs, threats and directives.
Highlight "strengths" and coping efforts	Be negative, critical.
Keep trying (If one strategy doesn't work, try another)	Give up. Blame the youth.
Conduct PSD on multiple occasions	Try and do too much at one time.

TABLE OF CONTENTS

Introduction

Phase I – PREPARATION PHASE
    Preparing The Youth To Talk
    Addressing The Youth Who Remains Silent
    Focusing On The Presenting Incident (Explore "What,
        Where, When, Who Present" And Obtain A TimeLine)
    Demonstrating Empathy
    Reviewing The "Story"
    Nurturing Collaboration

Phase II – PROBLEM-SOLVING PHASE
    Helping The Youth To Take The Perspective of Others
    Generating Causal Explanations
    Generating Alternative Solutions
    Noticing Warning Signs
    Fostering Responsibility ("Ownership")

Phase III – IMPLEMENTATION PHASE
    Conveying a "Challenge" And Bolstering Confidence
    Generating An Action Plan
    Anticipating Consequences
    Anticipating Possible Barriers To Change
    Reinforcing Effort
    Putting The Youth In A Consultative Role (Share, Teach, And Take
        Credit For Changes)

The present detailed script is designed to supplement the LIFE SPACE INTERVIEW (see page 166)

Phase I
PREPARATION PHASE

The <u>goals</u> of the PREPARATION PHASE are to:

(1) in a supportive way <u>acknowledge</u>, <u>affirm</u> and <u>validate</u> <u>feelings</u> that are appropriate under the circumstances

(2) help <u>de-escalate</u> ("<u>drain off</u>") <u>intense feelings</u>

(3) <u>engage</u> the youth in <u>problem-solving discourse</u>

(4) <u>understand</u> the youth's perspective by developing a <u>timeline</u>

(5) <u>nurture</u> a <u>collaborative working relationship</u>

- **PREPARING THE YOUTH TO TALK**

- **ADDRESSING THE YOUTH WHO REMAINS SILENT**

- **FOCUSING ON THE PRESENTING INCIDENT (EXPLORE "WHAT, WHERE WHEN, WHO PRESENT" – OBTAIN A TIMELINE)**

- **DEMONSTRATING EMPATHY**

- **REVIEWING THE "STORY"**

- **NURTURING COLLABORATION**

PREPARING THE YOUTH TO TALK

(Diffuse the situation. Deescalate intense feelings. Support the youth and give choices.)

I can see that you are very angry. Take some time to calm yourself down so we can talk about what happened.

Your actions (how you look) are telling me that something is bothering you. Do you want to talk about it?

It often helps if you can talk about what you are feeling.

I hear you are really angry. I'm here to understand what happened and see if I can be of help.

Why don't you take a moment and then we can try to work it out together.

I want to understand what happened so we can work on it together.

It is helpful to think about what happened before you talk.

Let's talk about what happened. I would like to hear more about ...

This situation is not going to go away, so let's talk about what happened and what you can do about it.

I know it is difficult to talk about what happened, but I need to hear what happened from your viewpoint.

It sounds like something has upset you; can we talk about it?

We wouldn't be here if something didn't happen. Let's talk.

Do you want to talk about it now or later?

ADDRESSING THE YOUTH WHO REMAINS SILENT

(Acknowledge feelings. Convey empathy and a desire to explore the youth's point of view.)

I have the feeling that our talking about what happened is upsetting you. It is okay for you to tell me that you don't want to talk. Maybe you can tell me the reasons you don't want to talk.

Some students don't talk because they don't trust teachers (adults) and they don't expect them to understand or help.

I see it is difficult to continue. I wonder if your silence is connected to something I said or did?

If this isn't a good time to talk, we can find a time later when we can talk.

Sometimes being silent provides an opportunity to think quietly to oneself about what happened and what can be done to improve things.

I need to be able to understand what has been happening in your class (residence, home). What has been going on?

It sounds like this is an ongoing problem, but let's discuss what happened today.

This sounds like a serious situation. It calls for some serious thinking about what to do.

I can see that you are figuring out how to handle things. Let me know if at any time I can be of help.

I can see how upset you are, but your behavior doesn't tell me what is making you so upset.

When someone is upset, it is often difficult to remember what happened, but let's give it a try. Okay?

I can tell you're almost ready to work on this. We can go at your pace.

FOCUSING ON THE PRESENTING INCIDENT
(EXPLORE "WHAT, WHERE, WHEN, WHO PRESENT" AND
OBTAIN A TIMELINE OR "MENTAL VIDEOTAPE" OF THE
EVENT)

(Ascertain the location of the anger provoking event, characteristics of the provoking person, details of any conversation that occurred, what happened, in terms of duration, intensity, frequency, what thoughts and feelings preceded, accompanied and followed anger-aggression, what, if anything, he did to control or manage his anger, what was the outcome for self and others. Begin at the point when the stressful event occurred and move forward in time. Conduct a behavioral chain analysis that connects feelings, thoughts and behaviors. Underscore the choices the individual made and options for the future.)

Let's talk about what happened step-by-step. Tell me what happened. What are you doing?

What was the first thing that happened? Can you remember how the problem got started?

Tell me when the trouble began.

How long did it go on?

What happened before that?

What happened after that?

And then what happened?

Who was there? Who else was there? Were others involved?

Where did this happen?

When did this happen?

When you did ... what happened then?

Where were you when he said (did) that?

What was going on?

Did this happen before or after you ...?

Tell me what you said, and how you said it.

So what did you do then?

Then what happened to make her say (do) that?

What did he do/say?

Who made the first move?

What did you do/say?

What did he do after you did/said that?

How did you feel when that happened to you?

How did that make you feel?

What went through your mind at that point?

You must have had some thoughts about that. What were you saying to yourself at that
point? Were there any self-statements that led you to choose X? What were they?

What thoughts go through your head when he says/does ...

Are you saying you thought ...?

How did you feel when that happened to you?

How did you show that feeling in your behavior?

On a scale from 1 to 10, how (hard did you hit, .. loud did you yell, .. etc.)?

How did others (offer names) react? ... Then what happened?

How often does this happen? (Look for patterns.)

Do you have any ideas about what set you off in these situations?

What do these situations mean to you?

Did your reactions (feelings, thoughts) help manage the problem or did they make things
worse? What did you (feel, think, do)? Did this increase your anger?

How did you come to choose (decide) to do ... ?

What happened to you as a result of your choosing to do ...? What happened after you
made the choice to ...?

Help me understand what you mean when you say ...

Think about what you told me a few minutes ago. Where does this fit in?

Let's review. Let's see if we can get the facts of what happened organized. First, everyone was supposed to ..., then ... Let's see if we can paint a picture of what happened.

Is that an accurate description of what happened?

What were you told to do? What was the rule you were supposed to follow and then what happened?

I hear that you think it wasn't fair so you ... Is that correct?

Now that you have a clearer picture of what happened between you and X, how do you feel about it?

What do you think should happen next?

As best as you can describe, what went wrong?

DEMONSTRATING EMPATHY

(Acknowledge and validate feelings that were appropriate under the circumstances and consider the impact of what "lingers.")

You seem pretty upset. When he did X that must have made you feel even more upset.

I can see how upset you are. Why don't we talk about it and see if we can work it out.

I can see you are angry. Can you solve the problem in a way that turns out to be best for both of you?

How tough was it?

How did that make you feel?

On a scale from 1 to 10, how angry .. sad .. embarrassed .. afraid etc. were you?

I can understand why you would feel ...

What I see is someone who is really upset. If we talk about it, it will help you feel better.

When you do X, it tells me you feel upset about Y. There is a way to make it better.

This just hasn't been a good day, has it? But it doesn't have to keep on being that way.

What is most important in our talking is you. What happens to you is most important and that will depend on what you do. I can see how upset you are, but I want you to know there are ways to solve this problem.

I am sorry you got involved with X, just when you were learning to behave differently (see things differently). Your new behavior was just beginning to pay off for you.

You lost control, when everything ...

It seems like ... (you are frustrated, annoyed, angry).

It sounds like ... (it made you angry when they didn't ...).

What did you do when you were feeling .. (so upset)?

What did you do with the feeling of ... ?

How did you show your feelings?

Do you think you were ...

Was he the great big guy who ...

Some people can really get under the skin of someone else.

When friends (family members) do X, it is natural to want to get back at them (not back down, run away).

When you do something for someone and they don't reciprocate, you feel betrayed. Understandably that makes you angry.

Some problems seem so big that it seems as if no one can do anything about them.

Sometimes things seem terrible, but there are always ways to make them better.

You said that you were "dumb" (an idiot, had no hope), but what I hear between the lines is a message that maybe with some help things could get better.

When he said X and you got mad and went on a rampage, it was like a little kid in you took over.

It's okay to feel like this. It will get better.

Other students who have had this same thing happen to them have often had the same feelings.

Sometimes when people feel like X, they think ... (nothing good can ever happen; they might as well give up). But there is a way to work it out.

Let me see if I understand. You did X because you wanted to ... because in your mind you were trying to .... Is that what you are saying?

It must have been difficult to do X when you were worrying about ...

Are you feeling disappointed about ... ?

It is often hard to hear new things about yourself when you are feeling so badly.

REVIEWING THE "STORY"

(Check out your understanding of the "story." Summarize the youth's view of the situation. In retelling, highlight "strengths" and coping skills. Ask clarifying questions.)

Let me see if I got this right (if I understand this correctly).

Let me see if I understand. From your point of view you were trying to ... and then he reacted by ...

Correct me if I am wrong, but it sounds like ...

It sounds like you think ...

Do these seem to be the reasons you got so angry?

So, what I hear you saying is ... Have I retold your story correctly?

So, in other words ...

It seems that ...

Is that a fair description (interpretation) of what happened?

This is what I hear you saying. Correct me if I missed anything.

You have described the situation clearly. Let's review what you have said.

Could you tell me again about the part that X played? I'm not sure I fully understand what happened. Please tell me once again so I don't miss anything.

Let me summarize what I have heard you say and you can correct anything I didn't get right.

Let me say it back to make sure I understand and see if that is the way you remember it.

You were upset and you made a decisions to ... Is that correct?

NURTURING COLLABORATION

(Help youth begin to see a way out. Nurture hopefulness.)

We are going to work this out together.

Every problem has a solution.

Let's see if we can make sense of what happened to you.

It is important for me to understand why you are so mad (angry, frustrated, sad).

This is a difficult situation, but we can work it out together.

This has not been a good day for you, but we know what's wrong so we can do something about it.

We know what the problem is, but we have to figure out what we can do about it.

When we talk together like this, we can work out ways to handle the problem.

It sounds to me that you have a good understanding about yourself and what gets you into trouble. It also sounds to me that you were trying to make X mad (get him into trouble, get back at him). Am I correct? If you do that, what happens? Is that what you want to have happen? What can you do about it? I am ready to help.

I am pleased that you felt comfortable (safe enough, had the courage) to tell me (show me) how you felt about this problem. Sharing that is an important first step in our working together.

Phase II
PROBLEM-SOLVING PHASE

The <u>goals</u> of the PROBLEM-SOLVING PHASE are to:

(1) help the youth perceive the events from <u>others' point of view</u> and recognize how he <u>contributed</u>, perhaps <u>inadvertently</u>, <u>unwittingly</u>, and <u>unknowingly</u> to the <u>problem</u> (behavior).

(2) recognize a <u>possible behavioral pattern</u>, if such behaviors have happened in the past

(3) engage the youth in the <u>problem-solving steps</u>

(4) foster a <u>sense of responsibility</u>

- **HELPING THE YOUTH TAKE THE PERSPECTIVE OF OTHERS**

- **GENERATING CAUSAL EXPLANATIONS**

- **GENERATING ALTERNATIVE SOLUTIONS**

- **NOTICING WARNING SIGNS**

- **FOSTERING RESPONSIBILITY ("OWNERSHIP")**

HELPING THE YOUTH TAKE THE PERSPECTIVE OF OTHERS

What do you think prompted him to say (or do) X?

Do you suppose that she ...

Do you think she was ...

Did she think you were ...

So what do you think he meant when he said ...

Do you think he knew about ... ? If he didn't know what was really bothering you then what does that mean? (Does that help explain his behavior?)

How do you think X (teacher, friends, parents) would describe what happened? People often have two views of the same event. How does your account fit with that?

Could she be thinking that you were ...?

Is there a rule about this? What is the rule? So when you didn't do that (follow the rule), what do you think she could do? What were her options?

Why do you think he was calling you ... ?

What sort of reaction would you have (how would you respond), if someone did that to you?

Do you think it could be possible that ... ?

So, it wasn't just you that she was upset with?

Can you think of a time when someone got angry with you? How did you feel when you were treated that way? Did you want to be his friend? Did you want to cooperate with him? How do you think people respond to you when you behave in that way?

If X did not stop you when you were really angry, what might have happened? So by stopping you, she protected you from doing something that would have caused you even more problems. Sometimes teachers have to control you until you can control yourself.

How do you think she feels about what happened?

Who decides what consequences will happen? What options did he/she have?

GENERATING CAUSAL EXPLANATIONS

(Help the youth appreciate that behavior has multiple causes.)

Do you think what you said (or did) had anything to do with the way he responded?

Why do you think he got so mad about that?

Are you sure that X wanted to … ?

Any other possible explanations? Any other ways of looking at it?

Could there have been something that set her off?

But what do you think made it all fall apart today?

If he calls you a name and gets you into trouble, then who is really in charge? It sounds like he really knows how to get to you. Do you think you were <u>set up</u> by him?

It seems that sometimes your so-called buddies <u>set you up</u>. They are puppeteers and you are the puppet. (They are fishing and you take the bait. They throw the switch and you light up.)

Is a friend someone who helps you get out of trouble or someone who gets you into trouble?

Do you think they are laughing with you or laughing at you?

It sounds like you were trying to teach him a lesson (get back at him), hoping he would react to you. But look at what really happened.

I think, what we are talking about is at the heart of the problem. Do you agree?

What was your goal in the situation? What did you want to have happen? How did your getting angry (losing control) help you get what you wanted? Did your anger help you achieve your goal? Is your anger getting you all you want?

I can understand why you became angry and why it was so important to you at that time. I wonder if there are other things happening to you that could add to your anger. Sometimes what happens outside of school, like at home, can affect how you react in school.

Sometimes people become angry because they are feeling afraid or sad or humiliated. For example, … Has anything like that ever happened to you?

Sometimes people become angry because they have had bad things happened to them in the past. They had been hurt and no one listened (understood), so they get angry. Has anything like that happened to you?

It sounds like you have something else on your mind today that makes school seem pretty unimportant. What's bothering you?

Has something like this happened in the past? How is this like what happened in the past? What is common about these situations?

Is fairness (following rules, accepting feedback, receiving criticism, getting respect) an issue for you? In what ways?

It sounds like the problem that got you sent here isn't the whole story. What else is bothering you?

Who are you really mad at?

What did you do, if anything, to make the situation worse? What do you need to do to make it better?

What is really important to you in all of this? What are the main issues you are struggling with?

We have talked a lot. Some of this is really important. Let's list the most important points.

What I hear in all of this is ... Correct me if I am wrong.

It sounds like you have been carrying around a lot of feelings like ...

Think about what you just said. What is the major issue?

It sounds like you have two different things to handle here. They are ... Am I correct?

I'm glad you value fairness. Fairness means going by the rules. That sounds like a guideline to live by.

You are clearly a person who values your reputation. And when you feel you have been dishonored ("dissed") you get angry. Is that the way you see it?

So talking about things can help. So does understanding what is really behind what you did.

GENERATING ALTERNATIVE SOLUTIONS

(Help the youth identify as many solutions as possible. Nurture a GOAL, PLAN, DO CHECK approach.)

What are all the things you can do when/in ... ?

It sounds like there are a lot of ways to go about solving this problem. Let's figure out how many different ways you can think of to solve this problem (handle this situation).

So getting angry (hitting others) is one way to try and solve a problem. What other ways are there to try to solve the problem?

What <u>choices</u> did you have?

How did what you said to yourself influence the choices you made?

What happened after you made that choice?

What did others (be specific) do?

Can your self-statements help you make choices that lead to good consequences?

What else could you have done?

What would happen if ... ?

That's one way, can you think of another way?

Sure, throwing an object (punching, cursing, throwing a temper tantrum) is one way to say you don't want ..., but are there any better ways to get your message across?

Can you think of a different way so X wouldn't happen?

If you choose to do X, what do you think will happen? What do you think will happen next?

Sometimes just plain calm talk can communicate ideas.

Understanding one's problem is the first step in developing a solution. What could be your next step?

This situation is beginning to make sense. When a person understands a problem, it is easier to solve it.

I believe that in your own way you were trying to tell (say, show) X. Is there another way you could have done that? What else could you have done?

Maybe there is a way for you to say the same thing without getting into trouble (without hurting others or hurting yourself).

What could you say (do) differently?

What is your goal in the situation? What are the different ways to achieve your goal?

Is there anything else you could have done to handle the situation (what could you have done instead of ...)?

How can you find out?

Can you improve on that?

What advice would you have for a good friend who has this same problem?

That sounds like a solution (strategy) worth trying.

What is a general rule that would help you with ... ?

It sounds like you have a new plan for this situation.

Do you think it would help if ... ?

That is one solution to keep in mind. How will you remind yourself to do X?

How can you remember to use what we talked about today out there on the playground?

Remember, some of the solutions you have chosen have "backfired" in the past. What will you have to be on the lookout for so this solution does not backfire? What will you have to tell yourself to get through that situation?

It seems clear that you have considered a number of choices. Which one do you think will work out the best for you?

It sounds like you have thought through this carefully. Let's review your options and how they will work.

What is your first step? Then what?

NOTICING WARNING SIGNS

(Help the youth become aware of <u>both</u> internal and external – interpersonal – cues or warning signs. Help the youth identify body signs, feelings and thoughts that he/she is "too hot" to act.)

When you are getting angry where do you feel it in your body?

How can you (others) tell when you are first getting upset?

Do you know when you are getting out of control or does it just happen?

Are you telling me that you go from being angry to going suddenly out of control?

Can you remember anything you said or did between the time you got mad and the time you lost control (had to be restrained)?

Is there any way you can learn to "notice," "catch," "interrupt," "stop yourself early on"? *(Use only one of these verbs at the time.)*

So when you feel upset, what is the first thing to do? Then what?

What would be a warning sign that this is a high risk situation?

What would be a warning sign that you are getting angry?

Highlight that getting angry and aggressive usually involves the help of others. Who is the "accomplice"? What to watch out for (warning signs) in others?

What would be a warning sign that X is getting angry? When you notice that he is getting angry, what do you usually do at that point? Do you really want to spend time with people who are willing to put you at risk (in danger, get you into trouble)? Can you tell ahead of time that this might occur? How?

What would be a warning sign that you have been set up .. taking the bait .. getting caught in a trap ... sucked in? *(Choose one)*

I have a thought o want to share, if that is okay. Do you think it is possible that X gets you to act out and gets you into trouble;?

It sounds like you're a pretty good detective. You can pick up on subtle cues and read the situation ahead of time. You are "street smart".

What are you saying to yourself at that time?

Let's write down any 'hot talk" you think or say to yourself in that situation. How do these "hot thoughts" cause you to feel/behave?

FOSTERING RESPONSIBILITY ("OWNERSHIP")

You have given a very detailed and thoughtful description of your problem and some of the possible solutions you can follow.

It sounds like you convinced yourself to ...

Let's review your choices. Of these options, which one do you think you will choose first?

If you choose X, what does that mean?

What can you do to make things better for yourself and for others?

Do you want me to speak to her on your behalf or do you want to do it on your own?

You are right! You now understand that you are responsible for keeping out of trouble.

You have made good choices in the past. How have you gone about that? What are your choices now?

Have there been other times when you have chosen not to ... ? How have you resisted the temptation to act out (get back at X)?

I hope you can make a good choice for yourself and for others.

Of all the things you could have done, how did you choose that way of responding?

Are there less angry ways to achieve your goals and still feel okay?

This shows us that you are beginning to take on more and more responsibility.

Does that mean you want to ...?

It is too bad that you have given up your freedom. If someone else can make a few gestures (or say something) and you go off and lose control, then do you give your control to them?

Being free is about being in control of one's own mind, reactions, feelings and not putting yourself under the control of someone else.

I want to see if you can be your own person with your own thoughts. Show yourself that you are in charge by not blaming your actions on someone else.

It sounds like you can <u>trick yourself</u> into thinking that it is okay to hurt someone. When did you first have the idea that it was okay to …? Do you want to keep on tricking yourself or do you want to take charge and begin to …?

Has anything like this happened before? In what ways are they alike? Is there a pattern here that we can learn from?

How did you get so good at (intimidating, scaring others, upsetting adults, avoiding …)? … If you had to teach someone to do this, how would you go about it? What do they have to watch out for? What if they wanted to not get into trouble, what advice would you have for them?

Phase III
IMPLEMENTATION PHASE

The goals of the IMPLEMENTATION PHASE are to:

(1) "<u>challenge</u>" the youth to use problem-solving strategies

(2) <u>generate a step-by-step action plan</u> that includes likely <u>consequences</u> and <u>possible barriers</u> and <u>role play</u> (rehearse) new skills

(3) <u>reinforce</u> effort

(4) ask the youth to <u>describe/explain</u> what he will do and <u>why</u> (put individual in a "consultative" role) and acknowledge what he has learned today

(5) ensure that the youth <u>sees the connections</u> between his/her efforts and the resultant consequences and "<u>takes credit</u>" for changes and plans for ways to address any <u>lapses</u>

(6) prepare the youth to <u>rejoin</u> ongoing activities

- CONVEYING A "CHALLENGE" AND BOLSTERING CONFIDENCE

- GENERATING AN ACTION PLAN

- ANTICIPATING CONSEQUENCES

- ANTICIPATING POSSIBLE BARRIERS TO CHANGE

- REINFORCING EFFORT

- PUTTING THE YOUTH IN A "CONSULTATIVE" ROLE
  (SHARE, TEACH, AND TAKE CREDIT FOR CHANGES)

CONVEYING A "CHALLENGE" AND BOLSTERING CONFIDENCE

(Convey the sense that it will be <u>hard</u> to make changes and that no one expects him/her to be "perfect.")

It won't be easy to do what we have been talking about.

It won't be easy to do "X," especially when "Y" won't be interested (or when "Y" continues to tease you).

Maybe its too early to ask you to try doing ...

You have a difficult situation, but it sounds like you have the right idea (that you are on the right track).

This is going to take a lot of courage on your part. How will you begin?

When he does X, that will give you an opportunity for you to practice Y.

That sounds like it might work. What do you think?

This is your chance to show the others what you have learned.

You know what to expect when you go back into the class. It is going to be tough. How will you be able to handle that? What will you be on the lookout for?

Like you said, this won't be easy.

Sometimes, it is hard for people to ...

It will be interesting to see how you choose from your many options. I am interested in seeing what will work for you.

This has been a tough talk, but its going to pay off for you.

I know it will be tough to handle that, but I have confidence that you can <u>spot</u> (<u>notice</u>) when trouble is coming; You can <u>catch yourself</u>; You can <u>notice</u> when you are getting worked up; You can <u>use your game plan</u> and <u>interrupt the cycle</u>.

You can take charge of your life so no one can get you into trouble, if you don't want them to.

Do you think you can do this next time? All I can ask is that you give it a try.

Do you think you can try this out?

I have seen you handle problems like this before and you did them well. Is there anything you did in handling those problems that you can use here?

Remember how calm you were when you told me about how you handled (anticipated) X? Do you think you can handle this one the same way?

Successfully reaching your goal will take time. It won't be easy or come quickly.

It won't be easy to <u>not</u> allow them to get you into trouble, but I believe you can do it.

I believe you are mature enough to face this and stay out of trouble.

Do you think you can ignore such set-ups? It won't be easy. Are you saying that you think you could avoid falling into the "trap" .. "taking the bait"?

How confident are you (on a 0% to 100% scale) that you can do X?

If you need help, I'll be right beside you. (You can check in with me.)

I am available to talk to you whenever you need me.

We will talk again.

GENERATING AN ACTION PLAN

(Help the youth select a solution to try and see that he has opportunities to try out new ways of behaving.)

That sounds like a good idea that might work.

You have a good idea. What will you say to him (do) when you leave here?

What do you think you can do to calm down? Do you think you can X?

Is it difficult to just let your anger go and let bygones be bygones?

Do you think about taking a time out … about compromising .. about negotiating?

What can you do to prevent yourself from becoming angry? (from getting into trouble)?

What has worked for you in the past?

Can you remember a time when you were really angry and you did <u>not</u> take it out on someone? How did you feel about that?

What advice would you have for a friend who has this same problem so he/she can handle the situation better?

How will you remember (remind yourself) to ... ?

What will you have to watch out for?

What will you have to tell yourself in order to ... ?

What will happen when you go home? How can you prepare for that?

When you go back in, what do you think she will say? What will you say if they ask you what we talked about?

Is there anything else you could say that might change her mind (change her behavior)?

If you handled it that way, what would he do/say?

Now tell me one more time; how you are going to handle (anticipate) any trouble.

It is clear that you have a good game plan. When you go back in the classroom, she will be expecting an apology. What will you say to her?

To be prepared is the best advice. Let's practice this. Imagine that I am "X," what would you say? (Use behavioral rehearsal.) Now that we practiced it, do you think you can try it on your own?

Let's practice together some of the other skills you have learned such as planned ignoring, use of "I" messages, time out procedures, relaxation exercises, etc.

So if X occurs, then you will be able to Y?

So whenever you notice, you will be prepared to do X.

Who can you talk to when you have problems with ... ?

What do you think X will do when you see him next time? How will you deal with that? That will not be easy to do. I guess you have a choice.

Have you gone through your "conflict cycle" before? What happened? What are the different ways you can break this cycle?

It is easier to learn coping skills than to change your attitude. Let's discuss this.

It sounds to me that you have the right idea, but the wrong behavior.

Let's practice what you can do to handle the situation. *(Role play the new skills.)*

This afternoon you will have a chance to practice what we worked on this morning. *(Prepare the youth to join ongoing activity and plan to use new skills.)*

ANTICIPATING CONSEQUENCES

If you do ..., then what do you think is likely to occur?

If you make the changes you plan, what do you think the consequences will be?

If you can do X, what do you think people will say (do)?

When you start to do X, who do you think will first notice the changes? What will they see and hear?

When you start to use your coping skills, how will that make you feel?

Do you know the penalty for not X?

What happens as a result of your getting angry in that way?

How do you think things would turn out if you did X instead of Y?

If this trouble starts again when you go back to your classroom, remember that you decided to ...

The next time he starts to X, what are you going to do differently so you won't get into trouble (so you can stay in charge of yourself, be in control, not allow someone else to get you into trouble, disappoint them so they can't set you up)?

Let's write out the decisions you can make and the list of benefits you will receive.

How might you avoid this type of conflict in the future? If you did that, what would be some of the consequences?

ANTICIPATING POSSIBLE BARRIERS TO CHANGE

What will you do if ...

What if he doesn't listen ...

What if she tells you ...

What will be different this time as compared to times in the past when you had to deal with ... ?

Do you think they will (trust you, give you another chance)?

It will be hard to say "no" to a friend when he tries to X. What will you do differently this time?

The next time they tell you to do Y, you may feel just as angry. What will happen then?

Do you think that you can pull it off when (even if) ... ?

And when things don't go the way you expect and it upsets you, what will you do then?

Let's suppose that ...

Do you think he will be X? And what if ... ?

How can you remind yourself to ... ?

When you go back into the classroom (ward), you can remember just how well you did it here practicing with me.

Each time that trouble comes up again, remember that you now know how to handle your anger, like you did when we were working together.

Are you ready to ...?

I have noticed you are really good at making some people afraid of you. When did you learn this? Is there a particular person that you learned this from? How does this learned anger get in the way of you doing Y?

Now that you know this, how can you use this information to control your anger?

Which of the skills we talked about will you be able to use in your real life situation (in your everyday experience)?

REINFORCING EFFORT

I am impressed with the way you can describe what happened and why it happened. You were able to tell it clearly and without getting angry.

That is a calm way to let someone know you understand the rules.

You are showing maturity when you can deal with X. (When you can make "smart" decisions.)

That is a productive way to handle problems. When you can talk to people about what is on your mind, feelings don't get out of control. Everybody wins!

That is a sign of maturity to face up to the consequences of your behavior.

I see so much self-control in your approach. You have learned so much that you can now teach it to others.

That sounds like an idea that is worth trying.

Good idea. Boys who are angry usually can't stop and think (or hear what others have to say).

Good job! Today you (specify behavior – told yourself to …, took a time out, walked away, ignored, asserted yourself, etc.). This is a big step.

Well done, you handled your disappointment without getting upset!

Even though you were upset, you managed to … instead of …

You have shown that you have matured. Instead of fighting, you did X. You told yourself that it just wasn't worth it.

You are showing that you understand a better way to handle things.

You have made a lot of progress. When you go back to your classroom, what will you have to tell others about what we did here together?

Remember everybody has problems, but not everyone knows how to fix them.

It isn't easy to accept consequences when you thought you were right (when you thought you were acting in a responsible fashion).

I noticed how you were able to control yourself even when others were loosing it.

I'm very impressed with you when you …

I appreciate the way you …

I give you a lot of credit for …

I'm really proud of you for thinking more clearly about …

Well done! You are now beginning to think more clearly about your options.

That's an excellent insight!

I am impressed that you figured this out on your own. Most students your age don't know that their feelings at home can cause problems at school, and vice versa. How did you figure this out? Usually, I don't get to this part of the discussion until much later.

When you are out of control like this, it tells me something is really bothering you. But when you use your words to tell me how you feel (what is bothering you), then your mature self is coming out.

There is a part of you that X, and another part that is able to take charge.

This shows that you had more self-control than you realized you did.

You have a real ability to read people, stay cool under pressure … be "street smart". You are a good psychologist. You are able to figure things out.

How did you get others to trust you (follow your leadership) at such a young age?

You have learned a lot today!

PUTTING THE YOUTH IN A "CONSULTATIVE" ROLE (SHARE, TEACH, AND TAKE CREDIT FOR CHANGES)

(It is __not__ enough to change. Need the youth to be able to <u>describe</u> how change came about and <u>see connections</u> between own actions and outcomes. Encourage the youth to explain how he/she will benefit from using new behaviors.)

Let's review what you did that was helpful.

Tell me in your own words what you need to do if there is a problem.

Tell me the steps that you can use to stay out of trouble and what you can do to practice your coping skills.

How can you make these techniques your own?

How did you get so good at …?

Why is it important for you to stay out of trouble?

With whom else can you share what you have learned?

Are you saying you want to do X? What are the skills you will need to …

Do you think you can teach what you have learned to someone else? Who?

What will you tell others about how you worked on your problems?

What have you learned that is important that you can share with others?

Are you saying that in spite of X, you can do Y?

We can fix problems, if we talk about them. Words are better than fists to solve a problem.

We can figure out a way to fix things so you will feel better.

When you go back to your classroom, what will the other students be able to learn from you? What will you tell them you learned?

The reason for this rule is … Does that make sense? How can you follow the rule, even if you don't like it?

How is what you are feeling here apply to other situations?

How did you come to the decision to do X instead of Y?

So all this meant … Is that correct?

Do you ever notice that in your everyday activities that you tend to <u>ask yourself</u> on your own, the kind of questions that we ask each other when we chat? .. I guess you are becoming your "coach," your own therapist and putting me "out of business."

APPENDIX B

WEBSITES RELATED TO ANGER AND VIOLENCE

Information About School Safety

California Department of Education: School Safety
http://www.cde.ca.gov/spbranch/safety/

California Healthy Kids Survey
http://www.wested.org/wested/lookup_services/treeHTML/wested_3_15.htm

Center for the Study and Prevention of Violence (University of Colorado)
http://www.colorado.edu/cspv/blueprints
> Safe Communities-Safe Schools Planning Guide: A Tool for Community
> Violence Prevention Efforts
> Bullying Prevention Program: Blueprints for Violence
> Prevention\Prevention Programs that Work for Youth: Violence
> Prevention
> Positive Peer Culture Programs

Columbine High School Review Commission: Lessons Learned
http://www.state.co.us

Early Warning Signs, Timely Response.
http://www.air-dc.org/cecp/guide/

Guide to Safe Schools
http://www.ed.gov/offices/OSERS/OSEP/#STUDIES

FBI Report: The School Shooter: A Threat Assessment Perspective
http://www.fbi.gov/library/school/school2.pdf

The Institute for the Study of Antisocial Behavior in Youth
http://www.iay.org/

National Alliance for Safe Schools
http://www.safeschools.org/

National Network of Violence Prevention Practitioners
NNVPPMGR@edu.org

National School Safety Center Report and Checklist on Identifying Potentially
Violent Students
http://www.nssc1.org/

President Clinton: Working To Reduce Violence Against Children
http://www.whitehouse.gov/WH/Work/1222998.html

Safe Schools, Healthy Students
http://www.sshsac.org (click SAMHSA Clearing house, then click KEN)
http://www.ed.gov/pubs/studies3.html

Search Institute: Practical Research Benefiting Children and Youth
http://www.search-institute.org/

Student Risk Factors in School Violence
http://education.ucsb.edu/~schpsych.html

U.S. Department of Justice and Education: 1999 Annual Report on School Safety (Early Warning, Timely Response: A Guide to Safe Schools)
www.safetyzone.org/pdf/schoolsafety2.pdf

General References on Violence Prevention

Adolescent Assault Victim Needs: A Review of Issues and a Model Protocol
http://www.aap.org/policy/00991.html

American Family Physician: Preventing Street Gang Violence
http://www.aafp.org/afp/990415ap/medicine.html

American Medical Association: Youth and Violence: A Report to the Nation
http://www.ama-assn.org/ama/pub/category/3536.html

Best Practices of Youth Violence Prevention: A Sourcebook for Community Action (Thorton, T. N., Craft, C. A., Dahlberg, L. L., Lynch, B. S., & Bark, K.) (888-252-7751)
http://www.cdc.gov/safeusa
http://www.cdc.gov/ncipc

Centers for Disease Control and Prevention: Best Practices of Youth Violence Prevention: A Sourcebook for Community Action
http://www.cdc.gov/safeusa/publications/bplink.htm

Crime and Violence Prevention Center: California's Attorney General's Office
http://caag.state.ca.us/cvpc

Crime Prevention Effectiveness Program
http://www.preventingcrime.org
http://www.bsos.umd.edu/ccjs/corrections

Department of Education: Safe and Drug Free Schools Office
http://www.ed.gov/updates/fact-209.html

Florida Department of Education Research and Statistics
http://www.firn.edu/doe/menu/ednews.htm

Gender Differences in Aggression (Pepler & Craig)
http://www.yorku.ca/research/lamarsh/index.htm

**Massachusetts Medical Society Violence Prevention for Children and Youth
    Parent Education Cards (Tip Cards) (800-843-6356)**
Email: dph@mms.org

Partnership for Preventing Violence
http://www.mcet.edu/peace/

Surgeon General Website: Youth Violence: A Report of the Surgeon General
http://www.surgeongeneral.gov/library/youthviolence/report.html

Agency Web Sites

**Adults and Children Together Against Violence (ACT – sponsored by
    American Psychological Association Public Communications Office.
    Produces informational publications, workshop materials and commercials
    against violence.)**
http://www.actagainstviolence.org/

American Academy of Pediatrics
www.aap.org

American Academy of Child and Adolescent Psychiatry
http://www.aacap.org/info-families/National Facts/99Violfctsh.htm

American Institutes for Research
http://www.air-dc.org/

Bureau Of Justice Statistics
http://www.ojp.usdoj.gov/bjs/

**Centers for Disease Control and Prevention: Division of Violence Prevention
    (Best Practices of Youth Violence Prevention: A Sourcebook for
    Community Action 888-252-7751)**
http://www.cdc.gov/ncipc/dvp/dvp.htm

Centers for Disease Control and Prevention: Adolescent and School Health
http://www.cdc.gov/nccdphp/dash/

Youth Risk Behavior Survey, United States, 1999
http://www.cdc.gov/epo/mmwr/preview/mmwrhtml/ss4905al.html
Center for Prevention of Adverse Life Outcomes: University of Colorado
KIVIALME@eathlink.net

Center for the Prevention of School Violence
http://www.ncsu.edu/cpsv/index.html

Center for the Study and Prevention of Violence
http://www.colorado.edu/cspv/

Children's Safety Network
http://www.edc.org/HHD/CSN

Coalition for Juvenile Justice
http://www.juvjustice.org

Crime Prevention Programs
http://www.preventingcrime.org/

Department of Justice Canada
http://www.canada.justice.gc.ca/

Florida Department of Education Research and Statistics
http://www.firn.edu/doe/menu/ednews.htm

Hamilton Fish Institute, George Washington University
http://www.hamfish.org/

Harvard School of Public Health: Violence Prevention Programs
http://www.hsph.harvard.edu/php/vpp.html

Institute of Violence and Destructive Behavior
http://interact.uoregon.edu/ivdb/ivdb.html

National Association of Attorneys General and National School Board
http://www.keepschoolssafe.org/

Youth Violence in the United States: National Center for Injury Prevention and Control
http://www.cdc.gov/ncipc/dvp/yvpt/newfacts.html

Facts and Myths About Youth Violence
http://www.cdc.gov/ncipc/dvp/yvpt/myths.html

National Consortium on Violence Research
www.ncovr.heinz.cmu.edu

National Crime Prevention Center
http://www.ncpc.org/

Fact Sheet: Mental Health and Adolescent Girls in the Justice System
http://www.nmha.org/children

National Mental Health Association – Juvenile Justice Section
http://www.nmha.org/chidlren/justguv/index.cfm

National Resource Center for Safe Schools
http://www.safetyzone.org/

National School Safety Center
http://www.nssc1.org/home.htm

North Carolina Center for the Prevention of School Violence
http://www.ncsu.edu/cpsv/

Office of Justice Programs
http://www.ojp.usdoj.gov/

Office of Juvenile Justice and Delinquency Prevention
http://www.ncjrs.org/ojjhome.htm

Parents' Resource Institute for Drug Education
http://www.prideusa.org/

The Prevention Institute
http://www.preventioninstitute.org/

Safe and Drug Free School
http://www.ed.gov/offices/OESE/SDFS/

Substance Abuse and Mental Health Services Administration (SAMHSA)
http://www.samhsa.gov

U.S. Department of Education
http://www.ed.gov/index.html

U.S. Department of Justice, Office of Justice Programs
http://www.ncjrs.org
http://www.ncjrs.org/fedgrant.htm#ojp

Specific Programs

ACT: Adult and Children Together Against Violence
(APA Public Communication Office, 202-336-5700)
http://www.actagainstviolence.org/

American Psychological Association: Warning Signs: Take a stand against
violence.
http://www.apa.org/campaign/mtvupdate.html

American Psychological Association: Controlling Anger – Before it Controls
You
http://helping.apa.org/daily/anger.html

Anger Management Programs: A Commercial Website
http://www.angermgmt.org/

Big Brothers / Big Sisters
http://www.ppv.org/bbbs.htm

Center for Safe Youth
http://www.safeyouth.com/

Domestic Violence Project of Santa Clara County
http://www.growing.com/nonviolent/index.htm

The Fast Track Project
http://www.fasttrackproject.org/

Girls' Advocacy Project: Juvenile Justice Center, Miami-Dade County
http://www.gapgirls.org/

Information on Popular Street Drugs
http://165.112.78.61/ClubAlert/clubdrugalert.html

Media Literacy
  Media Awareness Network
  http://www.schoolnet.ca/medianet
  Facing TV Violence
  http://www.cfc-efc.ca/docs/00001164.htm

Join Together: Communities Fighting Substance Abuse and Gun Violence
(617-437-1500)
http://www.jointogether.org

National Network for Family Resiliency
http://www.nnfr.org/

National Network of Violence Prevention Practitioners
NNVPPMGR@edu.org

National Resource Center for Safe Schools
http://www.safetyzone.org/

Parents and Friends of Lesbians and Gays (PFLAG) (202-467-8180)
http://www.pflag.org

Peer Support Network: Antibullying Programs
http://www.roehampton.ac.uk/support/rdio/research.asp

Positive Parenting Program: Triple P
http://www.triplep.org

Positive Youth Development in the United States: Research Findings on Evaluations of Positive Youth Development Programs (Catalano et al., 1998)
http://aspe.hhs.gov/hsp/PositiveYouthDev99/

Anger Management Program for Children and Adolescents: Think First Programs (Dr. Jim Larson)
e-mail: larsonj@uwwvax.uww.edu

Youth and Violence – Medicine, Nursing, and Public Health: Connecting the Dots to Prevent Violence (312-464-4520)
http://www.ama-assn.org/violence

School-based Programs: Instruction and Mental Health

About Our Kids: New York University Child Study Center
http://www.aboutourkids.org/

About Mentoring
http://www.mentoring.org/

American School Health Association
Federal activities addressing violence in school: A special report
(L. Barrios, 2000, Journal of School Health, 20)
http://www.ashaweb.org/

Bullying: Information for Parents and Teachers
http://www.yrbe.edu.on.ca/~safeschl/bullying1.htm

ERIC Program: Bullying in Schools
http://www.uncg.edu:80/edu/ericcass/violence/digests/banks.htm

Making a Difference in Bullying
http://www.yorku.ca/research/lamarsh/

National Center for Conflict Resolution Education
http://www.nccre.org

Conflict Resolution / Peer Mediation
http://www.coe.ufl.edu/CRPM/results.html
http://www.coe.ufl.edu/CRPM/pmprograms.html
http://www.coe.ufl.edu/CRPM/pmo.html

Center for School Mental Health
http://www.mentalhealth.org/specvials/schoolviolence

Comprehensive School Reform (has information on programs in different states)
http://www.ncrel.org/csri/

Correlates of School Violence
http://eric-web.tc.columbia.edu/monographs/uds109/reference.html

American Psychological Association
    Prevention of Mental Disorders in School-aged children
    (M. T. Greenberg et al., 2001)
http://journals.apa.org/prevention/

National School Safety Center
http://www.naspweb.org/

Preventing School Violence Resources
http://www.nga.org/Justice/SchoolViolence.asp

The Prevention of Mental Disorders in School-Aged Children: Current State of the Field (Greenberg et al., 2001)
http://journals.apa.org/prevention/volume4/pre0040001a.html

Prosocial Communities
www.resilience.net

Not Me Not Now: What Smart Kids Say to Sex
http://www.notmenotnow.org/

Reducing the School Dropout Rate
http://www.nwrel.org/scpd/sirs/9/c017.html

Screening for Child Psychiatric Disorders: Strengths and Difficulties Questionnaire
http://www.sdqinfo.com

Prevention of Elder Abuse

American Association of Retired Persons (AARP): A Profile of Older Americans
http://www.aarp.org/

National Elder Abuse Incidence Study (NAIS – 1998)
http://www.aoa.gov/abuse/report/

Questions and Answers about Older Battered Women (Linda Vinton, 1998)
http://www7.myflorida.com/doea/healthfamily/publications/elderissues/
doeaolderbatteredwomen.html

Canadian Network for the Prevention of Elder Abuse
http://www.mun.ca/elderabuse/

HelpAge International
http://www.helpage.org/

International Network for the Prevention of Elder Abuse
http://www.inpeabuse.org/

National Committee for the Prevention of Elder Abuse
http://www.preventelderabuse.org/

Web Resources on Elder Abuse
http://www.seniorlaw.com/elderabuse.htm

Clinical Applications

About Medications for Combat PTSD (Shay, J., 1995)
http://www.dr-bob.org/tips/ptsd.html

International Society for Traumatic Stress Studies
http://www.istss.org

National Crime Victims Research and Treatment Center: Medical University of South Carolina
http://www.musc.edu/cvc

American Academy of Child and Adolescent Psychiatry
http://www.aacap.org

Child Survivor of Traumatic Stress (Ken Fletcher, Editor)
http://www.ummed.edu/pub/k/kfletche/kidsurv.html

Managing Traumatic Stress: Tips for recovering from disasters and other traumatic events
http://www.helping.apa.org/therapy/traumaticstress.html

Talk To Someone Who Can Help
http://www.helping.apa.org

Civitas Child Trauma (Baylor College of Medicine)
http://www.bcm.tmc.edu/civitas

Expert Consensus Guidelines: Psychiatric treatment guidelines for the most difficult questions facing clinicians
http://www.psychguides.com/

Information About Dialectical Behavior Therapy (DBT)
http://www.behavioraltech.com/

List of Therapist Manuals for Empirically Supported Treatments
http://www.apa.org/divisions/div12/rev_est/index.shtml

NIMH: Suicide Facts
http://www.nimh.nih.gov/research.suifact.htm

The Behavioral Technology Transfer Group
http://www.behavioraltech.com/

Suicide Prevention Information
http://www.mentalhealth.org

American Association of Suicidology: CDC-AAS Media Guidelines
http://suicidology.org/mediaguidelines.htm

SUBJECT INDEX